Sinclair Lewis Remembered

AMERICAN WRITERS REMEMBERED

Jackson R. Bryer, Series Editor

Sinclair Lewis Remembered

Edited by
GARY SCHARNHORST
and
MATTHEW HOFER

THE UNIVERSITY OF ALABAMA PRESS
Tuscaloosa

Manufactured in the United States of America

Typeface: AGaramond

∞
The paper on which this book is printed meets the minimum requirements of American National Standard for Information Sciences—Permanence of Paper for Printed Library Materials, ANSI Z39.48-1984.

Library of Congress Cataloging-in-Publication Data

Sinclair Lewis remembered / edited by Gary Scharnhorst and Matthew Hofer.
p. cm. — (American writers remembered)
Includes bibliographical references and index.
ISBN 978-0-8173-1772-0 (trade cloth : alk. paper) — ISBN 978-0-8173-8627-6 (ebook) 1. Lewis, Sinclair, 1885–1951—Criticism and interpretation. I. Scharnhorst, Gary. II. Hofer, Matthew.
PS3523.E94Z837 2012
813′.52—dc23

2012008304

Cover photograph: Lewis in 1915 (by permission of the Minnesota Historical Society).
Cover design: Michele Myatt Quinn

For Imani and Payson, Andreas and Stian

Contents

Chronology

1885	February 7, Born in Sauk Centre, Minnesota, to Dr. Edwin J. Lewis and Emma Kermott Lewis
1891	Death of mother
1892	Father marries Isabel Warner
1902	Attends Oberlin Academy in Ohio
1903–6	Attends Yale University; edits *Yale Literary Magazine;* travels to England
1906	Works briefly at Upton Sinclair's cooperative utopian community, Helicon Home Colony; travels to Panama
1907–8	Returns to Yale and graduates
1908–15	Travels the United States; works in New York publishing houses; writes short stories and poems; sells plots of short stories to Jack London
1912	Publication of *Hike and Aeroplane* (as "Tom Graham")
1914	Publication of *Our Mr. Wrenn;* marries Grace Livingston Hegger
1916	Publication of *The Trail of the Hawk*
1917	Publication of *The Job* and *The Innocents;* birth of son, Wells
1918	Collaborates with Daniel Reed on a theatrical adaptation of the short story "Hobohemia"
1919	Publication of *Free Air;* unsuccessful production of *Hobohemia* in Greenwich Village
1920	Publication of Main Street
1922	Publication of *Babbitt*
1925	Publication of *Arrowsmith*
1926	Publication of *Mantrap;* declines Pulitzer Prize for *Arrowsmith;* death of father
1927	Publication of *Elmer Gantry*
1928	Publication of *The Man Who Knew Coolidge;* divorces Grace Livingston Hegger; marries Dorothy Thompson
1929	Publication of *Dodsworth*

1930	Birth of son, Michael; awarded the Nobel Prize for Literature
1933	Publication of *Ann Vickers*
1934	Publication of *Work of Art;* collaborates with Sidney Howard on a theatrical adaptation of *Dodsworth*
1935	Publication of *It Can't Happen Here* and *Selected Short Stories*
1936–42	Writes several plays, including *Angela Is Twenty-Two;* works as an actor
1938	Publication of *The Prodigal Parents*
1940	Publication of *Bethel Merriday;* teaches at University of Wisconsin
1942	Divorces Dorothy Thompson
1943	Publication of *Gideon Planish*
1944	Death of son, Lieutenant Wells Lewis, killed by sniper fire in Piedmont Valley, France
1945	Publication of *Cass Timberlane*
1947	Publication of *Kingsblood Royal*
1949	Publication of *The God-Seeker*
1951	January 10, Dies in Rome; buried in Greenwood Cemetery of Sauk Centre; posthumous publication of *World So Wide*

Sinclair Lewis Remembered

Introduction

He was the first American to receive the Nobel Prize for Literature, yet Harry Sinclair Lewis's life was not a particularly happy one. His biography reads like a cautionary tale. Born in 1885 in Sauk Centre, Minnesota, an outback village with a population of about twenty-five hundred, Lewis remained a staunch and uncouth midwesterner his entire life. As he wrote in a piece about his hometown in 1931, "I find myself thinking of its streets and the familiar friendly faces when I am on the great avenues of New York, or Paris, or Stockholm: when I am in the little stone hilly villages of Italy, or sun-basking villas of Spain, or the yellow ancient temples of Athens."[1] As an adolescent he was interested in religion and studied German in part because he wanted to speak with local German-born priests in their native language.[2] He also exhibited a voracious love of reading, and among his earliest literary heroes were Henry David Thoreau, George Bernard Shaw, H. G. Wells, and Charles Dickens. Lewis left the Midwest in 1903 to enroll at Yale, where his fellow students considered him a country rube; he was so unpopular he was virtually ostracized. In the lexicon of the day he was "fresh." "My university days at Yale," he later reminisced, "were undistinguished save for contributions to *Yale Literary Magazine,*" and even those pieces "reek[ed] with a banal romanticism."[3] After summer trips on tramp steamers to England and Panama and a month feeding the furnace of Helicon Hall, Upton Sinclair's utopian community in New Jersey, he graduated a year behind his class and, to his physician-father's chagrin, immediately turned to literature for a livelihood.

Lewis began his career as a hack writer. He hired his first agent in 1907, contributed several potboilers to an ephemeral New Thought magazine in 1909 and 1910, knocked out a pulp novel for boys in the summer of 1911, sold story ideas to Jack London, wrote advertising copy for a string of New York publishers, ghosted parts of several books, and sketched scenarios for Hollywood films. His first serious novels, he remembered, fell "dead before the ink was dry."[4] Following his initial success as a contributor of O. Henry–type formulaic tales to the slicks, especially the *Saturday Evening Post,* like Huck Finn he lit out for the territory to research *Free Air* (1919), his sixth novel and his first to be published by the ambitious young firm of Harcourt, Brace and Howe.

Over the next ten years—a *decade mirabilis*—Lewis wrote five of the most influential social novels in the history of American letters: *Main Street* (1920), *Babbitt* (1922), *Arrowsmith* (1924), *Elmer Gantry* (1927), and *Dodsworth* (1929). In them he created a gallery of memorable characters, particularly Doc Kennicott, George F. Babbitt, Sharon Falconer, Gustaf Sondelius, and Fran Dodsworth, and he coined terms and phrases (e.g., *main streeter, babbittry*) still in vogue. As E. M. Forster noted, Lewis managed to "lodge a piece of a continent in our imagination."[5] In 1998 *Main Street* was selected by the editors of the Modern Library the 68th best English-language novel of the twentieth century, ahead of such works as Edith Wharton's *The House of Mirth,* Hemingway's *A Farewell to Arms,* James Joyce's *Finnegans Wake,* Wallace Stegner's *Angle of Repose,* Joseph Conrad's *Lord Jim,* and Jack London's *The Call of the Wild.* The following year the readers of the Modern Library selected *Arrowsmith* the 78th best novel of the century, ahead of Thomas Pynchon's *V.,* Faulkner's *Light in August,* Hemingway's *A Farewell to Arms,* and Willa Cather's *My Ántonia.*[6]

For his five important novels of the 1920s Lewis was awarded the Nobel Prize for Literature in 1930, much to the consternation of such figures as Theodore Dreiser, Sherwood Anderson, Rebecca West, Thomas Mann, William Faulkner, Ellen Glasgow, and Ernest Hemingway. (In *Green Hills of Africa,* a Hemingway, character declares that "Sinclair Lewis is nothing."[7]) Most of the dissenters believed Dreiser or even Ezra Pound deserved the honor before the author of *Main Street* and *Babbitt.* On the other hand, Lewis received kudos from many other fellow authors, including Wells, Forster, Arnold Bennett, Wharton, Eugene O'Neill, and Sinclair. Even if we concede that Dreiser deserved the Nobel more than Lewis in 1930, at least Lewis deserved it more than did Pearl Buck in 1938. Lewis won the prize in the early months of the Great Depression and during the failed presidency of Herbert Hoover apparently because it suited the temper of the times, especially the anti-Americanism of many Europeans. Or as Mark Schorer has noted, Lewis's fiction and Nobel acceptance speech "found favor abroad because both gave back to a jealous Europe the dismal picture of American life in which it wanted to believe."[8]

Unfortunately, the remainder of Lewis's life was a decrescendo interrupted by an occasional drum roll. As Schorer explains, "His work, always flirting with social parody," after 1930 tended "more and more toward self-parody."[9] Like his friend and fellow Minnesotan Harold Stassen (1907–2001), elected the "boy-governor" of his state at the age of thirty-two and a perennial, pathetic, twelve-time candidate for president until his death, Lewis peaked early and careened downhill the rest of his life. The first novel he wrote after his receipt of the Nobel Prize, *Ann Vickers* (1932), was published simultaneously in thirteen languages and in sixteen countries—and is as easily overlooked or forgotten today as Faulkner's *A Fable* (1954) or Steinbeck's *America and Americans* (1966). In

1938 Granville Hicks titled his review of *The Prodigal Parents* "Sinclair Lewis' Stinkbomb."[10] Lewis eventually grew so bored with writing fiction that in the late 1930s and '40s he became an actor, a playwright, a theatrical producer, and a Broadway director. In all, he published twenty-three novels as well as a barrelful of short stories, plays, essays, and a smattering of poems. If he was not the most gifted writer of his generation, he was certainly one of the most prolific.

Yet for all his gifts as an author of topical fiction, the world changed more quickly than Lewis could adapt to it. Lewis "had caught Main Street just at the turning point, at a now vanished point," as Perry Miller observed at the time (chapter 115, this volume). The provincial Gopher Prairie of his imagination had utterly disappeared by his death in 1951, the victim of paved streets, four-lane highways, luxury automobiles, and radio and television. Even his last significant novel, *Kingsblood Royal* (1947), which seemed brave and controversial when it appeared on the eve of the modern civil rights movement, was a throwback to the "passing novels" of the 1890s, such as W. D. Howells's *An Imperative Duty* (1892), Frances E. W. Harper's *Iola Leroy* (1892), and Mark Twain's *Pudd'nhead Wilson* (1894).

To be sure, Lewis pioneered no new style and founded no new literary school. He disdained taxonomies, and his fiction resists neat and pretty categorization. He is more easily described by what he was not than by what he was. Alfred Kazin called him a "New Realist,"[11] though Lewis particularly derided academics' attempts to pigeonhole him. Certainly he was not an "old realist" like W. D. Howells, whom he had met in Florida in 1916 and with whose theory of fiction he had little truck. Whereas Howells had genuflected in the presence of Emerson and Hawthorne during his first visit to New England sixty years before, the iconoclastic Lewis would have none of this brand of hero worship. He went out of his way to ridicule Howells in his Nobel Prize speech in 1930: he "was one of the gentlest, sweetest, and most honest of men, but he had the code of a pious old maid whose greatest delight was to have tea at the vicarage."[12] Lewis contrasted Howells, who embraced the "smiling aspects of life," with what Wells called the "jolly coarsenesses of life,"[13] and he later joked to his friend, Ramon Guthrie, that he was "a photographic realist" like James Joyce, "only a hell of a lot less so" (chapter 87, this volume).

Lewis has also been called a social satirist. Certainly he was the author of problem novels about business, race and anti-Semitism, women's rights, marriage and divorce, socialism, medicine, religion, art, the "village virus," the threat of native fascism, American expatriatism, the plight of the "salariat" or office workers, and the "generation gap." But he was not a satirist in the Swiftian mold. "I'm not a satirist," he insisted to Betty Stevens in 1947. "You take a man like Swift—he was a satirist because he exaggerated" (chapter 109). Nor were his characters ever unqualified scoundrels. Lewis professed to love many of them, even the rascals, because they entertained him. "I like the Babbitts, the Dr. Pickerbaughs, the Will Kennicotts, and even the Elmer Gantrys rather better than anyone else on earth," he declared in 1928. "They are good fellows. They laugh—really laugh."[14]

Unfortunately, Lewis failed either to plan or to complete two novels he should have written. For whatever reason, he had little to say publicly about the First World War. Schorer remarks that "in his personal life the war did not touch Sinclair Lewis,"[15] and Richard Lingeman adds that "when America did go to war, Lewis retreated into political silence."[16] He apparently harbored reservations about the justice of the war, like many other socialists at the time. The leader of the Socialist Party of America, Eugene V. Debs, was sentenced to ten years in prison in 1918 under the Espionage Act of 1917 for his opposition to the war, and Lewis may have feared the same fate. He was less reserved in his support of the war effort against the Nazis during the Second World War, scripting a radio play to promote the purchase of war bonds. He also suffered the loss of his son, Wells, killed by a sniper in France in October 1944. Yet he never wrote a novel devoted specifically to war.

Most famously, Lewis never published an oft-projected and long-rumored labor novel based on the life of Debs, variously titled "Neighbor" or "The Man Who Sought God," though he made at least seven attempts to write it. He hoped it would be his masterpiece, and he collected material for years and drafted hundreds of pages, all of them eventually destroyed. He seems to have been blocked, partly because he never fully identified with the working class and could not imagine all the challenges of a blue-collar life, partly because he was unsure how to address the ideological turmoil on the political left during the Great Depression. His failure to finish the labor novel was one of the great disappointments of his career.

He resented assertions that he was merely a "stenographer" of life or a "journalist" or a sociological novelist. Such animadversions, he believed, denigrated his achievements as an imaginative writer. Still, in his own voice Lewis once admitted that in his fiction he scratched the "sociological itch which afflicts so many writers like myself,"[17] and he elsewhere joked with Maude Parker Child that eventually "I who peculiarly detest the sociological novel will go and 'do' the plumbers, the dentists, the communists, the authors . . . the chiropodists and the vermin exterminators, and with my last gasp be planning a chatty series of novels embodying the history of South Dakota."[18] The scholar Stephen S. Conroy averred in 1970 that Lewis was blessed with what C. Wright Mills called "the sociological imagination,"[19] and as recently as 2002 Lingeman argued that Lewis was a "literary sociologist" even while conceding that Lewis detested the sociological novel: "he approached the job like an anthropologist studying the mores, customs, and mating rituals of a primitive village."[20] Certainly, Lewis carefully researched his best novels. He outlined the plots, wrote capsule biographies of his characters, and drew elaborate floor plans of the houses where they lived and detailed maps of the towns where the stories were set. He conducted fieldwork, read insatiably on his subjects, and hired consultants to assist him. Alfred Harcourt once likened Lewis working on a novel to a PhD student writing a dissertation (chapter 69). Lewis understood long before the mass of sociologists, for example, that racial categories are socially constructed and fluid: "The races of mankind in every country run through a gradation of color from intense black to the almost pure white which is to be found only in alarming cases of anemia. No one has ever determined just where the line in this shading is to be drawn."[21] On the other hand, whenever he wrote on a topic that required little or no intensive preparation or when he neglected the basic carpentry of the novel, as in *Mantrap* (1926) and *The Man Who Knew Coolidge* (1928), or when his passion for detail and accuracy flagged, as in *Work of Art* (1934) and *The Prodigal Parents* (1938), he failed to write a very good book.

Lewis has also been fairly regarded as a transitional figure in the history of American modernism. Yet Schorer has gone even further, claiming that Lewis became "the spokesman for a literary generation."[22] Trouble is, he belonged to the same generation as many a greater novelist than he, among them Faulkner, Hemingway, F. Scott Fitzgerald, and Cather. By all accounts, Lewis was allergic to the modernist revolt in the arts. He attended the Armory Show in New York in 1913, but it made no impression on him. He was "deaf" to the experimental music of Béla Bartók (1881–1945) and Arnold Schoenberg (1874–1951).[23] He was repulsed by the avant-garde fiction of James Joyce and Gertrude Stein. That is, Lewis responded to the conditions of modernity without developing a modernist style. At most, he thought, realism and modernism "can co-exist,"[24] and to his credit he was not entirely ignored by the high modernists. T. S. Eliot remarked in a letter dated New Year's Eve 1921 that his wife Vivian "has read me some bits of Babbitt. It has some good things in it."[25]

Lewis is best understood, in our opinion, as a social comedian and provocateur in the Dickens tradition. Like Dickens, he was a social documentarian. In 1931, moreover, Constance Rourke called Lewis a "fabulist," or a teller of fables. "Lewis turns his abundant fables into critiques and challenges," she averred, "but the transcendent effect is the traditional effect: the American portrait, a comic portrait once more, has been drawn in amplitude."[26] Certainly the notion that Lewis wrote social comedy helps to explain his best work. His "mission in life," Lewis once told Frazier Hunt, was "to be the despised critic, the eternal fault-finder" (chapter 34). Lewis's admiration for Dickens's novels was also unbounded.

Both Allen Austin and Ida Compton, in their interviews with Lewis at his Vermont home in the late 1940s, remark on his ownership of the Nonesuch Press edition of Dickens's complete works. Allen noted that "*Martin Chuzzlewit* was open on the table in front of the divan" (chapter 112), and Compton quoted Lewis to the effect that if his own books "are read fifty years from now . . . it's because I did for America what Dickens did for England" (chapter 110). That is, Lewis displaced Dickens's London in a series of midwestern towns and cities populated by such Dickensian types as Chum Frink, Buzz Windrip, and Fred Cornplow.

To illustrate the point: Carol Kennicott in *Main Street* was a version of Grace Hegger Lewis, the snooty philistine to whom he was married when he wrote the novel. He even inscribed her copy of the novel, "To Gracie, who is all the good part of Carol."[27] She remembered many years later how in 1919 she advised him on the book by patiently answering his questions.

> He was grateful always for my professional experience with manuscripts, my knowledge of printer's signs and jargon, my instinctive good literary taste.
>
> The novel often intruded on my sleep. Fortunately I could always wake easily and cheerfully, if Hal came home late and wanted to talk, or if at six A.M., unable to sleep, he came to sit on the edge of my bed and ask: "Gracie, what kind of pictures would there be on the wall when Carol does over the living room?"
>
> I would push my hair away from my face, rub my eyes, try to take in what he was saying.
>
> "Uh—uh—why don't you hang up a piece of Japanese brocade—a sash—an *obi* I think it's called?" (Chapter 29)

In an interview with Lewis in the late 1940s but not published until 1958, three years after Grace Hegger Lewis published her autobiography, Lewis was asked whether he "meant [Carol] to be silly." Lewis replied, "Certainly. For example, I deliberately had her decorate a room in bad taste" (chapter 112). That is, he had used his wife as a model dilettante, and she failed to recognize his censure or his humor.

In addition, Lewis was a liberal humanist who aspired to the role of public intellectual. For six months, from autumn 1937 until spring 1938, for example, he wrote a weekly column for *Newsweek,* and he was an occasional contributor to the *Nation, American Mercury,* and *Esquire.* He was an intellectual but not an intellectual snob. On the contrary, he derided the cultural quackery of such highbrows as Bernard DeVoto,[28] Harold Stearns, Greenwich Villagers, and Left Bank expatriates. He stridently opposed what George Orwell termed "group-think," and to the extent his novels share a common theme they protest American middle-class complacency and commercialism and cultural standardization. As he wrote in his own fanciful self-portrait, he may have had "no virtues whatever save a real, fiery, almost reckless hatred of hypocrisy."[29]

He was also, unfortunately, a man of unpredictable opinions and a clutter of contradictions. Despite his Ivy League pedigree and an early ambition to earn a PhD in English, he scorned academic pretension and skewered the professoriate, especially teachers of literature. "Our American professors like their literature clear and cold and pure and very dead," he declared in Stockholm.[30] Ironically, though his novel *Main Street* epitomized the "revolt from the village" in American literature in the 1920s, after his turn to acting in the 1930s Lewis sometimes played the part of the Stage Manager in Thornton Wilder's nostalgic and sentimental "Our Town," a play that revolted against the revolt from the village. An erstwhile Fabian socialist in his early twenties, he became a social crank and a self-righteous scold, a self-described "counter revolutionary," in his sixties. Dorothy Thompson wrote that "he was basically apolitical, but insofar as his social ideas were articulate and consistent, he was an old-fashioned populist radical."[31] He once asserted, incredibly enough, that the two greatest people he had ever known were the socialist Debs and the Republican president Hoover (chapter 89). A religious skeptic, he nevertheless read Thomas à Kempis's *The Imitation of Christ* for pleasure. Although he could be charitable and charming, he also could be obnoxious and condescending, as petulant as a child. His readiness to take offense was legendary. To quote Henry Seidel Canby, he was "as little restrained by good taste as an angry cat" (chapter 5). He was a failure as a father to his sons, Wells and Michael, and all of his romantic relationships ended badly. His first wife, Grace, was a social climber who affected a British accent and bragged she had been conceived in Vienna. Theirs was, according to Lingeman, "a marriage of two narcissists."[32] His second marriage, to the journalist Dorothy Thompson, one of the most brilliant political commentators in America during the 1930s and '40s, suffered from a professional rivalry in which she bested him. Her public star was rising as his was falling. His affair late in life with Marcella Powers, an acolyte less than half his age, ended when she decided she wanted to become a conventional wife and mother.

The list of people Lewis alienated during his life reads like a Who's Who of Anglo-American writers and publishers. With his prickly temperament, he may well have lost more friends than he made were it not a mathematical impossibility. His reputation never recovered from his infamous row with Dreiser at the Metropolitan Club in New York on March 19, 1931. After Lewis publicly accused Dreiser of plagiarizing two thousand words from the serialization of his wife's book *The New Russia* (October 1928) in his book *Dreiser Looks at Russia* (November 1928), Dreiser slapped him. The incident made front-page news across the country and redounded to the benefit of neither man. By the end of his life he had become a social pariah. Only a handful of associates, such as H. L. Mencken and Fanny Butcher, remained loyal to him.

Central to his inability to maintain friendships was his alcoholism. Like almost all of the other American writers to receive the Nobel Prize for Literature—Hemingway, O'Neill, Faulkner, and John Steinbeck—he was a very heavy drinker most of his adult life. "I suppose hundreds of people in three decades have seen Sinclair Lewis drunk; no doubt he made a vast public spectacle of himself," Miller mused (chapter 115). Long before his lonely death in Italy in 1951, Lewis had exhausted his appeal, stained his reputation, and spent his talent.

Nor was he ever considered physically attractive. Tall and lanky, with a startlingly ugly and acne-scarred face, Lewis resembled Fred Astaire with pustules. In *Across the River and Into the Trees* (1950), Hemingway caricatured him as a "mediocre writer" who had "outlived his talents," a fellow with "a strange face like an over-enlarged, disappointed weasel or ferret. It looked as pock-marked and blemished as the mountains of the moon seen through a cheap telescope and . . . it looked like Goebbels' face, if Herr Goebbels had ever been in a plane that burned, and not been able to bail out before the fire reached him."[33] Similarly, in *You Can't Go Home Again* (1940) Thomas Wolfe described the face of Lloyd McHarg, modeled on Lewis, as so "puckered up" it seemed "all dried out and blistered by the fiery flames that burned in it.[34]

Lewis was, above all, a professional writer in the best sense of the term. While he was not a craftsman, he was disciplined. When he was working, he kept a strict routine, and he often told young writers that the secret to literary success was "the application of the seat of the pants to the seat of the chair."[35] When he was on his game, Lewis could easily write three to five thousand words a day. He occasionally described his study as a "factory," and George Horace Lorimer, the editor and publisher of the *Saturday Evening Post,* referred without irony to Lewis's "plant" in 1917.[36] He willingly tailored his stories to editors' specifications, but in the end he rarely compromised with the demands of the literary market. He courted readers, but not popularity at the price of his integrity. But there were some exceptions: He was not above "whoring," as he put it, as in many of his short stories and in such novels as *The Man Who Knew Coolidge* and *Mantrap.* He was occasionally willing to capitalize on his reputation, to publish a "swell piece of cheese to grab off some easy gravy."[37]

Even during his life Lewis became a persona of letters non grata. No self-respecting critic dared to discuss his fiction. Even today he seems a tempting target for the slings and arrows of the Neiman Marxists on the left. Ironically, Schorer's *Sinclair Lewis: An American Life* (1961), over nine years in the making and over eight hundred pages in length, gave the coup de grâce to his critical reputation. As Lingeman explains, "Schorer's book gave academics and general readers a license not to read Sinclair Lewis, if they needed one."[38] It also appeared in the heyday of the New Criticism and at the height of the Cold War and "the anticommunist culture war in academe,"[39] so it skews the record of Lewis's opposition to Marxism and his growing conservatism in later years. For whatever reason, Schorer's biography also betrays several biographical blind spots. He omits all mention of a woman who pursued Lewis, a former mistress of A. S. Frere, though he certainly interviewed her,[40] for example, and while Schorer mentions Dorothy Thompson's "friend," Christa Winsloe, a German novelist and playwright, several times in passing,[41] he was apparently as oblivious as Lewis to the fact that Winsloe was his wife's lover. Schorer's disdain for his subject is palpable, especially in the final chapters. He even concludes that Lewis was "one of the worst writers in modern American Literature."[42] and his "life, for all his millions of readers, is an allegory of uneasy, hapless waste, a life which, long before his death, had become the object of the world's pity and contempt."[43] Reviewing *Sinclair Lewis: An American Life* for the *New York Times Book Review,* Irving Howe scolded the biographer: "a reader looking back upon the shambles of Sinclair Lewis' years and reflecting that such tragic waste is far from unique to him, may feel for this brilliant and stricken man a more open sympathy than Mr. Schorer allows himself to express."[44]

There have been hints in recent years of a nascent critical rehabilitation. Richard Lingeman's *Sinclair Lewis: Rebel from Main Street* (2002) offers a necessary corrective to Schorer's biography. Once a toxic topic, Lewis's fiction also has been slowly regaining scholarly respectability. To judge by the column inches devoted to Lewis in the annual *MLA Bibliography,* there has been an uptick in the interest in Lewis during the past twenty years. Today there is even a scholarly Sinclair Lewis Society, founded in 1992 and affiliated with the American Literature Association, which issues a semiannual newsletter.

This volume offers yet another alternative, anecdotal account of Lewis's life. It is a type of collaborative biography published incrementally over a period of eighty years, with many of the entries recorded by friends, former friends, enemies, and acquaintances after his death. It gathers dozens of scattered sources about Lewis's life and career, illustrating the complexity of his personality in a way no single biographer could, and it offers unsanitized glimpses of him, warts and all. We have selected entries, including two interviews with Lewis new to scholarship (chapters 16 and 35), that have contributed to the narrative of his life we have constructed—not always a seamless one, but one that can be read coherently from start to finish. We have distributed some of the most important sources among many sections of the narrative in order to enhance its continuity. Our internal cuts from the entries, omitted passages that do not contribute to the narrative, are indicated with bracketed ellipses. We have also silently standardized the spelling of "Sauk Centre" and corrected misspellings, punctuation errors, and other obvious mistakes.

We are indebted to Steven Keller and Russell Cole of the Zimmerman Library staff at the University of New Mexico for their assistance in the preparation of this volume.

1
Sauk Centre
1885–1903

Growing up in Minnesota, the bookish Harry Sinclair Lewis was a loner. "Odd-turned" with pustulant acne, a favored butt of practical jokes, he was an unlikely candidate for fame and fortune. The youngest child of the village doctor Edwin J. Lewis (1849–1926) and Emma Kermott Lewis (1849–1891) and the younger brother of Claude Lewis (1878–1957), who also became a physician, he seems to have left few early footprints. As he later wrote, his "boyhood was utterly commonplace."[1] No one in Lewis's immediate family and none of his adolescent friends recorded memories of him as a child, though Hazel Palmer Lynam, the sister of one of his friends, and his niece, Isabel Lewis Agrell, collected some impressions later.

1 / Hazel Palmer Lynam

Hazel Palmer Lynam (1890–1963), an acquaintance of Lewis in his adolescence, attended Oberlin College and later taught school in Duluth.

Source: Hazel Palmer Lynam, "The Earliest Lewis," *Saturday Review of Literature,* April 14, 1934, 628.

Dr. Lewis was our family physician while we lived in Sauk Centre, and one summer arranged for Harry to work as night clerk in my father's hotel, the Palmer House. I imagine this must have been his first hotel experience and must have been about the time he finished high school or early in his college career.

Our small hotel circle and their friends found a great deal of amusement in the "fool" things Harry did, as it was generally recognized by this time that he would never amount to very much. They liked to recount how he called a traveling man at five-thirty in the morning to tell him that he had forgotten to call him for the five o'clock train.

I remember once he fell through the glass top of a cigar case for no good reason at all. He was standing by it and, I suppose, strayed so far away mentally that he neglected to maintain his center of gravity in a practical position.

My younger brother discovered him as a storyteller. He used to sit up on the desk behind the glass partition, where the bookkeeping was done, and listen to the stories Harry would tell. Sometimes I joined them. He would ask us what we would have, and no matter what subject we chose, he would start immediately and go on and on. My brother, by right of prior discovery, insisted on doing most of the selecting, so the stories were usually a little bloodthirsty for my taste. The only fragment of these tales that remains in my memory at all is one about a man tied in a cave and driven mad by the constant slow drip of water on the back of his hand.

I can remember once Harry spent a long time urging me to study and be valedictorian of my high school class. He was distressed because I was not taking a proper interest in my work. I was quite stimulated about the idea for three or four days, so he must have been rather convincing.

He was willing to put himself out, more than most adults, to amuse us; and we liked him very much in spite of the mild contempt with which he was viewed by our elders.

2 / Isabel Lewis Agrell

In her memoir, Isabel Lewis Agrell (1916–2000), Sinclair Lewis's niece, preserved personal accounts, family documents, and even a recipe for "Sinclair Lewis Cookies," which called for a shot of bourbon.

Source: Isabel Lewis Agrell, *Sinclair Lewis Remembered* (Crosslake, MN: privately printed, 1996), 35–36.

Sinclair used to say that the only person he really wanted to impress was his brother Claude, but he was never able to do so. Untrue. Claude was very proud of his younger brother. I'm sure that Sinclair exasperated Claude many times throughout their lives, but there was always a strong bond between them. I know that they both had great respect and affection for one another.

Because there was over a six-year difference in their ages, Claude undoubtedly had little interest in including a little brother in his boyhood games and pranks. By the time Claude left home for a year of teaching after high school graduation, Sinclair was still in grade school.

Claude maintained a good and happy relationship with his entire family throughout his life. I think Claude thoroughly enjoyed his friendship with Sinclair, in spite of the fact that he was much more conventional and even-tempered than his illustrious brother.

In a financial record of Claude's when he was at the University of Minnesota, one item mentioned was "Suit for Harry—$19.00." When I questioned my mother one time about the youthful Sinclair, her reply was that "he was a nice young man."

Claude was in touch with Sinclair throughout their lives by letter, by phone, or in person. Within my memory, during the twenties and thirties, whenever Sinclair visited Claude and Mary's home, he was treated as a very important guest. The best white linen tablecloth covered the dining room table. Large white linen napkins were a must.

The best glassware, silver, and china were used. We always had white linen tablecloths and napkins, fresh every Sunday, as did Grandfather Lewis, but when

Sinclair came, everything was a little extra special. Our dear German maid, Katy Meyer Lang, dressed in black or white uniforms with a white organdy apron on special occasions. She said that the only thing Sinclair ever complained of was the orange juice, which he thought should *not* be strained as she had been doing.

At one dinner party, which my mother gave for Sinclair when I was in high school during the '30s, our neighbors, Bishop and Mrs. Kemerer, were invited. Sinclair arrived very intoxicated. Mrs. Kemerer was a good sport and humored Sinclair although I am sure my parents were embarrassed.

Claude and Mary visited New York during the late '20s. Sinclair took them to a speakeasy and on a tour of the *Île de France,* the ocean liner.[2] These were the only events I remember, although I am sure there must have been more, knowing Sinclair's delight in showing provincial relatives the sights of the city.

2
New Haven and New Jersey
1903–8

After a college preparatory course at the academy of Oberlin College in Ohio, Lewis enrolled in Yale University in the fall of 1903. Some of his instructors and classmates there—Chauncey Brewster Tinker, William Lyon Phelps, Henry Seidel Canby, and Leonard Bacon—later reminisced fondly about him. Although a frequent contributor to student publications, he essentially remained an outsider during his years in New Haven. He was so disaffected he took off the academic year 1906–7 to live and work in Upton Sinclair's cooperative community in New Jersey and to travel before returning to Yale. He completed his undergraduate degree in the spring of 1908 while working part-time for the *New Haven Journal-Courier.*

3 / Chauncey Brewster Tinker

Chauncey Brewster Tinker (1876–1953) was professor of English literature at Yale University (1899–1945), where he was affectionately known as "Yale's Dr. Johnson." He was among the first to recognize Lewis's talent. Tinker, whose mind Lewis found "keen, appreciative, eager, humorous," inspired him to excel in his studies during his first year.

Source: Chauncey Brewster Tinker, "Sinclair Lewis, a Few Reminiscences," *Proceedings of the American Academy of Arts and Letters* n.s. 2 (1952): 65–67.

My own acquaintance with Lewis had been formed as early as September 1903. It began, oddly enough, as I was walking across the old campus on my way to the very first class which I ever taught at Yale College. I was accosted by a tall, red-headed boy, who asked, "Are you my Prof? My name is Harry Lewis." "Oh yes," I replied in some surprise. "I have your name on my list. How do you do?" He went on, "How about this fellow Yeats that's going to lecture tonight?" "Well," I answered, "he is an Irish poet, and his name is pronounced 'Yates.' You had better go and hear him." It was clear that the boy was interested in poetry. So was I. Here was a bond between us.

I was never dismayed by the presence in my classroom of this rather gawky and excitable person, whom his classmates presently called "Red Lewis." He sometimes wearied me, but he was my best student, and my eager helper. He enjoyed all the work and wanted to recite most of the time. His thirst was hydroptic. He often stayed after class to talk with me, and his classmates criticized him for it. But he did not care. He and I loved the same things, and that was enough for Harry. When he left me after one of these interviews, I was no better than a deflated balloon, but his enthusiasm won me, and we became good friends. This enthusiasm I shall always remember as his first and most conspicuous quality, and I am glad to have known him in his youth when the skies glowed with the dawn of a glad new day.

He was of course at the furthest remove from a sentimentalist. Nevertheless there was, I believe, at the heart of the creature a passionate affection that irradiated everything around him. But association with him was no quieting experience. He wanted in return as much as he gave, and this was of course a staggering demand. To supply it with anything like continuity was, for a young instructor, simply out of the question. After all, one had one's work to do, and it required most of one's time. I must beware of giving the impression that there could be any intimacy between a young instructor and a freshman in that forgotten world, but affection and respect were by no means incompatible with it.

There was a third passion that frequently held sway within him. I do not know how to name it, save to call it unexpectedness. With Harry you could never tell. To fit him into a category or to look for any principle that governed his behavior was to discover that nothing would serve to define him. The conventions and restrictions of good society—especially of good collegiate society—were offensive to him. His abiding temptation was to undermine them and blow them at the moon. He might in that process spread a good deal of discomfort and make the judicious grieve, but at least life ceased at once to be commonplace and dull. After all, he was *Red Lewis,* and friend as well as foe had to admit it. An anecdote from a later period of life will illustrate his utter waywardness. After the passage of a number of years, his classmates, in repentant mood, invited him to attend a class dinner at the Yale Club and make a few remarks. When his turn came to speak, he rose and began in some such way as this, "When I was in college, you fellows had no use for me, and I have to tell you that I have none for you." His remarks are said to have been received with thunderous applause. Lewis had cleared the air. He had purged the stuffed bosom, and thereafter much was forgotten and all was forgiven. Similarly, when membership in the Institute was offered to him he thrust the invitation aside with something like scorn. But thirteen years later he repented and gratefully accepted election. Later still, he even served as one of the Directors of the Academy.

4 / William Lyon Phelps

An eminent Boswell scholar, William Lyon Phelps (1865–1943) joined the Yale faculty as an instructor the same semester Lewis matriculated, and he supported the brash midwesterner throughout his undergraduate career. Phelps rose through the faculty ranks (instructor 1903–8, associate professor 1908–13, professor 1913–33). During the decade between his retirement from Yale and his death, he continued to be considered one of America's preeminent academic minds.

Source: William Lyon Phelps, "Men Now Famous," *Delineator* 117 (September 1930): 94.

I remember him well as a freshman at Yale. He came from Sauk Centre, Minnesota, in 1903. His name was Harry S. Lewis. He was very tall, incredibly thin, and his head was crowned with a mass of fiery red hair. Very few of his classmates knew his Christian name; he was universally known in college as "Red" Lewis, both because of his hair and because of his radical opinions, which he took no pains to conceal. At that time he was a disciple of Upton Sinclair.[1] He was not disliked in college, but was regarded with amiable tolerance as a freak. He took not the slightest interest in the idols of the place—athletics, societies, and so on; nor did he care to "make" any of the positions in extracurricular activities that are rewarded with social distinction. And as he took no interest in these things, he did not see why he should pretend to do so. In other words, he was a complete and consistent individualist, going his own way, and talking only about things that interested him. We at once found a common bond of friendship in our admiration for a Minnesota poet, Arthur Upson, whose brief life ended tragically, and who had written some beautiful verse.[2] On that ground of intimacy, we proceeded to have many long discussions on literature, the real passion of Lewis. I liked and admired him immensely, although our views on many subjects were and are irreconcilable. It was a pleasure to me to see a lad who thought for himself. In his senior year he became an editor of the *Yale Literary Magazine.*

5 / Henry Seidel Canby

Henry Seidel Canby (1878–1961), best known for his contributions to early American literary scholarship, began teaching at Yale after he graduated from that institution in 1899. He was editor of the New York *Evening Post* for four years, achieved professorial status in 1922, and became one of the founding editors of the *Saturday Review of Literature* in 1924. He was also the author of several books, among them *Classic Americans* (1931), *The Age of Confidence* (1934), *Thoreau* (1939), and *Whitman* (1943).

Source: Henry Seidel Canby, *American Memoir* (Boston: Houghton Mifflin, 1947), 307–9.

I have known [Lewis] well, though never intimately since our paths seldom cross, for forty years. I knew him first as a Yale undergraduate, a nonconformist, getting what he could—and he got a great deal—from that stronghold of intelligent conformity where radicals, once they are accepted as Yale men, can say or do what they please. (It is said that [Josiah W.] Gibbs, greatest of mathematical physicists, was saved for his university by some elder statesman who remarked that he might be incomprehensible, but he was a good Yale man.) Sinclair Lewis would often drop in for an evening in the room in "dirty Durfee" where I was living with Chauncey Brewster Tinker. This would have been in 1906. Tinker, a conservative in literature but never a reactionary, was a brilliant lecturer who could make tradition glow with life. The young man and the older were temperamentally alike, though worlds apart in their ideas of how to live. Both had ignitable minds which would explode at a hint of the cheap or the false, but as to what were true and what were false values, they could seldom agree. For Sinclair derived his emotional consents from nature as interpreted by the scientists, and Tinker from Doctor Johnson and the Word of God as validated by the Anglican Church. Thus it came about, as often with a child of nature, that Lewis worshiped Tinker's impeccable taste while distrusting his philosophy, and Tinker was increasingly annoyed by a writer whose idea was to lash sensual man into finding his own way to salvation. Santayana[3] would have enjoyed their conversation, then and later, and been supercilious to both. [. . .]

Too many easy judgments were formed of Lewis in his percussion-powder days. He had a face of boilerplate, but his mental skin was as sensitive as a baby's. If he drank, it was, as with Poe, to quiet his nerves, usually with contrary results. There was a noble independence about the man, to be respected even when he used it to sneer at the genteel age, which was his enemy. I have seen him rise from a dull dinner party, say "I'm tired," go through the nearest door, pop into the most available bed—and emerge two hours later in excellent humor. Once he chose an ambassador's room, which made difficulties with protocol.

But Lewis was always and essentially a realistic idealist, a true, if surprising, product of the liberal late nineteenth century in which he had his roots. He was always, you will note, on the side of the angels. But his eye and ear were too honest to please the respectable, who prefer *genre* paintings to candid photographs. The trouble was not his choice of characters—the country was full of Babbitts and Elmer Gantrys. It was the overpowering and often unpleasant reality he gave to them. Only in moments of intense perception do we see both type and individual in a person we like or hate. We are blind to the type, or do not recognize the individual. Sinclair's gift was for realizing, and always with a satiric point. Dialogue was his best medium. Some of his most brilliant dialogues were never written down. Once at my house he rode high on an imaginary conversation between Shakespeare and Ben Jonson. Jonson was the patronizing highbrow; Shakespeare was the popular writer, humble in a dangerous way before Art and Learning. He could give the people what they wanted, since he was not writing for posterity like his learned friend. To this day I see Lewis's quizzical Will and pompous Ben more vividly than in any historian's portrait. It is the art that Shakespeare himself practices in Polonius and Falstaff, and excellently adapted to letting society recognize its own warped or frightened soul behind an inescapable verisimilitude.

The best phrase for Lewis was written by Horace when he spoke of the writing world as a *genus irritabile.* He was a fighter, as little restrained by good taste as an angry cat. Yet when he was not irritated he was generous and fair. I have heard him defend and praise at a public dinner a fellow writer (equally irritable) who had but recently attacked his intellectual integrity.

6 / Leonard Bacon

The critic, translator, and Pulitzer Prize–winning poet, Leonard Bacon (1887–1954), was Lewis's younger classmate at Yale and, later, his close friend. He taught at the University of California at Berkeley until 1923, and he received the Pulitzer Prize for poetry in 1940 for his volume of satirical verse, *Sunderland Capture.* Lewis's short story "Young Man Axelbrod" (*Century* 94 [June 1917]: 188–98) is informed by a visit with Bacon, who was the model for the character of a wealthy young aesthete. See also James M. Hutchisson, "Sinclair Lewis, Paul De Kruif, and the Composition of *Arrowsmith.*" *Studies in the Novel* 24 (Spring 1992): 48–66.

Source: Leonard Bacon, *Semi-Centennial* (New York and London: Harper, 1939), 44–46.

The cadaverous, pale-freckled face and tomato-soup-colored hair of that singular Junior who was to be the first American to win the Nobel Prize for literature could not be ignored then any more than now. "Harry" Lewis was as different from the correct young types around him as Sauk Centre is from Tuxedo. He had none of their artificial constraints and far more real dignity of nature. He stormed and he damned, but again he might roar you as gently as a sucking-dove. And his hates and his loves were genuine and never compromised by ulterior and clandestine desires, although there was nothing he would not do to assist fellow-sufferers among the rocks and briars of the lower slopes of the two-horned mountain. His classmates I believe had viewed him with alarm, had been cruel with respect to his irascibilities, which were passionate, and had ignored his talents which were obvious to every "heeler" of the *Lit.* Our admiration, I feel sure, was not unpleasant to him and there was quite a group of us who instinctively endeavored to do him honor. This reflects some credit on us, for Harry did not belong to any society and never would, which does not add anything to the prestige of the classes of 1906 and 1907. He was apart from that kind of thing, and in one way from the college, for he did not even live in it. He had a room in a cheap boarding-house outside the pale of the university, where I perused a typed volume of his poetry four inches thick and discussed with him the merits of an equally fat book by an author who never won the Nobel Prize. The unfortunate's name was Swinburne,[4] to us at the time a figure who meant liberty and the casting-off of fetters.

Harry was a scarlet thread in the drab of my Freshman year, and after I returned from my enforced year abroad, in my Junior year. I never have had a better time with any man than when we sat over welsh-rarebits and beer at the Hof-Braü, and disposed of the past and the future with great impartiality and equal authority. Poetry was his love, and I am still astonished at the direction in which his fate took him. It was clear even then that he was a comer, but in 1905 I should have predicted for him the lyric, perhaps the epic, but not the photographic. In a satire twenty years later I adjured him to return to his early altars.[5] Furthermore, I believe he will before he dies. He came into the world not to turn a candid camera on Babbitt, but to revel in something as old as the Tale of Troy and as new as the aeroplane. If he finds it, he will create out of his unabated natural forces something that will force us to think at once of *War and Peace* and *The Three Musketeers.* And his sunset will be as surprising to the world as his dawn was to me.

I have a last vignette of him in New Haven. Harry in his senior year, 1906–7, had given up college in mid-term, for the delights of Upton Sinclair's Utopian experiment, Helicon Hall. Strange as it may seem to Marxian youth, many of the staunchest reactionaries they know were rampant socialists then, a fact that should give Marxian youth pause. Upton Sinclair appointed Sinclair Lewis furnace-man in the New Jersey Utopia, which led Harry to form a low opinion of that belated Brook Farm. He returned disillusioned in the autumn of 1907 after the graduation of his class, to round out his degree and become once more the delight of the slaves of the *Lit.* We had long walks and talks. And a strange fantasy of his about the sphinx became a symbol for me, which has been dominant in my thought, if I may call it thought, these thirty stricken years. I was a candidate for the *Lit* (last place) and everything hung on whether or not one final poem was accepted before the election. Harry Lewis, my delightful roommate Harry Beers[6] (also a candidate but a sure one), and I went down to read the bulletin of the chosen, which the Board would post in the window of the *Lit* office late that night. It was blowing a gale and black as pitch in the Berkeley Oval, and many lucifers went out before we were certain that "The Ballade of the Golden Horn" was safely on the list.[7] I have never known a moment of greater triumph, and no other Nobel Prizeman has struck so many matches in my behalf.

7 / Upton Sinclair

Upton Sinclair (1878–1968), Pulitzer Prize–winning novelist most famous for *The Jungle* (1906), wrote more than ninety books in the course of his long career. He was a strident political and social activist, an ardent socialist, and an advocate for reform in America, including Prohibition. Lewis lived and worked in his utopian community—Helicon Home Colony—in Englewood, New Jersey, from November to December 1, 1906. It was destroyed by fire the next year. Sinclair also ran for governor of California in 1934 on the EPIC platform (End Poverty in California). In later years, Sinclair Lewis often complained about people who confused him with Upton Sinclair.

Source: Upton Sinclair, *The Cup of Fury* (Great Neck, NY: Channel Press, 1956), 64–66.

We called him Hal. He was tall and lanky, a twenty-year-old eaglet who was fledging his feathers; he had vivid red hair, and an abnormally florid complexion. You know him as Sinclair Lewis—author of *Main Street* [1920], *Babbitt* [1922], *Arrowsmith* [1924], *Dodsworth* [1929], and a dozen other novels.

Hal was eager, talkative, and a good listener. And at Helicon Hall, there were many people worth listening to: a philosopher from Columbia University, William P. Montague;[8] a professor of manual arts from Teachers' College;[9] a Swedish writer, Edwin Björkman, who was translating Strindberg;[10] a couple of minor novelists;[11] a physician;[12] and others who could tell much about life and letters.[13]

Hal had quit Yale in order to learn about co-operative living. [. . .] He soon had enough of furnace-work and general education, and went off to New York. There, incidentally, he wrote a playful article about our Helicon "home-colony" life for the New York *Sun.* It has been reprinted in the collection of Hal's miscellaneous writings called *The Man from Main Street: A Sinclair Lewis Reader,* and you may enjoy reading it. [. . .]

Years passed before I saw Sinclair Lewis again. He had become editorial adviser to a publishing house, and I offered them one of my novels, *Sylvia.*[14] We met for lunch and Hal had the sad duty of telling me that the novel was declined. Then when I moved to California, he came to my house for an evening, bringing his first wife. More years passed, and I next saw him at his New York hotel. We corresponded sporadically and sent each other our books. Several of mine he praised, and I quoted his opinions; and I did the same for him. On a dust-jacket recently, I saw what I wrote about *Babbitt* when it was first issued: "I am now ready to get out in the middle of the street and shout hurrah, for America's most popular novelist has sent me a copy of his new book, *Babbitt.* I am here to enter my prediction that it will be the most talked-about and the most-read novel published in this country in my lifetime."

8 / Emile Gauvreau

A high school dropout, Emile Gauvreau (1891–1956) began his career in journalism along with Lewis at the *New Haven Journal-Courier.* In 1919 he became the youngest managing editor of the *Hartford Courant* in its history. In 1924 he founded the tabloid *New York Evening Graphic* (a.k.a. the pornoGraphic), which launched the careers of Walter Winchell and Ed Sullivan, and in 1929 he became managing editor of William Randolph Hearst's tabloid, the *New York Mirror.*

Source: Emile Gauvreau, *My Last Million Readers* (New York: Dutton, 1941), 43.

Our staff [on the *Journal-Courier*] was made up largely of Yale men working their way through college and there was a general exodus of editorial brains when Commencement arrived. Sloane[15] got a new staff together, year after year. Sinclair Lewis was one of Sloane's reporters and so was Waldo Frank, the brilliant liberal writer.[16] There were others, now nationally recognized. Lewis dropped in to smell the ink when I was a cub. The intellectuals on the paper carried on great discussions. I sat back in my corner, when my obituaries were done, and listened to verbal explosions, which were as illuminating as they were unprintable. I have heard Lewis tear the world to pieces, and as things turned out, his predictions were moderate. After he left the *Journal-Courier* he sent an autographed copy of his first novel, *Our Mr. Wrenn* [1914], to Sloane who let everything slide and locked himself up in his cubby-hole to read a book by one of his boys. Even then I understood the pride this unappreciated editor felt in his heart.

3
Bohemia
1908–19

After graduation from Yale, Lewis looked for a job without much success. He was fired from a series of newspapers, including the Waterloo, Iowa, *Daily Courier* and the *San Francisco Bulletin,* because he was temperamentally unsuited to daily journalism. In addition, as he admitted, he was "afflicted with Wanderlust."[1] Over the years he lived in Carmel, San Francisco, Washington, and finally the East Village in New York, where he worked at a series of editorial jobs and published several minor novels before becoming a regular contributor to the *Saturday Evening Post.* With this semisecure source of income, he bought a flivver and, with his new wife Grace Hegger Lewis, toured the country before writing *Free Air* (1919), the sixth and last of his apprenticeship novels.

9 / William Rose Benét

William Rose Benét (1886–1950), writer, editor, and Pulitzer Prize–winning poet, was Lewis's classmate at Yale, where he edited the student newspaper. They lived together during the summer of 1909 in Carmel and later moved in the same New York literary circle: Lewis worked for the publishing firm of Frederick A. Stokes Company from October 1910 to October 1912, while Benét was on the staff of *Century.* Benét was one of the founders of the *Saturday Review of Literature* in 1924 and worked for the magazine until his death. He married four times: his first wife was Theresa Thompson, sister of Kathleen Norris (see headnote, chapter 31), and his third wife was the poet Elinor Wylie (1885–1928).

Source: William Rose Benét, "The Earlier Lewis," *Saturday Review of Literature,* January 20, 1934, 421.

In certain formative years after leaving college—for I was late in developing a mature viewpoint—"Red" Lewis was one of the strongest influences in my life, and, I may say, a thoroughly beneficial one. That is not to say that we always got along well together. Our ideas often clashed. It is from such clashes, when you are young, that sparks are struck to kindle new ideas. The controversial battles of youth are necessary to growth.

I first heard of Harry Lewis, as he was called then—Sinclair being his middle name—when I was a Yale undergraduate. As he was in Yale College and I was in the Scientific School[2] we had no occasion to meet. Second to the historic *Yale Literary Magazine* in those days there was another small literary magazine modeled somewhat upon Stone & Kimball's *Chap-Book,* known as the *Yale Courant.* Lewis was already drawing more books from the Yale library than, I believe, any undergraduate has before or since, and trying his apprentice hand at writing, as he had doubtless done in school. It was quite natural that he quickly "made" both the *Lit* and the *Courant* and was elected to the Chairmanship of the latter. This office he almost immediately resigned to devote his literary energies to the *Lit.* I stood second in the *Courant* competition and succeeded to his vacated office. Therefore, one afternoon, passing the precincts of the *Lit* in a basement passage of White Hall, on the way to my own editorial cubicle, I happened to espy the fellow of whose brilliance and independence I had already heard. A long, gangling youth with a conflagrate head of hair was stretched out on a high-window seat smoking a pipe. He invited me in with a wave of the hand. We exchanged a few remarks, the usual "kidding," I think, of undergraduates.

A little later, of course, Lewis threw in his fortunes with Upton Sinclair's Helicon Hall, where he wrote poetry while tending a socialistic furnace. He wrote a lot of verse in those days. He caused quite a stir at Yale by his eminently characteristic espousing of the socialist cause so early in his career. It seemed to me at the time an interesting and sporting thing to do. It still does.

I am not going to dwell on Sinclair Lewis's undergraduate literary efforts. Henry Mencken,[3] who professes a low opinion of poetry in general is, I believe, still trying to suppress any reappearance of his own early poetic efforts. As a matter of fact, "Red's" undergraduate verse was not at all bad for those days. I have some of it still, clipped from old *Courants.* He soon began to sell verse here and there to New York magazines. I remember a most rollicking stave he wrote about a priest, highly laudatory of this priest's convivial spirit and called "Father Kileen" [*Yale Courant,* November 24, 1905]. It was modeled upon the late Richard Hovey's "Barney McGee."[4] At that time there was another man of literary promise in Yale College, Allan Updegraff.[5] He and Lewis were great friends and were associates later, I think, on *Transatlantic Tales* in New York, where they set themselves to translating foreign masterpieces of fiction. Updegraff has since become a well-known novelist.

I never saw Lewis again, that I remember, in college. It was after graduation, in California, that my best friend, Henry Hoyt[6] (Elinor Wylie's brother), wrote me that Lewis was coming to the Coast. I must meet him. At that time Henry and I had decided, with the arrogance of youth, that most people were bovine and that a soul could be discerned in very few. By that we meant, I suppose, that most people had very little independence of mind or spirit. "Red," however, quite evidently had.

I had lately come back from across the Pacific as deck yeoman on an Army transport, and I decided now to take a trip to Carmel, California, to meet this avatar. I arrived over a sandhill in a creaking buckboard of some sort to have a lanky individual, in corduroys and sweater or something of the kind, topped by the bonfire of his hair, hail me from the door of a shack. I lighted down, and "Red" introduced me to our mutual dwelling. As I remember it, we sat up all that first night discussing the Christian religion. I was quite controversial in my religious views at that time and Lewis proceeded to give me all the benefit of the higher criticism. On the other hand, I contributed a song I had learned from an

Army officer, a nonsense song which "Red" immediately caught up and proceeded to troll lustily. It became one of his favorites.

We spent some time in Carmel together. We got to know the late George Sterling, drank his muscade and ate his abalone.[7] We wrote and wrote. I was writing pretty bad verse and Lewis was, at the time, writing short stories considerably under the influence of Edith Wharton,[8] whose work he intensely admired. He was acting at Carmel as secretary for Grace MacGowan Cooke and her sister Alice MacGowan.[9] Mrs. Cooke's daughter, Helen,[10] whom we knew, later became the wife of Harry Leon Wilson.[11] We were all great friends, even though Mrs. Cooke dubbed me "William the Silent," and "Red" somewhat annoyed Helen Cooke, solely out of his admiration for her, by chanting a most complimentary song about her which he had made up, entitled "A Fugitive Queen." "Red" and I swam in the Pacific, picnicked on the beach, took long walks, did our own cooking, and even tried experiments with our own laundry. I was amazed then, as I have been ever since, at the man's ability to reel off stories. On the way home from George Sterling's, through the Carmel woods, of a summer night, he would launch into some yarn that he had made up on the spur of the moment, and before we were back at our cottage—we had moved into better quarters due to the benevolence of a grand old lady who was then one of the leading spirits in Carmel—the whole story would have been completed in recitative. It was a marvelous performance, and apparently his fund of invention was inexhaustible. Also there were, as doubtless there are still—as appears in *The Man Who Knew Coolidge* [1928]—the almost endless monologues in which he suddenly took on a character part, and the fantastic imaginings that would be worked out in the most intricate detail, till one almost screamed for surcease from the spate of words. From intense hilarity the man would also, at times, turn as grave and didactic as a Baptist minister and proceed to lay down the moral law, according to his own highly individual ideas, with an almost snarling earnestness that seemed to bode hell-fire for the unbeliever. It appeared as if Shelley himself could never have been more deeply stirred by the injustices and tyrannies of the economic order, or disorder.

My brain, to use Henry Hoyt's expression, was sometimes thoroughly "sandpapered" by the constant dissection of ideas, the questioning of every premise, the rovings of "Red's" insatiable curiosity concerning preconceived notions, and the constant challenge of his argument. And it did me a whole lot of good. This man was not content to stand and gaze at the horizon. He stalked forth immediately to crest the hill and find the next one. He may have come from Minnesota, but he was spiritually from Missouri, and had to be "shown." His intellect and his imagination were steaming up for the battle with life, and the ferment of young ambition in him shriveled up any "green sickness" of youth. The days of the making of a writer are days wonderful and absurd. "Red" himself has caught the yearning absurdity of such a period beautifully in his latest novel, *Work of Art* [1934], in the grand Swinburnian poem that the youngster in Black Thread chants from a rooftop.[12] We had great days—as they seem to me now—days of typewriter pounding with "great thoughts." Nights of conviviality and tremendous conversations. Once we "hiked" a long way down the Coast together, camping out at night. Then the time at Carmel came to an end.

Lewis took a job on the San Francisco *Bulletin* and I went back to Benicia Arsenal, the Ordnance post of which my father was then in command. I had "Red" out to stay at the Arsenal and meet my family. He took an immediate strong liking for my father whose enormous reading, individual mind, humorous disposition, and liking for discussion exhilarated him. My father retained a deep fondness for one he would always speak of as "Harry" Lewis, as he had known him. He admired the questing intelligence and the spiritual integrity of the man. Naturally they were usually on opposite sides of an argument—but then my father enjoyed that. In fact it was a habit of his to take the opposite side. Otherwise there was no sharpening of wits, no arraying of the whole armament of opinion. This was right up "Red's" street, and they would sit up half the night in an intellectual duello that fascinated them both.

Lewis returned to the East, and soon I followed him. He got me a hall bedroom next to his own larger room on Van Nest Place in the middle of Charles Street. That was long before the days when, as now, Seventh Avenue cut a swath through that section of town. So we lived in Greenwich Village, "Red" being employed by the Frederick A. Stokes firm of publishers, I as a cub editor on the old *Century Magazine.* The youth of that period was chiefly interested in sociological matters. It was some years before the war, and after the war the more or less disillusioned youth of America seemed to turn, in the Scott Fitzgerald[13] days, toward intense individualism and the "eat, drink, and be merry for tomorrow we may die" attitude. Not so in that earlier time. Most of the young people were out to reform the world in one way or another—and, by Golly, the world was going to reform or know the reason why!

It was the day of the old *Masses* with Max Eastman and Floyd Dell as editors;[14] of "the Working Girls' Home," namely the back room of O'Connor's old Café on the corner of Greenwich Avenue and Sixth, where beer flowed freely and music had charms—the place where John Masefield[15] himself once tended bar. It was the day of "The Old Grapevine," long gone, up Sixth Avenue a few blocks, where were checker players and bar philosophers and a cat that walked on the bar; it was the day of the Anarchist Ball, where I was introduced to Emma Goldman;[16] it was the day when Frances Perkins, now a member of President Roosevelt's cabinet, was laying the foundation for a notable career in labor matters;[17] when Edna Kenton lived not so far off;[18] when Union Square was a veritable Hyde Park for soap-box orators; when "Red" came home one day with news of a new Stokes author who had just swum into their ken, by name Edna Ferber;[19] when John Reed[20] managed to get some of my poetry into the *American Magazine;* when Sinclair Lewis, on his way from Sauk Centre to Stockholm, pounded furiously at his typewriter, in his Van Nest Place room, lit by a tattered weisbach, composing lyrics for a comic opera he was sure he was going to sell to George M. Cohan.[21] At the same time he had become fascinated by aviation and journeyed out to Mineola to renew acquaintance with Captain Paul Beck,[22] one of the first Army fliers, whom he had originally met in Benicia, California. He also took time off from the office and wrote Stokes a boys' book, about a boy aviator,[23] and he was as busy as a bird-dog doing a thousand and one literary jobs and sitting up arguing till dawn.

10 / Charles Hanson Towne

Charles Hanson Towne (1877–1949) was an influential editor, prolific author, and New York celebrity. From 1901 to 1929 he served as editor for the journals *Smart Set, Delineator, Designer, McClure's,* and *Harper's Bazar.* He was also one of Lewis's earliest supporters. As late as 1938, Lewis averred that to Towne and only a few others "I owe something that cannot be repaid except in lasting affection."[24]

Source: Charles Hanson Towne, *Adventures in Editing* (New York and London: D. Appleton, 1926), 85–87.

After we had moved to the Fifth Avenue offices, Colonel Mann[25] began the publication of another magazine. It was called *Transatlantic Tales,* and consisted, as its name would imply, of stories from other lands, done into English by experts. It was a splendid idea, but somehow it never quite "caught on." The late Edward Clark Marsh, who some years afterward became vice-president of the Macmillan Company, was editor-in-chief and on his staff was a young, red-haired lad from somewhere in the Middle West—a high-strung, nervous, tempestuous fellow who made swift movements with his hands and talked like a streak; a gawky, lank six-footer, who banged doors and lost his temper at the telephone, and seemed out of place, cooped up in an office. He was always longing to be off somewhere. He resented four walls and a roof more than anyone I ever have known; yet he had the will to work, and accomplished much during the fretful hours he was at his confining desk.

There was little at the time to suggest the writer of important American novels. None of us, I fear, paid much attention to the youth, or took too seriously his spasmodic dissertations on literature—of which he knew a great deal. Later, he came to the staff of *Adventure,* under the editorship of Arthur Sullivant Hoffman,[26] and one day he told me he had had his first novel accepted by Harper's. He was all excitement. He had written it nights and Sundays—in every spare moment he had[27]—and if it proved a success he intended to rid himself of the chains that bound him to an editorial job. But *Our Mr. Wrenn* did not create much of a sensation, full of charm though it was, and so our Mr. Sinclair Lewis stayed on. He tried again; four or five novels were industriously produced, and many short stories, before he took his courage in his hands and fled from New York to write *Main Street* [1920]. He became reader and literary advisor for Frederick Stokes, and later for George Doran.[28] I ran into him a little while ago; he was the same red-headed youth, apparently, the same "Hal" Lewis I had known so long ago—as carefree and jubilant, quite as in love with life, and as eager to be off to some new scene.

"And did you once see Shelley plain?"[29] I thought; and also I thought how seldom it is that one knows, at the time, that it *is* a Shelley encountered on the road of youth.

And Lewis was kind enough to remind me that when he wrote his first book, and told me of its four rejections, it was I who suggested that he offer it to Miss Elizabeth Jordan,[30] who was then on the editorial board of Harper & Brothers, anxiously seeking fresh talent. I think I was as happy as he over the incident.

11 / Mary Heaton Vorse

Mary Heaton Vorse (1874–1966) was an affluent New York feminist best known as a labor and social justice activist as well as a journalist, novelist, and poet. For her lifetime of service, she was honored—along with Eleanor Roosevelt and Upton Sinclair—with the first United Auto Workers Social Justice Award. She was also the model for the character of Mary French in John Dos Passos's novel trilogy *U.S.A.* (1930–36). Lewis later listed her among the people he saw most often during the period 1910 to 1915. According to Schorer, Vorse "was kind to him" and for her "all his life, he felt a rather special affection and loyalty, even though they were never intimately associated."[31]

Source: Mary Heaton Vorse, *Time and the Town* (New York: Dial, 1942), 95–96.

The nucleus of what was to be the Provincetown Players was forming that summer [1911]. Susan Glaspell and Lucy Huffaker[32] had taken Miss Roseboro's house. Hutchins Hapgood and Neith[33] had come back to Provincetown.

Sinclair Lewis was back, living at the Avellars' wharf. He was prodigious. He would come into the house, roaring that "he had a girl and her name was Daisy, when she sang the cat went crazy, with delirium and epilepsy and all sort of cataleptics." A stream of fantasies, of stories, of ideas streamed from him. He never stopped. He ate almost as much blueberry pie as Wilbur Steele.[34] He wrote a whole boy's book in three weeks, seventy thousand words, called *Hike and the Aeroplane* [1912], probably the first airplane book for boys. He wrote it to make money to begin his first novel, *Our Mr. Wrenn.* He raced through the first twenty thousand words of that in the next three weeks and when Joe [O'Brien][35] and I read it, we knew here was an author.

He was never still, his hair flamed, his blue eyes blazed, his long, sensitive hands gesticulated. He got himself sunburned to dull plum color over and over again and peeled. He galloped over the dunes barefoot. He shook sand into the picnic basket. He came in shouting he had an idea, and a flood of nonsense to float Noah's Ark would resound through Kibbe Cook's house.[36]

I would chase him out with a broom. The children would join in. The dog would bark. We would go slamming in and out Kibbe Cook's house doors, with Red leading all of us, looking like one of the earlier Sennett films.[37] Joe O'Brien, Wilbur Steele, and Art Hutchins[38] joined in these comic roughhouses and it was as if a herd of buffalo pounded through the little house.

12 / Harrison Smith

Harrison "Hal" Smith (1889–1971), another Yalie (MA class of '14) and a friend of Lewis's from his early employment with George H. Doran and Company, was Lewis's editor at Harcourt, Brace until 1931. Smith later edited a collection of Lewis's correspondence with Alfred Harcourt and others, *From Main Street to Stockholm* (1952).

Source: Harrison Smith, "Sinclair Lewis: Remembrance of the Past," *Saturday Review of Literature,* January 27, 1951, 7–8.

I awoke suddenly one night a week before he died and saw Lewis looking mournfully across his breakfast table at me, and my mind went back into the past, to my first meeting with him in his narrow room on Charles Street in Greenwich Village. I had been a freshman at Yale when he was a senior and an editor of the *Lit,* but I did not even know him by name until the evening I went over to Charles Street to visit George Soule,[39] who was employed by that time in the publishing house of Frederick A. Stokes, where Lewis was reading manuscripts. It was impossible to concentrate on what George was saying in his calm, wise way for a loud, intense voice penetrated the walls and echoed down the dusty stairs.

"That's Red Lewis," George said "You've got to meet him." And there he was, perched like a crane on a couch, tall, lanky, red-headed, all knees and joints, sawing his hand up and down in a wildly passionate attack on an anonymous young man who was unable to get a word in edgewise. "Good Lord," I thought, "here's a revivalist minister on the loose." I stayed silent in awe and admiration. For the first time in my life I was aware that I was listening to a man who violently and passionately cared about the same kind of things that had been vaguely concerning me, that here was a man dangerously aroused, brilliant. Part of my own awakening had come from reading Bernard Shaw[40] and H. G. Wells.[41] I thought of Lewis as a beardless, younger Shaw, or another Wells perhaps, and suddenly I knew that I had met my first genius. I had never liked to use this banal word, but then and later I attached it in my mind without embarrassment to Sinclair Lewis.

It was Lewis, as well as George Soule, who drew me to the musty old rooming house where, as one lucky enough to have a small income, I took the dark parlor downstairs. Cats, scarred and beaten up from battles and backyard love affairs, crept in on cold nights when I opened my window, until the black room around my bed seemed to be illuminated with the fire of green eyes. I began to know Lewis and to hear about the doctor father he worshiped. There were tales of riding with him on his rounds which I could match, because my own father had belonged to that noble and vanishing breed of general practitioners, and very different tales of Yale—where sleekly groomed and mannered youngsters from Groton, Exeter, and Hotchkiss passed the lanky red-headed Westerner on the campus with quick glances of mistrust.

13 / Edna Ferber

Edna Ferber (1885–1968), a novelist, playwright, and journalist, was a New York author and member of the Algonquin Round Table. She is best known today for her early Emma McChesney stories and her novels *So Big* (1924), for which she received a Pulitzer Prize, and *Giant* (1952).

Source: Edna Ferber, *A Peculiar Treasure* (New York: Doubleday, Doran, 1939), 191–92.

Editors of various magazines offered me more money for the McChesney stories, but I sentimentally stuck to the *American* where they had originated. Business was unimportant to me then. Sometimes the odd young man who was publicity writer for the Stokes company used to talk to me about it, whenever he managed to talk seriously at all, which was practically never. He was a gangling, redheaded, popeyed fellow; shambling, untidy, uproariously funny. Together we would go gesticulating and jabbering along the New York streets, leaving a procession of startled or shocked faces turned toward us as we went. The cuckoo young man's name was Sinclair Lewis, but everyone called him Red. He and I had built up two characters which we always assumed when together. Red was Gus, the janitor of a mythical office building, and I was Tillie, the scrubwoman. We talked in a bad German dialect, faintly Weber-and-Fieldsian,[42] and not very funny except to us.

"Tillie, you vas earning goot money on new chob, ain't?"

"Ja, only for my knees, them new kind stone floors."

This would go on for hours. Red was better than I at it—more outrageous. His linen was the grubbiest, he had no money, he would escort me to the door of one of those literary parties to which I had been bidden, but nothing could induce him to come in.

"Naw, I'd be turned out of there. They wouldn't want me in there." In a year or two I, too, learned that literary parties got you nowhere and were very dull stuff indeed.

14 / William E. Woodward

William E. Woodward (1874–1950), a historian and novelist, turned to writing after a successful career in advertising and public relations. Admired during his lifetime by historically inclined American modernists for his biographies of George Washington, Thomas Paine, and Ulysses S. Grant, Woodward is famous for writing debunking histories against the grain; he even coined the term *debunk* in his best-selling first novel, *Bunk* (1923). In 1912 he founded the Publishers' Newspapers Syndicate, a weekly book review page, and promptly hired Lewis to write the reviews. Woodward subsequently reviewed *Elmer Gantry* (1927) in the New York *Evening Post* and wrote a *New Yorker* profile of Lewis in 1934, "The World and Sauk Centre," which effectively ended their friendship.

Source: William E. Woodward, *The Gift of Life: An Autobiography* (New York: Dutton, 1947), 187–88, 197–98.

One day I had a talk with Rodman Gilder, son of Richard Watson Gilder, the famous editor of the *Century Magazine.*[43] I was telling him of my difficulty in getting an editor when he looked blank a moment, as if in a state of deep reflection, and then he said: "Oh, my goodness, I think I know just the man for you. His name is Lewis. He's a sort of editorial helper on *Adventure,* that little magazine published by the Butterick Company."

Naturally, I was interested, for I respected Rodman Gilder's judgment. "Tell me about him, Rodman," I said. "I've never heard of him. Lewis. Lewis. What's his first name?"

"They call him Red," Rodman said, "but that's a nickname. His name is Sinclair—or Sinclair Lewis, in full. He's a Yale man—worked his way through Yale. Comes from somewhere in the West, from Wisconsin or Minnesota—I forget which. And can he write! Young fellow, about thirty. Lives on First Avenue, in the tenement district."

"Do you think he'd like the job?" I asked.

"Listen, this Lewis chap has been knocked all over the lot by people who think they are his betters. He's had a hard life, and is dog poor, but he has ability. I'm sure he'd be a good man for you. Call him up and see him."

I called up the publishers of *Adventure* and asked for Mr. Lewis. They had to look for him, but eventually he came to the phone. I had him meet me at the Brevoort[44] for dinner that evening. He was a lanky, blue-eyed, red-haired fellow with a rough face and as homely as a rail fence, but he had a winning smile and a cordial handshake. I liked him the instant I saw him and I spent an hour or more in telling him of the review syndicate, of the newspapers in it, and of what he would be expected to do. He listened, crumbling bread in his plate. I had hardly finished telling him of my plan when he began to make suggestions, some of which were brilliant. I got him, finally, to talk about himself and his antecedents, of his life as a boy in Minnesota, of the poverty of his youth, of his various jobs, and of his constant and ardent desire to be a writer.

"Would you really like to have this job as editor of our syndicate?" I asked.

His eagerness seemed to wane a bit, and he sat a moment in a self-enforced silence. Then he said, "Yes, I think I'd like it, and I'm sure I could make good at it."

"All right," I said, "the job's yours."

"Yes, yes," he muttered, taken aback, "but you've left out one very important item. How much are you going to pay me?"

"Oh," I said hastily, "I'd forgotten. I'm sorry. The job pays sixty dollars a week."

Lewis looked at me across the table in utter surprise. It showed all over his countenance. "Sixty dollars a week!" he exclaimed, and jumped up, almost overturning his hair as he rose. "Sixty dollars! Shake." He reached across the table and seized my hand. "Shake on it. It's a bargain. When do I begin?" [. . .]

When I returned from my wedding trip around the middle of January in 1914, I found the business going along splendidly. Van Slyke[45] was bringing in quantities of advertising, and Sinclair Lewis was making the book-review page in our syndicate papers sparkle with life.

Lewis was also writing a novel, he told me, and he showed me some chapters of *Our Mr. Wrenn,* his first book. They were well written, and as I read them I felt that he had a delicate sense of character, and that he knew how to tell a story, a quality that is often lacking in writers of fiction.

I noted also that he was dressed in a clean, spick-and-span new suit. He told me that he had moved from his room on First Avenue and was living in a nice place in Greenwich Village. In short, his new job as our editor was putting him on his feet—novel writing, new suits, pleasant rooms, and a brighter outlook on life.

He had also made some new acquaintances, one of whom was Grace Hegger, a young woman who had a job as caption writer at the offices of *Vogue.*[46] Lewis spoke of her so many times and with such warmth in his manner that I felt he must be in love with her. He was, indeed, and he married her a year or two later.

I remember listening to him tell me of his first visit to the apartment on West Seventieth Street, near the river, where she lived with her widowed mother. I shall try to give the account in Lewis's own words, as I recall them.

"Well, Bill, she wrote me an invitation to dinner on an engraved card. Yes, written and sent by mail. How's that for being high class? I wondered why she didn't call me up on the phone and invite me. But I suppose she wanted to give the proper tone to the invitation, so she wrote it on engraved paper.

"I'll tell you one thing, old man. Miss Hegger is no ordinary run-of-the-mill office worker. She's accustomed to elegance, and polite society, and when I'm with her I feel always that I'll do the wrong thing.

"I went to dinner at her house. Didn't know what to wear, but Grace told me to come in my everyday clothes. I met her mother, a fine old lady. They have a tiny little apartment—only three or four rooms; they're poor, you know.

"They had candles on the dinner table. Yes, sir; just candles in pink shades, with the other lights turned out. Candles shining down on the white tablecloth and the spotless napkins. They're gentle folk, and I watched all their movements. I learned a lot about how nice people behave."

15 / Elizabeth Jordan

Elizabeth Jordan (1867–1947), author, journalist, editor, and suffragist, is perhaps best known for her relationship with the novelist Henry James, whom she persuaded to participate in the group novel *The Whole Family: A Novel by Twelve Authors* (1908). Ironically, she also rejected Mark Twain's "The War Prayer" for publication in *Harper's Bazar* in 1905. But she sponsored Lewis's novels for publication by Harper and Brothers during the 1910s.

Source: Elizabeth Jordan, *Three Rousing Cheers* (New York and London: Appleton-Century, 1938), 339–43, 346.

I was immensely interested in my efforts to draw new writers of promise into the Harper book family. There was always a thrill in the reading of the first novel of a new writer. Possibly here was another genius! I was fishing in strange waters, and I caught a large fish often enough to keep my enthusiasm alive. I shall always be especially proud of the biggest catch I landed for Harper's.

One day a young man in his late twenties came to the office with a letter of introduction to me from Charles Hanson Towne, the poet. Mr. Towne mentioned in his note, without obvious enthusiasm, that the bearer's name was Sinclair Lewis, and that he had with him the manuscript of his first novel, *Our Mr. Wrenn.* Would I read it?

I would, of course. Reading and judging the merit of novels and other book manuscripts was then my professional job. I looked at Sinclair Lewis. He was a tall, thin, red-haired youth with an effect of exuberant vitality, and with blue-gray eyes that worked overtime. No one could have called him handsome, but he had the widest and most engaging grin I had ever seen. Our first encounter was brief. I promised to read his book and he departed.

I liked *Our Mr. Wrenn.* Later Mr. Towne confided to me that the reserve of his introduction was due to the fact that several publishers had already declined the book. I can't imagine what they were thinking of. Inevitably, it had the beginner's faults, but it held great promise and a strong atmosphere of H. G. Wells, who was young Mr. Lewis's literary idol at the time. Any editor should have recognized its quality, and I deserve no credit at all for doing so. We agreed to publish the book with certain changes, and my long and delightful association with Sinclair Lewis began.

I worked with him on the manuscript, and some of the changes I had to ask him to make were the kind that break an author's heart. He took them all with entire good-humor, and he never lost his grin. When he had done all the reconstruction he thought he could endure at one session, he would sit up suddenly and say, "Now, *praise* me!"

The praise he liked best was my repeated prediction that he would develop into one of the great authors of his day.

"Are you sure of that?" he often asked.

"Absolutely," I always said. Then his grin grew wider. He was sure of it, too. Fortunately we were both right.

As it happened, that summer was especially hot and I had to pass most of it in New York. Our twelve-story apartment building on Gramercy Park had a nicely tiled roof with a safe balustrade running around it. I often invited friends to have a hot-night dinner up there with me—cold chicken, salad, ice-cream and claret cup. Then we reclined luxuriously in steamer chairs and settled the large problems of the day. Only the stars were above us, and New York, flaunting all her jewelry, lay below us. From the East River, a few blocks away, boats moaned up at us as they passed.

I invited young Mr. Lewis to this roof retreat for a conference and meal one hot evening, and he was enchanted. Apparently it was the spot he had been looking for all his life, and he couldn't say enough about it. He left reluctantly and very late, and the next evening he returned uninvited. He said, with a grin, that every one else was out of town, and this was the nicest place he knew of, and that he was sure I wanted him. I did, and he came very often. It is to this roof—now my New York roof for a quarter of a century—that he refers in his inscription in my copy of *Our Mr. Wrenn.*

During this first year he complicated our work by falling in love. He did it violently and tempestuously, as a red-haired youth of his type would be sure to do it, and his courtship was a whirlwind affair. He told me all about the girl, in great detail, and frequently when I thought we ought to be considering *Our Mr. Wrenn.* She was Miss Grace Hegger. He won her very soon, and immediately brought her to dine with me. She was a charming girl and I liked her from the moment we met. He had asked not to have any other guests the first evening she came. He said he wanted me to know Grace as well as he did. But immediately after dinner he turned to me imploringly.

"I've never danced with this woman yet," he said. (He always spoke of her as "the woman.") "I'm crazy to dance with her. Won't you play for us and let us get going?"

I sat down at the piano and the young things danced all evening, till the musician at least was worn out.

They were married just before *Our Mr. Wrenn* was published. They were very much in love and both were temperamental, and their first year of married life was an experience of alternate glory and storm. We kept in close touch. I visited them at their first home near Plandome, Long Island, and they frequently came to my New York apartment. When *Our Mr. Wrenn* was published the proud author wrote this inscription on a fly-leaf of my copy:

> To Elizabeth Jordan,
> Who accepted the MS. of *Our Mr. Wrenn,* suggested changes that were not just "editorial suggestions" but inspiring and creative finishing touches, and always by her kindliness and good-fellowship and trained knowledge, by hours in the office and on the roof that overlooks all the city, enabled me to make a book of this.
>
> Sinclair Lewis
>
> And with affectionate greetings from the girl to whom it is dedicated.

A year later Hal brought me his second novel, *The Trail of the Hawk* [1915]. He had become "Hal" by that time, because he didn't like his first name and because Hal was a name Grace liked. We accepted the new novel with three rousing cheers. It was a beautiful book. No revision was necessary that time. On every page of it a young genius had laid bare his heart and soul. Of all the books Sinclair Lewis has written, I still like that one best. Here's the inscription he wrote in my copy:

> To Elizabeth Jordan, friend and boss, discoverer and maker of *Hawk* as she was of *Our Mr. Wrenn,* with more gratitude than can be expressed on this one small page.
>
> Sinclair Lewis
> 20 October 1915.

This novel was in a way autobiographical. Hal himself was at heart a hawk, wild and untamed. Notwithstanding his devotion to Grace it was hard for him to accept responsibility and the routine of domestic life. But she, too, was devoted, and wise for her years.

Hal was an appreciative youngster, and in return for what he was good enough to consider my helpful interest he began to suggest plots for the short stories I was writing. His plots were not in my line. Their subjects called for certain technical knowledge which he had and I had not. I urged him to write them himself, as a way of increasing his income. At first the idea did not interest him. He was a novelist, not a short-story writer, he reminded me, but I finally persuaded him to work up a dramatic railroad yarn he had outlined to me, and to send it to the *Saturday Evening Post.* Mr. Lorimer[47] accepted it at once.

With his encouragement Hal wrote half a dozen short stories for the *Post* in rapid succession, and was paid five hundred dollars each for them. He always wrote and revised with extraordinary ease. I can still see him standing beside my desk, changing sentences and even whole paragraphs of *Our Mr. Wrenn* without even sitting down to it. He was publicity man for George H. Doran at the time, and was chafing over the need of giving his days to advertising work when every instinct in him was clamoring for freedom to write fiction. His short stories solved his problem. Within a year or two he was able to resign the Doran job and concentrate on his novels. After another short interval he and Grace were lolling on the Florida sands and sending me "valentines" of the bungalow they had rented. [. . .]

Hal's third novel was called *The Job* [1917] and was interesting because it contained his first definite intimation of the literary path he was to follow in later years. All his early books had good notices. Each, as he wrote it, had an exciting originality and distinction of style. But he was still far from *Main Street.* His books sold well for a beginner's novels. No one at Franklin Square[48] except myself saw all the possibilities for this engaging newcomer. I once said to him, "Hal, do you know what may happen? Here at Harper's we're doing all the planting, watering, and general development of this genius of yours. We'll bring out all your first books. Then, some day, you may suddenly decide that another firm might do more for you, and you may hand it a book. It would be quite on the cards if that book proved to be the 'bestseller' you and I are waiting for—and if that new firm got all the cash and credit of it, after we have taken you through the burden and heat of your first literary years."

Hal's blue eyes looked hurt. He assured me rather stiffly that he would never do any such thing, and that I ought to know him better than to suggest it. He remained with Harper's during my three years as literary adviser there, and even for a couple of years after I resigned. Then he wrote *Main Street* and gave it to another publisher.[49] He was immediately whirled to fame and fortune—himself rather incredulous and startled by the experience—on the flaming tail of that literary comet.

16 / W. D. Inglis

The New Thought that Lewis advocates in this interview with the physician W. D. Inglis (b. 1874), a graduate of Washington and Jefferson College, is an early twentieth-century metaphysical movement, frequently aligned with first-wave feminism since many of its proponents were women. New Thought also privileged the printed word, and its secular dimension was responsible for the publication of many self-help books during the early twentieth century. Lewis later satirized New Thought in *Elmer Gantry.* As in this interview, he also satirized the boosterism of "the average man" in the "Solid American Citizen" or "Regular Guy" in *Babbitt.*

Source: W. D. Inglis, "Where Lies the Hope of the Average Man?" *Lexington* (Kentucky) *Herald,* May 12, 1915, 13.

"Are you satisfied with your job?"

"Yes—er—n-n"—

"Well, ARE you satisfied with it? Of course not! No man worth a bean is ever satisfied with his job, Then what are you going to do about it?"

This was an interview, all right, but somehow it had got started backward. What business had Sinclair Lewis to shoot questions at me like that? I came not to talk about myself but to ask questions about "Our Mr. Wrenn," the mousey little clerk who kept on struggling and kicking till he got a better job and won the right girl.

"I'm not Willie Wrenn," I began (not forgetting business of scowl, also using deepest throaty growl). "Never you mind"—

"But you are a little Wrenn, just the same," Mr. Lewis interrupted me. "So am I. So is every fellow who isn't at the top of the heap. Good Lord! There are thousands of us right here in this city and tens of millions of us throughout the country. We've got to climb up and get what's ours. We've got to fight. We can't quit. Remember that young lawyer who left the "Big City" and went back to his Blue Grass farm 'because three men owned New York and all the rest were their dodgasted clerks'?"[50]

"Well, he quit cold; that's all. Maybe he was lucky to have a soft place to crawl off to. But you and I and a few million more of us haven't any place at all to crawl off to. We've got to stay. No use for us to plod along like dummies. We must fight and fight intelligently or we'll be knocked down and run over and wiped off the map."

The interview was all knocked into a cocked hat now. It was hardly worth finishing. You see, here was the author of a novel that the critics called "charming," "spontaneous," "original," "amusing," and all that sort of thing, and of course I expected to find a highbrow person with an "outlook" and "views" and learned admonitions; instead of which I had discovered a tall, wiry, red headed young fellow who frowned and walloped the desk—plain business desk—with his freckled right fist as he scolded and encouraged in the same breath. He seemed to be looking right into the eyes of thousands of plodders and urging them to do their level best.

"You know how you hate advice," Mr. Lewis went on. "You hate it, I hate it, we all hate it—and yet I often feel as if I'd like to get together a few thousand young fellows and girls and tell them that if they don't get better jobs and draw down more pay it's all their own fault. The man behind the counter and the girl behind the typewriter needn't take root and stick there if they really want to get out and grow up. How can they do it? By taking a dose of practical New Thought every day. Wait! This isn't preaching. You wouldn't call 'Johnny' McGraw[51] a preacher, would you, when he's showing a young player how to improve his batting average? He has been through it all himself, hasn't he? He's practical, isn't he? So am I. I speak from experience.

"There is no question, of course, that our present system of doing business has a tendency to hold down the majority for the benefit of the few. But that has been the tendency of all systems since mankind was born. America is the land of opportunity. A man or woman has more chance here than anywhere else on earth. The thing to do is to wake up and take your chance, fight for it, work for it!

"What's the first step? Look yourself over. If a clerk or salesman will take three minutes every day for a month and honestly examine himself he will be surprised to find how much new stuff he will discover. Suppose he wants to be a big advertising man. Perhaps he has taken a few weeks' course in a correspondence school of ad-writing and he thinks that settles it and the boss is a fool for not giving him advertising to write. But does he really know how to write the stuff that will coax people to buy? No. Now let him take stock in himself:—'What am I?' What am I worth? What do I really know? What do I want to do? How can I, equipped as I am, in the environment I'm in, do something to help myself up? It's a sort of application of New Thought in a practical way without any frills on it. It isn't the work in office hours that counts for climbing—unless you have thought it all out, away from the office; what you are, what you have and what you will do. It's the serene, honest view of one's whole abilities and ambitions, as sharply distinguished from the busy view one daily takes of the details of one's work, that enables a man to forge ahead. All of us more or less fail to see the woods for the trees. The man who can see the whole woods of a business as well as the individual trees of it is likely to become an executive.

"And what's he going to do once he sincerely knows what he wants to do? That's up to him. It differs enormously with each case. For I am firmly convinced that the average man differs as much from every other average man, except in the externals of clothes and manner, as do the sharply marked personalities you will find so clearly contrasting with each other in an artist's studio or a scientist's congress. Mr. Wrenn was mighty different from Samuel Ebbitt and 'Tom' Poppins and Horatio Teddem and the other 'average people' that took their commonplace food and played five hundred in his boarding house, yet the whole bunch of them would have been lumped together as 'just common people' by the patronizing observer from the avenue.

"And, each having an individuality, he has to solve an individual problem. Mr. Wrenn solved his by wanting to wander and shipping off on a cattle boat. I know of an office boy who is solving his by copying out chapters from really great books. I know of a stenographer who is solving hers by reading the dictionary. She's soon going to become a crack private secretary instead of a careless typist.

"But, first of all, Mr. Average Man has to do some real thinking. Perhaps it will lead him into rabid anarchism. Perhaps it will lead him to a savage desire to become one of the master class. But it will certainly do one thing—it will cure him of his unconscious supposition that he's just an undistinguished member of a commonplace bunch of uninteresting people.

"The ordinary, hard working man who can shake hands and tell a good story and stick on the job is likely to be as much afraid of the cant phrases of cults as he is ashamed of his romances, but if he'll think hard enough he'll suddenly find that it's sober fact that every man is a king, and Napoleon or Shakespeare were only men, and that therefore there's no reason why he should stop with being just a clerk. He may quite possibly find that by being a clerk he can do as much big and happy work as though he were a discontented millionaire. But even then he must consciously and sincerely realize the royal dignity of himself, who is that biggest of things, a Man!

"Let every fellow and every girl who wants to rise in the world do the job they have better than anyone else. You've got to do your level best at the thing that brings in the bread and butter NOW before you can begin to hitch your wagon to a star, and if you don't know how to do your level best hunt up some good book on Efficiency that deals with your business. Where? You can get it at the public library. Don't be afraid. Go after it. Dig for it. The librarian will help you get it. That's his business.

"And when you've worked out some suggestion to help the business you're in, don't be afraid to offer it to the boss."

17 / Albert Payson Terhune

Albert Payson Terhune (1872–1942) was a writer, journalist, and dog breeder. Much of his fiction, most particularly his novel *Lad: A Dog* (1919), involved the collies he famously bred. He published popular stories in such journals as *Redbook, Greenbook,* the *Ladies' Home Journal,* and *AKC Gazette.* Lewis ghostwrote two or three chapters of his novel *Dad* (1914).

Source: Albert Payson Terhune, *To the Best of My Memory* (New York: Harper, 1930), 195.

Sinclair Lewis and I used to argue hotly and at much length, years ago, as to where the big money lay in writing. From my own experience, up to then, I held that it was all in the magazine end of the game—if it were anywhere at all. Lewis believed there was more money in one successful book than in an armful of magazine work. It was his ambition, he said, to write best-seller novels, rather than well-paying magazine yarns, and he was certain that one day he would do it.

At the time, he had written *Our Mr. Wrenn* and *The Innocents* [1917]—both of them short novels of rare charm—and *The Trail of the Hawk,* an aviation book in which he spoke of me as the "big newspaperman over at Pompton."[52] All three books were good. None of them scored anything approaching a hit. But Lewis had a queerly unswerving faith in his star.

Owen Johnson[53] and I were ushers at Sinclair Lewis's wedding in the spring of 1914. George Soule was his best man. Lewis was married on the rainiest day in the history of deluges. The wedding was in an upstairs chapel of the Ethical Culture Building in New York. The chapel was reached by a long passageway with offices on either side. Part of the ushers' duty was to steer wetly arriving guests away from an undertaking establishment that stood with invitingly open portals at the head of the stairs.

18 / Harrison Smith

Smith reminisced about the earliest and happiest period of Lewis's first marriage, when he lived on Long Island and commuted by train to his job in the city. His literary career was advancing if not yet prospering, and to all outward appearances he seemed content.

Source: Harrison Smith, "Sinclair Lewis: Remembrance of the Past," *Saturday Review of Literature,* January 27, 1951, 8.

We had foolish times together. Both of us treasured small adventures and the human curiosities we came across. I can bring back to mind a trip to Cape Cod to visit Lewis. I am not sure now that he was at that time on his honeymoon with Grace Hegger, the tall, slim, blonde girl he had married, but maybe I was not so indiscreet and it was a few weeks later. He was in love with Grace Hegger—or perhaps in love with being in love with her. At any rate, I remember how gay we all were and that a silly, striped parasol and a broken-down bicycle from which all of us fell off were a part of it. Later they took a tiny house in Port Washington, where I was a constant visitor. Lewis had become George Doran's editor by that time and an excellent one, too. He had written *Our Mr. Wrenn* and when the *Saturday Evening Post* had published enough of his stories he cut loose from jobs forever and wrote at home. He worked hard, long hours and was always infuriated when at suburban parties the men inferred that he was a lazy, lucky dog, who stayed at home with the women.

19 / William Rose Benét

Benét, Lewis's near neighbor on Long Island, also remembered him during this period after his marriage to Grace Hegger and before his greatest literary successes.

Source: William Rose Benét, "The Earlier Lewis," *Saturday Review of Literature,* January 20, 1934, 421–22.

"Red" wrote his first novel, *Our Mr. Wrenn,* and got married. His second novel, *The Trail of the Hawk,* reflecting his still strong interest in flying—the conquest of the air took a strong hold upon his vivid imagination—dealt in 1915 with a character in some ways the prototype of Lindbergh.[54] In fact, when "The Spirit of St. Louis" did land at Le Bourget, taxying to a stop with no casualties in spite of the enormous onrushing crowd, it seemed to me as though an early Sinclair Lewis novel had come true. He had called the prophetic turn upon American history—I do not mean in exact achievement, I mean in the spirit of American aviation. Charles Lindbergh, with his upstanding liberal of a father, with his own Minnesota background, and his own sturdy independence, would have been just the sort of American "Red" could have novelized with vehemence and enthusiasm.

In my first marriage my wife and I lived hardly a stone's throw from the Lewises at Port Washington, Long Island. "Red" and I commuted on the same train of a morning; but I regret to say that his industry in that period quite put me to shame. While I was content to loll in the smoker with a newspaper, "Red" was in another car, secreted from the conversation of commuters, writing furiously upon a new book during the whole journey from Port Washington to New York. Was that *The Trail of the Hawk,* or could it have been *The Job*? At any rate, it was when he was still being published by Harper's, before Alfred Harcourt[55] had left Henry Holt and Company to set up his own shop and to become Sinclair Lewis's publisher. After jobs with *Adventure* and the Publishers' Newspaper Syndicate (under "Bill" Woodward, so well-known now as a biographer) "Red" had become editor for George H. Doran. He began to sell stories to the *Saturday*

Evening Post, and *The Innocents* and *Free Air* came along in their time. I am not, however, sure of my dates here—and the rest is history: how he took "time out" to write the novel Alfred Harcourt believed would be his most vital, how he went to Washington to do it (where Henry Hoyt and I once dropped in upon him at the room apart from his home that he had rented for a workshop), how he produced *Main Street* with only the motive of giving as true a picture of his own Middle West as a scrupulous artist could give, and then, surprisingly to him, the fame and the fanfare.

The simile one instinctively thinks of first for Sinclair Lewis is "dynamo." He is the journalist *par excellence.* He has that absorbing curiosity about life without which no great writer was ever born. I was lucky to hear something of that curiosity stated in his earlier years, to be in contact for a while with that keen and searching mind, to have my lazy thinking questioned and exposed by that searchlight intellect. Conversation with him was always intensely stimulating. He could suggest a myriad new ideas in half an hour. And there is one incident I remember well because it seems to me the essential Lewis. Not Lewis the critic of his country, though he has been a badly needed satirist of its institutions and the flame of his rage against our national stupidities has been a splendid cauterization.

We were dining together one night, and to our table came a stranger, a traveling salesman, whose conversation I thought a great bore and whose personality afflicted my intolerance. But "Red" plunged into conversation with him. Before he knew it the man was revealing all his characteristic ways of thinking and emoting, as well as giving us a good slice of his life. I can remember that I still maintained a rather annoyed attitude. The type didn't appeal to me. Then the man left and "Red" turned to me with a most quizzical smile. "Do you like that type of fellow?" I said—or words to that effect—believing my toplofty attitude to be inalienably the right one. "That's the trouble with you, Bill," said "Red" (or words to *that* effect), "you regard him as *hoi polloi,* he doesn't even represent the cause of labor or anything dramatic—but I understand that man—by God, I love him."

20 / Alfred Harcourt

The publisher Alfred Harcourt (1881–1954), who as an editor for Henry Holt and Company had lured Lewis away from Harper's, founded the firm of Harcourt, Brace, and Howe with Lewis's encouragement in 1919. Lewis became one of the most valued authors in Harcourt's stable, and between 1919 and 1930 he published eight novels with the firm, including all of the novels for which he would receive the Nobel Prize.

Source: Alfred Harcourt, *Some Experiences* (Riverside, CT: privately printed, 1935), 27–28.

My friendship with Sinclair Lewis started at about this time when he was with the publishing house of George Doran. We fell into the habit of lunching together in the grillroom of the old Waldorf.[56] He and Grace Hegger had just been married and were living on Long Island. He was spending all his time outside of office hours, on commuting trains, and at home, writing short stories and novels. His novels he had taken to Harper's because of Elizabeth Jordan, then in their editorial department, who was interested in his work. Those early novels, *Our Mr. Wrenn, The Trail of the Hawk,* and *The Job,* received scant attention, and their sales were small. Their unsentimental directness, the simple ordinary people he portrayed, the affectionate irony with which he treated them, made them ahead of their time.

We were both from small towns and swapped many a story about the people we had known—I in New Paltz, New York, and he in Sauk Centre, Minnesota. From those talks, I saw that he could write a first-rate novel about the small town, and I urged him to think about that. One day he came into my office at Holt's, closed the door, and said, "Alf, I am going to write that small-town novel which you have been pestering me about. I've got a title for it—'Main Street,' and don't you mention it to a single person. When it is done, you've got to publish it."

21 / Fanny Butcher

Fanny Butcher (1888–1987), editor, critic, and reviewer, worked on the *Chicago Tribune* for fifty years and served as its literary editor for forty. She became Lewis's pen pal almost by accident months before she first met him in 1916, and they remained friends for life. Butcher was one of the few friends, in fact, with whom Lewis never quarreled.

Source: Fanny Butcher, *Many Lives—One Love* (New York: Harper and Row, 1972), 383–87.

It was as an editor that I first knew him. He was with the George H. Doran publishing house, and the author of the most intriguing and stimulating book-promotion letters any P.R. man ever wrote. I was a very lowly tyro reviewer, without enough savvy even to recognize a letter as promotion. I answered one signed Sinclair Lewis that had been a masterpiece of the Dale Carnegie slogan, "How to Make Friends and Influence People."[57] Before I knew it, Sinclair Lewis and I had made friends on paper. I began saving the things he wrote to me because they were such fun. As we got to know each other better, they grew into enchanting letters, signed, not Sinclair Lewis, but Hal. Hal, he explained, was what he was called by friends, "a derivative from a name that was tacked onto Sinclair Lewis when I was christened." [. . .] Hal obviously pounded out his own letters on his typewriter, and they sounded as spontaneous as a first draft of a short story. They were never dated and they often had additions or corrections in longhand. One of the first he wrote suggests the literary style which was to become world-famous. He thought like a novelist.

In a letter to which his was an answer, I must have written him that I had a novel in my head, because he added words of editorial advice to his amusing description of himself. Some of his advice sounded as if it came from a Dutch uncle. He wrote:

> It's rather interesting, this way of getting acquainted. I wonder which of the publishing types you picture me, (I think an "as" goes in here—punk

> sentence)—the young enthusiast, just out of college; the old boy who being still a bachelor, has never really settled down to a dullness befitting his age; the person who writes letters that are a little different but, when met personally, proves to be unspeakably dull; the brisk advertising man? Gosh, I don't know which of 'em I am—for all my Greenwich Village radical friends—including the big Chicago contingent—assure me that I am a dull conservative because I am (fairly) new-married and live in a suburb and hold down a job; whereas all the people in that suburb feel shudderingly that I am a dread anarchist. Likewise, all the young authors regard me as a grim and sophisticated old editor, while my own publishers regard me as a naïve but promising young author. You takes your choice: age, thirty; format, a tall folio; hair, red; temper, bad.
>
> There's my portrait—and I'll be hanged if I'll tell you what my picture of [Burton] Rascoe[58] and yourself is!
>
> And do write your novel. But let me warn you of one thing—don't let it by any chance have either a newspaperwoman or an authoress in it! It's almost incredible, the number of novels by women—and, tho less frequently, men—which try with a fine sincerity to be original, but which sound all exactly alike because always their heroines are (1), at home; (2), broke and on a job; (3), breaking into the writing game and into "Bohemia," (4), in love. [. . .] That exact formula is so amazingly much used now that I'm imploringly begging every newspaperwoman I know not to follow it.

His advice about not writing an autobiographical novel was so to the point, coming from an editor of one of the most outstanding publishing firms, that I asked for permission to quote it in my column. He gave it, but asked me please not to sign his name, because his youthful vanity, he said, wanted him to be known chiefly as author, not critic—"Now that I've made a start," he wrote. His start at that moment was one book for young readers signed Tom Graham and two novels, *Our Mr. Wrenn* and *The Trail of the Hawk,* neither one with any signs declaring, "This way to the Nobel Prize."

Then he added, anent printing the letter, "You'd better rewrite it. I hustled it out and is [*sic*] probably got seven grammatical errors and one offense against good taste, with a lot of faults of diction and other things which I don't know their names."

Later in the same letter: "How do the novel? Gee, I dunno—the only way I get them done is by getting up at six or six-thirty, working till eight, then working again on my commuters' train, and probably on the train going out at night again, and Sunday mornings as well, and so by the end of a year and a half having enough copy—two or three or four times rewritten—to have a novel. But when it's done, it's fun to have it." The letters grew longer, more full of advice about life and work, more revealing of the happy dreamer that he was then, and more enchanting to a girl who was herself as permanently imprisoned by dreams of someday writing books as flies used to be in what was called Tanglefoot Fly Paper.[59]

Sometimes a letter would start with the disillusionment of overwork, but it never ended in a mere few lines. Letter writing—as it should be—was relaxation, not duty. For some, letter writing and receiving can be even more rejuvenating than eye-to-eye talk.

> I'm tired as the devil; my eyes hurt and I hate the sight of mss, with all that fervor I felt years ago when, during my first ms. reading, I discovered that Literachure can be turned from a delight into a demnination grind by the outpouring of little offerings from the industrious and conscientiously commercial mediocre, gosh, that's a lot of converted adjectives for that adjectiferous clause. I wish I'd been writing ads or publicity all day; but then, cheer up, had I been writing that rot I'd be wishing I'd been reading mss. I want to turn to and be commercial myself for an hour or two before going home, but I dunno's my eyes will let me.
>
> In other words I get, as you get, the feeling every so often of "what's it all about." You have it now especially with the man; doubtless too with the job at times. [. . .] I lunched with the Managing Editor of a Very Great Magazine today, and he confessed he hated his job and wanted to write a novel and had been able, after months of grinding between 6 A.M. and 8, to turn out 25,000 words of a novel. [. . .] Doubtless had I talked with his Owner instead of himself, Owner might—only owners don't so often confess, that's why they're owners and the rest of us work for them—but Owner *might* have confessed that he longed to marry or get unmarried, give up his magazine entirely and go chicken-farming, or else make his magazine into some totally different kind of a sheet, being bored with it, with his office, with his managing editor.
>
> What I'm trying to say is that I fancy there aren't any of us—except the drudges who're numbed and the fools who don't care—who don't have a problem of love or work or ambition dogging us all the while; a desire to be someplace else or with someone else. [. . .] You want the man; I want a white colonial house on a hillside overlooking a lake, and a cool quiet place in which I can write fool fiction for seven hours a day without a thought of finances.

In Hal's letters there was curiosity about what that girl who, he had decided, was to be his little sister, looked like. He wrote: "And when do you send me a snapshot of yourself? How in thunder do you expect me to speak on in my lordly and editorial terms when I don't know whether you resemble Marie Doro, Carrie Nation, Eleonora Duse, Queen Victoria, Eva Tanguay,[60] or a bathing girl on a Ladies Home Journal cover?" The nearest he came to a snapshot of me was when he saw a picture of the building I worked in and wrote:

> Saw movies—movies of the Germans, took by the photographer of the Chicago Tribune. One of them showed said photographer emerging from a grim stone doorway—with trolleys running just beyond—bound for Europe with his cunning little camera and his new hat and wrist watch. And says the caption, it was the Chicago Tribune building. Lord, I thought, out of that doorway Fanny comes every day. It was like going to Chicago and really seeing you. [. . .] And we'd start off on that tramp; run along country roads, hand in hand, like kids; and then discuss whether life is worth taking seriously and, if it is, what one shall think of it all. [. . .] What's the use of it all—when fame is empty and comes only so slowly that one isn't interested in it; when money can buy so little—just eats and clothes and travel; when friendship is a tissue of selfishness and love a tissue of misunderstanding. Yet there is use of it. If find love and friendship—eats and travel—terrifically worthwhile and call old Mother Philosophy a lying shrew and determine that I shan't sit about literary table d'hotes and be melancholy but just live and find something of that same joy that giggling kitchen wenches and drunken longshoremen and exquisite old men of silvery skins dreaming in gardens of canterbury bells do unquestionably find. We'd talk terrible much, wouldn't we honey! No, not would; rather *will.* We'll meet before long. What will you say then? Tell me, oh sage, who have created for me a lake to swim in and a fire to talk to us by night, tell me what we shall say and do when we do meet.

By that time, despite the fact that neither of us had the foggiest idea of what the other looked like, we had become lifelong friends. I had been told much about his wife, Gracie, whom he called "my chum" and who, I judged, must be the star of all the cherubim in what was plainly his private heaven. I had been given a key to it as an adopted little sister who needed counseling and affection and got both without constraint.

22 / Grace Hegger Lewis

Grace Hegger Lewis (1887–1981), Lewis's first wife (they married in 1914), worked initially as assistant household editor and later as beauty editor at *Vogue*. She had fading connections to high society and affected an English accent throughout her entire life. This recollection is excerpted from her novel, a fictionalized version of her life with Lewis in which she is "Susan" and he is "Timothy." According to Schorer, this novel and her autobiography "are substantially the same."[61] She and Lewis separated in 1925 and divorced in 1928. She was remarried, to Telesforo Casanova (d. 1981), in 1933.

Source: Grace Hegger Lewis, *Half a Loaf* (New York: Liveright, 1931), 79–81.

One midsummer evening as they sat on their veranda, Susan questioned:

"Why don't you start writing short stories again? It would be a change after the long novel."

"I don't think I have the short story mind," he answered. "I need room to think. That's why I was fired off every newspaper I was on—couldn't fit myself into an allotted space."

"Try just for fun. Shall I get your notebooks? They are swarming with ideas. And send it first to the *Post*. Do you know how much they pay?"

"It depends upon how well known the writer is."

"Well, you're beginning to be known with two novels."

"Fatuous woman!" and he pulled his chair closer to hers and gently bit her ear. "Except in my home town and to a few people here and in New York I am about as prominent as one of those carrots hidden in that row down there. But I will be known some day," his thin face hardened, "and I hope it won't come too late for us both to enjoy it. Do you think you can stand waiting, little playmate?"

She pulled a handkerchief out of his breast pocket, and tied their wrists together. "Handcuffed for life. Try and lose me. [. . .] On your feet, brother. Left, right, left, right, through the doors and into your room, and where's the notebook?"

And because the suggestion was born frivolously, it proved to be a gay story poking amiable fun at some of the Greenwich Villagers among whom he had once lived. He couldn't have written it two years ago, but now he was a married man, a householder, a commuter, and if his citizenship was not exactly solid, he at least no longer regarded all capitalists as fiends and all garment-workers as suffering angels.

At the end of ten days they began to wonder if there was a chance that it had been accepted. Did the *S.E.P.* make quick decisions or did it take a long time? Perhaps the story had been lost in the mails. Heavens, ten days was nothing when you realized how many manuscripts they must receive. "Gosh, you'd think this was the first time I had ever sent anything to a magazine—an old timer like me."

Two days later, Susan accompanied Timothy to his office.

"Stick around, old darling, for a bit, and watch Papa work. Sit over there where I can see you, and see you still after you have gone. Do you love me in my lil office jackik?" He struggled into a frayed and shapeless gray mohair coat. She saw the door was closed and gave him a possessive hug.

He shuffled through his mail. At least no large envelope with the returned manuscript.

"Sue! a letter from the *Post!*"

He tore at the envelope instead of neatly cutting it with a paper-knife. "A check! Oh, sweet, they've taken it! See, see, three hundred dollars!"

"Let *me* see," and she hung over his shoulder. "It's *five* hundred! The number 5 like a 3, but the writing says five. Nearly two months' salary. [. . .] What does the letter say?"

"'This is a capital yarn. Write us some more like this and we'll make you as famous as Irvin Cobb and Phoebe Snow.'[62] And it's signed by George Horace Lorimer himself!"

Timothy had never been happier. Success, money, love. He loved and was loved, perhaps not so passionately as he had dreamed it, but that would develop, and anyhow he didn't seem to know what to do to change matters.

"Write us some more like this." Of course he could, a cinch. He was simmering with ideas. Why if he only wrote a story a month that would be six thousand a year, more than he was making now and on the job every day.

"Susan." He solemnly took both her hands and looked straight into her eyes. "Do you realize this letter and this check may mean freedom for both of us? Freedom to write as I please and when I please, freedom from cities and communities and jobs!" Then his blue eyes left her and she knew his soul had also left her to follow the trail it must take alone.

"What do you want to do?" She was frightened.

"Chuck this job. Instanter. Leave suburbia. Wander—with one of those new portable typewriters—and you. What about it, panfish?" His face was red with excitement, his long body thrashed about in the small office as if he sensed for the first time how small had been his cage.

23 / Burton Rascoe

Burton Rascoe (1892–1957), editor, journalist, and critic, wrote for the *Chicago Tribune* until 1920 and, in 1922, became literary editor of the *New York Herald-Tribune.* Like his colleague, Fanny Butcher, he first met Lewis in 1916 when the novelist moved to Chicago for six weeks to research *The Job,* a novel about a realtor that anticipated *Babbitt,* and he remained a booster of Lewis's work for the rest of his life.

Source: Burton Rascoe, *Before I Forget* (New York: Literary Guild of America, 1937), 367–69.

One day sometime in 1916, a lanky, freckle-faced, sandy-haired, most amiable, most immediately friendly young man, vibrant with nervous energy, had come to the office to see Fanny Butcher, who wrote a column of book news and comment for one of the Sunday sections. Miss Butcher introduced me to him. He was Sinclair Lewis. He acknowledged the greeting with "Hello, Burt!" Soon afterwards I was calling him "Red," whereas Miss Butcher stuck to "Hal." He was in town to get a job in a real-estate office, out of the experience of which he wrote *The Job.* I had liked all of his published books, and I had never met anyone more agreeable or more entertaining as a person. We got together every time he came to Chicago until I left there; but it was not until 1920 that he had become a personage, famous for the authorship of *Main Street.* My wife and I gave a party one night, inviting Lewis and Sherwood Anderson,[63] Harry and Ruth Hansen, Keith and Etta Preston, Jerome and Florence Frank, and Gene Markey.[64] That evening we called upon Sherwood to tell his famous Mama Geighen story—his best unpublished story and his most hilarious story, published or unpublished. He was in top form about this fantastic binge he went on with George Wharton and about their encounter with the massive and marvelous woman who ran a saloon on the side of the road in Wisconsin, far from town or village. He sent us into gales of laughter, and he smiled modestly in satisfaction that his performance had been good. Lewis left the room. He came back after a minute or so. He had turned his collar and his vest hindpart before, parted his hair severely, powdered his face white. He held his hand before him, tips of fingers to tips of fingers. There was a look of severe piety on his face. He delivered an extempore sermon on the evils of drink and on the evil that women like Mama Geighen do in this world, so realistically that had he delivered it in precisely the same way in a Protestant church where he was not known I am sure it would have been accepted as a very elevating and ennobling sermon indeed. We all paid this manifest genius as an actor, improviser, orator as well as great novelist the tribute of complete silence until he had concluded. Then there was an uproar of laughter and acclaim. Lewis went into a bedroom to remove the powder and change his collar and vest. Sherwood was sitting beside me on a piano bench. Sherwood was jealous and mad as a wet hen because his performance had been capped. He turned to me and said, "It's a pity. He wants it so bad, and he will never have it." I did not ask Sherwood what he meant by "it." I knew. He meant "genius." There is in Lewis the least jealousy of his fellow writers of any writer I ever knew; no one goes out of his way to praise the contemporaries whose work he likes as much as Lewis does. His tribute to Thomas Wolfe in his speech of acceptance when he was awarded the Nobel Prize is but one of dozens of voluntary efforts to enhance the fame of his contemporaries and help them to gain wider audiences.[65] [. . .] Later on that evening there was dancing, and wines and spirits for those who cared for them; Lewis got exhilarated and demonstrated his ability as a "human fly" by climbing out the window and making his way around the three sides of the sunroom on a ledge not more than an inch wide, and then climbing cautiously down the wall to the ground, two stories below, oblivious of the frightened screams and supplications of the women that he desist.

24 / Grace Hegger Lewis

Nearly half a century after the event, the snobbish Grace Lewis remembered with ill-concealed condescension her first visit to her husband's hometown in 1916. Her impressions of Sauk Centre parallel Carol Kennicott's first impressions of Gopher Prairie.

Source: Grace Hegger Lewis, "When Lewis Walked Down Main Street," *New York Times Sunday Magazine,* July 3, 1960, 10.

Sauk Centre was a prairie town of 2,500 when we approached it by train in early May 1916 for a visit of about two months. We had been married for two years but this was my introduction to Hal's parents. (I called him "Hal" because he had been christened "Harry," which he had dropped at Yale. "Sinclair" was too formal, and I did not like the "Red" which, because of his red hair, came so easily to an acquaintance of even five minutes.) Nervously Hal kept telling me how small the town was, how modest his home, what a fine doctor his father was, how much good his stepmother did and that she came from Chicago. He hadn't been back in eight years and he would be as much a stranger as I.

However, mine was a warm welcome, although the uncompromising Dr. E. J. Lewis never ceased to look with suspicion upon his Eastern daughter-in-law. Hal's home was a two-story house of seven or eight rooms, with golden-oak furniture rendered comfortable by long use. There was a well-cut lawn with tall elms, and a stable without horses or automobile. (For country calls the doctor rented horses and later a car with a driver from the livery stable.)

There was a hired girl, and the daily living was conducted with the dignity demanded by the social standing of a doctor's family in a small town. The meal hours were dictated by his farmer patients, who came in early from the countryside, and by the customs of the town itself: 6:30 for breakfast, noon for dinner, and 6 for supper, and we were frowned on if we were five minutes late.

After the Dinner Party to Honor the Bride, with its agonizing preparations, to which were invited the president of the First National Bank, the owner of the Boston Store,[66] the Congregational minister, and the head of the largest furniture store (who to my amazement was also the town's mortician), we were delighted to accept all invitations which came our way—to card parties and lake picnics, to the high school baccalaureate and the Eastern Star dance.

I went to the current-events club with Mrs. Lewis and to a rest center she had established, with rockers and growing plants and hot coffee, for the wives of the German and Scandinavian farmers who heretofore had left the women to crouch in the farm wagons, regardless of weather, when they transacted their business indoors over drams of schnapps. Hal, by himself, called on the Commercial Club and appealed publicly for library funds. He received twenty-five cents.

25 / Fanny Butcher

The first time she met Grace, Lewis's "little sister" immediately sensed the problems that would destroy the Lewis marriage nearly a decade later—the two principals were basically incompatible. The birth of their son, Wells, in 1917 also complicated the marriage. Although Lewis was placing virtually everything he wrote for the magazines, often in the *Saturday Evening Post,* his novel *The Job* was a critical and commercial dud.

Source: Fanny Butcher, *Many Lives—One Love* (New York: Harper and Row, 1972), 387–93.

Madly, everyone thought, Sinclair Lewis chucked his very good job at Doran's and set out in an old Ford with his wife to wander around the South. She was to take orders for custom-made corsets, he to gather material. He had already been "discovered" by the *Saturday Evening Post* as a writer of popular short stories. Perhaps there were wander genes in his blood, because he had roved all across the map before he had settled down to being an editor in New York. He had, it was gleefully pointed out when his books became fabulous bestsellers, been fired from both the Associated Press and the *Bulletin* in San Francisco because he was no good as a reporter. In his whole life he had never really took root anywhere—never watched a sapling climb to his rooftop.

There had been a good deal of soul-searching and advice-giving in the letters that preceded the one in which he announced the gypsying. One bit of advice is as good—for anybody—today, as it was for me then in my early twenties: "So that you found that you could get along, in yourself and by yourself. I'm glad. It's absolutely necessary. Life is a failure until you do—it's a failure tho your name be blazoned before theatres and on magazines or on books or on empires. You must be able to get along for months without seeking or having a gentle word or a tacit good wish from any living soul."

In the same mood, he wrote:

> It isn't necessary to see the use of it all, the end of this weird game called human life, to be happy and self-controlled. I do know the fascination of

> watching people, the joy of reading, the deep and abiding satisfaction of affection, of friendship, of tenderness, the cool strong feeling of rising at dawn, seeing the expectant gray morning sky, and getting to work on my own real writing and so—what the devil do I care, so far as my practical daily concrete problems are concerned, whether we're immortal spirit or merely monistic functions of force whose consciousness is of quite the same kind as any other manifestation of energy. Regarding the future of this fool human race with its murderous "patriotism"—clean pessimistic; regarding me—and you and my chum and my friends—optimistic.

Finally, he wrote a farewell letter from his desk at Doran's:

> At last! Gosh, I have had one 'orrible two weeks in the office. I've been sitting here at the typewriter all day and every day, turning out copy so fast it's made my hand lame. They've stung me with all the work they could think up, to get it done before I get away and my experimental successor comes in. So I've been writing newspaper ads, magazine ads, circulars, book jackets, descriptions of books for next spring's catalogues, all most breathless-like. You see I'm through, a week from today.
>
> From all of which you may judge that your temperamental big brother, who alarms his friends by baldly running away, can also turn into grinding Office Person for a time, at least. It's a good thing to be able to do. I hate to agree with the platitudinous but it's certain that nothing helps a writer to succeed so much as being able to sit down and work. No, that is not a concealed sermon; it's a hope that, having that faculty, I shall climb up among the High Uns.
>
> I hope everything is pulling along, little sister. You'll have found a lot of yourself when you get to the position where you don't care a damn what anyone else but yourself does. I want you to have reached that position by the time I reach New Orleans, which will be about next April, I guess.

They were letters to dazzle anyone, especially a very young newspaperwoman who believed that words were mightier than broadswords. They built up a mental picture of someone who probably looked a little like the then irresistible Prince of Wales, or perhaps like that character who in my childhood had been the dream of every red-blooded American girl, the man who always leaned caressingly over the shoulder of the Gibson girl.

One day I had a letter saying that he and his "chum" had decided that he should come to Chicago before her, spend an uninterrupted month doing research on and writing a novel, which was to be called *The Job.* Why Chicago?

It was easy to make myself believe it was because he thought I might be able to help enlighten him on how a girl on the job, any job, thought and lived her life—although I didn't recognize any of my answers to his questions when *The Job* appeared. I was naturally atwitter over the prospect of actually seeing my very articulate writer-editor hero.

The great day finally arrived. The telephone rang and the voice from it squeaked, "This is Hal Lewis." I was crushed right there. The voice of my "temperamental big brother," as he had christened himself, was a high and edgy tenor. It didn't match his letters at all. However, worse was to come. When he appeared in the hall of the old *Tribune* building, on Dearborn and Madison street, he was the tallest, the thinnest, the reddest human being I had ever laid eyes on. He had a huge incarnadined handkerchief clutched to his profusely bleeding nose. And his words of tender greeting were, "Where's the men's room?" Just that romantic was my first meeting with the great Sinclair Lewis.

That month which Hal spent in Chicago alone, working, was my first and unforgettable lesson in what literary concentration can and must be. He worked day and night, he told me, and I'm sure he did, except when he knocked off for dinner at the Butcher home. My mother worried about anybody's being so thin and invited him to dinner anytime he wanted to come. He came, often and regularly. He lived in a cheap furnished room—to save money to spend on his chum, he said, when she arrived, and he certainly saved it, for, as I remember, just once during the month did he invite me and my current beau for dinner.

For three days before his wife's arrival, however, he did no work on his novel. He had found a pleasant little furnished apartment on the North Side, and he spent twenty out of every twenty-four hours there preparing a welcome for her. Those three days before her arrival, he was in transports of love, writing poems to her, love letters, wrapping dozens of little presents that he hid around the rooms, a chain of passionate adoration, the links bits of string leading from one present to another like the cobwebs of our childhood parties. When he showed me with almost bursting joy what he had done, everything seemed an expression of utter devotion.

Of all the man-woman relationships I have observed in a long life, I have never known a man more completely, utterly bewitched by a woman than Hal Lewis was by his Gracie. He literally adored her. She was for him the Venus of a summer night's star-spangled sky, which filled him with awe at both its beauty and its eternal remoteness. She was the first trillium of spring. She was to him the most beautiful, the most alluring, the most brilliant woman God had ever taken the trouble to shape, and, because she was his, he became a god, capable of anything. He wasn't maudlin about her, he was simply epically in love.

The night of her arrival was sacred to their reunion, but the next night he invited me and my beau to dinner to meet his incomparable "chum." What we expected to meet was an angel whose halo would blind us. Gracie, as she proved to be ineptly named, was by nature and practice, if not by birth, a duchess, with a veddy, veddy English accent, and a point of view apparently rubbed off from her association with one of the expensive women's magazines, where she had worked as a caption writer. She was half English, but when I met her brother, not long afterwards, he spoke with every R resounding, and he was as simple and American as Iowa corn.

One of the unforgettable shocks of my life was when she greeted us at the door with one of the most calculatedly deflating remarks I ever heard. Gracie's reaction to the days and nights of utter devotion that had gone into the transformation of an impersonal transient apartment into a spider web of entangling love, was—"O, did you see what Sinclair did? All those silly poems and presents. I told him the moment I realized what he had done that he shouldn't have spent his time so foolishly. Just wasted it. I was very cross with him."

Wrapped in that wet blanket, the four of us finally went on to dinner in a nearby neighborhood restaurant, where the table d'hôte was advertised as being very good. It was not a famous glamour spot, but after a month of living on heaven knows what rations, except for those evenings when he was plied with my mother's affectionate care, it was a potentially charming meal to Hal, as it was to us. My beau and I were happy that it *was* a neighborhood spot, and not too expensive. When the excellent soup came, Hal's dream girl took one delicate sip of it, pushed it away from her, and said, "I can't stand this place, Sinclair," and got up. Thus ended our dinner party. Where we went to please Gracie is an utter blank in my mind.

Gracie, all of his friends knew long before he realized the truth about their marriage, was not what the doctor ordered. Or perhaps she was, for without her his gorgeous and bitter satires might not have been written. She taught him to see life with irony. It took time, though he repaid her by making her the wife of the disillusioned Dodsworth, as well as the starry-eyed heroine of *Main Street.*

Incidentally the inscription he wrote in my copy of *Main Street* is, I think, the nicest thing anyone ever wrote in a book for me. "For Fanny Butcher," it reads, "impresario or impresaria, too busy being kind to lesser poets to write her poetry."

Gracie, by the way, was the only person who really knew him that I ever heard call him Sinclair. His oldest friends called him Hal, his later ones Red, inevitably because he had red hair, a red face, and a firey disposition. For a while he insisted he was going to write a "red" novel, but he never did.

When *The Job* was published, I got a long letter in his sprawly writing. The letter was from 309 Fifth Avenue, New York, dated only Monday. It read:

> Fanny, dear, I'm getting well panned for the new novel. After reading roasts in New York Sun & Tribune,[67] I dunno whether I'm a great young realist or a foul-mouthed old grouch with a cheap cockiness. Ouch! [. . .] We're settled and happy here with a small but rather nice place in one of the few old houses still left, among the loft buildings on the Avenue. It's been good to be back—not the lights and theaters, the old friend and people at the Brevoort alone, but the multitude of people doing such different things—packed boxes and guarding munitions, wharves, running subways and making pants. And every one of 'em a story—a whole novel—which one could write if one could only live a thousand years or so.

It was around that time that Hal's first son, Wells [1917–1944], was born. I was visiting friends in Woodstock, New York, and he and Gracie's brother came up to drive me down to New York, and, with me, Mabel Reber, who had once been society editor of the *Chicago Tribune.* The new father and the new uncle, it seemed to us, were very casual about the gift of God. Hal was more concerned about the baby's name than communicative about its charms. As editor for George H. Doran, Hal had been so enthusiastic about H. G. Wells as a novelist, historian, science-fiction dreamer, philosopher, and all-round literary marvel that he had insisted on naming the baby Wells.

26 / George H. Doran

George H. Doran (1869–1956), American publisher and author, founded the New York–based publishing firm George H. Doran Company in 1908, which merged with Doubleday, Page, and Company in 1927 to form Doubleday, Doran, then the largest publishing house in the English-speaking world. Lewis worked for the Doran firm from the summer of 1914 until November 1915.

Source: George H. Doran, *Chronicles of Barabbas* (New York: Harcourt, Brace, 1935), 339–41.

While Dawson[68] was still in editorial charge, a tall, red-headed, lanky, and somewhat threadbare individual, who was the most fluent talker I have ever met, called upon me from a publisher's advertising agency. He seemed to me much too intelligent to be a mere advertisement solicitor, in fact as a salesman he was practically a total loss, but as we talked from time to time, he revealed fine qualities of editorial judgment and publicity. He gave no evidence of financial success, indeed quite the contrary. One day I asked him how he would like an editorial job in my office at a salary of $60 weekly. He almost embraced me and was at his editorial desk on the following morning. Thus began the publishing career of Sinclair Lewis. The change from Dawson to Lewis was revolutionary. Dawson, calm and serene, wrote out his briefs for or against a manuscript in beautiful Addisonian[69] phrases. Lewis pounded out on a typewriter the crispest of American staccato opinion and criticism, literally reams of publicity stunts. He was a dynamo of energy and freshness of thought. After he had been with me a fortnight he came to me, and in the exuberance of his happiness volunteered that he was so contented that he was settled and located for life if I would have him. I was delighted, for while he was a bit too fast for my mental processes and thoroughly impractical in many ways, he had a commendable sound sense, indefatigable energy, and downright industry, which properly harnessed would go far to the making of a young publishing house. He had written and published two novels with Harper's, and with the Dawson experience in mind, I talked with him on the wisdom of his commending authors to publish with me while he published with Harper's; but that was a situation which time and loyalty would compose.

Meanwhile his strident tones and his clattering machine gave an air of intense industry and activity to my hitherto quiet sedate establishment. He exuded enthusiasm, particularly to my salesman. Then there was a week when a somewhat Sabbath calm settled upon my office. Lewis must be incubating. He was. Then came another week of renewed and still more impatient activity, and yet another week and a perfectly electrified Lewis came to me, brandishing a check received that morning from George Lorimer of the *Saturday Evening Post* for $500 for that silent week's work on a short story. My $60 now advanced to $75 weekly could not compete with Lorimer's $500. The lure of individual achievement was much greater than the quiet security of an editorial chair. The next week, Lewis had bought a flivver, and with wife Gracie was hitting the trail for the West and freedom and *Free Air,* shortly to be published by Harcourt, Brace. Even before *Free Air* was published Lewis told Alfred Harcourt, of the newly formed firm of Harcourt, Brace and Howe, that his books, himself, and such funds as he had accumulated were all at the disposal of Harcourt. After *Free Air* they published *Main Street.* I was beginning to learn that a publisher is not a genius to his editors. However, there was no change in the friendship between Lewis and me. From his present lofty heights, he every now and again descends upon me, and we fraternize. From out of the first 5,000 edition of *Main Street,* I had a copy, read it, and literally worshipped it. At that time the highest compliment I could pay Lewis and his book was that he had written *The Old Wives' Tale* of America, that he had captured American types with the same meticulous accuracy as A[rnold] B[ennett] had delineated Five Towns and their people.[70] And this was before 2,000 copies of *Main Street* of the ultimate 500,000 copies had been sold; not a genius, but a prophet. I took unction to my soul.

4
Main Street
1919–21

After years in the trenches, Lewis's career unexpectedly blossomed with the publication of *Main Street.* Friends and rivals alike were shocked and surprised. Nearly three hundred thousand copies of the novel were sold during its first year in print. It was recommended for the Pulitzer Prize for 1921 by the fiction jury, though the Columbia trustees overruled the recommendation and the award was given instead to Edith Wharton's *The Age of Innocence.* Lewis only half-facetiously joked in a letter to Joseph Hergesheimer that he had been "ruined" by the popularity of the novel. "An earnest young man, Yankee of physical type, comic and therefore the more humorless, writes a long book to slap the bourgeois—the bourgeois love it, eat it! It would make an excellent short story."[1]

27 / Alfred Harcourt

In 1919 Alfred Harcourt founded and began to build a publishing company, and Lewis enlisted in the cause. The convergence of their interests led to a mutually beneficial partnership for over a decade. The first Lewis novel that Harcourt published was *Free Air,* serialized in the *Saturday Evening Post* in the spring of 1919 and the last of his apprenticeship novels. Harcourt also remembered his enthusiasm for *Main Street* when he read the novel in manuscript in the summer of 1920.

Source: Alfred Harcourt, *Some Experiences* (Riverside, CT: privately printed, 1934), 35–36, 54–58.

When I left Henry Holt and Company, I hadn't any idea what I was going to do. Some jobs in other publishing houses were offered to me, and I had just about decided to take one of them. As I knew Sinclair Lewis would be interested, I wrote to him of all that had happened. He was in Minnesota at the time, for he had given up his job with Doran, and was devoting himself to writing. In reply to my letter, I received a telegram at my home in Mount Vernon, asking me to meet him at Grand Central Station early the next Sunday morning. I decided to drive into town for him. I supposed some developments with the *Saturday Evening Post* had brought him East. As soon as we got settled in my car, I said something to this effect, and that it was fine of him to plan his trip so that we could have Sunday together. He blasted out, "Hell, Alf, I got your letter. I wrote you a letter, I wrote you a long night letter, and then I said to myself, 'This is important.' I drove 125 miles to Minneapolis, put my car in a garage, bought a railroad ticket and berth, and sent you a telegram to meet me here this morning. What I came on to say is, 'Don't be such a damn fool as ever again to go to work for someone else. Start your own business.' I'm going to write important books. You can publish these. I've got a little money saved up and you can have some of that. Now let's go out to your house and start making plans." [. . .]

The first book of Sinclair Lewis's which we published was *Free Air.* This was one of the enterprises he and I discussed in that memorable visit in Mount Vernon. At that time, the *Saturday Evening Post* was just starting to print, under the title *Free Air,* a serial Lewis had written based on an automobile trip he and his wife had made to the Pacific Coast after he left Doran's. The serial covered only the trip out and would be finished in three issues. Lewis and I worked out a scheme to expand it to book length by extending the story to cover some action on the Pacific Coast and on the trip back to the East. As it would take Lewis several months to get the additional material ready, we thought further serialization would be impossible, for the *Post,* to our knowledge, had never printed continuations of serials after a gap of time. However, *Free Air* had been so popular with the *Post* readers that the *Saturday Evening Post* contracted for the second part. The book sold moderately well—better than his earlier novels.

On a Saturday morning in the summer of 1920, Sinclair Lewis brought me the manuscript of *Main Street.* I took it home to read over the weekend. When I finished it Sunday night, I telephoned without success to a number of places in New York where I thought I might find him. As a last resort, I called the apartment of my secretary on the chance that she might know where he was. She said, "He is sitting on the stepladder in my kitchen with an apron tied around his neck, pretending to help me wipe dishes. I know he has been hoping to hear from you, for he has been depressed and almost silent." I tried to tell Lewis how greatly moved I was by the novel. "Did I think it would sell?" I said I thought it would have the same sort of sale as Arnold Bennett's *The Old Wives' Tale,* about which we were both enthusiastic—perhaps 40,000 copies. He was incredulous over my hopes for so good a sale, but pleased by the comparison with *The Old Wives' Tale.* My secretary reported that he started talking like a geyser as soon as he left the telephone.

He came to my home to make final corrections. There were about 200,000 words in the original manuscript, and I felt cutting would be wise if it could be done without destroying anything inherent in the book. Toward the end of the novel, there was a 20,000-word episode which I thought belabored the plot, although it was amusing in itself. We talked about deleting it, but in an argument with Lewis, I didn't have a chance. I finally suggested that the number of changes required to take out the episode would be a fair test of whether it was deep in the fiber of the book. If he had to make more than ten changes, we'd leave it in. He agreed to this. When I came home the next evening, he rather sheepishly admitted that in taking out the episode he had made only seven changes—all but two after it. I was so relieved that I tore up the manuscript of that part and threw it into the wastebasket without a thought of its possible value as a literary curiosity.

Main Street was published on October 23, 1920. Heywood Broun's review in the *New York Tribune,* which appeared a couple of days before publication,[2] started a run on the bookstores, and there was a flare-up of public demand almost before we had made all of our first deliveries. The booksellers had ordered conservatively because of their record on Lewis's earlier novels, and they couldn't imagine that many people would want to read a novel about an American small town. Even after the demand started, they expected it to die down. For almost a week, Womrath,[3] then a concern that ran circulating libraries all over New York City, telephoned six times a day for the immediate delivery of twenty-five copies to this or that branch before they would give us a basic large order. The demand started in New York, and up to Christmas was largely confined to the Eastern seacoast, but by the New Year, the talk in the East had spread to Western literary circles, and the copies of *Main Street* sent as Christmas gifts all over the country were provoking discussion. As we had warned the Western booksellers of this, they had ordered considerable stock, but not enough. It was a mad scramble all that spring to keep the stores supplied. There was a binders' strike in May. Seventy thousand sets of unbound sets that couldn't be touched were lying in Quinn & Boden's bindery. We jockeyed a duplicate set of plates of the book around, and managed to get 20,000 copies ready at another printing plant, using odds and ends of paper stock and binder's cloth. It was a sorry lot of books, but the demand was so insistent that those 20,000 copies went into the bookstores and out as fast as they were supplied, and we never had a complaint. To be sure of keeping ahead of the demand we had, at one period, the equivalent of three freight-car loads of books available. If the book had suddenly stopped selling, the consequences would have been very serious for so young a firm as ours. But it didn't stop. The sales for the first six months of 1921 were over 180,000 copies, and we were never out of stock for more than a few hours.

It was heart-warming to me to see the enthusiasm of my old bookseller friends over this really big success. Charlie Ayres of the American News Company, who had ridden me hard in my early selling days at Holt's, told a friend of mine that the day he gave me an order for 10,000 copies of *Main Street* was one of the happiest days of his life.

28 / James Branch Cabell

James Branch Cabell (1879–1958), author of novels, short stories, and poetry, is remembered primarily for his works—popular in the 1920s—of ironic and satirical fantasy fiction, such as *Jurgen* (1919). He published stories in such esteemed venues as *Harper's* and the *Saturday Evening Post* and was named to the American Academy of Arts and Sciences in 1937. The last manuscript Lewis accepted for publication as a reader for Stokes was Cabell's novel *The Soul of Melicent* (1913), and later, as Schorer explains, "at Doran, he declined the work that was to be called *The Cream of the Jest*" (1917).[4] In the summer of 1919, Lewis invited Cabell to read an early incomplete draft of *Main Street.* In January 1920, Lewis reported to Cabell that he had "destroyed all but a few pages of the 30,000 words" Cabell had seen. The draft "struck me as incomparably clumsy—and at times vulgar when I read it. It was off on the wrong foot."[5]

Source: James Branch Cabell, *As I Remember It* (New York: McBride, 1955), 166–67.

Lewis I had known, and I had liked heartily, both as a person and as a youngster in whose genius I put faith, some two years prior to this spectacular success with *Main Street.* I was, I believe, when Hal Lewis—for I never called him "Red"—became famous almost overnight, one of the very few living persons who had read each of his five earlier novels, and who already possessed inscribed and autographed copies of them.

Well, and the general conception of *Main Street,* which I had heard all about of course from its not unduly taciturn writer when I read the novel's uncompleted typescript at the Rockbridge Alum Springs,[6] and prompted a few changes in it, during the summer of 1919, appeared to me a deal better than was its final printed expression in the autumn of 1920. I enjoyed, that is, parts of this book far more than I did a vast quantity of its other parts. I thought the novel too long, and the writing of it straggly. Nor, it was an odd thing, saving only myself could I ever find anybody, not even at the height of the book's fame, who had read actually all of *Main Street.* It was the general conception of the book—the impairments wrought by the unconquerable smug "village virus" of small town life—which, as we say, caught on and became proverbial.

29 / Grace Hegger Lewis

In her autobiography, written more than twenty-five years after her separation and divorce from Sinclair Lewis, Grace Hegger Lewis remembered her own role in the composition of *Main Street.* In her account, she was her husband's advisor, technical consultant, editor, and proofreader. She obviously did not recognize the extent to which she was satirized in the novel in the character of Carol Kennicott.

Source: Grace Hegger Lewis, *With Love from Gracie* (New York: Harcourt, Brace, 1955), 145–46, 190.

Main Street was with us day and night. We talked about it constantly when we were alone (though never with guests unless they had some information Hal needed); he often phoned me from his workroom to tell me some adroit situation which had just come to him or to discuss the right word to use when the *Thesaurus* failed him. He brought home a dozen pages at a time for me to read, never taking his eyes off me as I went through them, and demanding to know what in the pages had caused each change in my expression as I read, what had brought a smile or a laugh, what had made me cry. I was his barometer, but I was more than that, for after I had finished reading we would go over the pages line by line, Hal defending his point of view, his overfondness for certain words, his too-elaborate avoidance of the cliché, but giving in quickly on some things. He was grateful always for my professional experience with manuscripts, my knowledge of printer's signs and jargon, my instinctive good literary taste.

The novel often intruded on my sleep. Fortunately I could always wake easily and cheerfully, if Hal came home late and wanted to talk, or if at six A.M., unable to sleep, he came to sit on the edge of my bed and ask: "Gracie, what kind of pictures would there be on the wall when Carol does over the living room?"

I would push my hair away from my face, rub my eyes, try to take in what he was saying.

"Uh—uh—why don't you hang up a piece of Japanese brocade—a sash—an *obi* I think it's called?"

"Golly! Now *that's* an idea. Something absolutely different—abso*lute*!"

Hal had sold one last story to the *Post*—"Habeas Corpus" [published January 24, 1920]—and then there was to be a long silence. The novel must be finished. [. . .]

If Lewis had never read Masters's *Spoon River Anthology*[7] neither did he read the history of Emma Bovary until he was half through the final draft of *Main Street.* He did not need to read *Bovary* to discover Flaubert's method, which had left its mark on every generation of writers after 1870. But where the realism of Flaubert was coldly, clinically objective, Lewis was warm in his sympathy or hotly angry in his condemnation of his characters and the village where they dwelt. If Flaubert said, "*Bovary, c'est moi,*" Lewis could well have said, "*Carol, that's me,*" for he was more than approving of what Carol was trying to do to better Gopher Prairie whereas Emma Bovary only wanted to better life for herself; and he thought Carol's Chinese party a very fine party indeed and one he would have enjoyed attending.

30 / Heywood Broun

Heywood Broun (1888–1939), journalist and founder of the American Newspaper Guild, worked mostly for New York–based newspapers as a sportswriter, columnist, and editor. As Harcourt noted, Broun's enthusiastic review of *Main Street* in the *New York Tribune* presaged its critical and commercial success, though he would later scorn *The Man Who Knew Coolidge* and *Elmer Gantry.* Broun and his wife, Dorothy Hale (1882–1934), were also members of the Algonquin Round Table. He ran unsuccessfully for Congress in 1930 as a Socialist on the slogan, "I'd rather be right than Roosevelt." The annual Heywood Broun Award given by the Newspaper Guild honors his tradition of social activism.

Source: Heywood Broun, "Hewing to the Line," *Woman's Home Companion* 58 (February 1931): 26.

When I first met Sinclair Lewis he was a successful and prolific author of light fiction. There was a keen demand for his work but he told me that he had quit contributing and was eking out a meager and painful existence while working on a novel much more ambitious in plan.

"Of course," he explained, "it isn't the sort of book anybody will like and I'll be lucky to sell a thousand copies."

A few months later *Main Street* appeared and became an almost instantaneous bestseller. It is quite possible that people did not like it but at least they bought the book. That was obligatory, for editorial comment raged throughout America as to the validity of this criticism of small-town life. Every alert citizen was forced at least to dip into the story in order to hold his own in current conversation. [. . .]

Main Street was a difficult book in the sense that it made small concession to the reader who likes a fast-moving plot. The story was slight and the emphasis fell upon the painting of the background. Few authors have ever gone into greater detail of description. When Lewis undertook to set before his audience the look of some certain bypath he did not omit so much as a scrap of paper lying beside the road. He endeavored to present a complete catalogue of a community.

Indeed before he began the actual work of writing he had prepared huge scrapbooks filled with odd bits of information about small-town life. And in addition he drew maps to scale so that if one character went from a certain point to another the book would be accurate in its time schedule. In preparing for *Babbitt,* Sinclair Lewis went to even greater lengths and familiarized himself with the precise floor plan of the house in which his hero lived.

31 / Kathleen Norris

Kathleen Thompson Norris (1880–1966), novelist and short-story writer, was the highest paid female writer of her era, and her many popular romance novels are still highly regarded in that genre. She married the novelist Charles G. Norris (1881–1945), the brother of the novelist Frank Norris (1870–1902), in 1909. She met Lewis in San Francisco the same year. After 1910 she published work in the *Atlantic*, the *American Magazine*, *McClure's*, *Everybody's*, *Ladies' Home Journal*, and *Women's Home Companion*. William Rose Benét married Kathleen Norris's sister, Theresa, in 1912, and the Lewises moved into the house on Long Island they vacated in 1914. See also Richard Allan Davison, "Sinclair Lewis, Charles G. Norris, and Kathleen Norris: An Early Friendship," *Modern Fiction Studies* 31 (Autumn 1985): 503–10.

Source: Kathleen Norris, *Family Gathering* (Garden City, NY: Doubleday, 1959), 205.

Sinclair Lewis took Cigi [C. G. or Charles G. Norris] and me to lunch in Washington one day and asked us to come up to his apartment and hear the first chapter of *Main Street*, which was to set the world ablaze the following year and lead bestsellers for several years. But we begged off; we had something else to do. It was probably the all-important business of finding attractive tin cups for ranch luncheons. Red told us that day that it was the great American novel.

32 / George Jean Nathan

George Jean Nathan (1882–1958), drama critic and editor, was one of the foremost theater critics of his time, known for his cultured and often sardonic perspective. With H. L. Mencken he edited the *Smart Set* from 1914 and founded the *American Mercury* in 1924. As Schorer explains, "as a general impression," this account of his first meeting with Lewis "can probably be accepted."[8] H. L. Mencken recounts essentially the same version of events in *My Life as Author and Editor* (New York: Knopf, 1993), 328–29.

Source: *The Intimate Notebooks of George Jean Nathan* (New York: Knopf, 1932), 8–10.

Late one afternoon [in 1920], our mutual friend, T. R. Smith, then managing editor of the *Century Magazine,* telephoned Mencken and myself at our office and bade us come up to his flat that evening for a drink. When we got there, we found with Smith a tall, skinny, paprika-headed stranger to whom we were introduced as one Lewis. The fellow was known to neither of us save as the author of a negligible serial that had appeared in the *Saturday Evening Post* and that had subsequently been gathered between book covers [*Free Air*] and, to me specifically, as the author of a play called "Hobohemia" [1919], produced the year before down in Greenwich Village and exquisitely—if I may be permitted so critically indelicate a word—epizoötic.[9]

Barely had we taken off our hats and coats and before Smith had an opportunity even to fish out his *luxe* corkscrew from behind his *luxe* sets of the works of the more esoteric Oriental and Polack amorists, when the tall, skinny, paprika-headed stranger simultaneously coiled one long arm around Mencken's neck and the other around mine, well nigh strangling us and putting resistance out of the question, and—yelling at the top of his lungs—began: "So you guys are critics, are you? Well, let me tell you something. I'm the best writer in this here gottdamn country and if you, Georgie, and you, Hank, don't know it now, you'll know it gottdamn soon. Say, I've finished a book that'll be published in a week or two and it's the gottdamn best book of its kind that this here gottdamn country has had and don't you guys forget it! I worked a year on the gottdamn thing and it's the goods, I'm atelling you! Listen, when it comes to writing a novel, I'm so far ahead of most of the men you two think are good that I'll be gottdamned if it doesn't make me sick to think of it! Just wait till you read the gottdamn thing. You've got a treat coming, Georgie and Hank, and don't you boys make no mistake about *that*!"

Projected from Smith's flat by the self-endorsing uproar—it kept up for fully half an hour longer—Mencken and I jumped into a taxicab, directed the driver to speed us post-haste to a tavern where we might in some peace recover our equilibrium and our ear-drums, and looked at each other. "Of all the idiots I've ever laid eyes on, that fellow is the worst!" groaned Mencken, gasping for breath. Regaining my own breath some moments later, all that I could add was that if any such numskull could ever write anything worth reading, maybe there was something in Christian Science too.

Three days later I got the following letter from Mencken, who had returned to Baltimore: "Dear George: Grab hold of the bar-rail, steady yourself, and prepare yourself for a terrible shock! I've just read the advance sheets of the book of that *Lump* we met at Schmidt's and, by God, he has done the job! It's a genuinely excellent piece of work. Get it as soon as you can and take a look. I begin to believe that perhaps there isn't a God after all. There is no justice in the world. Yours in Xt [Christ], M." The book was *Main Street.*

As is sufficiently known, it not only became a best-seller over-night, but it promptly established its author as one of the most observant, penetrating, and significant writers in America.

33 / Fanny Butcher

Despite his sudden success, Lewis for better or worse refused to play the part of the literary lion.

Source: Fanny Butcher, *Many Lives—One Love* (New York: Harper and Row, 1972), 396.

He was unpredictable, sometimes pixyish, loving to play the bad little boy just to watch the results. I had casually mentioned to him when he was going to give a lecture for the building fund of Northwestern University that there was a rivalry between it and the University of Chicago. Hal had been paid, he told me, a thousand dollars for the talk, a practically unheard-of fee. The lecture was a sellout. Every seat in the vast Auditorium Theatre was filled, and the ovation that greeted the lanky author of *Main Street* was prolonged and clamorous. It was naturally expected that at some time the lecturer would pay some tribute to the great institution that was presenting him, and that he would point to its future growth. Hal talked delightfully and engagingly about how Chicago would always be his big city, not London or New York or Paris, because as a boy Chicago had seemed the center of the world to him. Then he began talking about Chicago's educational as well as cultural advantages, about its incomparable institution of learning. Suddenly the blood froze in my veins. He was talking about the University of Chicago. He never once mentioned Northwestern, and when he finished there was not enough applause to shake one small loose rafter.

Afterwards, when I told him I thought he ought to be ashamed, he said, "It served them right trying to bribe me to ballyhoo their campaign. I showed 'em. I'm incorruptible," and he laughed until he had to be slapped on the back to keep from choking. He deserved, of course, to be punched in his articulate jaw, and I got him away as quickly as possible lest he would be.

5
Zenith
1921–22

Main Street was not a fluke. Lewis's next novel, *Babbitt,* which he mostly wrote in England and Italy to escape the furor prompted by the publication of its predecessor, was more critically if less commercially successful. Still, a total of nearly a quarter-million copies of it were eventually sold. Alfred Kazin asserted a generation later that Babbitt had "entered as completely into the national imagination as Daniel Boone."[1] Lewis also insisted that he loved the character Babbitt, that he was not an object of the author's scorn: "Along with his Rotarian, right-thinking notions there was much that was fine and lovable."[2] As late as 1949 he told Perry Miller that he "wrote *Babbitt* not out of hatred for him but out of love" (see chapter 115).

34 / Frazier Hunt

Frazier Hunt (1885–1967) was a writer, radio announcer, and European correspondent for the International News Service. The Hearst Corporation owned both the INS and *Cosmopolitan,* so Hunt was pressed into service in London to recruit Lewis as a contributor. Lewis reminisced about his long friendship with Hunt in "Tom Sawyer on Dowling Street," *Newsweek,* February 7, 1938, 28: "I have known Spike Hunt for years, and I have truly seen that not merely in writing about the scattered Little People but in casual meetings with them has he a genius of sympathetic friendship."

Source: Frazier Hunt, *One American and His Attempt at Education* (New York: Simon and Schuster, 1938), 248–54.

Throughout the first three years of my total five years of London residence, Sinclair Lewis was to play a strong part and exert an inordinate influence. I had been back in London less than a month from my painful search for Irish "peace," when I received a cable from Ray Long[3] telling me that the author of *Main Street* had just arrived in London and that I was to approach him at once and try to land his next novel for *Cosmopolitan.* I found that he was stopping "in chambers" at the comfortable old Georgian House at 10 Bury Street, near Piccadilly Circus, under the wise and friendly wing of Dungar, the unapproachable major-domo. I telephoned Lewis for an appointment. I was to come at four o'clock.

There was a friendly smile on his battle-scarred face when he met me at the door. He welcomed me profusely, and introduced me to a somewhat cross-eyed European-Britisher named Bechhofer—later to be styled Bechhofer Roberts—who was by way of being a writer-critic-friend-and-philosopher.[4] We sat down and Lewis poured a tall drink. I was "Mr. Hunt" to him for a full ten minutes, and then I became "Frazier."

A little later he thundered: "Say! what in hell is your real name, anyway? You've surely got some other name besides Frazier. My name is Red."

"Friends and enemies call me Spike," I answered.

"Well, that's better. Let me get you a little drink, Spike."

That was all there was to it. We mixed like Scotch and soda. From that moment we were almost inseparables. When friends couldn't locate Red at his own diggings they would call up my house or office, and two-thirds of the time they'd run him down—or vice versa.

Main Street had shot Red to the very top of American authors. I always had a suspicion that the real reason he was so popular at this time with English craftsmen and the British public generally was because he had cracked down so frankly and brutally on the American small town. He painted just the sort of picture of the American scene and its crude intolerances that the average Britisher wanted to read. They welcomed him as one of their own kind—superior, a bit snooty, and extremely critical of inferior breeds.

But Red fooled them. He saw through their own sham and hypocrisy as easily as he could see through a freshly polished pane of glass. When great and near-great tried to patronize his own American self-criticism they were met by a stinging rebuff. Certainly he was not showing up the weakness and intolerance of his own land for the benefit of Englishmen.

The famous bohemian Savage Club asked Lewis to talk at one of their Saturday-night entertainments. Many distinguished American men of letters—Mark Twain, Bret Harte, Stephen Crane, Artemus Ward—had addressed the club and left behind them a tradition of friendly salute to "the mother country."[5] Club members naturally expected honeyed phrases for English literature and hopes that some day America might catch up. Instead, Lewis charged them like Pancho Villa's irregular cavalry.[6] He explained that he would like to write a *Main Street* about this self-satisfied and behind-the-times land. He had written *Main Street* for the good of America and not to make his country the misunderstood laughingstock of a people who were so placid and secure in their own ignorance that they seldom traveled or bothered to keep in touch with other people's points of view and accomplishments.

It left the good ale drinkers aghast. They had never heard such impertinence. But Red made them like it. He could switch moods as easily as an organ player could change the tremolo stops. In a way, he was not unlike the colored prize fighter who carried a horseshoe in his glove just for luck. Yet time and again I have seen him let one fly at some unsuspecting patronizer, when he was really aiming at himself. He was a many-sided genius, and when he caught himself aping his hosts in speech, thought, or intolerance he would strike out at them, when he was actually whipping himself back to his own amusing naturalness.

Largely through Red I was to be thrown feet first into a strange and talented group of literary, artistic, and newspaper radicals, who were principally Englishmen but had a healthy sprinkling of American expatriates. Many of them were to become tried and true, and friendships were to be cemented that neither time nor distance will ever break.

I had brought an American touring car to London that was to have a profound effect on the motor future of the British Isles. Certainly half of the ten motor mechanics practiced up on it. It spent a large part of its life in garages and shops. There it would be tinkered with, taken apart, and generally used as a mechanical guinea pig. Even its demountable rims were an endless source of delight: mechanics would spring on them at the slightest provocation, and on cross-country trips, we would often be delayed from two to four hours while brawny but thick-witted workmen wrestled with those newfangled rims. Gas stations were only just beginning to be introduced into the stubborn land, and we invariably carried extra tins of fuel on our running boards. Petrol was sixty cents an imperial gallon, but even that did not keep us from galloping time and again from the southern coast of England to the mountains and lakes of Scotland.

Red went along on many of these trips. Gracie Lewis was not always in England when Red was there, but I vividly remember one rather long and leisurely trip that we all took together. Gentle and beloved Walter Fuller[7] accompanied us as our guide and peacemaker. I had traveled most of the Continent in search of firsthand material for an "Is the World Going Dry?" magazine series.[8] I wanted particularly to do the Glasgow slums on a drunken Saturday night, so we started north. Red and I kept a list of the roadside pubs we passed. Some of the names were a bit poetic: the Three Graces, the White Swan, the Seven Virgins, the Stag at Eve. As I recall it now the Red Lion won over the White Horse by a score of nineteen to seventeen. Coach and Horses was third and the Duke of Wellington fourth.

I am a little afraid that we pulled up at far too many of these inviting havens and that my investigation might just as well have been a little less personal and inclusive. Late each afternoon we would choose an attractive, old-fashioned inn, and settle down for the evening. After supper Red and I would find a quiet seat in the taproom and buy mugs of ale for the village squire, the doctor, the butcher, and whoever would sit and discuss affairs with us. More than one evening we would remain with the innkeeper and an old crony or two long after the pub had officially closed, and argue the war, the debts, and the next slaughter.

At supper we would always decide the hour we would meet for breakfast the following morning, so that we might all be ready to start at the same time. One morning, following a rather prolonged night session in the taproom, the five of us were on hand save only Red. Gracie, quite lovely to look upon, was among the first down, and confidently ordered the master's breakfast. On came the porridge and the blue milk. But no Red. Next came the rubber fish and the cold toast. But no Red. Last appeared the stage eggs and the Irish bacon. Still no Red.

In front of Red's empty chair there now spread a semicircle of stone-cold, unhappy-looking dishes, topped off by an uninspiring pot of tea, tepid enough by this time to bathe in. Of course we had no drinking water: only unlettered American tourists drank water at their meals.

Gracie was certain Red would appear at any moment. Finally through the open double-doors at the far end of the room strode the lean figure of the novelist. His thin red hair had not been combed and he had obviously completed his toilet on the way downstairs.

He barked a frosty good morning, and sat down. His slightly bloodshot eyes glared at the awful array of English cooking that confronted him. It would have made a far stouter man cringe.

"Miss!" he shouted at the bucktoothed waitress, half scaring her out of her hide. "Miss, get me some water, please."

No one spoke. There was a feeling of impending tragedy in the air. Red looked again at his breakfast and quickly turned his head. The rest of us were not exactly afraid of him but we thought it best to leave him to his own thoughts: he had been in a vast ale-buying mood the night before.

Red moved nervously in his chair. Our eyes were glued on the kitchen door. A full minute dragged by. Then when we had all but given up hope, the bucktoothed girl swung open the door and hurried toward our table. We drew a deep sigh of relief. The situation would be saved: Red would get his drink of nice cold water and then he'd feel better.

"Sorry to keep ya woitin,' sor," she apologized, setting squarely in front of Red a pot of boiling hot water.

Red gave it one look. Then he half rose from his chair and threw out his long, lean arms in a gesture of despair. "My God, woman!" he screamed. "My God in Heaven! I want cold water. COLD WATER! C-O-L-D WATER!"

It was too much for us. We fairly exploded while Red only glared sullenly at the frightened girl. But we wouldn't be bullied. Finally a smile broke out on his thin lips. "Great God! What a country!" he swore. "I think they must boil their eggs in beer."

It was a Saturday afternoon when we reached Glasgow. That night Red and I wandered off to the slums. I had seen Chicago's red-light district and New York's Bowery, and I had watched men have the D.T.'s on the streets of Brisbane, Australia. I had seen opium dens in Shanghai and tequila and *aguardiente* bars in Mexico, but never had I seen anything to compare with this Scotch border town at the hour when the pubs closed for the weekend. Men, women, and children were fighting in the dirty streets; gin-drinking charwomen were lying helpless in the gutters and alleys; a quarter of the great city was overrun with hundreds of poor, helpless, drunken wretches whose only sin was poverty, and who for a few hours were finding escape from their everlasting fears and their defeats by the only road they knew.

Finally Red stopped and raised his clenched fists to high heaven. Tears were streaming down his cheeks. "I can't stand it any more," he cried. "I can't stand it."

All the way back to the hotel he cursed and raved, "God damn the society that will permit such poverty! God damn the religions that stand for such a putrid system! God damn 'em all!"

That was one side of this strange man, who seemed to spend half his time fighting his own intolerances and shortcomings. In many ways he was a spoiled boy. He always had to be the center of the stage. He could brook no other hero. There was a strong streak of the actor in his make-up, too. Times without number I have seen him impersonate a little German professor of philosophy; again, with his head wrapped in a bath towel, he would become an Indian yogi; with a false mustache he would be the villain about to rape the village hired girl. And I shall never forget an evening at the home of the famed literary agent, Curtis Brown,[9] when in blank verse Red improvised a complete saga of the winning of the West: the covered wagon trains, the start from Independence, the fording of the Platte, the Indian attack, the death of the baby, the wagon wheels grinding over the grave, the arrival in the rich lands of Oregon Territory. It was moving and beautiful. No one else in the world could extemporaneously have equaled it in drama and pathos. It was Lewis the artist, the imaginative American, exalted lover of his own land and its history. I was never so proud of him as I was at that moment.

It is difficult for me to stop writing about this extraordinary friend. I have always felt that the secret of his strange and diverse character lay hidden in his unhappy youth in the Minnesota town of Sauk Centre. The skinny, pimply-faced little Harry Lewis, brought up in stern old Doc Lewis's home by a kindly stepmother, had been a lonely, inadequate lad. He was backward at the rough-and-tumble games and sports of the tough boys of the town. He was a misfit. An old shoemaker was far more of a companion to him than were his schoolmates. With the aid of this odd codger and from books, the boy created a world of the imagination. Often even it was a bitter world, intolerant and cruel.

Years later when Lewis started to write *Main Street,* the fictional town he saw and hated was the real town of his own unhappy youth. He was not in the least to blame for the fact that he painted only half a town. His boyhood had been only half a boyhood. It had been the exact opposite of my own full and satisfying one.

Often in London I would chide him for his eternal faultfinding and his intolerant attitude toward a poor and faltering world. "Don't you understand," he answered me one evening when we were comfortably ensconced before my own fireplace in Portsea Place, "don't you understand that it's my mission in life to be the despised critic, the eternal faultfinder? I must carp and scold until everyone despises me. That's what I was put here for."

Red and I had a thousand amusing and colorful hours at this tiny house of mine near the Marble Arch. I remember an evening when George Slocombe[10] happened to be over from Paris, and I had Sir Philip Gibbs and A. S. M. Hutchinson[11] in to meet Red and George. Red came in late. His face was crimson and he was as high as a turkey gobbler's comb. I introduced him to the two shy and soft-spoken English writers.

At once Gibbs was "Phil" to him, but he had a little difficulty reducing the extremely sensitive author of *If Winter Comes* to a familiar nickname. He turned on him and shot out: "What do people call you, Hutchinson?"

The distinguished writer cringed before the blast. "My intimate friends call me 'A. S. M.,'" Hutchinson finally answered.

"My God!" Red thundered. "I can't remember all that. I'll just call you 'Hutch' for short."

And "Hutch" he did call him. But long before the night was done he had won both men to his warmth and honesty, and to his right to be different.

35 / Charles Phillips Russell

Charles Phillips Russell (1883–1974), journalist, southern writer, and member of the English faculty at the University of North Carolina (1931–37) and School of Journalism (1937–54), lived in England from 1920 to 1925, working in advertising and as a reporter for the London *Daily Express.* He interviewed Lewis while he was writing *Babbitt.*

Source: Charles Phillips Russell, "Sinclair Lewis Declares Americans, More Than Britons, Ruled by Main-Street Idea," (Portland) *Oregonian,* October 9, 1921, 3.

London, Sept. 15. [. . .] Sinclair Lewis did not invent Main Street, but he certainly put it on the map. I found Mr. Lewis "Main-streeting" in London, so to speak, and he has been telling me his impressions of Main street and Main streeters as they exist on this side of the Atlantic in comparison with that well-known thoroughfare as it exists in Uncle Sam's domain—at least in the eyes of Sinclair Lewis.

This does not mean that Mr. Lewis has deserted the Main streets of Gopher Prairies for the boulevards of European metropolises. He said so himself. He has simply left Main Street, U.S.A., temporarily for Main Street, England, in order to obtain that peacefulness and seclusion meet for a novelist in the throes of a new composition.

For in the quiet cottage of a Kent village in which he is now settled, after a stay of several weeks in Cornwall, he has been at work for some months on his new novel. Its theme he declined to disclose.

"That's a secret," he said, "and will be until it is finished in the spring. Publication, I suppose, will take place the following fall."

"Are you enjoying yourself?" he was asked.

"Immensely," he answered emphatically. "The atmosphere over here was made for writers. The differences, after the hustle and tear of our life in the states, is astonishing. The quietude of Main streets in the Old World—if you like to call them that—is almost uncanny. The sense of ease, of relaxation, of plenty of timeness is most grateful. How cool and steady the English are. There is something admirable in the calm with which they go about the business of living."

"Then you detect a difference between Main street, America, and Main street, Europe?"

Main Street's author reflected a moment and then said:

"There is something ridiculous to me in emphasizing the differences between peoples. Such differences are apt to be very superficial, especially between two peoples like the British and Americans. Every day I encounter incidents that reveal their astonishing likeness to each other. The Main street type of mind is, of course, not peculiar to America. The small-town attitude toward the world, I am convinced, is the same everywhere.

"And yet—yes, there is a difference. I think it lies in the fact that the American small town considers itself a part of the universe; over here the small town has no such belief—it is hardly even interested in the outside world. I would not call its attitude self-satisfied; it is simply not concerned.

"And that brings up another point of difference. I think it is fair to say that the chief characteristic of the English small town is its absence of interest in affairs in general. The American town is more alert. That is one of the things with which I have been most impressed—there is more eagerness in the United States. More and more I have the feeling that some big things of the future are to come from America. Friends of mine over here have told me that they feel the same expectation. Our people are more forward looking; sometimes they are almost pathetically anxious to keep abreast of what is going on in the world."

"Do you feel convinced, then, after observation on both sides of the Atlantic, that the Main street point of view is more characteristic of the American people than the English?" Lewis was asked.

"I wouldn't say that," he answered. "The Main street angle is not a matter of geography; it is a matter of physical size and living conditions. Where a community is small the people naturally know each other intimately and therefore are more observant of each other's affairs, movements and opinions. Criticism is therefore quickly heard and this has the effect of suppressing strongly marked individuality. The result is uniformity.

"But I think it is true that America is more governed by the Main street idea. Our legislators, congressmen, senators and other lawmakers and officials—even our presidents—are apt to come from small towns. Therefore, you cannot expect their outlook, their horizon, to be very broad.

"The weakness of the American small town is its mental tightness, its Puritanic inhibitions. So we get Comstockery and Sumnerism.[12] In literature this does not make for truth and honesty. The censor of morals becomes, in effect, the chief editor of the nation's books. The result is to prevent the growth of a literature of distinction. Think of an Edith Wharton trying to write with the pencil of a Comstock poised over her page!"

"When you refer to literary truthfulness," I asked Mr. Lewis, "do you mean realism?"

"Not at all." His reply was emphatic. "I object to these literary classifications. What is realism, anyhow? How draw a fine distinction between it and romanticism, say? Where does one begin and the other leave off? How would you classify a writer like Hergesheimer,[13] for instance? Is he a realist or a romanticist, and when and where?"

"Such terms are used vaguely. Often their intention is merely to detract. There is another phrase of the same kind that I consider equally meaningless—'photographic.' The implication is that his presentation is like that of a camera. But a writer can put down only what he has seen and it is impossible for the human eye to act like a camera. You look at a woman in a corner. If you are observing her features, you cannot take in the details of her frock at the same time. The camera is mechanical and exact. If not interfered with, it presents everything before it impartially and down to the last detail. But the human eye is compelled to concentrate. It sees one thing clearly and the rest vaguely or impressionistically. It is the business of the writer to see and to present the essential thing in each subject or situation and that alone. His observation is selective and the more acute his selective gift or training, the greater artist he is."

At this point the author of a novel which has sold to the extent of 300,000 copies in the United States was asked how it had been received in England and whether, as a picture of a phase of life peculiarly American, he thought it would be understood in England.

"I don't know," he said. "I have no reports. It has been out only a very short time here. Besides, I have been out of touch with things in London. I have spent all my time since arriving here in the middle of the summer in the provinces, except for a brief trip to Paris. I only came up from Kent for the day. The only new thing I know about *Main Street* is that it is now being translated into Swedish. I think I see troubles for the translator. How would you translate American slang into Swedish? Suppose, for instance, a character says: 'Say, where do you get that stuff? What's the big idea, anyhow? It's time you took a new line. I'm offa all that dope.' How will that passage look in Swedish? Again, how is a man going to translate Swedish-American dialect into Swedish? How would he render such a sentence as 'Ay tank so'?"

"Did you find any Main streeters in Paris?" I asked.

"Yes, they are all collected around the tables of cafes on the *rive gauche.* Some of them are old inhabitants and seem to know their way about Paris pretty well, but the more they try to be French the more they are American."

36 / Charles Breasted

Charles Breasted (1897–1980), the author of a memoir of his father, the archaeologist and historian James Henry Breasted, also befriended Lewis in London.

Source: Charles Breasted, "The 'Sauk-Centricities' of Sinclair Lewis," *Saturday Review of Literature,* August 14, 1954, 7–8.

I first met Sinclair Lewis in the United States, when he was capitalizing on the success of *Main Street* by lecturing far and wide; but our real acquaintance and eventual friendship dated from a February afternoon in 1922, when we both happened simultaneously to converge upon the American Consulate General in London to have our passports extended. Lewis was then completing *Babbitt* in a bare-walled, single-windowed room, furnished with a table and two chairs, which he had rented in the Middle Temple in London. During those days he used to join me periodically for dinners and simple soirées at the homes of old friends in the Holland Park and Camden Hill sections of London, where we met such diverse personalities as George Peabody Gooch, the English historian;[14] Hermann Gollancz, the Semitist[15] Maxwell Armfield, the sadly crippled yet extraordinarily active artist;[16] Cyril Scott, the composer;[17] Edmund Dulac, the illustrator;[18] and many others. Lewis had already struck up a warm friendship with H. G. Wells (which was to prove sadly short-lived), and had met Galsworthy,[19] Claude Lovat Fraser,[20] Barrie[21] (his historic visit with Conrad,[22] which Wolfe so witheringly described in *The Web and the Rock,* came much later), and other leading figures of the day. He was greatly impressed with what seemed to him their un-British easy informality, and with the fact that their social gatherings included every age level and that the young people in their teens seemed genuinely to enjoy such association with their elders. He would always compliment his hosts especially on this latter aspect of their social life, which was in such contrast to the separation between generations in the United States. This in turn would lead him to expound upon the foibles and fortes of life in America. If the occasion included games, he was likely to be in the middle of them, usually on the floor; and as often as not he would end up by teaching a group of guests, including the prettiest girl present, the subtleties of poker.

One evening when we were on our way in a taxi to some such gathering I asked Lewis if *Main Street* wasn't largely autobiographical. He answered that of course Doc Kennicott was a portrait of his father. Then I said, "What about Carol Kennicott—isn't she a portrait of you?" He seemed startled and said that only a very few people has guessed her identity. "Yes," he added, "Carol is 'Red' Lewis: always groping for something she isn't capable of attaining, always dissatisfied, always restlessly straining to see what lies just over the horizon, intolerant of her surroundings, yet lacking any clearly defined vision of what she really wants to do or to be."

37 / C. R. W. Nevinson

C. R. W. Nevinson (1889–1946), English painter, was a friend to the Italian Futurist, F. T. Marinetti (1876–1944), and, for a time, associated with the writer and painter Wyndham Lewis (1882–1957) at the Rebel Art Centre in London, though he was never a member of the avant-garde Vorticist group. He painted Lewis's portrait in June 1924, and Lewis bought Nevinson's painting of the Brooklyn Bridge soon after.

Source: C. R. W. Nevinson, *Paint and Prejudice* (New York: Harcourt, Brace, 1938), 236–38.

Another sitter of mine was Sinclair Lewis, the strangest literary man I have ever known. He was restless, clownish, and intense as only Americans can be, and he prowled round my studio incapable of sitting still, while all the time he poured out the most remarkable monologue of love and hate, shrewdness and sentimentality, that it can have been the lot of any portrait painter to hear. He used to leave me with a sense of exhaustion and elation that I have never known any other human capable of producing.

He was obsessed with a dread of the future and of his own in particular, fearing that his creative faculties would dry up; and all this before he wrote *Babbitt, The Man Who Knew Coolidge,* and *It Can't Happen Here* [1935]. His irony was devastating and I wish I dared write some of the thrusts he made at contemporary writers, French, English, and American, but I have been warned that it is possible in this country to write the truth only of the dead. All the time I am struggling with the awful fear that something I have said will be held in evidence against me.

I have sometimes wondered if Sinclair looks back on that particular visit to England with dissatisfaction. Never have I met a man so sensitive and yet with such a gift of putting his foot in it. He would break all the snob rules laid down by the mumbo-jumbos of English literature, and infuriate everyone with a taint of preciosity. Sometimes it would seem that a devil possessed him, although I recall two occasions when he was worsted.

Once we were at dinner with Somerset Maugham, and among those present were Mrs. Maugham, Knoblock, McEvoy, Osbert Sitwell, and Eddie Marsh.[23] There was nobody in the party to whom Sinclair Lewis could take exception; and as for our host, I have always noticed like many others that he is the one man admired by all authors. After dinner, Sinclair Lewis took Eddie Marsh's monocle, stuck it in his own eye, and began parading up and down with Eddie Marsh following like a dog on a string. Then, to amuse himself, he parodied high-brow conversation in the best Oxford manner, at times imitating McEvoy's cracked voice, which was sometimes bass and sometimes treble. All of us were embarrassed, as the parody was grotesquely realistic, and I saw McEvoy pull his hair over his forehead and begin to look like a village idiot, a danger signal in him.

I knew it would come, and sure enough McEvoy suddenly interrupted the parody and inquired if Sinclair Lewis was an American. Sinclair Lewis looked taken aback by the question, but fell right into trouble.

"Yes," he said. "That is what makes me so sick with you condescending Englishmen."

"I don't care if you are sick," replied McEvoy calmly. "In fact I should be rather pleased. But you are just the man to tell me why old Americans are so much nicer than young ones."

Poor Lewis. The eyeglass fell from his eye and he was silent until we left.

I took him on to a night club and he began to regain courage. A little Chelsea girl joined us; and, still sore, he began boasting. I knew this Chelsea girl to be a terror and by no means as innocent as she looked, but in spite of all my efforts to silence him he would talk about himself. With murmurs of disbelief the girl urged him on until he was announcing to the world at large that he was the author of *Main Street,* which had the largest circulation, bar the Bible, of any book in America. The wicked little girl looked at him with wide-open eyes and asked, "Are you a writer?" By now he was in a mood to repeat himself. "Sure I am," he bellowed. "I am telling you I wrote *Main Street,* that has the largest circulation, bar the Bible, throughout America." With a look of complete innocence the girl went on, "You an author? I thought you were an American! But surely you were a publicity agent once?"

Another time talking with Lord Beaverbrook,[24] Sinclair Lewis kept on saying, "What do you think, Max?" Beaverbrook grew tired of this form of address after the eighth time and suddenly snapped at him, "What do you think, Sinc?" Little humiliations, maybe; but Americans are very touchy, and to be worsted by "a limey" is no fun.

38 / Harold Loeb

Harold Loeb (1891–1974), Princeton class of 1913, founded with Alfred Kreymborg and others the little magazine *Broom* in 1921. Lewis was an immediate subscriber. Loeb was also Ernest Hemingway's sparring partner, the model for the character of Robert Cohn in *The Sun Also Rises,* and a cousin of Peggy Guggenheim (1898–1979). Crossing paths with the Lewises in Rome, Loeb sketched their crumbling marriage in disturbing terms.

Source: Harold Loeb, *The Way It Was* (New York: Criterion Books, 1959), 84–86.

Early in November [1921], Sinclair Lewis, who had come to Rome to work on *Babbitt,* paid us a visit. He had red hair, a triangular face, long legs like a grasshopper's, and tremendous enthusiasms. We used to meet at a small terrace café where German beer was on draft and sit and talk as the sun went down. By himself Lewis was good company, but if a woman were present, or more than a few people, he seemed to feel it necessary to entertain them. This could be wearisome, especially when there was drinking.

Like most writers who have achieved a popular success, Sinclair was not satisfied with it. He wanted also to be recognized as a *littérateur.* I tried to avoid the subject because I doubted that *Main Street,* the one book of his that I had read, belonged in this category. I did not tell Red this, but one day, when talking about America, I said that he was unduly hard on our small towns: life was nearly as dull among the rich metropolitans, and with less excuse because they had the means to change it; and I believed that it was even duller in Italian villages, where everyone wore the same clothes, ate the same foods, indulged in the same pleasures. It was different in America, where the interplay of many nationalities and the continual moving about induced an intellectual ferment even in frontier communities such as Empress.[25]

Red did not want to hear about Empress. The talk veered to another subject.

On my way back to the hotel, I accused myself of perverseness. I recalled the many times I had agreed with Red's viewpoint: I, too, deplored the tendency of

Main Street to imitate the virtues and vices of Wall Street. Yet when I might have enlisted a stalwart supporter of *Broom,* I had seen fit to attack him for maintaining that sentiment. No matter what viewpoint was encountered, I seemed always to come up with an opposite.

The next time I saw Lewis, I invited him over for cocktails to meet Blaise Cendrars,[26] who was back in Rome with his *petite amie* and wanted to translate *Main Street* into French. I had hoped to do Sinclair a favor, but the party was a flop. Both Cendrars and Lewis insisted on holding forth in loud voices at the same time. Lily[27] found it difficult to get a word in. Foiled in their attempts to drown each other out, the "tomcats," as Lily called them, drank too much. Then Lewis discovered that Cendrars did not like to speak German. Thenceforth he would speak nothing else, except, from time to time, to sing a verse from "Barnacle Bill the Sailor." Through it all, Blaise's little friend continued to chat with Lily in a ladylike voice about the weather.

Perhaps Lewis felt he had been inconsiderate, for a few days later, when Gracie arrived from London, he invited us to dinner. In evening dress and silver slippers, Gracie exhibited the shining shoulders which Ford Madox Ford,[28] some ten years later, remembered as the most beautiful in the world. She had been staying with H. G. Wells and Rebecca West,[29] and named her baby "Wells." I found her attractive.

Asked to suggest a good restaurant, I recommended the Ulpia, an ancient grotto near Trajan's Column, which served good food and local red wine. From a row of niches high up near the dome portrait busts of the old inhabitants looked down upon the dining parvenus with calm disdain.

At first I didn't know what was wrong with Red. Instead of being the life of the party, he was subdued, apologetic. And Gracie proceeded to pick on him; she was contemptuous of his Midwestern mannerisms. I thought Lewis would explode, but he didn't. We managed to get dinner ordered. Then Gracie, assuming that Lily came from Greenwich Village, harped on the "cruelty of village intellectuals." Lily tightened her lips and looked hard at the silverware.

Everything went wrong, even the food. The breaded turkey cutlet tasted as if it had been cooked for luncheon. Red did not like the wine although I thought it superior to his favored Chianti. Gracie flatly contradicted everything he said.

Thinking a bit of "side" might help, I asked Gracie if she had run into Irene Castle[30] in London. Gracie came back with Edith Wharton and told us about having had tea with her in Paris. Lily couldn't stand it any longer. She opened up with the Prince Yussupov and the Grand Duke Dmitri, Rasputin's murderers,[31] whom we had met in a night club two nights before—they were drinking champagne bottoms-up as if it was vodka. Lily was magnificent. She kept on talking, and the evening ended.

And so, eventually, did the Lewis marriage. That night I wondered how much of Red's contempt for small-town life was due to Gracie. Could it be that Red was blind to the stuffiness of Carol Kennicott because she resembled his own wife? I hoped to find a hint of an answer in *Babbitt,* which, Red had told me, was to be about businessmen.

39 / Lillian T. Mowrer

Lillian T. Mowrer (1889–1990) was a British-born journalist, theater critic, and author of articles and books on foreign affairs. In 1916 she married the journalist Edgar Ansel Mowrer, who was awarded a Pulitzer Prize in 1933. After the Lewises arrived in Rome, the Mowrers sought them out.

Source: Lillian T. Mowrer, *Journalist's Wife* (New York: Readers League of America, 1940), 98–100.

During this period there were many interesting visitors, for though Rome seems a village, everyone comes there sooner or later.

"Who are you?" called a loud voice, as Edgar knocked at the door of a room at the Hotel de Russie in December 1921.

"I am the Middle West, and you are my prophet," shouted Edgar.

"Come in, Middle West," answered Sinclair Lewis. He was working on *Babbitt* that winter, writing steadily from early morning till tea-time, as is his custom. He is an indefatigable worker, and Zenith, the scene of his novel, was a real city to him. He had rolls of maps with every section of it planned and drawn to scale. He knew the history of each one of its inhabitants and could have written three books from the material he had prepared for one.

One night, when he was to have dined with us, the cook went on strike, so we took him to Al Vero Alfredo, a little *trattoria* almost next door, a place which, we had discovered, made excellent *fettuccini al burro,* noodles served with butter and cheese, but of a succulence that proclaimed Alfredo to be an artist. Sinclair Lewis loved the place, went there often and mentioned it in *Babbitt.*[32] And thereby hangs a tale. Dorothy Thompson,[33] his wife, tells it, and though it is her story I am going to repeat it, for it characterizes one of his most lovable qualities. The restaurant became immensely popular with Americans; they flocked to watch Alfredo—who looks exactly like a youthful Kaiser Wilhelm,[34] moustache and all—give the final touches to every portion of *fettuccini,* stirring butter and cheese with delicate precision as though each dish were the first he ever seasoned.

Years later when Sinclair Lewis revisited it, he hardly recognized the old place, so fashionable and full it had become. He sat in a corner, eyeing a little wistfully the elegant crowd, and toying with the menu, on which the passage from *Babbitt* was proudly quoted. You could order other dishes there, but *fettuccini al burro* was what the waiters expected you to take, and Alfredo, with two forks poised like *banderillas* in the air, darted to perform the final ceremony. So Sinclair Lewis ordered some and afterwards had a *saltimbocca,* another famous dish, fine veal scallops in Marsala wine. As he lingered over the meal and the restaurant emptied, the proprietor came to chat with the tall stranger who sat alone. He referred casually to the number of Americans who always visited him, boasted of having been written about by one of the most famous novelists in the world, and tried to impress his visitor.

Over a glass of wine he became more confidential, showed Sinclair Lewis some of his guest books. "There is hardly a celebrity visiting Rome who doesn't dine here," he proclaimed, proudly pointing to his collection of autographs. Then as a mark of extreme favor he said, "Perhaps the *Signore* would also like to put his name among the famous ones?" It was a kindly gesture to a lonely stranger. Sinclair Lewis drew out his fountain pen, signed, wished the man good night and went out. He had written "John Smith."

40 / Alfred Kreymborg

Alfred Kreymborg (1883–1966), editor, poet, novelist, and playwright, founded and ran such major small journals as *The Glebe, Others,* and *Broom.* He was a major proponent of innovation in the arts, promoting transatlantic modernism from both sides of the Atlantic. Throughout his autobiography Kreymborg refers to himself in the third person as "Krimmie."

Source: Alfred Kreymborg, *Troubadour: An American Autobiography* (New York: Boni and Liveright, 1925), 297–98.

The offices in the palace [one of the old palazzi in the Trinità dei Monti] became the headquarters of a number of artists from other countries. The few American writers in Rome quickly looked upon *Broom* as a consular haven. One of the first to stride straight in was the long-legged, red-headed author of *Main Street,* Sinclair Lewis. The novel was then at the zenith of its popularity, and no one was more flabbergasted than the man from Minnesota. He had come to Rome with the air of a bewildered conqueror and, finding Krimmie in his path, walked up to him with the unexpected query: "Hello, what do you mean by attacking *Main Street*?"

It devolved that Lewis had read about an address Krimmie had delivered at the Dutch Treat Club in New York just before his departure for Europe. The topic of his talk before this famous group of journalists had been "The Sunny Side of Main Street." Krimmie assured the novelist the speech had been a defense of Main Street itself and not an attack on the book. Lewis could not be convinced that anything good could come from such a street. The two men, the one from a remote small town, the other from the metropolis of American cities, argued from positions that had become comically juxtaposed. The novelist was a more accomplished dialectician than the poet and delivered himself with so much speed and gusto that the latter resigned the argument—as he usually did anyhow—and parted with the skyrocket on friendly terms. Lewis had descended on Rome to start a new novel, eventually to be known as *Babbitt,* and rented a magnificent suite in that most luxurious of hotels, the De Russie.[35] It was a strange *dénouement* in view of the Minnesotan's confession that when he sat down to *Main Street* he had done so supported by the residue of his earnings from the *Saturday Evening Post* and had expected to spend these savings on the time required for composing a devastating denunciation of America and its most characteristic offspring, the small town. His publishers had agreed that if the book went through one small edition it would be doing remarkably well. Something uncanny had happened to the American reading public. Trained and cajoled into perusing and clinging to happy endings and sweetly optimistic accounts of itself, one might have inferred that only the radicals would have touched the thing. But most of these fire-eaters rejected it, while some two hundred thousand copies had passed into the outstretched hands of Main Street inhabitants.

41 / George Jean Nathan

Nathan remembered an evening at Lüchow's, a popular German restaurant at 110–112 East Fourteenth Street in New York, that Lewis disrupted with a long satirical speech after he returned from Europe in May 1922. Nathan discovered later that the speech appeared nearly verbatim in part III, chapter XIV of *Babbitt.*

Source: George Jean Nathan, *The Intimate Notebooks of George Jean Nathan* (New York: Knopf, 1932), 10–14.

It was more than a year before I ran across our friend again. I had dropped in late one night at a beer conference of four or five literary compeers in a mughouse off Union Square, where we were then in the custom of gathering. We were in the midst of a quiet, if somewhat malty, conversazione when the door flew open and our friend entered. Who had bidden him to come or how he had learned of our meeting-place, no one knew. Jamming down his hat on one of the wall-pegs, he yelled for a Seidel, grabbed a chair and pulled it up to the table, bounced himself up and down on it for three minutes as if it were a mechanical gymnasium horse, and began loudly to sing something in pig-German, accompanying his melodic gifts with gestures that swept two glasses, three Schweitzer cheese sandwiches and one sizable order of Bismarck herring off the table. The song concluded and paying not the slightest heed to our grunts and maledictions, he next yelled for a fresh Seidel (fondly embracing the waiter, whom he addressed familiarly and endearingly as leetle Owgoost), complained bitterly of the slowness of the service, demanded of the assemblage if it did not regard him as the best gottdamn writer in this here gottdamn country, got down at one big gulp three-quarters of the contents of his delivered pipkin, pushed his chair from him, mounted to his feet, cleared his throat several times, and launched into the following declaration:

"Ladies und Chentlemens: It is gewiss a great pleasure, gottinhimmel, für me to have been envited to shpeak to you diss eefining. In rising to address mit you, mit my impromptu shpeech in mine vest pocket, I am reminded uff der shtory uff der zwei Irishers, Pat und Mike, who was riding on der choo-choo car.

Pat und Mike, I forgot me to tell you, vas sailors in der Navy. It seems Pat had der unter berth und by and by he heard such a noise von der ober berth und he called oop asking warum? Und Mike he answered, 'Shure und begorra how can Oi ivver get a night's shlape at all, at all? Oi've been tryin' to get into this damn hammock ivver since eight bells!'

"Now, ladies und chentlemens, shtanding up here before you great folks, I feel me a whole lot like Mike und maybe after I've sprechen along für a while, I may feel me so darn shmall I'll be able to crawl me into a choo-choo hammock mineself mit no trouble at all, at all."

At this point, he paused just long enough to shout for another Seidel and to drop what he evidently desired us to believe were rich German and Irish dialects. Then—"Gentlemen," he proceeded, aiming an imaginary hunk of chewed plug-cut at a remote corner of the wall, "it strikes me that each year at this annual occasion when friend and foe get together and lay down the battle-ax and let the waves of good-fellowship waft them up the flowery slopes of amity, it behooves us, standing together eye to eye and shoulder to shoulder as fellow-citizens of the greatest city in the world, to consider where we are both as regards ourselves and the common weal. It is true that even with our two hundred and fifty-two or practically two hundred and fifty-three thousand population, there are by the last census almost a score of larger cities in the United States. But, gentlemen, if by the next census we do not stand at least tenth, then I'll be the first to request any knocker to remove my shirt and to eat the same, with the compliments of yours truly! It may be true that New York, Chicago, and Philadelphia will continue to keep ahead of us in size. But aside from these three cities, which are so overgrown that no decent white man, nobody who loves his wife and kiddies and God's great out-o'-doors and likes to shake the hand of his neighbor in greeting, would want to live in them—and let me tell you right here and now, I wouldn't trade a corner lot in this fine city of ours for the whole of any one of them—aside from these three, gentlemen, it's evident to anyone with a head for facts that this grand city of ours is the finest example of American life and prosperity to be found anywhere on God's earth! I don't mean to say we're perfect. We've got a lot to do in the way of extending the paving of motor boulevards, for, believe me, it's the fellow with four to ten thousand dollars a year, say, and an automobile and a nice little family in a bungalow on the edge of the town, that makes the wheels of progress go round! That, gentlemen, take it from yours truly, is the type of fellow that's ruling America today; in fact, it's the ideal type to which the entire world must tend if there's to be a decent, well-balanced, Christian, go-ahead future for this little old planet. Once in a while I just naturally sit back and size up this Solid American Citizen with a whale of a lot of satisfaction."

For at least twenty-five minutes more he kept on in this vein, occasionally lapsing for a few seconds into dubious German, Irish or French dialect and interrupting himself only with admonitions to leetle Owgoost. Finally exhausted, he dropped with a bang into his chair, spilling half the contents of his Seidel over himself, and waited for some sign of approval of his great comedic gifts. There bloomed only a grim silence, save for a quiet remark from one end of the table that the lock on the outer door, evidently defective, had better promptly be replaced with a triple-Seigel. Not in the least disconcerted by the captious lull, our visitor pulled himself together, mopped up the hop moisture from his trousers, and—getting to his legs—lifted the remains of his Seidel above his head and clamorously proposed a toast to the novel he was then working on [*Babbitt*].

Concluding by this time that there was nothing to be done about it, the assembled literati decided to make the best of things. One got up and raised his Seidel "To our distinguished guest, Sinclair Lewisohn."[36] Another "To Upton Sinclair, author of *Main Street*." A third observed that it was an honor to have Alfred Henry Lewis present,[37] while a fourth ventured to inquire if the guest could by any chance be May Sinclair.[38]

"Well, anyway, what did you guys think of my speech?" demanded leetle Owgoost's best customer.

The answer was a volume of inelegant mouth-noises.

A few months later the speech was found to be the keynote of one of the sharpest, most bitingly satirical and best novels ever written by an American. Its name, if you haven't already identified it, was *Babbitt.*

42 / Alfred Harcourt

Because he had a background in marketing books, Lewis was a welcome presence in the Harcourt, Brace offices in the early 1920s.

Source: Alfred Harcourt, *Some Experiences* (Riverside, CT: privately printed, 1934), 58–59.

Sinclair Lewis was one of the familiar figures around the office in those days. Everyone liked him, and he was interested in everything we did. His work at Stokes's and Doran's had made him familiar with publishing problems, and he thought of himself as one of us. He and I had a chuckle one day when I abruptly left him—by then the famous author of *Main Street*—standing at my desk while I went to talk to a Chicago buyer who might give us an advance order for 5,000 copies of *Babbitt.* That book was written more around a central character than around a scene. Almost at once, Lewis fixed on the name of Babbitt for his hero, and found himself fascinated by him. There was some question about the title. Lewis suggested: Population, 300,000; Good Business; Sound Business; A Good Practical Man; A He-Man; The Booster; A Solid Citizen; Zenith. He always preferred "Babbitt," for he said: "One remembers *Ethan Frome, Nicholas Nickleby, Martin Chuzzlewit, Madame Bovary, Clayhanger, Hilda Lessways, Jane Eyre,*[39] and many other name-titles really better than one remembers apparently more striking titles, and it so causes the public to remember the name of the central character that he is more likely to be discussed."[40]

We agreed with him that "Babbitt" was the best title, but we pointed out that as the book was probably going to stir up the same sort of controversy as *Main Street,* there might be a good many George Babbitts around the country who would dislike being identified with the book. So Lewis added the middle name of "Follansbee." Before the book was published, we had a letter from a George F. Babbitt, complaining of the ridicule leveled at him,[41] and another after publication from a man whose name was Babbitt, but the "Follansbee" protected Lewis. *Babbitt* was much more popular in England than *Main Street,* and really introduced the American scene and speech to the Britishers. The British edition had an introduction by Hugh Walpole[42] and included a three-page glossary listing and explaining typically American phrases.

6
Hartford and England
1922–25

After the success of *Main Street* and *Babbitt,* Lewis had become one of the most visible literary celebrities in the country as well as something of a pariah. After all, as Emile Gauvreau allowed, whose town would he target next? Mencken urged him to write a satirical novel about a college president. Ironically, he had decided that his next novel instead would feature an unambiguous hero, a medical doctor, and that he would write it in collaboration with a bona fide medical researcher. He was more peripatetic than ever during this period, settling in Hartford, then going on a brief lecture tour through the eastern United States, visiting New York, taking a two-month voyage to the Caribbean and Latin America, moving to London, returning to New York, visiting Chicago and Sauk Centre, traveling with his brother, Claude, through Saskatchewan, then moving again to Paris.

43 / Emile Gauvreau

In the fall of 1922, Lewis hoped to settle indefinitely in Hartford, Connecticut, the former home of Mark Twain, Harriet Beecher Stowe, and Charles Dudley Warner and the home at the time of the poet Wallace Stevens. But no. *Babbitt* was published in September, and Lewis soon regretted the decision. As he wrote Mencken on September 13, "We seem to have settled in this town which has no virtues except that one can live in a lordly manner on not very much money, and that though it's quiet for work, it's only three hours from NY."[1]

Source: Emile Gauvreau, *My Last Million Readers* (New York: Dutton, 1941), 74.

Sinclair Lewis, who had become the literary sensation of the nation, moved to Hartford with his wife and young son. He appeared as a guest of honor at a banquet of the Hartford Press Club and following a number of speeches praising his genius, he got up and compared the people of Hartford with the Babbitts he had written about. He said it was regrettable that Hartford, in which he proposed to live, could be known only as the richest city of its size in the country and for no other reason. I agreed with him and printed his speech under a two-column heading on the first page of the *Courant.* Lewis then was as completely ostracized as a man with the plague—and moved out.

44 / Morris Fishbein

Morris Fishbein (1889–1976), physician and managing editor of the *Journal of the American Medical Association,* was an influential and controversial figure in the history of medicine. He is best remembered for his efforts to regulate medical devices and expose unscrupulous medical practices. After he favorably reviewed *Main Street,* Lewis sought him out. Fishbein in turn introduced Lewis to the microbiologist Paul De Kruif (1890–1971), who had completed his PhD at the University of Michigan in 1916 and was employed by the Rockefeller Center until it was discovered that he had anonymously published an exposé of the center's flawed science and commercialism. As Lewis later remembered, the first evening he spent with De Kruif and Fishbein the "three of us fell to debating. De Kruif and Fishbein hurled ideas about medical education at each other as though they were bricks. We planned to go to dinner together—an early dinner and home at nine—certainly nine, at the latest—lots of work to do. At two the next morning we were still shouting philosophy."[2]

Source: Morris Fishbein, *Morris Fishbein, M.D.: An Autobiography* (Garden City, NY: Doubleday, 1969), 99–103.

In 1921, Harry Hansen asked me one day to review a forthcoming book, *Main Street* by Sinclair Lewis. I received my copy about three weeks before the date of publication. I became so excited about the book that my review took about a half page of the Chicago *Daily News.*[3] I reviewed *Main Street* also in the *Journal of the American Medical Association,*[4] and I wrote a special review of it for the *Yale Review.* [. . .]

I introduced Lewis to Paul De Kruif one afternoon soon thereafter. Dr. Kruif had left the Rockefeller Institute after a battle with Simon Flexner[5] and had been employed by Hearst International Magazines to write a series of articles about alcoholic nostrums. He came to see me, with a letter of introduction from H. L. Mencken.

In the department of the AMA, headed by Dr. Arthur J. Cramp,[6] a considerable collection of such nostrums had been accumulated together with all of the information about their alcoholic content. During Prohibition manufacturers raised their alcoholic content and for many people these served as a substitute for unobtainable liquor. Among them were Lydia Pinkham's Vegetable Compound, Swamproot, Tanlac, 27 Indian Herbs, Peruna, and Liko. I sent De Kruif to see Dr. Cramp, and he was gone for a long while. As I learned later, he sampled most of the specimens.

Toward the end of the afternoon Sinclair Lewis came to see me and I invited him to meet De Kruif. About five in the afternoon they accompanied me to our apartment, which at that time was on South Michigan Avenue. My brother Harold was also there. Anna[7] was about to leave for a trip to Indianapolis. After she left, Lewis and De Kruif continued to take some appetizers until De Kruif suddenly became so ill as to be almost incapacitated. During this episode he got rid of practically all of the afternoon's intake that had not yet left his stomach. While we talked Lewis told us that he was working on a novel about labor and that the protagonist would be Eugene Debs,[8] famous presidential candidate of the Socialist party, who had just been released from a prison in Atlanta and was at the moment in a naturopathic sanitarium in Elmhurst, Illinois. The sanitarium was conducted by a naturopathic leader who had another institute in Chicago on Ashland Avenue near Harrison Street. Lewis suggested that we all go out to see Debs.

The trip to Elmhurst was long. I suggested that we call a taxi for the drive. We started north on Michigan Avenue to Jackson Boulevard and then west. As we neared Ashland Avenue an argument developed between Lewis and De Kruif. With a gentle shove De Kruif pushed Lewis through the side of the cab, cutting him slightly in the seat of his pants.

I suggested that we stop at the pharmacy of a man named Wilson at the corner of Van Buren and Ashland so that I could obtain the necessary material for repairs. We then proceeded west on Jackson Boulevard, and after leaving the Chicago city limits found ourselves in a heavy thunderstorm with rain and high wind. We decided to stop at a tavern for a few moments of refreshment and while there to telephone to Debs to tell him we were coming. While I was at the telephone, I observed some excitement in the tavern. The lightning had short-circuited the electricity so that the tavern was in darkness except for a dozen candles. Lewis had approached some drinkers at the bar and apparently had said to them, "My friend"—pointing at De Kruif—"can lick you."

Fortunately Debs had told me to come right out. I gathered my colleagues as quickly as possible and took them out to the cab. In the meantime, the driver, who had started to turn the cab around in the darkness, had been struck by a car going in the opposite direction and suffered the loss of one fender and a cracked windshield. However, we got in and away we went.

As we traveled from the tavern toward Elmhurst, we came upon five men walking slowly in single file along the road. Lewis said to the cab driver, "Stop a minute. Let us talk to these men." We stopped and he asked them where they were going. They said they were striking streetcar men from Buffalo and that they were working their way to St. Louis, where they could get new jobs. Lewis said to them, "Do you men know where you are?" The answer was "No." Lewis said, "Do you know that you are near Eugene Debs?" "Who's he?" they asked. Lewis said, "Do you mean to tell me you don't know Eugene Debs!" One man said, "I think I wore a button of his at one time."

That might have been a turning point in Lewis's decision not to write a labor novel. He turned to De Kruif and me and said, "Give these men some money," but I observed that he gave them none of his own.

We arrived at Elmhurst about midnight. We telephoned up to Debs and he came down with a fresh supply of liquid inspiration. We sat on the steps of the sanitarium until dawn broke, talking about a number of subjects.

We decided then to visit Carl Sandburg,[9] who lived nearby. When we reached the Sandburg home, we found Mrs. Sandburg already awake, but Carl had not come home that night. She offered to make breakfast for us, but we regretfully declined and drove back to Chicago.

En route I persuaded Lewis not to write a labor novel but instead to do a medical story. I pointed out that with his father and brother he would have little difficulty in getting all the necessary material. He asked me if I would go to Europe with him to help him with the background for such a novel. I had to tell him that I could not possibly leave my work at the AMA. I then suggested to him that De Kruif might well be able to help him.

We traveled along and agreed to stop at the Bismarck Hotel[10] for breakfast. At this point I decided to pay off the cab driver. I asked him how much we owed. He pointed at the fender and the windshield. I assured him solemnly that these no doubt were insured and that he would be fully compensated by the insurance company. I then asked him what he really thought it was worth since we had spent about ten hours with him. In those days one could use a taxicab for about $2.50 an hour. He remarked that he had had such a good time that he would settle for whatever we would give him. I gave him $30. We had breakfast, and I left my colleagues to go to their hotels.

Not long after this incident I received a note from Henry Mencken that Lewis and De Kruif had been with him in New York City for three nights and that they had departed for Europe. What Mencken actually said was: "Just poured De Kruif and Lewis on the boat for Bermuda."[11]

45 / Alfred Harcourt

By all reports, Lewis's collaboration with De Kruif on *Arrowsmith* went swimmingly, at least until Lewis or Harcourt or the two together decided against acknowledging De Kruif's full role in producing it. The novel was subsequently awarded—though Lewis declined—the Pulitzer Prize. In a statement to the press, Lewis explained that the terms of the award prevented him from accepting it, though his resentment over the denial of the award to *Main Street* five years earlier also was a factor.

Source: Alfred Harcourt, *Some Experiences* (Riverside, CT: privately printed, 1934), 79–81.

Even while he was working on *Babbitt,* Lewis decided his next novel would be nonsatiric. For a long time, he had wanted to write a medical story—his father was a country doctor—but he hesitated to start, because he knew little of the field. Soon after *Babbitt* was published Lewis met Paul De Kruif, who had just resigned from the Rockefeller Institute. Paul and he decided to take a trip together among the islands of the Caribbean, and while there to visit tropical research stations. Before they started, Paul wanted to marry Rhea Barbarin, to whom he was engaged. He and Lewis dropped into the office at 1 West 47th Street at lunch time to get some money so that Paul could take an early train for Michigan, where Rhea lived. Neither Don[12] nor I was in, but my secretary gave Paul her personal check for $1,000, which he and Lewis took to the Guaranty Trust Company where Lewis had his personal account. When the check came back from the bank, it had the signatures of both Paul De Kruif and Sinclair Lewis on the back. That check became my personal property.

The Caribbean trip, started partly for a lark, had developed into a serious study of medical work in the tropics. After that, Lewis and Paul went to England and the Continent together, where Lewis got to know some of the great medical scientists of our time. He then settled down in England to write his book. He had many titles for it: The Barbarian; Horizon; White Tile; Civilized; Merry Death; The Savage; Test Tube; The Stumbler; MD; The Shadow of Max Gottlieb (one of the characters); Strange Islands; and variations on the name of the central character, Martin Arrowsmith. As he got deeper into the writing, however, he was growing personally attached to his hero, and referred more and more to the manuscript as "Arrowsmith." By the time it was nearly finished, all of us were calling it "Arrowsmith." Lewis suggested "Dr. Martin Arrowsmith," and when we objected to the length of that, agreed to drop the "Dr.," but for a time held out for "Martin Arrowsmith," for he wrote, "He is so definitely Martin, more than 'Dr. Arrowsmith,'" but we all finally decided to follow the policy that had been so successful with *Babbitt,* and call the book just *Arrowsmith.* It was published early in 1925.

This was the first novel by a popular author to take medical laboratories as a scene, and to make a research scientist the hero. Martin Arrowsmith had a consuming passion for scientific truth, and he and his wife, Leora, were warm, idealistic people in contrast to the sordidness around them. The book was awarded the Pulitzer Prize, but Lewis refused it. He did this as a protest against the terms of the award, which required that the prize-winning novel should represent "the wholesome atmosphere of American life and the highest standard of American manners and manhood." This restriction, he felt, put too much stress on purpose, and not enough on art, in fiction.

46 / Frazier Hunt

Lewis and De Kruif initially seemed to Hunt and others to be ideal collaborators. Fishbein offered to open the files of the American Medical Association to them if they would write a medical novel together. They signed a contract with Harcourt in December 1922 with three-fourths of royalties assigned to Lewis, a ten thousand dollar advance, and one-fourth of royalties to De Kruif. Mencken ridiculed the idea, however. He thought it was "the damndest nonsense I have heard for years" and alleged that De Kruif was "in the pay of the Turks."[13] Still, during a two-month sea voyage from Barbados to Panama to Europe, working five to seven hours a day, Lewis with De Kruif as his technical advisor wrote "25,000 words of plan,"[14] and he assured Mencken on 9 May 1924 that De Kruif's "greatest pleasure was to be called on for some damn hard problem, involving not only sheer scientific knowledge but also an imagination."[15]

Source: Frazier Hunt, *One American and His Attempt at Education* (New York: Simon and Schuster, 1938), 254–56.

With *Babbitt* finished, Red returned to the States. In January of the following year I received a letter from New York announcing that he would soon be arriving "with the greatest guy in the world in tow." I got hold of Bechhofer and we formed ourselves into an unofficial welcoming committee. Trilby Ewer[16] and one or two others made up the cheering section. At the time I had a cocktail shaker that would hold a quart. I charged this to the brim and hauled it by taxi to Waterloo Station. By luck we posted ourselves directly in front of the spot where Red's coach stopped. As he stepped to the platform he walked squarely into a dry Martini. He was followed by a heavily built six-footer, with an immense head and a round face; his dark eyes flashed behind thick-lensed glasses, and his generous mouth broke out in a most friendly smile.

"This is Paul," Red shouted. "You don't have to bother with his last name."

Thus it was that Paul De Kruif was harpooned into my life. Red threw him hard and sure because he was never to get out of it. At the time, this Michigan giant was thirty-two years old and could whip his weight in wildcats, eat his weight in red meat, and drink his weight in beer, wines, and liquors. If Red might be called the Restless Seeker, Paul could rightly be termed the Tireless Searcher. I think it was Dr. Morris Fishbein of Chicago who had introduced them, and at once they had joined up. Paul's immense energy, his scientific approach, and his roaring strength appealed to the rather frail but inexhaustible Red. Red's crusades against sham and his devotion to tolerance made him an immediate blood brother to the highly talented writing bacteriologist. Then, too, they were fellow explorers—lone wolves forever roaming the vast borders of man's familiar world, searching for new patterns of life, new guideposts for man's destiny.

De Kruif had been born in a Dutch settlement in Michigan and ended up as a "radical scientist"—if such a term is acceptable. Taking up writing after a brief but exciting career at the Rockefeller Institute, at the close of the war Paul had run into Red. They consumed a vast amount of wine and high-priced Scotch, and decided that together they would map out a great novel that would be a complete exposé of organized science. Paul would supply the science and much of the fire, and Red would do the actual writing. Paul had just married a talented and attractive young bacteriologist, but Red dragged him away from his honeymoon, and the two roistering dreamers took ship to the West Indies. Plotting, arguing, creating their great novel *Arrowsmith,* they sailed for London. It was there at Waterloo Station that I met them.

47 / Paul De Kruif

For his contributions to *Arrowsmith,* another bestseller, De Kruif (1890–1971) received in addition to royalties a half-grudging acknowledgment. He had asked for the phrase "In collaboration with Paul H. De Kruif" to appear on the title page, but Lewis apparently thought the phrase would hurt sales—or his own reputation. So Lewis thanked De Kruif "for his help" on the book. As Schorer adds, the negotiation "robbed the collaboration of its luster" for De Kruif and "he lost interest in the book they had worked out together, and Lewis lost another friend."[17]

Source: Paul De Kruif, *The Sweeping Wind: A Memoir* (New York: Harcourt, Brace and World, 1962), 65–66, 75–76, 85–86, 102–3, 108.

Red Lewis could be a terrific listener. He asked a hundred canny questions and they were never silly. He roared with laughter at my desecration of sacred scientific cows. Medicine and medical science? It seemed it was like *Main Street,* and many of its greatest names turned out to be oafs like Babbitt. He drew me outside myself, stirring me to talk like a real writing pro, though what I'd written up till now amounted to next to nothing. My narrative seemed to him to be an epic of medical debunkology, skeptical, yes, cynically satirical; and debunking—that was what Red Lewis truly loved, and of muckraking in other fields Red Lewis was the master.

In the gray of the morning Red asked me a question: why shouldn't we collaborate on a book? About doctors? About what was alleged to be medical science? What would be funnier? What would be more sensational? What could be more timely? I did not hesitate. Why shouldn't we, indeed? When do we start?

"There's a detail we've got to settle, first," said Red. "I've been talking to Morris Fishbein, asking him wouldn't he like to work with me on a book about doctors. But the trouble about that is he's their spokesman. He's *official.* He's brilliant and learned. But *you*—" His interrupted sentence meant that I was the final opposite of official, a man who gave not a hoot, who'd try anything once, who was reckless, who could floor himself with a bottle of bitters and come back for more, who knew where scientific bodies were buried, who hauled medical skeletons out of closets and could tell about esoteric medical matters with buffoonery.

I left the little ethical detail of settling matters with Morris Fishbein to Red. I do not know if he ever talked about it to Morris. Indeed, Dr. Fishbein is said to maintain that he suggested me to Lewis as a collaborator. We parted, sentimentally, as conspiratorial brothers. We must get together right after I came back east with my divorce from Reno. We drank one for the road to the man who was for us as if a pope. "To his Holiness, Father Mencken," said Red Lewis, lifting his glass with reverence. I left his apartment in a haze, floating as if on air, safe on the side of the turbulent river. A writer, or a collaborator on a novel. A writer at last, or so it seemed. [. . .]

I was then wrong in my doubts about Red Lewis; he would not let me down either. He had promised to see me in New York and he did, the day of my arrival—by accident. I hadn't the least notion of where to find him. To get information on his whereabouts I went to the offices of Harcourt, Brace and Company, his publishers. Would they bother the great Lewis on the town on the celebration of his *Babbitt*? Had he left word about me? Providentially, as I reached the top of the steps the front door flew open and there was Red. He greeted me with a whoop, hugging me.

"By God, here is the boy who'll try anything once," he cackled. "Let's go to the Gotham for a drink. You've got to meet Gracie."

This was the first of the Mrs. Sinclair Lewises, and together Mr. and Mrs. Lewis were terrific in this heyday of the best-selling novel, *Babbitt.* In my life I'd never seen such a determined, dashing lady. She greeted me with a somewhat British "Hah d'y'do." She scrutinized me. So this was the young man that Hal—her name for Red—said would try anything once. She was stunning. She was like an American duchess. She was a mixture of haughty and democratic cast in a bohemian manner. I had never seen the likes of her. She was *sui generis.* It was plain that Red worshipped her as a stylish, sophisticated luminary of the emerging international world of café society.

I'd hardly recovered from my awe of her spectacularity before Mrs. Lewis—"call her Gracie," said Red—asked my medical advice. "I'm putting on too much weight, with all this *pawtying* around over Hal's new book. What can I do?" I gallantly assured her she was not an ounce too heavy and then she mowed me down. "Nonsense. You can see my rump's too big," and with a pirouette she displayed her rump in profile. "How do I take it off?" she asked, and her question was an imperious demand. "Your rump's just right as it is," I said. It seemed as if my retort was a bit forward. Gracie looked at Hal narrowly. She seemed to know little of Hal's intention to work with me. [. . .]

We boarded the train to Hartford, Connecticut, where Mr. and Mrs. Sinclair

Lewis were in residence. Mark Twain long ago had set the precedent for celebrated authors to mitigate the dullness of staid old Hartford; and I'd heard that this was why Red had gone to live in that conservative city.

Red had no sooner let us in the front door of his elegant rented mansion—there wasn't even time for us to take off our wraps—before he wheeled on me, giving me bad news in a tone of sincere regret. "I'm so sorry to have to tell you this," he said, "but Alf Harcourt says there's liable to be a seventy per cent drop in the advance sales of our novel if your name's on the cover along with mine." "Why's that?" I asked, puzzled and lacking privity to the theory behind such predictions in publishing. Red's red face became redder than ever. "Well, you see," he explained, "Alf dopes it out this way. If the critics and the book buyers see Lewis and De Kruif on the cover, they'll say Lewis is finished. He's hiring an unknown to help write his book for him."

This sounded like what's on the floors of stables to me, but I know little about the book trade. Paranoid thoughts raced through my head—is this celebrated author trying to provoke me? Does he want me to blow my top? Does he bank on my wounded pride making me call off the deal? Doesn't he remember our joint top billing is written in the contract? What will this do to the kudos I'd expected from my name appearing on the cover of the first truly scientific medical novel ever written?

This was the first time the ninth beatitude was to sustain me: "Blessed are they who expect nothing for they shall not be disappointed." It worked.

"Does this change our royalty arrangement—75 to you, 25 to me?" I asked Red coolly.

"Of course not, Paul, that stands firm as ever." Now Red summoned up his real talent as a rationalizer. Didn't Rhea and I see how disastrous it would be for all of us financially to have the book get off to a bad start in the advance sale? The critics and the trade would be sure Sinclair Lewis was slipping, et cetera, et cetera, and et cetera. When Red came to an end of his admirably syllogistic oration, "It's okay with us, Red," I said. "Isn't it, darling?" I asked, turning to Rhea. "Of course," she said with equanimity and a faintly dangerous smile. [. . .]

In our work on *Arrowsmith* Red and I were true collaborators; sheets of yellow foolscap kept pouring out of Red's typewriter and we made the landfall at Plymouth [England] with more than sixty thousand words of a complete scenario of the life and times of Martin Arrowsmith; we had down on paper the scientific philosophy of Max Gottlieb (who was a blended Jacques Loeb and Frederick Novy)[18] but who would have been much more Novy if Gottlieb was meant to portray the soul of a true searcher; we had sketched the life and death of brave Leora who was worth the whole kit and caboodle of all the characters. Despite ruinous rum swizzles, despite the perils of planter's punches, despite dangerous Holland gin and bitters—despite this voyage in a vapor of ethyl alcohol in all its forms—Red had brought off a miracle and knew it and I knew it and there once more was a singing in my heart. To have kept my promise to Alf Harcourt and Don Brace and to Gracie and Rhea—to keep our genius, Red, this side of delirium tremens. He had been kept this side of going off a deep end—though there were times, mornings, when his shaky hand poured some of his Scotch onto the table and some into the glass. Yet he'd got the nub of his novel down on paper; and now the task of dialoging it, for so great a writer as Red, ought to be coasting.

Red and I were never so close, before or after, as when we leaned on the ship's rail, shoulder to shoulder in the dark, and peered toward the lights of Plymouth. "England," said Red with choky emotion, as if coming back at last to a long-lost home. [. . .]

What about the credit for who wrote *Arrowsmith*? Over the years it has become plain that the majority of people who have talked to me about *Arrowsmith* had no idea I'd had anything to do with it at all. Then there is a small school of friends who erroneously believe it was not really Sinclair Lewis but De Kruif who wrote it. Nothing could be farther from the truth. Sinclair Lewis wrote it. Yet there is evidence that, during the early phases of the book's composition, Red thought I'd been of some help to him.

Just after our knock-down-and-dragout, in the glow of our reconciliation, Red showed me what was to be a letter to our publisher. "*And in all this there's a question as to whether he (De Kruif) won't have contributed more than I have.*" Who could have asked more? Who could have been more generous than Red, admitting this, or, rather, writing it? Yet it was not true.

But as he went at the dialoging of our scenario he corrected his opinion; and as he sweated through two complete drafts of the novel, Red's memory dimmed. And so when *Arrowsmith* reached the page-proof stage in 1925, on the page after the title there was a little acknowledgement that left not much more for me but thanks for technical assistance.

"Take it all out, to hell with it," I told Alf and Don and Ellen Harcourt. "Skip it all, I don't need it." Such was my paranoia. It was dear old Don Brace who then wrote to Red and extracted a broader acknowledgement.

48 / George Jean Nathan

Nathan, too, believed Lewis's collaboration with De Kruif was productive, even if Lewis's behavior had become increasingly erratic. Nathan remembered in particular a meeting with Lewis in London in the spring of 1923.

Source: George Jean Nathan, *The Intimate Notebooks of George Jean Nathan* (New York: Knopf, 1932), 14–16.

I began to meet our friend more frequently. He would stop in at my apartment in the late afternoon for a Florestan cocktail, sometimes so moody that he didn't speak five words and at other times so excited and voluble that he would stand up and, apropos of nothing at all, make speeches at me for an hour on end. These speeches, generally couched in dialect of one species or another, were invariably on one of two subjects: himself—in terms of a facetious self-appraisal predicated upon critics who did not sufficiently appreciate him, and myself—consisting for the most part in deplorings of the unhappy facts that I didn't drink enough, that I didn't have the sense to recognize "Hobohemia" for a swell play, that Mencken and I were nice enough fellows all right but that we ought to get married, and that something ought to be done about our recognizing Stuart Sherman[19] anyway. At other times I would call on him in whatever hotel room he was occupying that week. He never used a chair in any such room, but always favored a far end of the bed, the rest of the bed usually being taken up by a varying and various assortment of individuals who gave one the impression that he had run down into the street and herded them in indiscriminately a few minutes before. Who most of them were, I never had the faintest idea. Many of them looked like a comic-strip artist's idea of anarchists; they all talked at once about everything under the sun; and they all drank his liquor very proficiently. He called them all by diminutives of their Christian names, always duly announced in introducing each one of them that each was a great guy, and confidently and enthusiastically predicted to me on each and every occasion that no less than six of those present were virtuosi of one sort or another who one day would take the critics off their feet. None of them—there were at least eighty or ninety he thus eulogized in the period of my visits—has yet been heard of.

He had been living in London for several weeks with Paul De Kruif, his collaborator, working on *Arrowsmith*—originally called *Dr. Martin Arrowsmith*—before I got there on my annual spring trip. The day I arrived I went to a lunch party, where I found myself seated between John Drinkwater[20] and Philip Guedalla,[21] neither of whom I had previously met. I had not sat down before Guedalla said to me, "You are an American and I have a message for you. If your country doesn't recall Sinclair Lewis at once, there will be war between England and the United States!" It did not take a confidant of the oracles to imagine what had been happening. Our friend Red, as his nickname goes, had all too evidently been living up to his sobriquet, if not its communistic implications, at least in its taurian. It developed that the moment he had set foot on the English shore he had begun to make speeches. These speeches—according to Guedalla amounting up to the hour to something like two or three hundred and delivered in dialect on every conceivable occasion at the rate of a dozen or so daily, or rather nightly—had mainly to do, it appeared, with the shameful failure of the English critics, excepting only Hugh Walpole, to take a proper interest in American literature. Our friend, despite the German, French, Italian, Cockney and Way Down East dialects in which he couched his diatribes, may have minced words but certainly not meanings. He not only, while calling loudly for 'arf and 'arf or a spot of whiskey old top, named names, but dates, places and weather conditions. Every now and then, by way of prolonging international amity for a little while longer, it had been necessary for De Kruif, a veritable Sandow[22] of a man, to grab hold of his colleague, pull him down into a chair, and sit on him.

On one occasion, I was informed, our genial friend, being entertained by a lady of title and being congratulated by those present on his literary gifts, had indicated his wholehearted concurrence in the wisdom of the encomiums by running around the room and imprinting a very moist buss on the lips of all the female guests. On another, during a fathering of celebrated English men of letters, he had—after, as is his custom, promptly addressing every one by contractions of their given names—wound his arms around two of the sedate valetudinarians present and insisted that he be allowed to teach them the American jazz dances. On a third, invited to a dinner in his honor by an English woman essayist and novelist, he had brought along with him two strange Germans, a Russian, three Americans whom he had picked up at the American Express Company that afternoon, and two taxicab drivers, both boiled.

49 / Morris Fishbein

As early as 1925, as Fishbein recalled, Lewis seemed liable to become a victim of his own success.

Source: Morris Fishbein, *Morris Fishbein, M.D.: An Autobiography* (Garden City, NY: Doubleday, 1969), 105–6.

Having finished *Arrowsmith,* Lewis was considering doing a novel about a university president in which De Kruif was to participate with him. Lewis came to see me and at that time we visited Karl Harriman of *Redbook.*[23] Harriman offered Lewis a tremendous advance for a novel. Lewis was planning a trip to Canada with his brother Claude. While on the trip he conceived a less-than-good book called *Mantrap* [1926], which Harriman refused but which was then purchased by *Collier's* for double what Harriman had offered. This made an indifferent movie.[24]

Lewis had also more or less promised a book to Ray Long of Hearst. At the time he was extremely busy helping Harcourt in every way to push *Arrowsmith.* He did not want it reviewed as a scientific book but primarily as a novel.

I understand that a lump sum was given to De Kruif for his participation in *Arrowsmith,* in addition to having all his expenditures paid while abroad. However, by January 1925, De Kruif and Lewis discontinued their friendship. Lewis had not heard from him for four months. As far as I know, he and De Kruif never spoke to each other again.

Harrison Smith also quotes a letter from Harcourt to Lewis telling him about reviews of *Arrowsmith.* Harcourt says "Fishbein and Keith Preston of Chicago have come up to scratch."

Many people are convinced that *Arrowsmith* is the acme of all of Lewis's writing, although quite certainly *Main Street* and *Babbitt* had far more social influence and *Dodsworth* was perhaps more entertaining. The movie rights for all of these stories and their subsequent reprints must have given Lewis a great fortune.

Probably Lewis will be remembered also for his extraordinary attachment to hard liquor. He was a hearty drinker. I have seen him tip up a pint of Scotch and drink it down in a continuous swallow. Then he would stand and talk almost like one inspired until suddenly he would collapse and go to sleep. I am sorry to say that the nature of the times conduced to encouraging this habit. He could hardly attend any kind of meeting or party without someone searching at once for a supply adequate to his needs. One night we had a men's party at our house, attended by Lewis, Bart Cormack, Henry Justin Smith, Keith Preston, Ben Hecht, James Weber Linn of the University of Chicago,[25] and myself as host. (On later visits he used to have dinner with us and other friends.) Once he left a dinner to visit our children in their bedrooms. I found him after a long absence from the dining room telling them little stories. On this occasion the conversation was profuse and sometimes highly controversial. Lewis, then somewhat maudlin, said: "I'm just an acolyte at the altar of literature"; a pause ensued; then Bart Cormack said, "Don't you mean an alcoholite?"

7
Paris
1925

Never a part of the Left Bank literary coterie, Lewis was an outsider in Paris while he was working on *Arrowsmith,* just as he had been snubbed in the fraternal culture of Yale twenty years before. The high modernists considered him a clown, and he understandably resented them, as the comments by Harold E. Stearns, Samuel Putnam, George Slocombe, Nina Hamnett, Robert McAlmon, and Sisley Huddleston make clear.

50 / Harold E. Stearns

Harold E. Stearns (1891–1943), critic, essayist, editor of the ironically titled *Civilization in the United States* (1922), and former editor of *The Dial,* was a dilapidated and disaffected expatriate of the 1920s who, for many Europeans, represented the decline of American civilization. Although Lewis and Stearns had been friends, Lewis ridiculed him, albeit not by name, in an article in *American Mercury* in October 1925 as one of the "geniuses and their disciples who frequent the Café du Dome at Montparnasse." Stearns retaliated with an ad hominem attack, and the friendship was never repaired. See also Mark Orwoll, "A Battle in Bohemia: The Sinclair Lewis–Harold Stearns Feud," *Lost Generation Journal* 9 (Fall–Winter 1989): 2–5.

Source: Harold E. Stearns, *The Street I Know* (New York: Lee Furman, 1935), 204–6.

Sinclair Lewis was living down in some old town in Surrey finishing up, if I am not mistaken, *Arrowsmith.* He invited me down for a weekend. [. . .] Sinclair said he had been working hard. Before dinner we took a walk around the countryside—the train from London had got me down just in time for tea—and Sinclair kept on reiterating that he needed a bit of rest. "Fine," I said at length, "why don't you knock off for a few days and take me for a little trip with you over to Paris? I know the ropes; you'll have a good time. And I'll introduce you to some nice people. Probably it will do your work good, too."

Anyway, we did it—Sinclair providing me with a few extra clothes, for I had not brought down anything except overnight things from London. It was the first time he had ever been on the Continent, let alone to Paris, and he was as excited as a young man donning his first pair of long trousers. There was no sleeping either in the train down to the boat, on the boat, or on the French "rapide" that took us swiftly to Paris. Whenever and wherever we could lay hands on a brandy or a whiskey, we did so. We arrived so groggy and sleepy that there was nothing for us to do for the first few hours but to go to a hotel—I think it was the "Oxford et Cambridge," not far from the Rue Royale off the Rue de Rivoli—

and get some rest. After a snooze and a cold shower, Sinclair was ready for any great adventure that Paris had to offer. I rang up Lewis Galantière[1] and asked him to come to my aid and help me pilot Sinclair around—which he graciously did. It was as hectic a five days and nights as I have ever put in; Sinclair was full of vitality. He wanted to go everywhere at once, to see everything, to visit every bar, explore the "Quarter"—and we cut quite a dash in Montparnasse those few nights, too. How much he saw, or remembered, of historical Paris that first visit might be put into a very small page of a very small notebook. But I saw nothing to object to in that. He was on vacation; and, after all, where can one better spend a vacation than in Paris?

Yet most things have to come to an end, and Sinclair's vitality was not inexhaustible, though sometimes it seemed so to me during those five days and nights, when even two hours of sleep was the exception. He had to get back to England and finish *Arrowsmith.* But, he pointed out to me, why should I have to go back? He would lend me any money I needed, and I could write for my things and have them sent on or brought over from London. I said that would be great, for I had no desire to go back to London anyway.

51 / Samuel Putnam

Samuel Putnam (1892–1950), translator and scholar of Romance languages, is most famous for producing the first translation of Miguel de Cervantes's *Don Quixote* into contemporary English, though he was also a noted translator of François Rabelais. His palpable disdain for Lewis is representative of the opinion of the American literary expatriates in Paris.

Source: Samuel Putnam, *Paris Was Our Mistress: Memoirs of a Lost and Found Generation* (New York: Viking, 1947), 101–2.

A bright, sunny day in Montparnasse, bright between the unfailing Parisian showers. The terraces are crowded, with the exception of the Rotonde, which is deserted as usual. Things have been a bit dull of late, but, fortunately, it does not take much to provide entertainment. Conspicuously seated at the Dôme is a gaunt-looking chap with a shock of reddish hair. He is obviously expecting that he will be noticed. I say obviously, for we have seen his kind before and know the symptoms. We are in the habit of calling this type, as distinguished from the ordinary summer tourist or vacationing college boy, the "big shot from home." Now, there is a curious telepathy, a kind of grapevine, that operates between those terraces, and within a very short while everyone on all three of them is aware that the visitor is none other than Sinclair, or "Red," Lewis. At the same time, through a seemingly tacit and simultaneous understanding, all those at the Dôme appear to be agreed that no notice whatsoever is to be taken of Mr. Lewis's presence.

It is the slap direct from the Joyce and Stein[2] brigade to the literature that is being produced in their native land; it is their retort to *Main Street* and *Babbitt* and, as they see it, the stenographic, Pullman-smoker school of writing, which they do not consider writing at all. It would be hard to say how much, if any, of this Mr. Lewis gets; but, in any event, he very soon makes his exit, and as he does so his face is about the color of his hair. There is an unuttered snort as he stamps out, and a giggle, becoming a laugh, runs around the tables and spreads down the street to the Coupole and across the way to the Select. It is sufficient amusement for the next couple of hours, something to tell the latecomers about.

This incident, perhaps, may have something to do with the violent feeling which Mr. Lewis later displayed toward the Parisian variety of American aesthete. At any rate, it brings out a characteristic attitude on the part of the "exiles." Even Montparnasse and Greenwich Village did not mix.

52 / George Slocombe

George Slocombe (1894–1963), a friend of Frazier Hunt and Sisley Huddleston, was the chief foreign correspondent for the British leftist newspaper the *London Daily Herald* during the 1920s and later wrote for the *Evening Standard.* He befriended Lewis in Paris.

Source: George Slocombe, *The Tumult and the Shouting* (New York: Macmillan, 1936), 215–17, 219.

The reaction against the nationalism of the war and the immediate postwar years had brought [British Prime Minister Ramsay] MacDonald and the British Labour Party to office in England, a Radical and Socialist coalition to power in France. In the United States the intellectual reaction had taken the form of satire, and had reached its most remarkable expression in Sinclair Lewis's novel *Babbitt.*

I had met Lewis soon after the publication of his earlier work, *Main Street,* the first of his considerable successes. Many subsequent encounters have not revised my first impression of him. Tall, red-haired, with very pale blue eyes, a long upper lip, an extraordinary energy of speech, a very great diversity of ideas, a certain air of frenzy in his look, speech and gait, a frenzy half comic, half melancholy. He might have been poet or actor, so novel, so wild, so rhetorical were his sudden enthusiasms, his genial affectations, his native power of invention, mimicry and gesture. He had the rare art of living, for the moment, the character he portrayed. He entered into his mood; he borrowed his idiosyncrasies, his outlook, his gestures and his dialect. Once, at a public dinner given in his honor in London, at which his hosts had, formally or informally, wittily or soberly recited his praises, he chose in his speech of reply to assume the part of an American Senator. The imitation was life-like, a work of genius. Ten years later he was one of the guests at a luncheon of American correspondents in London. Another guest, a celebrated raconteur and widely traveled writer, the charming and much-loved Bob Davis of the *New York Sun,*[3] had spoken at inordinate length, as it seemed to Lewis. When it came his turn to speak he capriciously refused.

The chairman unwisely insisted. Lewis rose to his feet and harangued the audience, to its astonishment, in German.

One night he came to dine at my apartment in Montmartre. Among the other guests was Walter Duranty, the celebrated Moscow correspondent of the *New York Times.*[4] Duranty had never before met Lewis, and found him enchanting. He was in one of his happiest moods. Suddenly, *à propos* of the most trifling reference to British Royalty, he extemporized the narrative of an American traveling salesman from the Middle West who met a royal aide-de-camp in a public-house in London and persuaded himself that he had been taken by his chance acquaintance to visit Buckingham Palace and to meet the King. The tale was fantastic, but it had the art of verisimilitude. We saw the imaginative traveler and his boastful friend. We heard their long, friendly, maudlin dialogue. We saw the traveler return to his native city, improving upon the tale until it gained the dimensions of legend. Something of the same technique Lewis subsequently employed in his farcical novel, *The Man Who Knew Coolidge.*

53 / Nina Hamnett

Nina Hamnett (1890–1956), Welsh artist and writer, was intensely unconventional as well as sexually unrestrained. She was known in her lifetime as the "Queen of Bohemia." She also crossed paths with Lewis on the Left Bank in Paris.

Source: Nina Hamnett, *Laughing Torso* (New York: Long and Smith, 1932), 237–38.

I met Sinclair Lewis at the Dôme. He was with Stacy Aumonier,[5] who is now dead. We had an amusing evening, and told stories of all kinds. Sinclair Lewis tells stories very well and has the most remarkable ones about life in the Middle West. He would come from time to time to the quarter and bring Mr. Howe of Ellis Island fame.[6] One evening I came into the Dôme and found Sinclair Lewis and Mr. Howe. I was sitting with them when in came two American "College boys." They were so impressed with meeting the great man that they sat silently and listened to him. This was quite right as he is well worth listening to. I had to go out and dine with someone, and came back about nine-thirty. I found, sitting at the back of the Dôme, the two "College boys," alone and looking very frightened. I said, "What has happened to you?" They unfolded the following extraordinary story. They had a good many drinks, and foolishly opened their mouths. One of them said, "Say, Mr. Lewis, I guess that as far as style goes Flaubert has got you all beat, but as far as characterization goes you've got Flaubert all beat."[7] Whereupon apparently an appalling battle started and Sinclair Lewis left the Dôme having practically won on a "knockout."

54 / Robert McAlmon

Robert McAlmon (1896–1956), publisher, author, and poet, joined William Carlos Williams to begin the little magazine *Contact* in 1920. The next year he married the English writer and heiress Annie Winifred Ellerman (Bryher), and the couple expatriated to Paris. There McAlmon founded Contact Editions in 1922, which published works by Ernest Hemingway and Gertrude Stein. He also became acquainted with Lewis, not entirely to his pleasure.

Source: Robert McAlmon, *Being Geniuses Together, 1920–1930* (1938; rpt. Baltimore: Johns Hopkins University Press, 1997), 32–34.

One night Djuna Barnes[8] and I were at the Gypsy Bar when Sinclair Lewis barged in, some three sheets to the wind. He had once written a story about hobohemia and evidently feared Djuna would believe he had used her as one of the characters in it. Or perhaps he merely had an admiring eye for Djuna or a respect for her undoubted talent, however uneven it may be. But Djuna was well up with drink too and was not going to get chummy. I recall that Lewis looked wistful and went away from the table, with Djuna not having introduced him.

Another night a group of us sat on the terrace of the Swedish restaurant, the Stryx, Mina Loy,[9] Harriet Monroe,[10] and others were at the table. Sinclair Lewis came by and said to me, "Bob, I want you to meet Gracie. People say she is difficult, but maybe you won't find her so." One had heard of Gracie, and there seemed no reason for my meeting her particularly. However, I answered, "Rot! You aren't, are you? Come into the bar and have a drink where your husband can't pick on you."

We went to the bar and ordered gin fizzes, and then suddenly she fired three questions at me: if I thought Lewis the greatest American writer, a fine artist, America's first. Her questions were too fast, and I said so, whereupon she flew out the door, refusing to drink with me. At the time I had read neither *Main Street* nor *Babbitt,* and had read only the short stories of Lewis written in his pulp-magazine days. His hobohemia had struck me as a concession to the newspapers' ideas of Greenwich Village and Bohemia, and I conjectured that he didn't know a bit more about Main Street, or Minneapolis, or Babbitts, than I did. Our backgrounds were not unlike. I did, however, suspect that he carried Main Street about in his own mind, and that he chose to write the dullest aspects of small-town life and types, while I had memories of rather alert and lively people in those Middle Western towns. They were types who later went away, and they were as ironic about the pretentious village intellectuals of the sort Lewis depicted as Lewis could be. No, Gracie, I didn't then and I don't now, after having read *Babbitt,* think Lewis even a good second-rater. He gives to the traveling salesman, the fake-superior pseudo intellectual, and to the Europeans, a picture of America which they like to believe in order to feel their superiority. He fits in with Mencken and his Americana, but before him there has been Stephen Crane, Henry James,[11] and, at the same time, Dos Passos[12] had drawn wholly and in a characterized way several human beings in his *Three Soldiers* [1921]. Edith Wharton's *Ethan Frome* [1911] is worth more than all Lewis has written.

Another season Lewis was silenced at the Dôme. An admirer was assuring him that he drew better characters than Flaubert, but that perhaps Flaubert had the better style. Lewis, a bit intoxicated, insisted that he depicted character better and also had a better style than Flaubert. He asserted it while standing, and someone shouted, "Sit down. You're just a bestseller." Again Lewis was crushed, and old quarterites were amazed that he bothered to boast in the Quarter or the Dôme. Even if he were the world's greatest artist, some nobody would be likely to shout him down there.

It appears that at one time Lewis thought Wells great, and Wells smilingly admits himself not of the first rank. He is still more interesting to read, however, than Lewis. Lewis might better have read a bit of Trollope[13] to learn how to depict character and situation and also to placate the mores of the larger public. As he writes his penetration is not keen, for he misses all but the hick uplifters and the boobs of American small towns and cities, and Europe also produces a great variety of sappy and pretentious morons. So far as art or writing is concerned, I recall not a paragraph written by Lewis which gives one a joy in its velocity or suggestive quality. He is too intent on types to depict character. However, the world has become accustomed to seeing the Nobel Prize given to writers of second or third rank. It is pleasing to the populace, the mediocre.

55 / Sisley Huddleston

Sisley Huddleston (1883–1952), British journalist, writer, and revisionist historian, edited a British forces newspaper during World War I, then lived and worked in Paris into the 1930s as a writer for *The Times* (London) and the *Christian Science Monitor*. More than most of the American expatriates, he tolerated Lewis's idiosyncrasies. During World War II Huddleston collaborated with the Vichy regime in France until 1944, when the Free French imprisoned him.

Source: Sisley Huddleston, *Paris Salons, Cafés, Studios* (Philadelphia: Lippincott, 1928), 113–15.

Now an American: Sinclair Lewis. Red Lewis as we called him in his Paris days. Tall, angular, jerky in his manner, subject to fits of moody silence, and then breaking out into interminable talk, he was a lively person, and he was perpetually the center of lively incidents. Yet I remember on our first meeting, when he had just come from England, he gave me the impression of a country parson who was trying to look as sober as possible. He was dressed in solemn black—severe clothes of the English cut. He actually wore a monocle—or rather he made great play with this eyeglass, twirling it round on its cord. That too was English. Also, he had white spats. Another English touch. He carried a cane. Still more English. At that stage of his career the most American of writers was the most English. [. . .] Certainly Sinclair Lewis shattered my conception of the American.

That night he was, presumably, under the influence of his visit to England, solemn, restrained, and silent. His little head he carried aslant over his elongated body. It was crowned by his flaming red hair. By his side sat George Slocombe, an English newspaperman who had taken a tremendous interest in Russia, his pink face decorated by a magnificent red beard. The red beard was the only Bolshevik feature of Slocombe, but it sufficed to earn him the friendship of Chicherin, Litvinov, Rakowsky, Krassin,[14] and the rest.

Red hair and red beard. We were in an atmosphere of redness. But Slocombe's redness, I remarked, is like that of a radish: it is on the surface. Scratch it and you will find that inside he is very white.

There sat Red Lewis of whose exploits everybody was talking—of scenes in the conventional haunts of polite society, of unorthodox behavior which had amused London—and he was as demure as a clergyman who does not possess the habits of Elmer Gantry. Slocombe, on the contrary, was singing old sea chanties, of which he had a stock. The spirit was willing if the voice was weak, and we were asked over and over again what we should do with the drunken sailor, and were frequently informed that he had a dark and rolling eye.

The next time, however, Red Lewis woke up with a vengeance. We were at dinner. He monopolized the conversation. He spoke of everybody by their Christian name. I was Sisley for him and he spoke much of Gilbert [Chesterton][15] and of Hugh [Walpole]. I had to think hard to put the surnames on his personages.

"We are getting fed up with these English novelists who come on lecture tours and get away with good American dollars. I am not saying that for you, Sisley, but I told Hugh himself that it was too thick. Last year there was Bertrand [Russell][16]—whom, of course, I like, and he is in a different line. I don't think Gilbert quite went down. A lot of silly women laughed when he poked fun at America, but he certainly overdid it. I am not going to say anything against Philip [Wylie],[17] but perhaps we've had enough of him. As for James [Stephens],[18] he is a likeable fellow. No, good luck to them! Only we are rather idiotic to stand for it."

So it went on, but he presently drew me aside, and we had a talk about his methods.

> "People think I write glibly, but I don't. I make a thorough study of my subject. I live among the people I describe. I have spent a year studying medicine and medical men. Went through everything. I don't stick down the first thing that comes into my head. [. . .]
>
> "It's terrible how people expect you to remember them. They come up to you wherever you are and say, 'I'll bet you don't know who I am and where I met you.' Yesterday I replied to one of this tribe 'You win.'
>
> "That reminds me of [James] Whistler,[19] who used to hang around these parts, didn't he? Somebody came up to him and said, 'I would just like to say good day to you, Mr. Whistler.' So Whistler replied: 'Well, now you've said it. Good day.'
>
> "No, I don't care what the critics say. The more they say, the better the book sells. Here's one of them who says my last book is a compound of bunk, ignorance, and lies. Don't they wish they could put over bunk, ignorance, and lies!"

He was voluble but always sensible. He flung himself on a couch and his long loose limbs grew longer and looser. He jumped to his feet, strode across the room, and he was taller and lankier than ever. His face glowed and his hair caught fire.

Lewis told me of his beginnings. He had written, as I remember, a good deal for newspapers, and had published a novel or two which made little stir. Then one year he found he had made ten thousand dollars, and had spent only five. Thus he was a year in hand. What should he do? Most people would have reckoned that they were going ahead, and could by perseverance make fifteen thousand dollars, and perhaps work up to twenty. Not so Sinclair Lewis. He figured out that he could afford to take a year off, and write a really good novel. He did. He wrote *Main Street.* It caught the current. It stated what many Americans had obscurely felt. *Main Street* was a huge success. Since then each of his books has been an event. But it took pluck to do what Lewis did.

To coin familiar expressions is a test of success. Everybody knows what is meant by Main Street. Everybody knows what is meant by Babbitt. They have definite connotations. They have come to stay.

I saw much of him especially during the period of his matrimonial perturbations and liked him immensely. Most people like him. But occasionally he fell foul of the so-called American intellectuals of Montparnasse. His quarrel with Harold Stearns made a great commotion in the Quarter. Lewis went back to America one year, disgruntled by the celebrities of the Quarter. For some reason or other he picked on Harold Stearns, who had made a promising beginning with his *America and the Young Intellectual* and his *Civilization in the United States,* but who afterwards became interested in racing, and stayed in Paris without producing. In Mencken's *American Mercury* Lewis attacked the "geniuses and their disciples who frequent the Café du Dôme at Montparnasse."[20] The main attack was on a person whom Mr. Lewis referred to as the "very father and seer of the Dôme," [. . .] "an authority on living without laboring."

8
Katonah
1925–26

Upon their return from Europe in the spring of 1925, the Lewises leased Loudon Farm near Katonah, New York, in Westchester County, as their marriage continued to deteriorate. Lewis returned to potboiling during these months, knocking out a few magazine pieces and his novel *Mantrap,* based in part on the diary his brother, Claude, kept during their Canadian trip. But life in Katonah soon became intolerable for Lewis, who abandoned both his home and his wife.

56 / Grace Hegger Lewis

In her autobiography, Grace pulled no punches in detailing her husband's peccadilloes and blaming him for the failure of their marriage.

Source: Grace Hegger Lewis, *With Love from Gracie* (New York: Harcourt, Brace, 1955), 324–25.

I had thought that Katonah was too far from New York for casual acquaintances to drop in, but drop in they did without telephoning and they expected to be fed, given many drinks, and to sit about for hours talking. And Hal welcomed them, for *Mantrap* was not the absorbing, fact-finding job that the previous novels had been, and he was not enjoying the Edith Wharton atmosphere of this community of old New Yorkers related by blood or business interests who were fast becoming relics of a changing order. "Relics," that's what Hal thought they were and he was not interested in them even as copy.

Hal had chosen the empty chauffeur's cottage to work in, and at midday I would sometimes bring a picnic basket and thermos bottles and Wells, and we would eat lunch on a hilltop out of sight of the house. In the late afternoon if there were no unexpected guests we would play tennis for an hour, tennis which had never progressed farther than ball-batting, or we would drive in the car until we came to one of those beckoning dirt roads which the motorist flashes by regretfully, and leaving the car we would walk for several miles in the deep country.

Cocktails before dinner had become a habit and Hal liked the mellow haze of three or four which enveloped him after his walk or tennis sweat, his cold shower, and a clean shirt. There was no doubt he was drinking more, much more, than he did in Europe. Everyone we knew did. When we had guests there were more drinks after dinner, and then Hal would be doubly amusing, then argumentative, then a nasty remark, an abrupt exit, and my embarrassed good-byes to discomfited and often angry guests. Hal was asleep.

Equally bad were the evenings when we were invited out to dinner, and I would go to his room and find him sitting on the edge of the bed in his underdrawers, his face vacant with drink, and muttering: "Grace, I will *not* go to this goddamned stupid party. They only want me to make themselves important. You go." And go I would, but how I dreaded the lies I would have to tell.

Hopefully I suggested that we have only two cocktails at dinner and nothing else during the day when we were alone and that I keep the "cellar" in my bedroom instead of his. Skeptically he agreed but on the third day he was so wildly voluble at lunch that afterward I counted the bottles in my bedroom closet and found two missing. Obviously this was the wrong way to go about it. I felt degraded by the whole maneuver.

Degraded, too, by his not very skillful surreptitious kissing of the casual wives of his casual visitors. Also by the unknown female voice which had been calling him frequently only to ring off when I came to the telephone. What did he get out of this philandering? I have been told that what he aroused in women was the mothering instinct, which must have been a disappointment to him and yet at bottom that was what he was seeking. On many a lone woman's door did he bang at midnight, demanding noisily to come in, demanding a drink, then talking until dawn about his dissatisfaction with life though with no definite complaint, and suddenly falling asleep. If he had been very tight he would remember nothing when he awoke, and if the woman were very pretty and she told him that she had listened to him talk, and nothing more, he would be furious at the lost opportunity. He seemed unable to recognize that the sexual act was not important to him, that making love was rather a nuisance, and though he was essentially masculine and abnormalities of any kind were shocking to him, he could not supply the confident and robust elements which make for success in a love affair. As he did not believe in his own capacity to evoke love, it was to be that this realization of his inadequacy drove him to the solace of drink.

In his novels there are no truly passionate love scenes because he did not know how to create the truly passionate men or women to inspire them. He had the smirking attitude toward sex characteristic of his times, which reached its height, or rather depth, in *Elmer Gantry.* In the first draft of this book, considerably subdued later, the bigness of the theme, the vast research, the devastating satire, were blanketed by a lechery which caused one to read with nasty curiosity rather than with literary appreciation.

57 / Matthew Josephson

Matthew Josephson (1899–1978), leftist journalist, biographer, literary critic, and economic historian, was briefly associate editor for *Broom* and contributed regularly to the *New Republic,* the *Nation,* the *New Yorker,* and the *Saturday Evening Post.* He was not enthralled with Lewis's fiction, which he considered bourgeois.

Source: Matthew Josephson, *Life among the Surrealists* (New York: Holt, Rinehart and Winston, 1962), 303–4.

The only literary figure in Katonah, so far as I knew, proved to be the long-legged, red-haired Sinclair Lewis, who rented one of the large estates in the neighborhood during the summer of 1925. With Malcolm Cowley,[1] who was visiting me at the time, I went over to call on Lewis one evening, and found him with his wife and two guests. The house was a big, overstuffed Victorian mansion. They were sitting at dinner on stiff-backed Italian Renaissance chairs, Lewis looking almost feverish with discomfort, but very cordial and evidently happy to see Malcolm and me.

In truth, "Red" Lewis was drunk, as oftentimes happened. His handsome, Junoesque wife, Grace Hegger Lewis, seemed constrained and unhappy; a few weeks later Lewis was to leave the Katonah house and begin proceedings for a divorce. After a while the master rose unsteadily to his feet, brusquely made his excuses to the others, and asked Malcolm and me to accompany him to his room upstairs. There, still in his dinner jacket and with his shoes on, he flung himself upon his sumptuous bed and ordered a servant to bring us some whiskey.

"I don't like those people, don't want them; they're stuffed shirts," he exclaimed. "I much prefer to spend a little time with you boys." He then settled back and talked with us in a very friendly and sensible manner.

Lewis had been a nonconformist in earlier life, and even a Socialist for a while. Now that he was America's "millionaire novelist," his wife would have liked him to behave with the decorum of other members of the high-income class into which they had risen, or somewhat like the "old New York families" of Westchester County. But sudden fortune had made "Red" less tractable and more opinionated than before. What was the use of selling a million copies of your books if you could not tell people you disliked to go to hell? I used to see Lewis occasionally thereafter, roaring about the offices of Harcourt, Brace & Company like a very egotistical literary lion, exploding with anger because his last book had not received sufficient publicity or even having a row with his old friend Alfred Harcourt. "Send me a check for fifty thousand this afternoon at the Hotel Plaza," he would demand suddenly, and Harcourt would almost jump out of his skin.

On the other hand, although he was very impetuous and contrasuggestive by nature, Lewis had a lively intelligence and showed a warm interest in other writers. After blowing off steam at the editors of Harcourt, Brace, he would take me aside and in a gentle and avuncular manner talk with me about something I had written, expressing disapproval, or sometimes approval, in a very forthright and heartening way.

At Katonah both Malcolm and I had expressed admiration for *Babbitt* as a trenchant satire of America's business class. Lewis counseled us against becoming "too literary" and "too intellectual" in our writing. He thought that the Younger Generation who went to Paris were given to affectation, and felt aggrieved at some of them who criticized his novels as poor imitations of Zola's naturalistic works.[2]

58 / James Branch Cabell

Lewis by his own admission fell into the trap of potboiling in such negligible novels as *Mantrap* and *The Man Who Knew Coolidge,* a mistake the rival novelist Cabell exploited.

Source: James Branch Cabell, *As I Remember It* (New York: McBride, 1955), 167–68.

Lewis rather too often for his own good as a writer resorted consciously to what he termed "whoring"—by which he referred to no bedroom activities, not hereabouts at least, but meant the rapid and facile writing of mediocre tales which his being famous enabled him to sell at a handsome rate to this or the other periodical. It was his notion, as he assured me more than once, that a practiced author could do this whensoever he elected, and then, in his novels, return at will to writing in his best vein.

I did not argue about the matter. But nowadays I am quite firmly persuaded that the career of Sinclair Lewis disproved this notion. And, at any rate, I thought that *Mantrap* and *The Man Who Knew Coolidge* were almost unadulterated "whoring" in book form, and that in *Elmer Gantry,* an exaggeration which, by and large, I enjoyed, there was a great deal meritorious of the same Scriptural doctrine.

59 / George Jean Nathan

Nathan recalled a "boudoir harangue" that provided the basis of Elmer Gantry's Sunday School declamation to the children of Banjo Crossing Methodist Church, which follows the text of *Galatians* 5:22–23, in section 4, chapter XX of the novel.

Source: George Jean Nathan, *The Intimate Notebooks of George Jean Nathan* (New York: Knopf, 1932), 16–19.

With the completion of *Arrowsmith,* which further established him as one of the most important American novelists of his time, our friend returned to his native land and, finding himself in need of some ready money, applied himself to the writing of a deliberately commercial novel, *Mantrap,* that would need only a camera-man standing behind it and a peroxide blonde in front of it to make a popular moving picture. Always forthright and completely honest with himself whatever the effect of the forthrightness and honesty may be on the delicate sensibilities of such as leetle Owgoost, Englishmen, Pulitzer prize committees and suddenly kissed dowagers, he made no bones of what he was doing, but frankly announced to anyone who would listen that he was, to use his own locution, turning out a swell piece of cheese to grab off some easy gravy.

His literary cheese duly manufactured, he disappeared from New York for a number of months, traveling the West to gather material for his next piece of work. The night that he got back, he was put to bed with a high temperature, but the next morning—the temperature having dropped to 102—he telephoned Mencken and me to come to dinner with him that night, assuring us that he was in great shape and never felt better in his life. We arrived at about quarter to seven and found that he was still in bed, now with a temperature of 103. No sooner had we entered his bedroom and hardly had we begun to denounce him for a mule for having asked us to dine with him when he was obviously a pretty sick man, than he jumped out of bed, the tails of his short white old-fashioned nightgown flapping about him, and—striking an attitude—began:

Brothers and sisters, don't you listen for one second to these wishy-washy fellows that carry water on both shoulders, that love to straddle the fence, that are scared of the sternness of the good old-time Methodist doctrine and tell you that details don't mean anything, that dogmas and discipline don't mean anything. They do! Let me tell you, brothers and sisters, that justification means something! Baptism means something! It means something that the wicked and worldly—and here I point to some of our fellow-citizens—stand for this horrible stinking tobacco and this insane alcohol, which turns men into murderers, but we Methodists must keep ourselves pure and clean and undefiled. But tonight, on this first day of getting acquainted with you, brothers and sisters, I don't want to go into these details; I want to get right down to the fundamental thing that details merely carry out—and what is that fundamental thing? What is it? I'll tell you, brothers and sisters. It is the Lord Jehovah and His love for each and every one of us, big or small, rich or poor, drunk or sober. Love! Love! Love! How beauteous the very word! Not carnal love, not love of the flesh, but the divine presence. Love is the rainbow that stands out in all its glorious many-colored hues illuminating again the dark clouds of life. It is the bright morning and the evening star that, in glad refulgence, there on the awed horizon, call our hearts—and that goes for yours, Georgie, and yours, Hank,—to an uplifted rejoicing in God's marvelous firmament! Round about the cradle of the babe, sleeping so quietly while o'er him stands in almost agonized adoration his loving mother, shines the miracle of Love, and at the last sad end, comforting the fond hearts that bear its immortal permanence, round even the quiet tomb, shines Love. What is great art—and I am not speaking of ordinary pictures but of those celebrated Old Masters with their great moral lessons—what is the mother of art, the inspiration of the poet, the patriot, the philosopher and the great man of affairs, be he business man or statesman—yes, brothers and sisters and Georgie and Hank, what inspires their every effort? Love! Do you not sometimes hear, stealing o'er the plains at dawn, coming as it were from some far distant secret place, a sound of melody? (Shut up, you two bums, and listen!) When our dear sister here plays the offertory, do you not seem sometimes to catch the distant rustle of the wings of cherubim? And what is music, lovely music, what is sweet melody? 'Tis the voice of Love! 'Tis the magician that makes royal kings and queens out of plain folks like us! 'Tis the perfume of the wondrous rose, 'tis the strength of the athlete, strong and mighty to endure 'mid the heat and dust of the valorous conquest. Ah, Love, Love! Without it, we are less than beasts; with it, earth is

> heaven and we are as the gods! Yes, brothers and sisters and you two lice, that is what Love—created by the Almighty and conveyed through all the generations by His church, particularly, it seems to me, by the great, broad, wholesome, democratic, liberal brotherhood of the Methodist Church—that is what Love means to us!

His temperature having now evidently shot up again, he let out a loud whoop, informed us that we were both low infidels bent for Hell, fell back into bed and, exhausted, was sound asleep a few moments later.

At dinner in a nearby restaurant shortly afterward, Mencken contented himself with a single word of comment. It was: "Bughouse!" At dinner in the same restaurant not very much later as time goes, we were congratulatingly buying our friend drinks on the elaboration of the boudoir harangue—where it figured almost word for word—into his novel, *Elmer Gantry.*

One can always tell a new novel coming on when the oratorical mood in any one, single thematic direction assails our friend. *The Man Who Knew Coolidge* was nothing more than a series of such orations gathered together, with not a word changed. They had been delivered in a variety of places and at a variety of times, including the corner of Fifth Avenue and Fifty-sixth Street at high noon, a beer-house in Hoboken at eleven o'clock at night, another beer-house in Union Hill, New Jersey, at two in the morning, the bathroom of my apartment, the men's lavatory at the Rennert Hotel in Baltimore, a publisher's tea at the Sherry-Netherland, several taxicabs, two New York theatre lobbies on opening nights, and the steps of St. Ignatius' Church. *Dodsworth,* a year later, was heralded both before and directly after our friend's European material-seeking trip by innumerable vaudeville performances in the British dialect, aided and abetted by a monocle that he had purchased for the further embellishment of his histrionic talents.

9
Kansas City to Berlin
1926–27

In middle age, rebelling against his adolescent faith, Lewis jumped at the chance to beard the lion in its den in his novel *Elmer Gantry.* He spent months researching the topic, living in Kansas City for much of the time, where he attended Samuel Harkness's church, and the effort paid off: the first printing of *Elmer Gantry* consisted of 140,000 copies, "the largest first printing of any book in history."[1] The novel was also the most fractious work of Lewis's career—so controversial, in fact, that it was not made into a movie until 1960, over thirty years after its publication and nearly ten years after his death. In February 1927, to escape the anticipated firestorm of controversy among evangelical Christians, he embarked for London.

60 / Samuel Harkness

Samuel Harkness was a liberal Presbyterian minister in Kansas City and a consultant of sorts on *Elmer Gantry.*

Source: Samuel Harkness, "Sinclair Lewis's Sunday School Class," *Christian Century,* August 5, 1926, 938–39.

He came to Kansas City to do the preliminary fashioning of a missile intended for a bulging hornets' nest. He was perfectly frank about it. He gathered a group of preachers of all shades of theological opinion to meet in a series of weekly luncheon-conferences. He demanded that the ministers call him "Red"; he had their first names at his tongue's tip, and graduates of the greatest schools of religion in the old and new worlds, who preach to some of the largest congregations in the city, liked the experience so well that his suite became a rendezvous for the strangest "Sunday school class" in the history of the Christian church. These ministers lent him books with such titles as "Aids to Sermon Building," "How to Promote a Successful Revival," and "Why I am a Presbyterian," and gave him samples of the crude and incredibly silly song books used by evangelists. He attended tent revivals, read church papers and church year-books, listened to radiocast denunciations of himself, and then went on a two weeks' trip, motoring through Iowa and Minnesota with a former national chaplain of the American Legion that he might call on small-town preachers as a book agent and get their unguarded views. If he should use the data he has gathered thus far, he would be more verbose then Theodore Dreiser.[2] The writer was a train companion recently of a man who said, "I am writing a novel with a Presbyterian preacher as the hero. Will you give me a little information about the Presbyterian Church?" A "little" satisfied him, and he made no notes. Lewis would learn the shorter catechism and dissect the "form of government" into shreds. He gets everything knowable together and feels it to the bone. He writes from the "inside."

He shakes words as a terrier worries a rat. In the meetings of the "Sunday school class," he probed through the vague and platitudinous words that preachers so often use: "What is religion?" and the answer is "The art of living!" and the rest of the "pupils" smile approvingly—but not "Red." "What do you mean by 'art' and 'life'?" and soon he has one of the "class" floundering in a descriptive morass. [. . .]

The last session of the "class" was gay and sad. The Sage of Emporia[3] and the Buddha of Kansas City newspapers[4] were guests of honor. Every man present had been stabbed and shocked into new realizations, and the author of *Arrowsmith* sheathed his stiletto with these words: "Boys, I'm going up to Minnesota and write a novel about you. I've going to give you hell, but I love every one of you." And as the "class" disbanded, the man who had called himself an atheist flung his arm about each one in turn and said, "Good-bye, old man; God bless you!"

61 / George Seldes

George Seldes (1890–1995), journalist and media critic, served as editor and drama critic for the important small journal *The Dial* and was the New York correspondent for T. S. Eliot's influential journal, *The Criterion.* He nominated Lewis for *Time*'s Man of the Year in 1935. In the 1950s he was persecuted by Joseph McCarthy as a suspected Communist and was blacklisted.

Source: George Seldes, *Witness to a Century* (New York: Ballantine, 1987), 292–93.

Of his first wife he made a sort of fictional character; he may have been trying out the stories for a future novel about her. I always had a feeling Lewis never wasted words. He said Gracie came from a simple background, and later when he began making money and they were getting ahead, she had delusions of grandeur. He illustrated his point with this story: One of her high school classmates was in the hospital for an appendectomy. "Gracie called on her and asked the usual question. 'It was nothing,' the classmate replied. 'I'll be out in no time.' Gracie then said, 'I know. It's your healthy American peasant blood.'"

On another occasion Gracie was very critical of everything American. One of her listeners asked, "But you were born in America, weren't you?" "Oh, yes," Gracie replied, "but I was *conceived* in Vienna."

62 / Charles Breasted

As Gary Alan Fine and Amy Campion have explained,[5] while the citizens of Sauk Centre were initially offended by Lewis's representations of their town in his fiction, they soon capitalized on its notoriety: "What Lewis said was secondary to the fact that he made Sauk Centre the first truly famous small town in American literary history." Still, Charles Breasted remembered, to the end of his life Lewis's father apparently did not approve of his son's satire.

Source: Charles Breasted, "The 'Sauk-Centricities' of Sinclair Lewis," *Saturday Review of Literature,* August 14, 1954, 33–35.

In the summer of 1926, Hal and I had unexpectedly met again, as fellow guests at a house party on one of the ten thousand islands in Rainy Lake, Minnesota. He was at work on *Elmer Gantry.* His father, old Doc Kennicott of *Main Street,* was at the moment gravely ill, and one night Hal's almost feminine intuition suddenly warned him that the coming morning might bring news from Sauk Centre of the old doctor's death. He was unable to sleep, and so came and roused me and asked me to sit with him in the dressing room of our guest house and talk—which for me meant listening. We sat on a bench, he with his knees drawn up and his arms resting on them as he smoked incessantly.

"My father has never forgiven me for *Main Street,*" he said. "When I saw him a few weeks ago, we shook hands—but he can't comprehend the book, much less grasp that it's the greatest tribute I know how to pay him. He felt that I should have served an honored profession by becoming a doctor myself, instead of derogating and besmirching it in a book libeling my own birthplace. *Main Street* condemned me in his eyes as a traitor to my heritage—whereas the truth is, I shall never shed the little, indelible 'Sauk-centricities' that enabled me to write it—that make the unbridgeable difference between me and my son Wells."

Suddenly he rose, went to a mirror, and, turning his head from side to side, studied his face for some time. Then he said quietly: "You know, as the fire dies down inside of me and I grow old, I shall resemble somewhat a dignified old gentleman of the old school, but actually I shan't be. It takes three generations, and I'm only the second. My son Wells is the third. I think he *is* a gentleman, and perhaps he may create literature—as I have not. I've already done my best work, and of that *Babbitt* will probably be rated my best book—though my own favorite will always be *Arrowsmith* and, incidentally, my favorite character will always be old Max Gottlieb. Oh, in the future a book of mine will probably always be good for a sale of fifty thousand—but neither the critics nor the author will be fooled. The best of what I'll ever have produced will bear the same relation to true literary achievement that a jacket blurb does to the text of a really great book."

The next morning a speedboat brought a telegram: even as we had sat talking in the night Old Doc Kennicott had died. The same boat took us back to the mainland, where we parted, and Hal turned southward to bury the stranger who had sired him in Sauk Centre.

A fortnight later I saw him in Chicago on his way to Washington, D.C., where for reasons I cannot now recall he had asked Gracie, his first wife, to rent a house in which he would finish *Gantry.* His father's death, and the entire Sauk Centre community's heart beating as one at the funeral services, had moved Hal profoundly, and left him for the moment again in a subdued mood of clear self-perspective and genuine humility. Just as on the island on that last night, he spoke of his best work as already accomplished and he seemed unimpressed by the prospect of whatever he might produce during his remaining years. Although he began to regain some of his natural buoyancy, it was in this mood of unaccustomed gravity that he had left Chicago for Washington.

Business shortly took me to New York and Washington, where I spent a day with Hal and Gracie. They were trying valiantly, actually quite desperately, to carry on together, but the futility of their effort was continually betrayed by the underlying tension of their badinage. When we were alone together for a moment Hal told me I might soon be seeing him in New York; and when Gracie drove me to the station she said, without breaking her tone of feigned gaiety, that the future of her relation to Hal appeared at the moment even more problematical than ever before. It was their last attempt, and the cumulative bitterness their incompatibility had engendered was to find vent, respectively, in his *Elmer Gantry* and in her book *Half a Loaf.*

Not long afterwards, in New York, I received a telephone call from him, urging me to come to his room at the Hotel Shelton. I found him in a bleak, gray tower room, in a state of abysmal depression and near-collapse. After a final flare-up, he had rushed away from Washington with virtually nothing save his current manuscript. The only other personal effects I noted were three brandy bottles, two of them empty.

I asked him if he had any definite plans. Only to complete *Gantry,* he answered, a matter of three or four months. He expected to leave for Europe before its publication because he was certain that once it had appeared he would be thrown out if he didn't leave voluntarily! At this point I asked him if he would care to share my bachelor apartment in lower Fifth Avenue while he finished the book. For some reason this sent him rather to pieces, and it was several minutes before he tried to speak. Finally he said that this seemed a very kind proposal, which he would probably accept, but he would like a few days in which to think it over.

Considering his general condition at the moment, I wondered whether he would even remember this proposed arrangement. To my surprise, he not only did, but decided that in order to be really fit for this last lap of his latest job he would attend some famous health camp or other, up the Hudson [Billy Brown's Harbor Sanitarium in Garrison-on-Hudson, New York]. Then, just as he was departing for the latter, he startled me still more by asking me to agree that we should have no alcohol whatsoever in the apartment and should, furthermore, entertain as few people as possible!

He returned ten days later, looking healthier and more relaxed than I had ever seen him. During that time he had, of course, been forbidden tobacco and alcohol, been made to exercise all day long, and to be in bed and asleep by nine o'clock each night. He felt so exuberantly well that even before unpacking his bag he telephoned his bootlegger and gave him a sizable order. And within a few days the familiar procession of people began milling through our living room at any hour between two P.M. and three A.M., almost never between seven-thirty A.M. and midday, for during those hours, no matter when he had gotten to bed, the writer Sinclair Lewis kept extraordinarily faithful tryst with his work.

He now began to indulge his love of books, and seldom returned from a walk or a trip uptown without an armful of them, or without there appearing messengers in his wake laden with parcels of two or three books at a time. He never took a book from such parcels without also removing the dust jacket. I had always been in the habit of preserving book jackets, partly for the brightness they gave to a book shelf, but largely because of the interesting and illuminating data they usually contained about the author; and I was the more distressed when he removed all the jackets from my own little library, insisting that they made a book look unread. Books were to him as much a necessity as food—and, alas, drink—and his continual purchase of them did not, therefore, make him conscious of his comparatively recent economic emancipation. But when he came home one afternoon with a parcel filled with new shirts, socks, and numerous neckties there was a curious, almost boyish pleasure in his face as he contemplated the neckties, and said to me, "You know, I can't get over the strange feeling it gives me to be able to *afford* to go in and *buy* some good-looking neckties I've seen in a shop window, and to do it without a sense of worry about the money, and without the feeling that I was depriving Gracie of something I ought to have bought for her instead!"

During the first month or two Lewis seemed to take great pleasure in our living arrangements. We took frequent walks together and saw many of our old mutual friends of evenings. Later at night he liked occasionally to revisit the Greenwich Village cafes and speakeasies he used to frequent in his pre-success days, even though he knew he would be plagued with requests for "loans" by the same down-and-out habitués who were there in his day, like Maxwell Bodenheim,[6] whose nauseatingly unctuous flattery never failed to arouse Lewis's pity to the tune of a generous sum.

At this time I was an "associate" in the office of the already legendary dean of public-relations counselors, an order destined to pullulate indefinitely in more or less his own image. There were definite reasons why I wanted to become familiar with public-relations techniques, but they were unapparent to Hal, who said I was dissipating the best years of my life and that I should concentrate on creative writing.

"It's utterly true that to learn to write," he would say, "one has to write and write and write and *write*! And if you can possibly avoid it, don't waste your energies on short stories and stuff for ephemeral publication. Write *books*. Be known as the author of 'Such-and-Such.' No matter what else you're doing, write at least eight hundred words a day, if possible a thousand—work in a bare room with nothing in it but a table, a chair, and a typewriter, and enough light—but *no view*! I wrote *Our Mr. Wrenn* while commuting on Long Island Railroad trains to my blurb-writing job at Doubleday, Doran's. One competent full-length book will do more to establish the prestige of a potential writer than a flood of short pieces."

In this connection, Lewis put up to me time and again—partly with the idea that in my case it might serve as excellent training and experience—his plan for gathering the research material for his long projected novel about labor. I suppose there was no younger man in whom he had seen the slightest literary promise who had escaped this proposal to join him in a Model A Ford tour of most of the leading industrial centers of the United States, and while he himself would engage typical working men in presumably revealing conversations, his younger collaborator was to take careful notes of the gist of each such encounter. I was still too unfamiliar with Lewis's major vagaries, and with the extent to which he had made the same offer to others, not to have been at the outset rather flattered by this repeated proposal; but instinct led me not to commit myself. I believe that in one or two instances he actually initiated such a tour; but, as might have been expected, they foundered almost at the outset. So far as I am aware, he never produced even a portion of a novel primarily concerned with labor.

Even had I then been free to follow Lewis's advice to devote myself exclusively to creative writing, there were at the moment certain obstacles which he was inclined to ignore. For after a full day in lower Broadway, capped with a final pummeling in the subway, there was no telling what I might find in our living room. More likely than not, Lewis would be surrounded by a welter of hopeful artistic strays from neighboring Greenwich Village, some of whom were certain to touch him for loans; girls who ran basement book shops; undergraduates from here and there, ostensibly doing research for English term papers, trying to look at ease in an atmosphere which left them puzzled and incredulous; a foreign correspondent or two, and at least one professional adventurer; and always a number of what Alf Harcourt described as "recurrent bevies of human alley cats and queers," odds and ends of humanity Lewis had met somewhere in his travels and had urged to be sure to look him up in New York, and who now, out of context, appeared lost and unassimilable.

To the least of these Lewis would listen with genuine deference—or more likely he would use the entire roomful as an audience for his clowning or his speeches in dialect—striving endlessly to stimulate a lively give-and-take, too often achieving no more than a rather hollow and specious kind of camaraderie.

Then again, by way of an enchanting interlude, one might find Elinor Wylie (whom he adored, and I shall never forget) peacefully having tea. Or of an evening there would gather, at one time or another, Rebecca West, the Van Dorens,[7] Bill Benét, Hugh Walpole, George Jean Nathan, Osbert Sitwell, Laurence Stallings,[8] Lewis Browne,[9] William Seabrook,[10] old Bill Woodward, Arthur Hopkins,[11] and many, many others I can't now recall. In the presence of these Lewis usually restrained his histrionics and made a definite effort to entice his guests to lead the conversation. For these were individuals whom he respected either for certain skills or attributes, or because they had something to teach him—for, with all his egotism and occasional arrogance in other directions, I was always impressed by his open-mindedness and readiness to learn about his craft.

Although so frequently at the price of sleep, the general talk, critical opinions, and discussions of their various professions which such personalities exchanged when they thus gathered informally together were, of course, tremendously stimulating and instructive to a young man with tacit hopes and visions. In addition, at every opportunity when he was in the mood, I asked Lewis technical questions about his own methods and findings. He always answered most willingly and with great clarity, usually citing exceedingly apt examples from his enormously wide reading to illustrate his meaning. As he was drawing within sight of the completion of *Gantry,* I asked him what he regarded as some of the most difficult and arduous technical problems of writing a novel.

He answered at once: "In my own experience, one of the toughest and stubbornest problems is to evolve natural, smooth 'connective tissue' between the incidents, sequences, and divisions of my story, so that the reader will follow its transitions without being conscious of them. Another phase which frequently involves some of the hardest work is to dress characters, rooms, and scenes accurately and convincingly, and at the same time to make the process interesting enough to hold the reader's attention. Then there's the fundamentally important matter of unobtrusively familiarizing the reader with the locale of the story, so that, ideally speaking, he unconsciously acquires a sense of eyewitness, *living* participation in it. I've always made detailed maps of the more important fictional towns in my stories—let me show you the ones I made of Gopher Prairie, Minnesota, and of Zenith and Elk Hills in the State of Winnemac, and of a whole atlas-and-gazetteer-ful of places!" From his file he brought out a folder full of maps all of which he had drawn, becoming progressively more detailed as the atlas of his Middle Western world expanded. Here were the towns in *Our Mr. Wrenn, The Trail of the Hawk, The Job, The Innocents,* and *Free Air.* Between Gopher Prairie and Zenith the detail increased until it was almost like an annotated commercial map, as for instance the ones of the business district, and of Floral Heights, the residential district of Zenith, whose outer fringes marked the horizon of Babbitt's daily life. By this folder full of maps Lewis had translated the world of his imagination and experience into something so close to reality that in listening to him one promptly became wholly convinced of their actuality. He was very proud of this distillation of his years of roaming and of photographic observation in every corner of the Middle West and in much of the rest of the United States; it was as real to him as *Bartholomew's World Atlas.*

63 / Ramon Guthrie

Ramon Guthrie (1896–1973), another of Lewis's friends in Paris in the 1920s, urged him to write the novel that became *The Man Who Knew Coolidge.* He later became a professor of French and Comparative Literature at Dartmouth College, not far from Lewis's home near Woodstock, Vermont.

Source: Ramon Guthrie, "Sinclair Lewis and the 'Labor Novel,'" *Proceedings of the American Academy of Arts and Letters* n.s. 2 (1952): 68–73.

Although he seemed to enjoy living in an atmosphere of unpredictableness, there was a streak of almost spinsterish neatness in Sinclair Lewis's make-up that abhorred leaving things unfinished. Once he had set his mind to a piece of work, he was almost certain to carry it through with reasonable dispatch. "Novels," he was fond of saying, "are written by keeping the seat of the pants applied to the seat of the chair." By following this formula, he turned out twenty-two novels.[12] It failed him only in the case of the one book that, judging from the effort that he gave to it and the faith he felt in it, lay closest to his heart.

A number of people worked with him in his attempts to write the much talked of "Labor Novel." I happened to be in at both the birth, and what turned out to be the death, of the project. The story of his struggles with this phantom novel, which exists only in a few sheaves of notes and the memories of those of us who heard him "talk it out," may be a key to Sinclair Lewis's personality and importance as an artist.

Late in March 1927, Red—nobody but Arnold Bennett called him Sinclair—hired a chauffeur-driven car in Paris and asked me to accompany him on a trip to Spain. Of course we never got to Spain; Red rarely held to his original destinations. We did end up in Venice, about the 10th of April, as I recall, and spent about a week there.

It was in Venice that I first heard him mention the labor novel. The story was still nebulous in his mind, but the essential concept was approximately the same as it was to be nine years later when I worked with him on it in Connecticut and

Vermont. Eugene Debs was the prototype of the hero. The title was to be *The Man Who Sought God.*

The world-wide excitement over the Sacco-Vanzetti affair[13] was at this height at the time and may have had a part in suggesting the novel to him. Although he felt no militant interest in the case, Red talked about it frequently and saw analogies between Sacco and Vanzetti, as martyrs to a reactionary society, and Debs persecuted and imprisoned by similar interests.

From Venice, Red decided to go on to Ragusa and Athens, but since I had a novel of my own to finish up, I turned back to France.

I next heard from him a couple of months later, when I was established in a small village in Dordogne. Red had a way with telephones. I was so awed by the miracle of his getting a call through on the primitive local switchboard at one of the rare moments when the postmistress happened to be on duty and the fat, ancient postman sober enough to pedal down to the far end of the village and fetch me, that I could only bellow a bewildered "yes" when I understood that he wanted me to drop my work and come to Paris to go on a walking trip through Alsace. Before the connection finally sputtered out, he managed to add that a specialist in Vienna had warned him that he was facing a complete collapse unless he entered a hospital immediately.

It took two or three days of patient insistence to get him out of Paris and on a train for Strasbourg.

From Strasbourg to Basel, switching from Alsace to the Schwarzwald and with zig-zags to avoid tourist centers, is about a hundred miles. What with stops wherever, as Red said, "church steeples and the bright prattle of little children" promised beer, we did it in about ten days. It was the longest stretch over which I ever saw Red completely happy. His brief account of the trip in *Dodsworth* makes it sound more strenuous than it was.[14] Red did "find himself breathing deeper, sleeping better, brooking less, and drinking beer instead of cognac." But he didn't "sweat and ache" too much under the weight of his rucksack. He did carry a rucksack, but its entire contents were a Bible, *The Imitation of Christ,*[15] a recent number of the *Bookman,* and a toilet kit. The problem of socks, shirt, and underwear he solved by stepping into the bathtub—when we stopped at hotels that had bathtubs—with them on and lathering them thoroughly. In the morning, they were often "sort of almost nearly dry enough" to wear again. On the second day, he threw the *Bookman* away.

It was characteristic of Red that, while America was ringing with pulpit-thumping denunciations of *Elmer Gantry,* its godless author could have been found lying under a tree along a road in Alsace, absorbed in either the Bible or Thomas à Kempis.

During our trip, the labor novel began to take on definite shape. Building around the theme, "Blessed are they which are persecuted for righteousness sake," Red would develop long segments of the story, weaving and expanding episodes as they came into his mind, without any thought of composing them. In one scene Clarence Darrow[16] (fictionalized, of course), knowing that the hero has been framed, tries to convince him that his only hope lies in pleading guilty and throwing himself on the mercy of the court. In another outstanding passage the hero suddenly sees himself as a self-dramatizing charlatan, reveling in his martyrdom. Sometimes another character, "the international waiter," a sardonic, picaresque, wise expert on life (Montenegrin by birth, Viennese, Parisian and Swiss by education), would slip into the story as a foil to the innocence and idealism of the hero. There were scenes between Clarence Darrow and the "international waiter" that were so splendid that any attempt I might make to describe them would only garble them. Eventually Red came to feel that the "international waiter" deserved a novel of his own.

Although the Sacco-Vanzetti affair may have provided the first inspiration for the labor novel, it would be a mistake to attribute to Sinclair Lewis any kind of sustained political conviction. He had been, briefly, during his college days, a socialist. He still took for granted that, by and large, politicians are scoundrels and governments more or less consciously contrived swindles to enable small cliques to exploit the masses. But, in his mature years at least, he did not believe that anything could be done about it. Eugene Debs might be a saint in his eyes, but that did not mean that either Debs's or Marx's or anybody else's social doctrines would ever be a panacea.

The title, *The Man Who Sought God,* also needs explaining. Whether or not Sinclair Lewis had a religious mind depends on one's concept of religiosity. He had scant use for Yahweh and the God of Caiaphas or of high priests in general.

"God is the *lacrimae rerum,*" he said, "the eternal tears of things."

In keeping with these concepts, the hero of the labor novel was to be a workingman who came to social and political awareness flounderingly, in the course of his search for what he himself would perhaps never know to be God. Inevitably he was to run afoul of Church and State on the charge that "he stirreth up the people." But the final crisis of the story was to be his inner struggle against an insidious messiah complex that threatened to destroy his humility and integrity.

Our trip ended, we went back to Paris. Red took an apartment in Auteuil, but he was too restless and unhappy to settle down. Paris never agreed with him for long. Around the first of July he began his wandering again. My wife and I accompanied him as far as Munich and spent a week with him there. When he saw us off for Paris, he seemed so forlorn and at loose ends, so in need of help and companionship, that only the necessity of my earning a living kept us from changing our minds about leaving him. Fortunately, the train that was to take him to Berlin and, as it turned out, to his first meeting with Dorothy Thompson, pulled out from the station within a few minutes of our own.

Some weeks later Red telegraphed asking me to join him and Dorothy at Cologne for a walking trip up the Rhine. At Mainz, I think it was, Dorothy had to leave us. Red and I wandered about the Rhineland for a few days longer before joining her at Berlin.

All during this period, the labor novel was shaping up in his mind. As he told it, in disconnected episodes, for the most part, but with enough links to give it a unity, it was a powerful and beautiful work that promised to become all that he hoped for it.

Red never boasted of what he had done or was going to do. In most ways he was extraordinarily modest. When I suggested that he could stand comparison with an H. G. Wells or an Arnold Bennett, both of whom he admired extravagantly, he was quietly shocked at my irreverence. He did, however, say that this novel was going to be better than anything that he himself had ever written—"even better than *Arrowsmith.*" He felt that he was not ready to write it yet. He wanted the experience of writing at least one more major novel first, while letting the labor novel ripen gradually in his mind.

Anyone who knew Sinclair Lewis remembers the unending monologues that he could improvise for hours at a time. During my first stay in Berlin with him, either Dorothy or I—or perhaps both of us—suggested that he put one of the current monologues on paper. Within a few days, he had written *The Man Who Knew Coolidge.*

It must have been in November that Dorothy asked me to come from Paris to Berlin to keep Red company while she covered an assignment in Moscow. She was living in Charlottenburg and invited me to use her apartment during her absence. Red had taken a suite in a small hotel a mile or so away. We met every evening for dinner and often at noon for lunch. Although he had begun work on *Dodsworth,* the labor novel was still very much in his mind. We talked much more about it than of *Dodsworth.* Shortly after I left Berlin, he received a letter from J. B. McNamara,[17] then serving a sentence in San Quentin, concerning his project and urging him to go through with it.

64 / Vincent Sheean

Vincent Sheean (1899–1975) was an American journalist and novelist who befriended Lewis in the mid-1920s and remained in Lewis's orbit the rest of his life.

Source: Vincent Sheean, *Personal History* (Garden City, NY: Garden City Publishing, 1937), 278–79.

By that rule of contradiction which operated upon me all through this time—I could not stop talking about Moscow. I must have been a great bore to everybody I met, and sometimes they did not hesitate to tell me so. [. . .] Sinclair Lewis was in Berlin, too, and his response to my obsession was an incomparable one; I still laugh sometimes when I think of it. Dorothy Thompson, who became Mrs. Lewis soon afterwards, asked me to dinner one night with some assorted German countesses and her prospective husband. Lewis—"Red," we called him—was in fine form, and at his best he was one of the funniest people in the world. I had been particularly tiresome about Moscow that evening, for I was leaving the next day to see the celebration of the tenth anniversary of the Bolshevik Revolution. I kept on telling everybody, including the surprised German countesses, that they ought to go to Moscow for the seventh of November, for the spectacle alone, if for nothing else.

Catching, for about the five hundredth time, the sound of my voice informing some hapless German lady that she had to go to Moscow, Red suddenly burst forth.

"Oh you must come to Moscow for the seventh of November," he chanted, giving the sentence the obvious contour of a line by Vachel Lindsay.[18] He went on without a pause, and in five minutes he had recited a whole poem by Vachel Lindsay—all about what was going to happen in Moscow on the momentous day (with a boom, boom, boom!) and how it was imperatively necessary for everybody to go there to see it. When we had recovered from this he went on and did the same thing in three other styles: Longfellow,[19] Swinburne, Tennyson.[20] The rhymes and metres were perfect, the parodies so keen that even the Germans did not need to be told what they were. The Tennyson parody was a triumph of ingenuity and wit, for it is always more difficult to hit off a good poet than a bad one. I have never heard anything like those improvisations; even Red could never do them so well again. They not only delighted their audience, but they performed one of the best offices of parody—showed up an absurdity. The most humorless enthusiast could scarcely have spoken of Moscow on the seventh of November after that.

65 / Claud Cockburn

Claud Cockburn (1904–1981), English journalist and novelist, was known for his communist sympathies. He was foreign correspondent for *The Times* (London) in America and Germany, but quit in 1933 in order to start *The Week,* a newsletter that was banned in London for his criticism of appeasement strategies during the onset of the Second World War. He was the cousin of the satirical novelist Evelyn Waugh (1903–1966). He also crossed paths with Lewis in Berlin in 1927.

Source: Claud Cockburn, *Cockburn Sums Up: An Autobiography* (London: Quartet, 1981), 43.

German friends begged me to take them to a party to meet this present Voice of America. Their earnest intention was to spend an hour or so happily cross-questioning Mr. Lewis on such matters as Americanism, Babbittry, and the Philosophy of Main Street. Lewis, however, was tired and turned up rather drunk. From beneath his jacket hung the ends of two towels clearly marked with the name of his hotel. He had them knotted round his waist to keep his trousers up. Some German at once thought this significant of something or other—the American revolt against convention, perhaps. But when he mentioned it to Lewis, the novelist looked at the knotted towels with an air of surprise as if he had only just noticed them and merely said he supposed his belt must have got broken or lost.

10
At Large
1928–30

After *The Man Who Knew Coolidge,* Lewis turned from potboiling to the international novel *Dodsworth,* the last major work of his career. In this roman à clef, he dissected from his own perspective the failure of his marriage. Two months after Grace obtained a divorce in April 1928, Lewis married Dorothy Thompson in London. They returned to New York that September, the first time he had set foot in the United States in eighteen months, and they soon rented an apartment on West Tenth Street in New York and bought a three-hundred-acre farm near Woodstock, Vermont. During these years, Lewis also interviewed a number of labor leaders and repeatedly started and abandoned the "labor novel" he hoped would be his masterpiece, and he quit Harcourt, Brace in a fit of pique because he thought the firm no longer paid enough attention to him.

66 / Charles Breasted

Lewis was among the first readers to celebrate the talent of the novelist Thomas Wolfe (1900–1938), whom he praised in an interview with the *New York Times* on November 6, 1930, as well as in his Nobel Prize acceptance speech. On his part, Wolfe fictionalized his meeting with Lewis (as Lloyd McHarg) in book 5 ("Exile and Discovery") of *You Can't Go Home Again* (1940). Breasted remembered one of their early encounters in London in 1928. See also Frank W. Shelton, "Thomas Wolfe and Sinclair Lewis," *Thomas Wolfe Review* 12, no. 1 (1988): 7–12.

Source: Charles Breasted, "The 'Sauk-Centricities' of Sinclair Lewis," *Saturday Review of Literature,* August 14, 1954, 8.

One morning in the spring of 1928, when [Lewis] was again keeping bachelor quarters in London at No. 10 Bury Street, I happened in, en route home from Egypt, and found him completely enthralled by a typescript, about which in his overwhelming enthusiasm he was for once almost inarticulate. "If this isn't it," he burst out, "I predict that the young giant who wrote it *will* eventually write *the* American novel, and anyway some of the finest work of our generation! His name's Tom Wolfe, and he's absolutely superb! I want you to meet him—he's dropping in tonight about two A.M."

When I returned late that evening "Hal" Lewis (as he was known to his older friends) was still sitting amongst the typescript of *Look Homeward, Angel* [1929]. He continued to expatiate upon it and towards two o'clock glanced at his watch and remarked that Tom should be along any minute now. "He'll announce himself long before he gets here," Hal said. He had hardly spoken when from the far end of Bury Street the stillness was shattered by an unholy clatter as of ash and refuse cans being dragged across sidewalks, emptied into the gutter, and tossed high into the air, to roll booming and clanging down toward St. James's. From the speed with which the cacophony was approaching, it was evident that more than one man was at work. We leaned out of a window and watched the methodical, efficient Halloween rampage of a pair of young Americans, one of whom, in the light of the street lamps, looked like a titan. When they reached

No. 10, they dusted each other off, and, leaving Bury Street looking like a prophecy of a future "blitz," started upstairs in the lift, which they insisted on operating themselves.

"After midnight," Hal said, "Tom upsets ash cans all over London, and the bobbies on the beat always politely look the other way!"

Tom Wolfe and the other marauder, a young American musical-comedy librettist, appeared at Hal's door, greeted him cordially, apologized for being so late—"We had to work our way over from Leicester Square," Tom explained—and after washing up, poured themselves double drinks and settled in for some of the best talk I had ever heard. They were still going strong toward five in the morning when I finally left my first, and only, meeting with Tom Wolfe.

67 / Vincent Sheean

The wedding of Lewis and Thompson in London was, as their friend Sheean remembered, surprisingly conventional.

Source: Vincent Sheean, "The Tangled Romance of Sinclair Lewis and Dorothy Thompson," *Harper's* 227 (October 1963): 136–38.

The first Mrs. Lewis obtained her divorce decree on 16 April [1928]; on April 23 Red, passing through Rome on his way to London, announced his engagement to Dorothy. [. . .] The frabjous day arrived: 14 May 1928. Dorothy had come to London promptly for the civil formalities, which were completed that morning by the ceremony at the registry office—S. Martin's in Henrietta Street, surrounded by book publishers. Jonathan Cape[1] and his wife were the witnesses; Jonathan was then Red's London publisher. A church ceremony (with all the vows, as both Red and Dorothy had wished) took place immediately afterwards in the Savoy Chapel[2] in the presence of a score or more guests, friends new and old, who repaired to the Savoy Hotel for a wedding luncheon afterwards.

There is something rather touching in Red's desire to have a thoroughly conventional wedding with all the "old" vows. It made the whole thing more "real," just as being married in England did. His first marriage, at the Ethical Culture Society's Lecture Room in New York, had been nothing like this. It is not too much to suppose that by doing things in the prescribed manner he hoped (consciously or unconsciously) to make his marriage more certain to endure. Neither then nor at any other time did he show signs of religious feeling—indeed, his ferocious *Elmer Gantry* had been published only the year before. It was the proprieties, rather than the religious ritual, that seemed valuable to him in solemnizing the event.

Neither Dorothy nor Red ever spoke to me, so far as I can remember, about their own feelings on that day, their hopes or fears. Red was probably so elated, so proud of Dorothy, so anxious to show off the prize he had won, that he had no moment of relaxation, much less of anxiety. We know that he could not resist the chance to deliver one of his monologues when it came time for the toasts after lunch as the Savoy. This one was (or so I have heard) quite funny, but many in London were wearying of Red's incessant performances: only two weeks before Arnold Bennett, after a dinner party, had written in his journal, "Sinclair did too many imitations."

The guests at the Savoy and at the luncheon afterwards included Mrs. Bertrand Russell (Dora),[3] Hugh Walpole, Rebecca West, Anita Loos,[4] Gilbert Frankau,[5] and a good many others. With this marriage Dorothy was entering upon the phase known as celebrity, in its fullest sense, with the American press (and on this occasion also the English press) out in force to observe. [. . .] To Dorothy it was a transference of role, as if she had suddenly stepped up from the audience into the limelight; and if Red ever did grow weary of his public personage (which he probably did toward the end), there was no hint of it in the zest with which he played himself in those days.

68 / Eileen Agar

After their marriage, Lewis and Thompson rented a villa near Naples where they planned to live and work for several months before returning to the United States. The British painter and photographer Eileen Agar (1899–1991) by chance lived nearby in Portofino and visited them.

Source: Eileen Agar, *A Look at My Life* (London: Methuen, 1988), 80–82.

After rejecting a dilapidated forty-room barracks of a place, Dorothy and Sinclair had settled into a little guest house in a huge park. There was a salon, and a great glass verandah looking over Naples and the sea; the kitchen was on one floor, with a not very desirable bedroom (being parkward, green and cool, instead of seaward, blue and warm), and up above, three bedrooms in a row; and the whole resting on a big stone terrace. Hal, as we called Sinclair, was hard at work on *Dodsworth,* using the villa Galotti (of which this guest house was a tiny appendage) as the setting for parts of this novel. Tall, with brushed-back carrot-colored hair, a global forehead and informal rubbery face, he was an intelligent octopus, with large pop-eyes, an electric vitality and long lanky limbs which spread everywhere like tentacles.

As we were still in Portofino, it did not seem far to hop across the water from Genoa to Naples, and we accepted their invitation hoping that things would go as smoothly as the crossing. For the first few days, everything in the garden was gorgeous, including the panoramic view of Vesuvius across the bay, even though we were woken up at seven o'clock every morning by the insistent tapping of two typewriters. Both Dorothy and Hal were hard at it, their mechanized muses demanding to be fed. But then one night at dinner all hell broke loose. Dorothy got up from the table saying that she must find some missing pages from the manuscript she was writing for a syndicated newspaper. Lewis was very drunk, and obviously feeling that his work was of more moment than Dorothy's, he erupted bitterly. After all, he said, he had written a few books himself in his time that were somewhat more important than her bloody manuscript. He was completely plastered and ended up by stalking out of the room into the garden, where he tripped in the dark among the rose bushes and fell into an intoxicated sleep. It was Joseph[6] who had to rescue him, pick him out of the thorns and put him in his ex-wife's bed. Apparently, Dorothy later recorded in her diary that she felt Hal had denounced her to Joseph that night. [. . .]

Dorothy and Hal missed their train and Joseph had to put them up for another day. He said they were all smiles and friendliness towards both of us, charming and uncomplicated. In the same letter he told me he rather liked Hal this time, though he still thought him neurotic and unsure of himself. He recognized Lewis's courage, and his brilliance as an interpreter of America, but feared he had nothing to offer as an alternative to the stupidity he exposed. Joseph wrote to me that he saw Lewis as a weeping interpreter, whose mouth would grin and scold and ridicule, but whose heart wept because all the time he was exposing his own self. He probably drank to ease the ache, for later, reading another Lewis novel, Joseph remarked: "You can smell the whisky between his lines."

Mixed feelings about Hal were the order of the day. Joseph recalled a time when he had been reading Lewis's novel *Main Street* aloud to Dorothy Thompson (they were still married then). She tore the book out of his hands and stamped on it. "I hate that book," she said. A few years later she was Lewis's biggest admirer. Sinclair was often criticized for his meanness, but at one point he offered to support Joseph for a year or two so that he could get on with his writing. Joseph never accepted this generous offer, but he certainly appreciated it.

69 / Alfred Harcourt

Harcourt was characteristically diplomatic in recording Lewis's departure for Random House. As he wrote Lewis on February 3, 1931, "If I've lost an author, you haven't lost either a friend or a devoted reader."[7] As Richard Lingeman adds, however, "The impression is unavoidable that Harcourt was relieved at no longer having to cope with Lewis."[8]

Source: Alfred Harcourt, *Some Experiences* (Riverside, CT: privately printed, 1934), 83–85.

After *Dodsworth,* we did not publish any more of Lewis's new books, but we kept the old ones. Although I saw him less frequently—and for a number of years not at all—nothing ever interfered with our personal feeling for each other. We had some long and intimate visits when he was in Santa Barbara in 1949.

Sinclair Lewis earned his success step by step, and paid for it. When he had an idea for a novel, he put as much study into the subject matter as a graduate student preparing a Ph.D. thesis, and he spent months living among the kind of people that were to be the figures in the book. If he couldn't feel himself part of them so that he could write from within, he would give up the idea, no matter how much time he had spent on it. Time and time again he tried to write a novel about a labor leader, only to throw away what he had written. Before he started the actual writing of a book, he had its structure worked out with the greatest care. I remember an elaborate and detailed map of the imaginary city of Zenith where Babbitt lived. As Lewis was finishing a book, he would work eighteen or twenty hours out of the twenty-four, day after day. Like a man possessed, he couldn't stay still, he couldn't lie down, he couldn't sit down, except at the typewriter. When, after the award of the Nobel Prize, a newspaper reporter asked him the typical question about his formula for success, his reply was, "The application of the seat of the pants to the seat of the chair."

He was one of the most generous-spirited men I ever knew. With some of the earlier books, he insisted that we take a larger share of some of the rights than I had proposed. Where people had given him substantial help in enabling him to get a proper background for a book, he saw that they got generous recognition.

He grew lonelier and lonelier. He longed for human companionship but he was so brilliant that he was soon bored by the people who could have given him affection. His sharp mind penetrated fast to the core of anything, and what he saw there was often disillusioning to him. He had none of the humdrum amusements and putterings most of us have that keep us steady. Sometimes it seemed as if his only relief was in drink. At times, he would collapse to the point where he scared everyone, including himself, and then he'd recover with amazing vitality. When I last saw him, he had gone for a number of years without drinking at all. His death, alone in Rome, caused a widespread sense of loss that would have astonished him. A force in modern literature went with him, but it is fitting that in his lifetime he attained the nearest thing there is to "contemporary immortality."

70 / Ramon Guthrie

Lewis planned for many years to write a "labor novel," at different times tentatively titled "Neighbors" and "The Man Who Sought God," that would feature a heroic labor leader modeled on Eugene Debs. He often started the novel but never finished it, the first time shortly before he received the Nobel Prize and left Harcourt, Brace. His friend Guthrie, who lived only an hour away from Lewis by car, recalled how his wish to consult experts on the project impeded his work.

Source: Ramon Guthrie, "Sinclair Lewis and the 'Labor Novel,'" *Proceedings of the American Academy of Arts and Letters* n.s. 2 (1952): 73–74.

It was in 1929 that Red made his first serious attempt to write the labor novel. He and Dorothy were living on their farm in Vermont. A number of authorities on labor, economics, etc., were in residence as a consultant staff. One of the experts was the late Ben Stolberg;[9] I have forgotten who the others were. Everybody except Red was buckled down to the job of writing the book. Red himself seemed rather baffled and disconcerted by the invasion. He would take naps, go for walks, read detective stories, get quietly but purposefully drunk, turn out potboilers for the *Saturday Evening Post,* while the board of experts sat in solemn conclave laying out the novel.

His original concept of the story had been ruled out as a childish fantasy. Thus far, all that he had really learned from their extensive tutoring in the history and theory of labor-unionism was: that Debs was an insignificant dreamer of no possible interest to any serious student of labor; that there *was* no real labor movement in America; that if there had been one he was too ignorant of Marx, Bakunin, Liebknecht,[10] and a host of others to write a novel about it; and (this much on his own) that he didn't *want* to write the kind of novel that they insisted he *must* write.

In the end he wrote *Ann Vickers* [1932] instead. One day in the fall of 1930 I drove over to see him. Red came out on the terrace to meet me. "You'll be glad to know that I'm writing a novel about a business woman," he said drily. "You don't know anything about business women, do you? Good! Neither do I, and I don't want to."

From a creative point of view, the years between *Dodsworth* and *It Can't Happen Here* must have been rather harrowing ones for Red. *Ann Vickers* was a passable novel perhaps, but he knew that it was not a good one. *Work of Art* was an underdeveloped negative of the "international waiter" novel. Whatever his inner anguish may have been, Red kept it to himself. He was the world's most assiduous brooder, but he never did his brooding on any one's shoulder. One day in the fall of '34 he did remark that most writers had at most a decade of real productivity in their lives. "After that, they are through." He cited Irvin Cobb, Dreiser, Jack London.[11] "Of course, a man can never know about himself."

A few days after this Red began answering his own question by writing *It Can't Happen Here.*[12]

71 / Morley Callaghan

Morley Callaghan (1903–1990), Canadian novelist, short-story writer, playwright, and journalist, became a friend of Ernest Hemingway while working as a reporter for the *Toronto Daily Star* and associated with Lewis, Hemingway, F. Scott Fitzgerald, and James Joyce on Paris's Left Bank during the 1920s. He once beat Hemingway in a contentious boxing match refereed by Fitzgerald. Lewis wrote privately in December 1928 that "Callaghan seems to me particularly to have a really authentic power of making his impressions of life—mad life or lugubriously sane life—completely vivid."[13]

Source: Morley Callaghan, *That Summer in Paris* (New York: Coward-McCann, 1963), 68–70, 74.

The door was opened by a grinning, balding man. It was Lou,[14] the secretary, the Lewis man. In the drawing room a writer, Mary Heaton Vorse, sat talking to Lewis, who looked almost frighteningly like a picture I had seen of him. A gaunt thin sandy man, with staring protuberant blue eyes, many freckles on his flushed face; the forehead broad, the face tapering sharply—skin over a skull. This strange excited wild face lit up as he came to me with his arms out. "Well, well, well," he cried, pushing me back a little. "Let me get a good look at you." And then, laughing, he looked at my wife. "You're charming," he said to her. "Just right for him." He sent the grinning Lou scurrying for drinks. All the time we were there Lou kept on grinning. "Do you know, Morley," Lewis said earnestly, "Flaubert would have loved your work. Yes, old Flaubert."

His approach, his appraisal, were so candid, his pale blue eyes still so full on me, I couldn't get my bearings. I was a young man who liked to play things down. [. . .]

Then suddenly his manner changed, that light in his eyes changed too, and though his tone was aggressive, almost magically he became defensive. It was not likely, the way I wrote, that I would be called a journalist. Someday, though, someone may say it of me. Don't ever let it bother me. His startling blue eyes, now troubled, on me, he said, "They call me a journalist, you know. Well, H. G.

Wells told me once that they called him a journalist, too, and he said, 'Don't ever let it trouble you that they called you a journalist.'" Then there was a solemn silence. The gaiety all gone, he sat brooding, and I too. And in the silence, I, the young writer, caught a glimpse of some gnawing discontent in this enormously successful novelist. When I grew older was I to know this discontent? I wondered. What was he communicating to me? Then, suddenly, he looked up as if aware he was out of character. If we had been alone and drinking he might have told me about his lonely life as a writer; the way he wanted to be seen; the way others actually saw him. Then the spell, the desire to be in comfortable protective character, was again on him. "No matter," he said, trying to recover the now slightly spurious gusto. How was my book doing? How was it received? [. . .]

Before we left he gave us a copy of his new book, *Dodsworth.* He told us we would love Paris. We were to let him know if he could help us.

Outside, my wife and I started to laugh, then fell silent. We were both still bemused. All Lewis's energy, change of mood, goodwill, gaiety, had left us feeling a little drunk. Was the literary life all on this grand, opulent, and theatrical scale? But after we had joked and shared our pleasure in Lewis, I remember I wondered with some pain, since I liked and admired him, why he used all his frantic energy in cultivating unreality? Why was he so bent on protecting himself that people might have no chance of judging his worth as a human being? I think he was really a shy man being afraid of his own shyness, his own natural warmth and generosity; he clowned his way out of his loneliness.

We were staying at the old Brevoort on lower Fifth. In the morning, letters of introduction came from Lewis, and a note saying he had sent his man Lou to St. Patrick's Cathedral to light candles for our safe journey to Paris.

72 / Gordon Sinclair

Gordon Sinclair (1890–1984), a Canadian commentator and reporter for the *Toronto Star,* covered the AFL (American Federation of Labor) convention in Toronto in early October 1929—as did Lewis.

Source: Gordon Sinclair, *Will Gordon Sinclair Please Sit Down* (Toronto: McClelland and Stewart, 1975), 25–26.

I had one assignment with another Nobel Prize winner who seemed like a frightened zombie. For some obscure reason a syndicate sent Sinclair Lewis to Toronto to cover the convention of the American Federation of Labor on one of the few times that that convention was held outside the U.S.A.

The *Star* had one guy doing think pieces about it and another writing whatever spot news came along. I drew the latter assignment a few times and the chair next to Lewis.

He always looked as if he was about to wet his pants. He had this drawn-in face with bad skin and eyes that seemed to stare all the time. He'd already written *Babbitt, Main Street,* and *Arrowsmith,* all of which I'd enjoyed, but in the long dull sessions of the labor unions I could never get him to talk about them.

Usually he was late getting to the meetings but he always stuck it out to the end and even when there was a recess and delegates slid off to their rooms to get a drink. [. . .] Toronto had no bars at this time. [. . .] Lewis sat there in silence, rebuffing anyone who came to speak to him and reading nothing. I never saw him even glance at any of the newspapers that were scattered around. I'd heard he was a pretty fair hand with a jug of rye but so far as I could see the man was a silent loner, sober as a vice president of A.A.

73 / William E. Woodward

By the late 1920s, Lewis's drinking had become pathological. Woodward remembered a visit Lewis and Thompson made to southern California in early 1930, when Thompson was pregnant with their son Michael, born in June 1930 (d. 1985).

Source: William E. Woodward, *The Gift of Life: An Autobiography* (New York: Dutton, 1947), 342–44.

Sinclair Lewis and Dorothy Thompson, who was then his wife, wrote us that they were coming to Los Angeles and Helen asked them to stay at our house, where we had plenty of room for guests. "Red" and Dorothy drove up one day early in April and we welcomed them. I liked both of them, "Red" from years back and Dorothy since I had met her in 1928. We had a lively reunion.

When Mac heard that Sinclair Lewis was to visit Los Angeles he said he would like to meet him, and so next day we had McAdoo and Eleanor[15] come to dinner.

"Red" was at his best. Maybe Dorothy kept him sober. As to that I cannot say, but I do know that his practice was to get drunk whenever he was to meet strangers, especially strangers of distinction. Anyway, he was as sober as a judge and his talk was fascinating.

On the following day Louis Bromfield[16] drove up and said he would like to meet Sinclair Lewis, and he was followed almost immediately by a couple of newspapermen who wanted to get an interview with the author of *Main Street.* We looked for Lewis and found him lying in a hammock on the lawn, but we were unable to awaken him. A bottle of Scotch and a glass were on a little table by the hammock, and Lewis was snoring. Bromfield stayed until seven o'clock, hoping that Lewis would get up. But he slept on and Bromfield went away without meeting him.

Dorothy was pregnant, her child due in a few months. When she learned that [Woodward's wife] Helen had to go to a hospital for a few days for a tonsillectomy, she declared that she could not cope with the confusion and the excitement of the situation. And next morning she left for a visit with Rose Wilder

Lane[17] in the Ozarks. Helen went to the hospital and Red and I remained with the servants.

That afternoon "Red" went to a cocktail party at Samson Raphaelson's house.[18] I was invited, but I was too busy to go. It was understood that, after the cocktails, a half dozen of the guests were to come to our house for dinner. We waited and waited for Lewis long past the dinner hour, but he did not show up. Then, at last, Raphaelson got me on the phone. He said that Lewis, as soon as he got to the party, lay down on a couch and went to sleep. He added that they had been trying to get him up, but had not succeeded. I said that I would come for him. When I got to Raphaelson's house, Lewis was snoring on a sofa in the living room. After much effort, I managed to get him down to a taxi, and he seemed to revive wonderfully on the way home. The fresh air, probably, was a help.

After we had been at the table awhile I said, as a joke—at any rate, I meant it to be funny—that we had learned who wrote *Ten Nights in a Barroom.*[19] Somebody at the table asked who and I pointed to Lewis. I had no idea that he would take it seriously, but he did. He rose from the table, said that he had been insulted, and walked out of the room. We saw him no more that evening, but before I went to bed I looked into his room and he was there, asleep.

Around two in the morning he came into my room and sat on the edge of the bed. "Bill," he said, "I love you, but I must go. I don't fit in here. I want to hire a chauffeur for my car. I don't trust myself in driving. Can you let me have Robert for a few days?"

I said I could not spare Robert, and I told him that he could get a chauffeur in the morning by calling up an agency.

Next morning I went down to breakfast at eight o'clock and there was "Red," sitting at the table and eating his oatmeal. He looked as lively and pleasant as one could wish. He never had a hang-over, as I knew. Outside, in the street, his car was throbbing with a chauffeur at the wheel. He said good-by cordially, and we parted on good terms.

11
Stockholm
1930–31

On November 5, 1930, Lewis learned he had been awarded the annual Nobel Prize in Literature. The award was controversial, to say the least. His friends George Jean Nathan, Carl Van Doren, Fanny Butcher, and Louis Adamic celebrated with him, while neither Ernest Hemingway nor Sherwood Anderson thought Lewis deserved it. Anderson (1876–1941), the author of *Winesburg, Ohio* (1919), wrote a friend to protest Lewis's receipt of the prize: "The Lewis thing was very depressing to me as it must be to all thoughtful men. The man has never touched American life, except to make it uglier by his touch, and now he is given this honor that should, if it were to go to an American, have gone to Dreiser. Dreiser has had real tenderness in him, Lewis never. It seems to me that Lewis must have got it rather out of European dislike of America rather than liking."[1]

Lewis and Thompson departed on November 29 to attend the ceremony in Stockholm on December 10, and the Nobel laureate addressed the members of the Swedish academy on December 12. His speech, "The American Fear of Literature," is reprinted in *The Man from Main Street,* 4–17. After spending the holidays in Germany, Lewis and Thompson returned to the United States in early March 1931.

74 / H. Allen Smith

H. Allen Smith (1907–1976), journalist and humorist, wrote books that were popular during the 1940s and 1950s and contributed many articles to a wide range of literary and popular venues, from *Esquire* and the *Saturday Evening Post* to *Playboy* and *Reader's Digest.*

Source: H. Allen Smith, *Low Man on a Totem Pole* (Garden City, NY: Doubleday, Doran, 1941), 39–41.

On the day that Sinclair Lewis was awarded the Nobel Prize for Literature his publishers telephoned that he was driving in from Connecticut with his wife, a Miss Thompson, and that Mr. Lewis would sit for an interview within the hour.

I started out of the World building and was walking toward the subway entrance, when Bowen[2] of the I[nternational] N[ews] S[ervice] swished past me. Twenty minutes later I found him in the small crowd at the publishing house. There was a hard glint in his eye.

Sinclair Lewis came in and sat at a desk. The ladies and gentlemen of the press faced him, sitting in folding chairs brought in from a nearby funeral parlor. As the first American to win the Nobel award took his seat Bowen of the I.N.S. seized one of the folding chairs, marched up to the desk, placed it alongside Lewis, stuck his face into the novelist's face and announced firmly: "I'm Bowen of the I.N.S. Congratulations."

Lewis looked at him, then at the rest of us, shrugged his lean shoulders and grinned. Whereupon Bowen of the I.N.S. sat down, back turned to the other reporters, and sprawled himself out on the desk so that he could gaze directly, at a distance of two feet, into the features of Sinclair Lewis.

Alarm came into the eyes of Lewis. He stared at Bowen of the I.N.S. for a long time, then slowly stood up.

"Perhaps," he said to Bowen, "perhaps you would like to sit in my chair."

"Ha!" cried Bowen of the I.N.S. "That's a good one! No, I'll stay right where I am. How does it feel?"

"How does *what* feel?" asked Lewis, slipping back into his chair.

"To win this prize," said Bowen of the I.N.S.

"Well," said Lewis, trying to make the best of an uncomfortable situation, knowing the rest of us were sitting there watching the little drama, realizing that he had to handle himself carefully or run the risk of making an ass of himself. "Well . . ."

Bowen of the I.N.S. didn't wait for an answer.

"Listen," he said, leaning even closer to Lewis. "What're you gonna expose next?"

Lewis glanced appealingly over the room.

"What do you mean, what am I gonna expose next?"

"I mean," persisted Bowen of the I.N.S. "what're you gonna expose next?"

"What have I exposed already?" challenged Lewis.

"Babbitt," snapped Bowen of the I.N.S. "You exposed Babbitt and all the others, and now I wanna know what's next on the list."

Lewis was patently irritated.

"Young man," he said, "I'm not, as you have it, gonna expose nothin' next. I'm not in the exposin' business. I'm—"

"Oh yes, you are," cried Bowen of the I.N.S. "I want a yarn out of this about what's next. Now, come on. What'll it be next?"

"God damn it," said Lewis, "I told you I'm not in the business of exposing things. I'm a novelist. I write novels. I don't go around—"

"Ah-h-h-h!" said Bowen of the I.N.S. and, turning to face the rest of us, grinned knowingly and winked, letting us know he was in control of this situation. Then he turned back to the furious winner of the Nobel Prize. "Let's have it," he insisted. "What're you gonna expose next?"

Sinclair Lewis sat and looked at Bowen of the I.N.S. for a long time. Then he got up from his chair, walked around the desk and faced the rest of us. Someone—I think it was Louis Sherwin[3]—went up to Bowen of the I.N.S. and whispered in his ear. What he whispered I don't know, but Bowen of the I.N.S. abandoned his quest for an answer to that question, and the rest of us took over. It was pretty dull, too, after Bowen dropped out.

75 / George Jean Nathan

Nevertheless, Lewis's friends feted him before his departure.

Source: George Jean Nathan, *The Intimate Notebooks of George Jean Nathan* (New York: Knopf, 1932), 20–21.

When some months later the news was flashed over the wires that our friend had been awarded the Nobel Prize, the immense gratification that a number of us felt was slightly modified by qualms as to how the fellow would conduct himself in the presence of Swedish royalty. It was our firm conviction, based upon years of close intimacy, that he would in all likelihood run right up to the Queen, call her by her first name and lodge an aqueous smack upon her lips, and that when he was presented to His Majesty he would promptly and affectionately whack him on the back, put his arm around him, and call him "you old son-of-a-gun." Consequently, on the night the award was announced, some of us gathered together with him and solemnly engaged to offer him sage counsel and instruction in the finer shades of the punctilio.

"For example," we asked him, "what are you going to say to the King when you meet him?"

"What am I going to say?" he roared, waving his arms in the air and knocking over two lamps. "What am I going to say? Well, just you guys listen! 'Your Gracious Majesty and Officers of the Coldstream Guards: It is a great pleasure, let me tell you, for a little feller from Sauk Centre to meet you big Swedes. I feel proud and honored, believe me, boys, and when I get back home and tell the folks of the swell reception you've given me, they're going to be not only proud of me but of you, too. After all, we're all brothers in Kiwanis, whether we're Swedes, Americans or Bohunks, and our hearts are in the right place. So what do you all say to going out, King, and having a little drink?'"

Yet once again our friend fooled us. Just as his whistle, however wet and riotous it may be when he is not in the grip of literary labor pains, is ever of an unremitting and almost Pythagorean aridity when he really sits himself to work, so his conduct in Stockholm turned out to be so formal and proper—indeed, so dismayingly formal and proper—that His August Majesty, together with several members of his court, privy to the eccentricities of American comportment, actually inquired of our hero if he was not, at least on one of his parents' side, partly British.

76 / Carl Van Doren

Carl Van Doren (1885–1950), Pulitzer Prize–winning biographer and critic, earned a PhD at Columbia University in 1911 and continued to teach there until 1930.

Source: Carl Van Doren, *Three Worlds* (New York: Harper and Brothers, 1936), 267–68.

After the dinner for Sinclair Lewis before he left for Sweden to receive the Nobel Prize late in 1930 a few of his friends took him away to a smaller party. It was like old times, we said. He and I recalled another dinner in the days of Babbitt when three or four writers had been invited along with Leopold Stokowski[4] and a tableful of musicians. Then Lewis, after dinner, organized an impromptu meeting of a Rotary Club. As chairman he introduced Mencken as General Pershing[5] with a message from the Army, George Jean Nathan as a representative of the Ku Klux Klan, me as the bishop who had come to dignify the revels. Now he organized an hour on the radio, with a standing lamp for a microphone. I was the announcer and he was most of the entertainers. Like old times. The whole company had the odd sense that there were classics present. Writing books had been the day's work. Had some of the books got into history?

Lewis was conscious of this, as he always is of whatever may be in the minds of anybody near him. He told the Swedish Academy: "There are young Americans today who are doing such passionate and authentic work that it makes me sick to see that I am a little too old to be one of them." He mentioned names: Ernest Hemingway, Thomas Wolfe, Thornton Wilder,[6] John Dos Passos, Stephen Vincent Benét, Michael Gold,[7] William Faulkner.[8] "I salute them, with a joy in being not yet too far removed from their determination to give to the America that has mountains and endless prairies, enormous cities and lost far cabins, billions of money and tons of faith, to an America that is as strange as Russia and as complex as China, a literature worthy of her vastness."

77 / Dorothy Thompson

Dorothy Thompson (1893–1961), journalist, married Lewis in 1928 and divorced him in 1942. She was, in 1934, the first US journalist to be expelled from Nazi Germany. In 1936 she began to contribute a thrice-weekly column, "On the Record," to the *Herald Tribune* syndicate and became, as Schorer explains, "the first woman to publish regularly on international affairs."[9] In 1938 she published an influential book, *The New Russia,* based on a trip to the Soviet Union, and in 1939 *Time* named her, with First Lady Eleanor Roosevelt (1884–1962), one of the two most influential women in America. She also was the ostensible inspiration for the character of Tess Harding, played by Katharine Hepburn, in the movie *Woman of the Year* (1942). See also Vincent Sheean, "The Tangled Romance of Sinclair Lewis and Dorothy Thompson," *Harper's* 227 (October 1963): 136–38; and Marion K. Sanders, *Dorothy Thompson: A Legend in Her Time* (Boston: Houghton Mifflin, 1973).

Source: Dorothy Thompson, "At the Court of King Gustaf," *Pictorial Review* 32 (April 1931): 17, 45, 50.

Writers, if they enjoy any success, are more accustomed [than scientists] to publicity. But what writer can really expect to receive the Nobel Prize? No matter how highly he may evaluate his own work, he can certainly think of dozens of other writers more worthy, in his own estimation, than himself. In thirty years only thirty persons have received the prize for literature, and the chances of any writer are therefore extremely small. Every year, for a few weeks in advance of the award, there are numerous rumors that this writer or that is being considered. But the history of the award itself ought to teach everyone not to rely upon these rumors.

In 1929, for instance, the international press was full of reports that my husband was being considered. He himself paid no attention to them, and was not in the least surprised when the award went to the great German novelist Thomas Mann.[10] In 1930, on the other hand, he never heard mention of his name. So it was a fairy story for him when the correspondent of a Swedish newspaper in

America waked him out of a late morning's sleep, called him, tousled and in dressing gown, to the telephone, and asked him whether he was going to accept the Nobel Prize just conferred upon him in Stockholm.

We have, as it happens, a friend who is extremely fond of practical jokes. More than once we have received letters, usually written in green ink, bearing postmarks from remote parts of the world, and offering to return money borrowed many years ago, or proposing brilliant schemes for making a fortune. We therefore suspect immediately an unknown voice or an unknown handwriting, if combined with some bizarre idea, and it would be just like our friend to decide on a dull morning to confer the Nobel Prize on his friend Red. Extreme wariness, therefore, in my husband's replies. He isn't going to be caught!

He withholds comment and waits for further news. But his publisher is on the telephone in another few minutes, then the Associated Press, and then a messenger delivers a telegram from the Swedish minister in Washington. And then the deluge! With a French cook going mildly crazy while she tries to answer correspondents of German, Spanish, Swedish, Danish, and even American newspapers, my husband desperately tries to pursue his dressing beyond the pajama-dressing-gown stage and to retrieve a slipper which in the excitement of the news has disappeared.

He limps upstairs to announce the news to his five-month-old son. "Golly, golly," is Michael's intelligent comment.

I suppose that the members of the Swedish Academy know more about world literature than any other group of people anywhere. As a Nobel Prize winner my husband can himself nominate candidates for the prize. In Sweden, talking with members at a small dinner attended only by the Academy members and himself, he suggested certain names.

"My dear Lewis," wailed one member, clasping his brow, "I beg you to think twice before you suggest a candidate. Do you know that if you suggest three or four people in all seriousness, I shall have to read every line they have ever written? It does not matter that I may already have read all their works. I had already read all of yours, and yet, this year, I have had to read them again, from cover to cover, and in the original language."

Considering that next to Theodore Dreiser and the author of the New York telephone book my husband writes the biggest books on the American continent, a certain sympathy must go out to the conscientious Academy members.

The prize is not a joke! The Swedish American Steamship Line has suggested a boat which will bring us to Sweden in time for the presentation of the prize. The American press has expressed itself pro and con on the matter of the literature award.

Oh happy men of science! The public knows so little about their works, anyway!

Another American, or rather Austro-American, Dr. Karl Landsteiner, of the Rockefeller Institute,[11] is also on his way to Sweden to receive the Nobel Prize. But his field is medical research. No one has cried that the award to him is an outrage. Editorial writers have not vied with one another in suggesting other scientists whom it would have pleased them more to see rewarded. No one has written to the papers to object to Dr. Landsteiner's religion, and the color of his hair, and that a movement ought to be started against his receiving the prize.

We are on our way, very happy, excited, and just a little rueful. Tremendously pleased at the warm telegrams from friends all over the world. What a charming letter from Hugh Walpole! How spontaneously generous the congratulations of Francis Brett Young![12] How proud my husband is of the note from E. M. Forster,[13] how happy in the cable from Thomas Mann, how touched and pleased by the cordial good wishes from Willa Cather,[14] from Louis Bromfield, from Joseph Hergesheimer, from Eugene O'Neill,[15] from Paul Morand,[16] from André Maurois,[17] from Lion Feuchtwanger![18]

But there are friends and colleagues whose congratulations are noticeably absent. There are others whose intense amazement reveals what they really think. One cables all the way from England, "Well, I'll be hanged!" And there are always, every day, the newspapers!

"You know, I don't think I ought to have got it—it's a mistake," says my husband in a rueful voice, quite convinced by a columnist's brilliant polemic against him.[19]

Afterwards, in Sweden and Germany, we met some other Nobel Prize winners in literature. What a lightening of the heart! All of them, without exception, had had the same experience. In Berlin an enterprising young newspaper woman called upon my husband for an interview and began by saying, "We young people are so happy that you got the prize, Mr. Lewis! We thought it awful when the committee gave it to Thomas Mann."

"Young woman," came the roaring answer, "you are an ignoramus! I would give the Nobel Prize twice over to have written *The Magic Mountain* [1924, translated 1927]. It contains the whole tragedy of European culture. Have you anything further to ask me?"

On the *Drottningholm*[20] we are already in Sweden, and for the first time we begin to apprehend what receiving the Nobel Prize really means. We are not going merely to get a diploma, a gold medal, and a check. The Nobel Prize festivities, preceding the Christmas celebrations, belong to the brilliant events of Stockholm's winter season. Cables arrive: You must accept the following dinner or reception invitations—from the king, from the Nobel Committee, from your publisher, from the Foreign Press Association, from a group of United Societies, from the Swedish Academy, from the American Club, from the American chargé d'affaires.

Our heads begin to swim. I wonder whether I have sufficient evening dresses. My husband groans in anticipation of successive struggles with shirt studs to be pushed through boardlike surfaces. We begin to wonder whether Rabindranath Tagore[21] and Bernard Shaw, who took the prize but avoided the ceremonies, weren't wise.

More cables: Will you lecture in Copenhagen? In Gothenburg? In Berlin? Will you speak on the radio? "No! No! No!" cries my husband.

But the captain of the *Drottningholm* prepares us for the exquisite courtesy which we are to learn is characteristic of Sweden.

"As a Nobel Prize winner you are already a guest of my country," he says; and no visitors in a great private house could be more generously served than we by Captain Renstrom, who is the very prototype of all sea captains.

We study Swedish. This we have already begun in New York, using a method which has taught us that "the wagtail is a small, lively bird with a stiff tail"; that Rurik was a mighty chieftain in Sweden; that he sailed across the sea to Russia and was one of the first organizers of the Russian Empire. All this we can convey in quite convincing Swedish. But we have not mastered the art of ordering a dinner or asking the way to the railroad station.

At the Nobel Prize banquet, in the Stockholm Town Hall, I was taken in to dinner by Prince Sivgard, the young grandson of the Swedish king. "I understand that you have studied a little Swedish," he said politely in his perfect English.

"The wagtail," I replied in what I like to think was quite perfect Swedish, "is a small, lively bird with a stiff tail."

The young prince looked at me thoughtfully for a moment. Then he grinned. "That *is* the way one gets taught languages, isn't it?" he asked.

After that we chattered about America, where he had been a guest at the wedding of Miss Manville to his cousin, Count Bernadotte.[22] "I had a wonderful time," he said. "But are you so terribly hospitable to all foreigners? We never got a moment's rest. And your reporters!"

I thought of the Swedish reporters, who had come aboard the *Drottningholm* from the pilot ship at one in the morning, waking my husband out of a sound sleep, to ask him what he thought of prohibition, the League of Nations, international peace, Swedish food, and literature prizes, and grinned in my turn. "And Sweden—is it always so hospitable to foreigners?" I asked.

1. Birthplace and boyhood home of Sinclair Lewis in Sauk Centre, Minnesota (By permission of the Minnesota Historical Society)

2. Lewis at Yale (By permission of the Minnesota Historical Society)

3. Lewis in 1915 (By permission of the Minnesota Historical Society)

4. Grace Hegger Lewis (By permission of the Minnesota Historical Society)

5. Photograph of Lewis by Man Ray, January 1925 (Courtesy of Man Ray Photos.com and Artists Rights Society)

6. Lewis and his son Wells (By permission of the Minnesota Historical Society)

7. Lewis and Thompson depart for Stockholm in 1930 (Courtesy of the Library of Congress)

8. Lewis upon his receipt of an honorary Doctor of Letters degree at Yale in 1936 (By permission of the Minnesota Historical Society)

9. Dorothy Thompson testifying before the Senate Foreign Relations Committee in 1939 (Courtesy of the Library of Congress)

10. Lewis and Marcella Powers, 1939

11. Sinclair Lewis, David Shirer Jr., Joseph Hardrick, and Michael Lewis at Sherwood Forest Lodge in 1941 (By permission of the Minnesota Historical Society)

12. Lewis at his desk in June 1944 (By permission of the Minnesota Historical Society)

13. Lewis in his Duluth home in 1945 (By permission of the Minnesota Historical Society)

14. Lewis at chess (By permission of the Minnesota Historical Society)

15. Lewis on the portico of his Florence home in 1950

78 / Fanny Butcher

Never one to stand on ceremony, Lewis did not display his prize medal. In fact, he had trouble even locating it in his study.

Source: Fanny Butcher, *Many Lives—One Love* (New York: Harper and Row, 1972), 396–97.

The highest accolade of the literary life is the Nobel Prize for Literature, and that honor was made even more sparkling for Sinclair Lewis because he was the first American to receive it—in 1930. When the news came over the *Tribune* wires that the Nobel had gone to my "big brother," I rushed a letter of congratulations to him. He rushed back a note that said, characteristically, "Dearest Fanny, a million thanks for your letter. Little did we think in the days when we used to hold hands on the shore of Lake Michigan that I would have anything like this inflicted on me. Golly, I've got to grow a red beard and be dignified, and the beard won't grow and I can't be dignified."

I judged from what he told me later that the Nobel Prize really was a shock to him. He and Dorothy Thompson were married then, but he was out of town when word of the award came to her over the ticker tape, sometime in the middle of the night. She called him immediately, rousing him from a deep sleep to tell him the news, and, he said to me, "I thought she was guying me, so I told her what I thought about her for playing such a cheap joke on me and slammed down the receiver."

Soon after his return from Stockholm, where he had proof that it hadn't been a joke, I was in New York, and, curious, I asked him if the Nobel award itself looked like anything more than a check for thirty thousand dollars (which was its fiscal glamour at that time). "I'll show you," he said, and he began going through drawers, first in his desk, then in a tall secretary. "I haven't looked at the darn thing since I got back," he said, as he continued what proved to be a fruitless search. He called in his secretary, who had been with him fifteen years. "I've never seen it," was his helpful reply. Dorothy was out talking to a visiting prime minister, so she couldn't help in the search. Finally, by digging out every possible hiding place in the apartment, it was turned up. It was in a leather case about the size of a writing portfolio, its cover beautifully tooled with a replica of the New York skyline, and the citation itself was beautifully hand lettered. You can see it at Yale, if you're curious. He willed it to his alma mater, where he had gone a shy, gawky redhead from the Sauk Centre, Minnesota, high school.

79 / Louis Adamic

Louis Adamic (1899–1951), author, critic, and journalist, immigrated to the United States from Blato, Austria (now Slovenia), when he was fourteen years old. He learned English while working in the American West, became a naturalized citizen in 1918, and entered the US Army during the First World War. He first met Lewis in 1931 on the occasion he described in his autobiography.

Source: Louis Adamic, *My America, 1928–1938* (New York: Harper, 1938), 97–98.

Ben Stolberg, a close friend of his, brought Sinclair Lewis—"Red," as everybody called him—to the first Literary Rotary evening after his return from Sweden. The date was 1 April 1931. I think it was only our second party, and the group happened to be small that evening—about a dozen. We were all sitting about the vast round table in the corner, and had given our orders, when neat, round little Ben and tall, reedy, gangling Red entered.

Red had had cocktails somewhere else, and his eyes seemed to stick out of the narrow red face like a beetle's. He was forty-six, and his red hair was graying above the large ears. His hands were long, slender, beautiful; the hands of an artist. His manner was intensely self-conscious, uncomfortable.

Ben introduced him around the table. Red knew Harry Hansen, Lewis Gannett,[23] Henry Hazlitt,[24] and Walter White[25] and had heard of some of the others. His eyes stabbed into Hansen and Calverton.[26]

I scarcely knew most of my fellow rotarians, and was embarrassed when, as I was introduced to him, Red exclaimed, "Christ, Louis, you wrote a grand book!—*Dynamite* [1931]—just read it—jeez, a grand book!" He kept this up for half a minute or longer, holding my hand. I said, "Thank you," and saw the others smile at my embarrassment.

Red sat next to Ben, across the table from me. He ordered a wiener-schnitzel, which he hardly touched. He drank a seidel of beer.

The meal lasted about half an hour and everybody was uncomfortable. Red talked only to Ben and Lewis Gannett, and was almost antagonistic to all the rest, except me. There was very little conversation at the table, no joking or kidding, no telling of funny stories. Most of the men tried—vainly—to ignore Red. They did not dislike him, but were self-conscious before Ultimate Success in Literature in person.

Red kept looking at me; and when our eyes met, he winked. To Ben, who told me later, he mumbled, "I don't like this bunch. Louis is the only proletarian here. All the rest of you are highbrows."

He tried to talk to me, but it was next to impossible across the wide table. Scheffel Hall was a large, dinful place, with a small German orchestra playing a piece every five or ten minutes.

Embarrassed at being singled out by Lewis like this, I said, "Why don't you eat. Your schnitzel will be cold."

Red's face went into a grimace; he shook his head. "Say, Louis," he raised his voice when the orchestra stopped, "what do you say we go to Detroit and Chicago, you and I. We'll tour the industrial Middle West."

"What for?" I asked.

"A trip," said Red. "I asked Ben to come with me, but he's a highbrow—doesn't want to come. What do you say?"

I said, "It's hard to talk here. Let's wait till we get out."

He nodded and, folding and unfolding his long arms and clasping and unclasping his long hands, he continued to mumble to Ben about not liking this bunch, to stare and wink at me, and to look the picture of self-conscious discomfort.

Red's gaze suddenly fixed itself on Calverton, who had lately written an article, "Sinclair Lewis—Babbitt," for the *Literary Review,* published in Paris.[27] He looked at him for several minutes, then said sharply, "So I am Babbitt, am I?"

Calverton tried to laugh it off, unsuccessfully. He said something I could not hear. Red's eyes burned holes into him.

Thereupon Red turned to Harry Hansen, who was still on the *World.* "And you, Harry, what do you mean by printing in your 'Book Marks'—and on the day I return from Sweden, as if to greet me with it—that piece of gossip as to why I left Harcourt, Brace and went over to Doubleday, Doran?"[28] He was referring to a brief item Hansen had published about a week before, explaining why America's first Nobel Prize winner in literature had changed publishers. The item had seemed harmless enough when I read it, but had evidently been salt on some raw spot in Red's makeup. He ripped into Hansen, who replied calmly, trying to reason with him. Ben had his arm around Red's shoulder, saying, "Now, don't be a damn fool, Red." Lewis Gannett—typically of him—poured oil on the waters, saying to Red that now he was big news and all sorts of things would get into the papers—even into his friends' columns; and by the by the storm subsided.

As we were all leaving, Red took me by the arm. "I don't like this bunch. Do you? Highbrows!"

"Most of them," I said, "I met just recently, and really know only Ben, but some seem very nice fellows."

"Highbrows!" he repeated. "You come with me."

"Where?"

"We'll go somewhere."

I said: "I'm supposed to go with the group. We're having a sort of party. It's a monthly affair. Why don't you come with us?"

"No, no. [. . .] Highbrows! They think they know so much. Nothing worse than a highbrow. You come with me. I want to talk to you about taking a trip to Detroit and Chicago, Gary, Indiana, and places like that, and look at industrial conditions—workers, proletarians—not highbrows!" As I learned later, he had been thinking for some time of writing a labor novel and was working himself into a mood for the task. Hence his constant reference to "proletarians."

80 / Harrison Smith

Smith later remembered the comedy of errors when he and Lewis drove to New Haven to deposit the Nobel medal in the Yale library.

Source: Harrison Smith, "Sinclair Lewis: Remembrance of the Past," *Saturday Review of Literature,* January 27, 1951, 8, 36–37.

Then there was that fabulous and disastrous and finally well-publicized journey to Yale one Saturday morning, with Lewis carrying in his oldest overcoat an elegant box lined with satin in which was enshrouded the huge, solid-gold medal, the result of his Nobel Prize in literature. He was motoring up from Vermont with me for the summer in the farmhouse he had taken with his second wife, Dorothy Thompson, the brilliant journalist and the only human being I had ever seen who could talk Lewis down. I had picked him up at this house in Bronxville. "I can't leave the medal here," he said. "Everybody loves gold. How about giving it to the Yale Library?"

I thought that was a splendid idea, and in our combined innocence neither of us had sense enough to know that that was not the way to present anything of value to a great university. There should have been letters, an exchange of compliments, a committee at the New Haven station, and a banquet in Lewis's honor. Besides we were not dressed for it; we looked like a pair of tramps, and Lewis had had too much to drink the night before and showed it. But he was immensely cheerful on the way up the Post Road, embroidering in his best manner the shocked surprise, delight, and admiration with which Dr. Rush, the librarian,[29] would greet us. It was to be done with the greatest modesty, as if he had Nobel medals to hand out every day, and I was to make a short speech of introduction while Lewis flashed the gold platter before Rush's eyes.

Well, it was a shock most certainly, but it was delivered to the wrong parties. We waited on a marble bench, Lewis with increasing impatience. "Don't you suppose he knows who I am?" he muttered. When we were admitted to the presence there was a man at a desk who resembled a distinguished librarian sitting at his desk. He looked impatient, I thought, for his lunch and the football game later.

The dialogue went something like this. Dr. Rush: "What can I do for you gentlemen?" Considering our travel-stained appearance, this was polite of him. I made my little speech. "Dr. Rush, this is Sinclair Lewis, and I am an editor of Harcourt, Brace, his publishers. We have come to Yale from which we have both graduated to give you for your great library—" at this point Lewis flashed the gold medal, which looked as large around as a grapefruit, in front of the astonished man's eyes and I added at the perfect moment—"the medal of the Nobel Prize in Literature."

The performance was perfect theatre but, like some of Lewis's dramatic adventures later, it was a complete failure. "Are you interested in our collection of medals?" Rush said. "I can have you taken to see them." At that point Lewis blew up. I had never seen him so mad. The librarian would not be convinced, nor did he ever look at what was under his nose. We left, we fled down the marble stairs, and drove in silence for the next fifty miles. Lewis deposited the medal that summer with the Vermont Historical Society as a temporary loan, and it is now on permanent exhibit in the Yale Library, along with most of his manuscripts.

12
Grub Street
1932–39

Lewis was largely written out by the age of forty-five. The reasons are many: his drinking, the slow collapse of his marriage to Thompson and their eventual separation in 1938, the pressure to satisfy the expectations of a new publisher, the troubling rise of fascism in Europe and the start of a world war. Although he still wanted to write his labor novel, instead he published such poor if popular books as *Ann Vickers* (1933), *Work of Art* (1934), and *The Prodigal Parents* (1938), as well as the topical *It Can't Happen Here* (1935). Strangely, Lewis also took a long detour from his career as a novelist by scripting several plays, including adaptations of *Dodsworth* and *It Can't Happen Here* and a May-December romance titled *Angela Is Twenty-Two* (1938). He even launched an acting career.

81 / William L. Shirer

William L. Shirer (1904–1993), journalist and historian, broadcast for CBS from Germany during the first year of the Second World War and became famous for his *Berlin Diary* (1941), which covered the years 1934–41, and for *The Rise and Fall of the Third Reich* (1960). He knew Lewis and Thompson in Vienna during the winter of 1932/33 and in his memoirs remembered the stresses on their marriage.

Source: William L. Shirer, *20th Century Journey: A Memoir of a Life and the Times* (New York: Simon and Schuster, 1976), 449–50, 451–52.

Dorothy and Red arrived in Vienna at the end of the summer of 1932 and rented a large apartment in the Wohlebengasse and a spacious villa on the Semmering, two hours by train south of Vienna in the mountains. At first they seemed quite happy, especially Dorothy, who was soon holding forth, as was her wont, in her salon crammed with admiring journalists, diplomats, statesmen, and what was left of the German, Austrian, and Hungarian aristocracy, discussing everything under the sun—art and love, but above all politics. This had been a problem for the Lewises ever since they were married four years before in London. Dorothy was much at home in Europe among Europeans; Lewis was not. Much of the conversation at Dorothy's gatherings was in German, in which she was extremely fluent but which Red scarcely understood. He felt shut out of the talk, and his inevitable reaction, which was mercurial, was to stomp out and leave not only the party and the dwelling but the city. He was always taking off in a huff for other parts. Except for the American correspondents, Red could not stand Dorothy's friends. Nor, even when he understood it, their talk. Politics did not interest him and he developed a phobia for her obsession about "The Situation."

"If she would just stop talking about 'The Situation,' for Christ's sake!" he would say as I followed him to a bar, after he had made a hasty exit from one of Dorothy's talkfests. "If she'd just call it off for five minutes! But she can't. I've got to listen day and night to her prattle about the *goddamn Situation.*" [. . .]

All through the winter in Vienna and on the Semmering he grew more irritable and drank more heavily, spending most of his time in the villa in the mountains, away from Dorothy. Already in their New York apartment, someone remembered, they had reached a point where they needed not only separate bedrooms but separate living rooms.

"Sometimes I think you don't see me at all," Dorothy would write him from Vienna after he had taken off for Italy following a quarrel, "but somebody you have made up, a piece of fiction, like Ann Vickers." It was his excessive drinking that bothered her most, and she would confide to his biographer of their life at this time that when he came to her room, late at night and drunk, he smelled of rotting weeds.

82 / Dorothy Thompson

Notwithstanding her concern about Lewis's drinking, Thompson admired his integrity. Even after his death, long years after their divorce, she allowed that she harbored a "bleeding pity" for him that was "a deep and ineradicable form of love."[1]

Source: Dorothy Thompson, "Sinclair Lewis: A Postscript," *Atlantic Monthly* 187 (June 1951): 73–74.

I recall that, early in the Nazi regime, Klaus Mann (son of Thomas) started publishing in exile (as I remember, from Amsterdam) an *émigré* monthly.[2] He wrote Sinclair Lewis describing the paper as a vehicle for young exiled German writers, and asking S.L. to allow his name to be used on the masthead as a "contributing editor." Red refused on the ground that he was not "a young German writer," was unwilling to sponsor a publication which he would be unable to follow, and believed that publications should stand honestly on their own feet. Klaus Mann, however, came out with the first issue without waiting for Red's answer, with his name on the masthead—a fact which was first called to Red's attention by a cabled protest from his German publisher, Ernst Rowohlt.[3] Red's books were still selling extremely well in Germany, and Rowohlt cabled him that the Mann publication was a "disgusting *émigré* sheet" and that his continued association with it would lead to the suppression of his books in Germany.

Now, it would have been simple and truthful for Red to have replied that Mr. Mann had used his name without his consent and despite his refusal—and Nazis or not, Red, as you know, wanted his books read. Actually, also, he was thoroughly annoyed with Klaus Mann. But his immediate reaction was that his relations with young Mann and his publication were none of Rowohlt's (or the Third Reich's) business! He cabled Rowohlt:—"DEAR ERNST HAVE YOU GONE CRAZY QUESTION MARK DO YOU HONESTLY THINK I WILL LET YOU OR YOUR GOVERNMENT OR ANY OTHER GOVERNMENT TELL ME WHAT I SHOULD WRITE OR WHERE I SHOULD PUBLISH"

Now, Ernst Rowohlt (as his record has shown) is no tower of civil courage.

But, right from the heart of Nazi Germany, he cabled back:—"THANK GOD THERE ARE STILL SOME MEN AMONG WRITERS."

Red, I later heard (from Rowohlt), was the only writer among those whose names had been exploited on the Mann masthead, and whose works were still published in Germany, who did not yield under similar pressures from their own German publishers. And actually Red's books went on being published and circulated until he wrote *It Can't Happen Here.*

His hunger for "culture" was really deeply moving. Like most writers he was a poor linguist. But there is something wholly admirable in his determination to learn Italian at the age of sixty. Until he was over fifty he had no interest whatever in music. Suddenly he "discovered" it, and thereafter, for years, the phonograph was playing the classics five or six hours a day—sometimes it could be maddening! He hated all games, until in his late middle age he determined to master chess. (This was after our separation, and I don't know what kind of chess player he became.)

But the fanaticism you noted extended to everything. He never did anything for fun. He was a peripatetic self-improvement association—dragging his intimates with him, too, and insisting they share his earnest efforts, often until their nerves were screaming in rebellion!

83 / Fanny Butcher

In the fall of 1933, as Butcher remembered, Lewis began to collaborate on a pre–Civil War play set in "Bleeding Kansas."

Source: Fanny Butcher, *Many Lives—One Love* (New York: Harper and Row, 1972), 394.

During our long friendship, he never railed at me, even during the years when he was bitterest, and his drinking seemed to make him want to hurt everyone. [. . .] His drinking did not seem to interfere with his work. That was plain to me one day which I spent with him and Lloyd Lewis[4] when they were writing a play together. It was about the Civil War and was called *The Jayhawker*. It was an unforgettable experience listening to them battling over a word, getting up and acting out a scene, rejecting it, revamping it. Hal was a paragon of sobriety while they were working. Before the word battle began they read me what they had already written; we emerged from the 1860s for lunch, took up arms again afterwards, and I left with stirring words jangling in my head, fascinated by the way that two of the most articulate people I knew could pick words out of and implant ideas in each other's mind. But I went home to write in my diary, "Hal looks sixty-five instead of forty-eight, and thick—it made me sick to see what drinking had done to him." When *The Jayhawker* opened in Washington, I was one of what was plainly a delighted audience, but the play didn't last in New York.[5]

The stage had an irresistible allure for Hal. In one way his best novels were essentially dramas, for much of their unique appeal was in the dialogue. He had a kind of electronic recording mechanism in his mind that caught nuances of speech and could reproduce them. He loved pretending he was a Babbitt or an Elmer Gantry or a gas-station operator in Okmulgee, Oklahoma, and often he would go on for hours in his act. Sometimes it was stitches-in-the-side funny—though sometimes it was boring.

84 / George Seldes

At Lewis's insistence, Seldes became his near-neighbor in Vermont and remembered him with unqualified affection. He had been expelled from Italy for his criticism of the fascists, and Lewis often talked politics with him while he was writing *It Can't Happen Here.*

Source: George Seldes, *Witness to a Century* (New York: Ballantine, 1987), 289–90, 292.

In 1933, my wife and I, who had been guests of the Paul Osborns[6] in Brattleboro, Vermont, decided to stay on that summer at a nearby boardinghouse. One day Lewis and his wife, Dorothy Thompson, driving home to Barnard, Vermont, from New York City, stopped by and urged Helen and me to buy a house in their neighborhood. Lewis said, "You'll be near the best college library [Baker, at Dartmouth] and the best hospital in New England [Mary Hitchcock Memorial and Hitchcock Clinic, Hanover, New Hampshire]."

I replied, "That's great, except for the fact Helen and I haven't got any money."

"But I have too much," Red replied, and persuaded us to come with him to Woodstock.

We liked the first little house the real estate agent showed us: it was built in 1783, the last year of the Revolutionary War, and had wooden pins, not nails, holding it together. It had a gravity water supply. It had no heating except fireplaces, no electric light, no telephone within miles. It did have 125 beautiful acres, and a view of the entire Green Mountain range. The price was $4,500.

Mr. Lewis took out a checkbook and made out a check to me for two thousand dollars. He then told the agent he would guarantee the mortgage—which was also two thousand dollars. Helen and I, with help from Gilbert,[7] [Seldes, his brother], raised five hundred dollars, and later that summer we moved in, bought an automobile, which Helen knew how to drive, and registered as voters.

Of all the great writers I have known in my seven European and American working decades, only one became a real friend. Hemingway chose to exhibit his dislike of my brother by attacking me; Theodore Dreiser was too difficult for anyone but adoring women to call more than an acquaintance; but of the great men of the literature of our time Sinclair Lewis was the one easy to become friendly with; and when my wife and I were his neighbors in Vermont we became good friends even before we had the chance, not once but several times, to save him from delirium tremens, perhaps even to save his life. He became so good a friend he could in sober as well as alcoholic moments confess the most intimate details of his life and still remain a friend. [. . .]

There was never any small talk at the Lewis table in Vermont. Sometimes there was an obvious subject—doctors for *Arrowsmith,* preachers for *Elmer Gantry,* Nazism and Fascism for *It Can't Happen Here.* But a recurring topic over many years was the great American labor novel that was to be the Lewis masterpiece. It haunted him, it was discussed between each successful book, and labor writers were at Lewis's table year after year. He probably accumulated filing cases of notes, but he never wrote the book. Perhaps it was because he had not come from a working-class family.

Sometimes, when not trying out parts of his work in progress, Lewis would talk about anything at all—from religion to his relations with his first wife. He once said, "God is *lachryma Christi*"—or Christ's tears of doubt—and once he said something that so impressed me I wrote it down immediately: "The Christian Church today is either an apology for no God at all or for God's mistakes."

85 / Malcolm Cowley

Malcolm Cowley (1898–1989), novelist, poet, critic, and journalist, spent three years in Paris after the First World War. There he met Lewis one evening at the Café Dome just when the sales of *Main Street* passed two hundred thousand. Or as Cowley later remarked, "In the year 1921, if you visited the parlor of almost any boarding house, you would see a copy of *Main Street* standing between the Bible and *Ben Hur*."[8] Later, Cowley worked in New York as an editor at the *New Republic* and an editorial consultant for Viking Press.

Source: Malcolm Cowley, *The Dream of the Golden Mountains* (New York: Viking, 1980), 296–97.

I learned that the most argued-about of the fall [1935] books was Sinclair Lewis's *It Can't Happen Here*—not much of a novel, I thought on reading it, but a vigorous antifascist tract. Many of the left-wing writers were delighted with its success and hoped that its author, the Nobel prizeman, would become their champion. Somebody in the League of American Writers conceived the notion of holding a semiprivate dinner with Red Lewis and his wife, Dorothy Thompson, as guests of honor. I wasn't enthusiastic about the proposal, knowing Red as I did, but still (with Henry Hart, who was in publishing, and the poet Genevieve Taggard)[9] I signed the letter of invitation. [. . .]

The dinner in the big room above John's Restaurant[10] was a disaster, even though half a dozen speakers abounded in praise for Lewis and his novel. Lewis kept glancing around suspiciously; his face was like a rubber mask drawn tight over a skull. Had he been drinking again? Clearly he did not propose to be inveigled into joining the League. Dorothy Thompson, seldom a quiet woman, this time had few opinions to express. Finally Lewis burst out with a speech. I forget his words, but I was sitting near the poet Horace Gregory,[11] who quotes him as saying: "Boys, I love you all, and a writer loves to have his latest book praised. But let me tell you, it isn't a very good book—I've done better books—and furthermore I don't believe any of you have *read* the book; if you had, you would have seen I was telling you all to go to hell. Now, boys, join arms; let all of us stand up and sing, 'Stand Up, Stand Up, for Jesus.'" The boys and girls stood up embarrassedly. Horace and I made our way to the door without saying good night to the guests of honor.

86 / Benjamin Stolberg

Benjamin Stolberg (1891–1951), a Marxist author and journalist, was particularly active in the field of American labor. He was an editor of *Bookman,* a columnist for the *New York Evening Post,* and contributed to the *New York Times,* the *New York Herald-Tribune,* the Scripps-Howard newspapers, and many magazines. He was also an unofficial advisor to Lewis on his aborted labor novel.

Source: Benjamin Stolberg, "Sinclair Lewis," *American Mercury* 53 (October 1941): 450–53, 459.

When Rebecca West, the well-known English writer, first met Sinclair Lewis, she was exhausted. "His talk is wonderful," she said, "but after five hours I ceased to look upon him as a human being. I could think of him only as a great natural force, like the aurora borealis."

Lewis takes no exercise, he plays no games, he has no hobbies. His main relaxation is his own talk. Even his silences seem like rest periods between torrential monologues. He goes on at top speed in a high, flat, midwestern voice, driven by a sort of *furor satiricus.* Yet his talk is curiously impersonal. It lacks all intimacy and is singularly free of private gossip or personal references. When now and then he does dwell on some personal problem, it sounds like a page from *Dodsworth*—for anyone to hear. Some comparative strangers have listened to what seemed very private revelations, until they realized that these revelations were not really private. They were merely stories of the tribulations and experiences of a character named Sinclair Lewis in a preposterous universe.

Lewis's conversation deals chiefly with the human fauna—its amusing or amazing customs, its gregarious imitativeness, its love of gadgets, its ridiculous fears and hopeless hopes and endless misunderstandings. Now and then he touches on its capacity for decency, even tragedy or heroism. But always he discusses this human fauna with the objective air of a natural scientist—in a constant stream of brilliant reporting, uproarious burlesque, superb mimicry, and shrewd, often wickedly shrewd, observation. He has a genius for making people remind one of human beings—just as monkeys do.

His usual method is to inflate the pompous, the trivial, the false, and then let some imaginary character do the deflating for him. And his characters are so preposterously lifelike because he has the gift of picking out, and pumping dry, their stereotypes in real life. Finally it dawns on the listener that it isn't talk at all; it's work. Lewis's discourses are the workouts of a great satirist. They are an expression of his perpetual obsession with the folkways of American life.

One afternoon three of us were sitting on the porch of his Vermont farmhouse, when a stranger drove up and introduced himself as Elmer Whoozit, the local representative in the state assembly. Immediately Lewis was galvanized.

"Why, hello," he said. "You're just the man I want to see; I'm thinking of going into politics myself. One of these days I may run against you."

"That's fine," grinned Mr. Whoozit. "I plan to run for the state senate this fall, and you can take my place. Sinclair Lewis succeeds Elmer Whoozit! Why, that's wonderful! Be glad to help you all I can."

The two of them promptly launched into the campaign. Under Lewis's hypnotic guidance, Elmer spilled all the tricks of local politics—whom to see, what to promise, what to avoid. We got the lowdown on the neighboring farmers, storekeepers, politicians. His vernacular was priceless.

With the greatest of ease Elmer Whoozit and Red Lewis got themselves elected. Then Lewis decided that Elmer mustn't get stuck in the senate. He must run for governor; and Lewis would succeed him in the senate. But only on one condition: the Whoozit-Lewis machine must reform the state. They would clean house, introduce the most enlightened legislation, turn Vermont into a model commonwealth. For just a moment Elmer hesitated, then he agreed. And he obliged us with a detailed, and quite cynical, analysis of the state machine, told us who's who and how they got that way and how to handle them.

Again Whoozit and Lewis were elected. Vermont became the most advanced state in the Union. The thing to do was to get the nation to catch up with it. And so Elmer went to the United States Senate, while Lewis followed him into the governor's mansion.

At last Elmer began teetering on the verge of the Presidency. Would Lewis back him up? Would he be willing to run for the Senate? Would he lend his genius toward making this country a *real* democracy? Elmer enlarged on national Republican politics, gave us his views on what this country needs. The scene was incredible, unforgettable. Here was a small-time politician unconsciously—even better: half-awarely—satirizing his own kind.

Finally Lewis got tired of the game. "Hell," he said, "who wants to be a senator? I should never have gone into politics in the first place." Later I met Elmer Whoozit again, fleetingly and in various disguises, in the works of his ephemeral political pal of that afternoon.

This episode sounds cruel. But it wasn't. It was a hilarious game in which we all partook. What Lewis really did was to get himself and Elmer so wound up that they couldn't stop, they had to go on vying with each other in the verisimilitude with which they enacted their rise in American politics. And in acting out his part, Elmer gave all he had as a professional politician. Lewis gets so fascinated with people, so excited by what interests them—and he is so assimilative—that he enters their world as one of them. [. . .]

Last summer Lewis was very angry with me for suggesting that Britain is our first line of defense. "Sure," he raged, "sure, the English are our first line of defense—ever since Valley Forge. And they anticipated the Monroe Doctrine by burning down Washington in 1812." Soon after the election—he voted for Roosevelt—he was for aid to Britain short of war, and still is. But should the country rapidly drift toward belligerency, he'll go with it. He moves with the Mississippi Valley. He doesn't change his mind—not any more than a thermometer changes its mind about the weather. [. . .]

The preparation of Lewis's last book, *Bethel Merriday,* which deals with the career of a young actress, drew him into the theater. He started in his usual way to gather all the material he could about the stage, and soon became part of it. He wrote two plays, *Jayhawker* (with Lloyd Lewis) and *Angela Is Twenty-Two,* a May-December romance, in which he played the part of December. He acted in other shows all over the country. He also dramatized *Dodsworth* (with the late Sidney Howard)[12] and *It Can't Happen Here,* which was put on simultaneously in twenty-one cities by the Federal Theater Project.

The Germans wanted to produce *Dodsworth* and asked Lewis and Howard to prove their Aryan purity. The authors regretfully notified Dr. Goebbels[13] that their "real names" were Levy and Horowitz.

87 / Ramon Guthrie

According to Guthrie, Lewis worked for several months on his "labor novel" in 1936 before again abandoning the project.

Source: Ramon Guthrie, "Sinclair Lewis and the 'Labor Novel,'" *Proceedings of the American Academy of Arts and Letters* n.s. 2 (1952): 74–79, 81–82.

In April 1936 Red asked me to start serious work with him on the labor novel. He was in good shape. *It Can't Happen Here* had restored his confidence in himself. He had not tasted so much as a glass of beer in twenty-six weeks. During the spring we had several sessions together on the book.

Basically the plot was the same as it had been nine years earlier in Venice. Roy (as we called the hero tentatively) was to be a home-grown Gene Debs. In the course of his groping for a God who is at once the tears and the meaning of things, he was to become a radical and to suffer the penalty for his convictions. Because of *The Man Who Knew Coolidge,* the original title would have to be changed. We considered a number of alternatives, among them *The Unconquerable* and *Roy against the World,* neither of which we liked much.

As soon as I could get away in June, we set out for Connecticut to gather documentation. My experience over a period of half-a-dozen years as a semi-skilled laborer in various Connecticut factories qualified me as enough of an expert for Red's purposes. I had worked on most kinds of machine-tools and still remembered enough to know a shaper chuck from a collet. As a refresher course, Red acquired a small library of machinist's manuals and set me to studying them.

Working on a book with Red, as I already knew from what little I had done on *Dodsworth,* was always a hectic job. One had to be on tap twenty-four hours a day. Red himself could get sufficient sleep by snatching naps, of anywhere from a few minutes to a couple of hours, between ideas. Whenever a new idea occurred to him, he dropped everything else and started off in full cry after it—on the quite valid theory that the surest way of getting the thing done was to do it immediately.

We covered the Naugatuck and Connecticut valleys from a variety of angles. The program of a typical day was a morning of conferring, getting notes into order, reading local newspapers for names, activities and interests, lunch with a factory owner or executive; an afternoon spent inspecting a factory or two and a C[ivilian] C[onservation] C[orps] camp; dinner in a beer garden with a group of workmen; a post-midnight snack and a prowl through some of the more obscure quarters of town with a police reporter. One of our closest friends was a mountainous triple-chinned German chief mechanic named Emil whose artistry on a milling-machine fascinated Red. On the night of the first Louis-Schmeling fight,[14] Emil took us to a combination gambling joint and speak-easy—though prohibition had been repealed a good two years earlier—to listen to the bout.

Although Red was incognito only to the extent that he signed hotel registers as H. S. Lewis, in order not to be hounded by reporters, most of our acquaintances among the workers knew nothing about this Mr. Lewis except that he was good company and had something to do with books. They talked naturally and easily with him. Once when he protested at never being allowed to pay for any part of the several meals he had with them, one of the men explained, "Hell, Mr. Lewis, you're just too swell a guy for your money to be any good around here."

Around two or three o'clock in the morning, when I would manage to get to bed with more hope than expectation of getting some sleep, Red was apt to drop into my room for a last cigarette and a few final questions such as:

"What kind of an operation is a buck-grinder used for?"

"Tell me once more the difference between a pawl and a dog. How do you suppose dogs ever came to be called that?"

"Would an educated mechanic—one who had a high school education—say 'morphadite' for 'hermaphrodite'?"

"How much difficulty would a boy of Roy's intelligence have in understanding *Das Kapital*?"

"When did conveyor belts first come into general use?"

"Can an ordinary lathe-hand read a blueprint? How long does it take to learn to read a micrometer—a 'mike'?"

"Do you think we should have Zoe join the CP?"

"What would the population of Torrington have been in 1910, and what did they make there beside needles and skates?"

"What did you say the difference between a dog and a pawl is again?"

Sometimes I was afraid that we were getting too much documentation. Red shook the suggestion off. "The main reason for having documentation is to know how much of it you can leave out. I may not even mention a turret-lathe once in the whole book, but I must know why I don't."

As a matter of fact, it irritated him to be thought of as belonging to the "slice of life" school of literature. "Sure, I'm a photographic realist," he said. "Like James Joyce—only a hell of a lot less so."

Warned by the debacle of 1929, I took particular pains not to seem to be writing his novel for him. Occasionally, after he had been thinking aloud about a character or a situation for a while, he would ask me to take over. Now and again, he would interrupt to say, "That's not a bad idea. Let's get it down on paper." Other times he would cut in with: "No, he doesn't do that. Here is what he does, though!" and take up the story again himself. Talking things out in this way was no more than mulling around in the general atmosphere of the novel and not serious enough for us to argue about. We had talked over *Dodsworth* in its earliest stages in the same way.

He always solicited suggestions, on plots, characters, episodes and dialogue as well as details of documentation. He took them for what they were worth and nothing more. As an instance of the basis on which we worked, one of Red's notes to me reads:

> Drrmn
>
> much thanks for your letter abt strike—I shan't follow it exactly, but it gives me lots of ideas. [. . .] You make Zoe [the heroine of the novel] a little too flip; she is slow-spoken, brooding, accurate.

In a subsequent note, he wavers on Zoe's character: "Let's get away from the skinny young heroine of today; but Zoe is in danger of being too lush." Another memorandum defines her as being "attractive in cynical gaiety."

Actually the personality of Zoe was not overly important to the story. Roy was the character that counted; and Roy, the gangling boy with "red, almost orange hair," born in a New England Sauk Centre, of parents who used Dr. E. J. Lewis's favorite catch-words against him, was Red Lewis himself.

The end of our trip, and as it happened of the labor novel, came suddenly. We had invited some of our friends—mostly workers in a Naugatuck plant—to dinner. It was Red's idea, and until within an hour before we were to meet them, he seemed enthusiastic about it. Suddenly, for no reason that he could think of, he made up his mind not to go. Simultaneously he declared that, since my wife was planning to come down from Vermont to spend the Fourth of July with friends of ours, it would be a gracious gesture if, to spare her the hot train ride, we drove up to get her. His plan further called for us to stop overnight at Provincetown on our way and then drop in for lunch with Sidney Howard who was living in the Berkshires.

When I pointed out that what he was proposing was a jaunt of some seven to eight hundred miles and that, since he disliked traveling more than a hundred miles a day in a car, it would take us a week to do it, he was unimpressed. His contention was that since Provincetown was in Massachusetts, it *must* lie somewhere along the direct route from Connecticut to Vermont. In the end, he agreed to my suggestion that I stay on in Connecticut long enough to fill in some of the gaps in our notes. He insisted on leaving his own car with me and hiring a car and driver to take him to the Berkshires.

Next morning, as he was getting into the hired car, he spoke enthusiastically of how much we had accomplished and how much fun we had had doing it. Then, as the car started up, he added a final word that is still something of an enigma to me. Here it is, verbatim: "And now I am sorry I have to go home and be a fascist." He said it as if he really *was* sorry—sorry for himself and that it had to be.

Nothing was said, then or ever, about abandoning the project. It was understood that we were to meet in Vermont and go on with our work. As a matter of fact, we did put in a few more sessions on it, but by the end of the summer he had already begun writing *The Prodigal Parents.* [. . .]

One of the principal reasons why Red abandoned the labor novel seems to be that, consciously or not, he had come to regard it as a book that he "ought to" write. [. . .] In the hero [of *The Prodigal Parents*], Frederick William Cornplow of Sachem Falls, Red did a sympathetic caricature of a small-town Babbitt in revolt against not only the new-fangled highfalutin-ness of his children and their demands on him, but also against society's, and even his own, concept of what he "ought to do." Plaintively he wants *somebody* "in this doggone family to do what they want to do for once." [. . .]

Red seems never to have put the labor novel entirely out of his heart. In 1947—twenty-two years after it first occurred to him, he revamped the original title into *The God-Seeker.* When Aaron Gadd, the hero of this historical novel of early Minnesota, invites his employees to form a union, it is almost surely a faint resemblance of the novel he never wrote.

88 / Budd Schulberg

Budd Schulberg (1914–2009) was the son of B. P. Schulberg, the chief of Paramount Pictures, and grew up among screenwriters and filmmakers. He later received Academy Awards for his screenplays of *On the Waterfront* (1954) and *A Face in the Crowd* (1957), though he is perhaps best known for his novel *What Makes Sammy Run?* (1941). As an undergraduate at Dartmouth, he visited Lewis in late fall 1935.

Source: Budd Schulberg, *The Four Seasons of Success* (Garden City, NY: Doubleday, 1972), 31–53.

Nearly forty years ago, when Lewis published *It Can't Happen Here,* I was at Dartmouth College in Hanover, New Hampshire, editor of our daily paper and, naturally, bristling with antifascism. [. . .] *It Can't Happen Here* was the high sign we had been waiting for: Lewis was one of ours. [. . .] My own enthusiasm for Lewis, and for his welcome commitment to the antifascist cause, was brewed to the boiling point when the avant-garde poet and Proust scholar, Professor Ramon Guthrie, a close friend of Lewis's in those Paris Left Bank days ten years earlier, asked me if I realized that "Red," as he called him, was living just over the mountain, near Woodstock, Vermont, an easy hour's drive. Practically a neighbor!

The following weekend I decided to combine the pleasure of a day-off excursion with some editorial business by driving over to call on Sinclair Lewis and interviewing him for the school paper. Most of my English professors, along with a pride of sophomore lions, put it down as a foolhardy mission. Lewis had become virtually a recluse. His ill temper was notorious. I would find a small army of servants, secretaries, bodyguards, and castle dragons to run me off. "So what's the worst that can happen to me?" the boy in me countered. "After all, he can't eat me!"

"On the contrary," said an aging bachelor professor of English who specialized in obscure modern poetry and acidic notes on our earnest literary efforts,

"I am under the distinct impression that roasted undergraduate is one of the favorite dishes on his menu. I'm not joking, Schulberg. I wouldn't risk it."

Nevertheless, that Friday afternoon I found my way across the White River and into the trees protecting a large white clapboard estate house a few miles beyond Woodstock. I took a deep breath and knocked on the door. I had to knock several times before anyone answered. Then the door swung open and a tall, skinny man with long arms and legs and one of the ugliest faces I had ever seen looked out and barked at me, "Well? What d'ya want?"

A small voice that sounded stuck in its throat hesitatingly identified me as the editor of the Dartmouth College daily and a friend of Professor Guthrie's.

"What the hell are you stammering for?" he barked again.

"I'm stammering because [. . .] I stammer," I stammered. "Makes me sound more frightened than I—I really am."

"Huh. All right. Come in."

The house was warm and inviting and lonely and empty. There was a wonderful, long living room lined with books and looking out through a wall of glass onto a seemingly endless terrace that dropped down in a series of broad, grassy steps. I kept looking around, surprised to find no one else in sight. No servants, no secretaries, no wife. "Mrs. Lewis"—that was the well-known Dorothy Thompson—"is off on a lecture tour," he answered my silent question. "Wanna drink?"

I followed Mr. Lewis into the kitchen to help get the ice and the mixings. On the way back I paused to look at the shelves of European editions of Lewis novels. I felt a sense of awe and youthful envy. Then we went out on the veranda overlooking those grass terraces, and started drinking together. It was easy talking because we shared, from opposite ends of the telescope of age, an enthusiasm for Ramon Guthrie. "I'm crazy about Ramon," Lewis said in a voice rather loud for an audience of one. "He c'n do 'em all—paint, fly, write novels, poetry [. . .] The only thing I thought he couldn't do is hold down a job in a conservative New England college like Dartmouth. You know I got 'im the job. Never thought he'd hold it more'n a year or two. Good old Ramon! Of that whole nutty crowd over in Paris he was one of the few who had genius. Only trouble was, he was a genius in so many different directions. If he ever settles down to one, he'll take it all."

We went in and refilled our glasses and I paid my courteous and sincere obeisance to the Lewis novels that I had enjoyed. They were books, I tried to say, that had made me laugh uncomfortably at the cultural wasteland of Middle America. "Oh, George Babbitt isn't such a bad guy," Lewis said. "Actually I kinda like him." He seemed pleased, but not particularly anxious to talk about the old ones. The only book alive for him at that moment was *It Can't Happen Here.* I addressed a self-conscious, or, rather, socially conscious, tribute to the book: how important it was that an author of Lewis's stature—our first and then our only Nobel Prize winner—had taken so firm and uncompromising an antifascist position. That was the way we talked in those unalienated days. "We've just formed a campus chapter of the League Against War and Fascism—Ramon is one of our faculty advisers—and *It Can't Happen Here* has given us some valuable ammunition, Mr. Lewis," I said. Eased by the highballs and his informality, I was hardly stammering any more.

"Oh hell, call me Red," he said. And then completely ignoring my mouthful of social significance, he said, "That Charlie Coughlin,[15] he's really something, isn't he? Christ, but he gives me a kick!" [. . .] Taking stage in the middle of the living room, Lewis delivered an impersonation of Father Coughlin and his radio rabble-rousing that reduced it, or elevated it, to first-rate vaudeville. I had known some novelists before, mostly those who had come to Hollywood to mend their fortunes,[16] but I had never encountered one who could act out and mime his material this way. The way he talked of "Charlie" Coughlin reminded me of once having seen Charlie Chaplin[17] do an impromptu Schickelgruber[18] routine at a party, years before his classic charade as *The Great Dictator*. Looking back it may seem odd to compare the comedic talents of Sinclair Lewis with those of Charlie Chaplin, but on our third highball, as he racked up Coughlin and moved on to Huey Long, William Dudley Pelley, Fritz Kuhn,[19] and our other American would-be Führers, it struck me as an inspired, satirical performance. We made an oddly assorted pair that afternoon. I had been sternly and perhaps immaturely incapable of taking our homegrown Gauleiters[20] lightly, while Red Lewis seemed congenitally incapable of taking them any other way.

Although I had come with a headful of questions, somewhere during the interview—which grew inadvertently into a visit—my host became the more aggressive questioner. The marble workers were on strike in the nearby Rutland-Proctor area, and Lewis—by this time at his insistence I was tentatively calling him "Red"—wanted to know all about it. [. . .] Only a few miles from where Red was living, I told him, were company towns, feudal in structure and fascist in effect, where indigenous storm troopers were terrorizing foreign-born quarry workers with shotguns, clubs and patriotic threats. *It Can't Happen Here,* I warned my host with undergraduate zeal, was not only a prophetic book but its dire prophecy was already *happening,* and practically on the doorstep of this luxurious farmhouse.

An eager listener as well as a great talker, Lewis responded with the sharp, staccato questions of a crack reporter, pressing me for *details,* not *theories.* He had a passion for the former, and a loathing for the latter. Now I found myself taking his place, taking stage and pacing up and down that spacious living room as I went on with my story of the boy journalist aiming his sling shot at the all-powerful Goliath of Vermont. [. . .] It all sounded like the plot of one of those righteous Depression novels then coming into fashion, and Red's reaction was a characteristic amalgam of serious interest and vast amusement. He plied me with good questions and good Scotch and I warmed to my subject, describing the native humor of the quarry miners that I was trying to work into a college play.[21] [. . .]

Red's laugh was like the bark of a seal. He warmed to the idea that the strikers didn't take themselves too seriously. One of the things that he despised about fascist movements was their lack of humor. He thought Hitler and Goebbels and the Brown Shirts were able to take over Germany because "the goddamned krauts never had a sense of humor." In spite of the doomsday novel he had just written, he really didn't believe that Americans would fall for the applesauce of a Hitler or a Mussolini.[22] The reason "Hooey" Long had gone as far as he had was that he had never lost touch with the earthy humor of the Louisiana rednecks who took to his slogan, "Every man a king." Red saw the assassination of Long as a sign that tyrants might find the going harder here in America than in Europe, since we were freer of ritual and dogma in a land where the independent, inquiring spirit still survived. He saw hope in the cussed independence of the Vermonter, despite the moneyed hierarchy and its hired troopers that I had come up against in Rutland. When I told him about Archibald MacLeish's efforts to rally fellow writers to the strikers' cause,[23] Red said he wouldn't go anywhere to please Archie MacLeish because he had no use for poets who wrote about Democracy with a capital D. Instead, he wanted to hear more from me about the facts of the case: how much the marble workers earned an hour, how much the marble was sold for, and what kind of profit the Proctors[24] enjoyed?

Sharp questions. And full answers. Another hour passed. It had begun to grow dark. We moved inside and when I saw what the hour was, I told Red I was afraid I had overstayed my welcome. On the contrary, he assured me, he had begun to wonder about this new left-wing "Farrell and Steinbeck" generation[25] and I was the first on-the-hoof example of "whatever the hell this new thing is" that he had a chance to know. I thanked him and said I'd like to drive over again some afternoon. Any time, he said, but if I had no plans for dinner, why not stay on and take potluck with him?

So we drank and talked on. Swapping stories and political notions. Disagreeing now and then, but congenially. Neither one of us was pie-eyed, as we used to say then, but the mood was mellow. He told anecdotes of his now-forgotten early fling with socialism, his adolescent attachment to Upton Sinclair's communal farm, and his prewar season of idealism when he was a dues-paying member of the Socialist Party. He scoffed at the young believer he had been when he was twenty-one, a quarter of a century earlier—gently mocking my own condition.

He talked of his fascination with hotels, whiskey, people—especially Americans. Like H. L. Mencken, his fellow member in the league against boredom and "boobocracy," Lewis had a big love-hate thing going for Americans: "If you wanna write, stay put, stay near what you know best, don't let yourself get trapped over there with the Ritz Bar oh-boy-are-we-having-fun-and-ain't-we-artistic! Set. I say 'Write American First.'"

The telephone rang and since he picked it up in the hallway off the living room where we had been sitting and made no effort to lower his characteristically boisterous Midwestern voice, I could eavesdrop unashamedly. I wish I could play it back word for word, as I was able to with some of his literary pronouncements. Alas, John O'Haras[26] come one to a lifetime. But it went something like this: "'Oh, hello dear, where are you now, Philadelphia?' I realized it was his indefatigable lecturer-wife Dorothy Thompson. 'Oh fine, I'm awfully glad the talk went so well, yes, I called the plumber and he's coming to fix that leak tomorrow, no, I won't forget to tell him about the powder room too, yes, the painter was here this morning to put on the second coat and the garage looks swell, I think you'll be pleased. Where do you talk tomorrow night? Oh, that's right, Baltimore, fine, dear, fine.'" [. . .]

As I listened, I began to hear a different Lewis from the all-powerful, all-confident Nobel Prize winner I had conjured on my way over to Woodstock. I may have been reading too much into it, but on the phone he had sounded subdued almost to the point of subservience. A different, more complicated image had begun to superimpose itself on the bolder and apparently oversimplified one that had first taken form in my hero-worshipping mind. To the authoritative, busy opinion-maker Dorothy Thompson, Sinclair Lewis seemed to have become the man who kept the home fires burning. I found myself wondering if the arrogantly famous figure that had been projected for me was simply a lonely man rather desperate for company and perhaps even for reassurance.

"Dorothy's packing 'em in everywhere she goes!" he was saying with what struck me as forced cheerfulness as he returned to the living room. "Seems like nobody knows what to think of Adolf [Hitler] and Benito [Mussolini] and FDR until she sets 'em straight." I felt the pride and the sarcasm were about equal measure. "Come on, let's look in the icebox and see what we can find for supper."

After dinner there was more talk and whiskey, while we took turns pacing the big living room and leaning on the classical white mantel in front of the crackling fire. Red kidded me, but good-naturedly, about what he called my "sophomore socialism." He said the worst thing about it was that it seemed to make us "Ivy League Marxists" so damned pompous and closed-minded. Hell, he said, even Gene Debs didn't carry on about it the way we young doctrinaires were doing. But then, he added, Gene Debs was an American original. He admired men who spoke their minds and took their lumps like Gene Debs. The way he said it came out as one word, *GeneDebs,* and it took me some moments to realize that his casual GeneDebs was the same man I had thought of in capital letters as The Great Eugene V. Debs with a Socialist halo around his head. Red told me of a train ride he and GeneDebs had taken together, when all the railroad workers had dropped by to shake their leader's hand, and while I was still marveling at this, he said, almost in the same breath, that of all the outstanding Americans he had known he thought "the two greatest were probably Gene and Herbert Hoover."[27] In those years, for most of us, Hoover was a dirty word. We still called the Depression shantytowns *hoovervilles.* Hoover was the bloated plutocrat in the top hat in Gropper's *New Masses* cartoons.[28] So I told Red that comparing Debs to Hoover was like comparing Joe Louis to Kingfish Levinsky.[29] To admire one would be to despise the other.

Lewis laughed at what he called my innocence and then vigorously defended his free-wheeling position. I wasn't sure that night and I've been uncertain ever since as to whether or not Red tossed Hoover in with Debs just to get that rise out of me. To dent my pretensions, my absolutism. He took a Huck Finn's delight in puncturing balloons. It struck me that he had a wonderfully quick intelligence that was not at all concerned with ideas. If his GeneDebs was an American original, so was my RedLewis. [. . .]

By this time my firsthand research on Lewis had enveloped a full eight-hour day plus a few hours' overtime so I apologized for overstaying my welcome and moved toward the door. But there was the drink for the road, and then another, and finally an hour later Red was saying, "It's a helluva long drive over the mountain at this time o' night. Might as well stay over, I've got plenty o' room." So we talked and drank our way into the dawn, and then adjourned until the early afternoon. Saturday was a repetition of Friday, even to the phone calls from the peripatetic Dorothy and his dutifully domestic reports. By Sunday I was definitely the boy who came to dinner. Lewis's luxurious white frame farmhouse had become a home away from home and dormitory life at Dartmouth seemed years ago and far away.

Back in Hanover, I was to discover on my return, my friends had become so anxious about me that they actually had called the police stations in various towns along the way. I was a notoriously erratic driver in those days, given to speed combined with absentmindedness. [. . .] But all of this time the only risk I was running was from an oversupply of Red's very fine Scotch. By Sunday night we were bosom bottle companions, fairly wallowing in companionability, both acknowledging how well we complemented each other—youth and age, radical and conservative, fledging writer and world-famous literary figure—both agreeing it was one of the best damned stimulating weekends we could remember. The early hours of Monday morning found us moving on to personal confidences, the quick-witted twenty-year-old dancer back home I wanted to marry, and his various complicated wives and his concern for his young son Michael. By the time I finally drove away around noon on Monday, feeling like a flagpole sitter coming down from my record seventy-two-hour interview, I remember even feeling a little guilty at leaving poor Red alone, with his wife busy pontificating all over the country. He stood in the doorway and waved me off, a lonely figure against that big empty house.

At Dartmouth the following evening I reported my adventure to Ramon Guthrie, who told me he already had heard of the talkfest from Lewis himself: I had scored a tremendous hit with Red, who instinctively hated or loved people on sight. What Red had not told me—with typical literary slyness, as I was to learn from other authors in time—was that he had been planning a labor novel, and already had done considerable factory and union research under Ramon's guidance. In fact, over the past six years this would-be novel had become something of an obsession with Red, his quest for the great white whale, the big novel of political idealism that seemed constantly to elude him. He had even thought to use Debs as a central figure, and the reason he had not confessed this to me in the course of our long weekend was that as much as he admired and worshiped Debs, there was something about the subject matter that defied and defeated him. Ramon Guthrie, of course, who knew Red Lewis far better than I, having been close to him both in France and in Vermont, now speculated that his friend suffered from a split social conscience. Genuinely aroused by injustice, he responded to Debs, Sacco and Vanzetti, Clarence Darrow, and Tom Mooney.[30] At the same time the inborn skeptic in him prevented him from making any deep commitment to their causes. In our bibulous discussions far into the night, apparently Lewis had been partly in earnest, reflecting his natural suspicion of any organized causes and partly baiting and devil's advocating me to see how well I could defend my position, which in many ways had once been his own, and for which he still held a flickering allegiance.

Now I began to realize something more complicated. I had not quite walked into Mr. Lewis's parlor like the innocent fly I had thought myself. Ramon Guthrie, that gentle, sly, benevolent Machiavelli, concerned for his friend's literary health and wanting to see Red achieve the labor novel that had been frustrating and haunting him so long, saw me as the ideal young catalyst who could recharge Lewis's enthusiasm for this on-again-off-again mission. My involvement with the marble strike—how an upper-middle-class college boy gets drawn into the labor struggle, moving from academic theory to active participation—was the perfect grist for his timely but temperamental mill. I had become, in Red's absorbent mind, the model of the generation coming of age in the depth of the

Depression. Red would like me to drop in as often as possible, Ramon said, more or less to sit for my literary portrait.

Flattered and intrigued, I drove over to Woodstock a number of times after that. Red seemed to be moving vaguely left again in his own highly individualistic way, and I threw all my missionary zeal into encouraging him. Ramon Guthrie was delighted with the progress I seemed to be making. Admittedly a hard-shell skeptic, Red Lewis was prone to question any social movement, even one as all-embracing as the New Deal. But Ramon thought he saw signs of his famous friend's gradual reconversion to a more humanitarian, socially engaged point of view. Beginning to pierce his armor of iconoclasm, I now sensed in Lewis a kindness, a genuine affection even for the people he pretended to despise. Although Mencken is often considered his mentor—his "antisoul brother," we might call him today—there was hidden in Lewis a love of humanity clearly not shared by the bourgeois-baiting curmudgeon from Baltimore. I did my youthful best to tap this hidden spring. I told him human-interest stories of the marble workers' lives that overlapped with his memories of Debs and the railroad strikers. I knew his loathing for hypocrisy and I evoked the smug college majority, those children of the well-to-do who studied Social Problems in the abstract while an honest-to-god social crisis was right under their noses but somehow beyond their sight. I reminded him how generous the Proctors were, as benefactors of the College, while refusing to give an inch in their negotiations with their underpaid marble workers. I tried to put this in my own words, without resorting to the Marxist jargon that the *New Masses* and the other communist organs had borrowed from the prose style of Stalin[31] and Eastern Europe. I didn't mention "the toiling masses" and I carefully avoided "surplus labor value," a concept from *Das Kapital* I had never fully digested anyway. It seemed to be working. Red, that fantastic talker, seemed to be listening. He even agreed to accompany me to Proctor, talk with the miners, and lend his name to their cause.

When I thought he was ready I suggested to Lewis, rather tentatively, that he come over and speak at Dartmouth. We—us liberals, deep thinkers, and social philosophers—had a long-hair discussion group called the Junto, modeled on Benjamin Franklin's old philosophical circle, and I thought it would be a fine idea if Lewis would lead a group discussion on "Fascism and the Novel." Somewhat to my surprise, Red accepted. Enthusiastically. If all the Hanover undergraduates were like his new young friend, his manner now seemed to suggest, he was ready to embrace them all. In addition there was his insatiable curiosity. What were these children of the Depression and our spreading fascist wars *really* like? By this time Red had begun to conceive of a young Ivy League leftist as the hero of his labor novel, in fact had decided to broaden his work from a strictly labor to a "hopeful new generation" approach. It seemed his search for the "big novel of political idealism" at last was coming into focus.

On the campus the coming of Sinclair Lewis was considered quite a coup. I was congratulated even by a few of the varsity football intelligentsia, who promised to be on hand for this celebrated occasion. I served as chairman and by way of introduction told the now legendary story of "my weekend with that ferocious recluse, Sinclair Lewis." Red chuckled appreciatively, the audience laughed and smiled with him and we were all one happy, mutually admiring family. Red did his Charlie Coughlin routine, and then his Huey Long, and quoted from his fictionalized Senator Windrip, and our young highdromes of the Junto were amused. But as he went on with his vaudeville, almost exactly the same act he had played to an audience of one on my first visit to Woodstock, I grew a little uneasy. I knew my fellow-members and I could read their faces. This was too serious a matter for spoofing. They were waiting for the Nobel Prize winner to say something profound and socially significant about Fascism. Instead, Lewis wound up with a well-told jest. I asked if there were any questions.

Alas, there were: those deep, theory-ridden, humorless, classroom-scented questions that can spring only from the mind of the teenage intellectual elite.

Did Mr. Lewis realize that fascism was not an isolated, historical phase but the final, inevitable, decadent, death-rattle stage of capitalism?

Mr. Lewis cleared his throat and muttered something about not having to be a social scientist. He was just a goddamn novelist.

But how could Mr. Lewis be so politically naïve as not to relate his novel on fascism to this final stage of capitalism in which the crumbling democratic façade reveals the decadent and inevitable violence of dictatorship as the last stand of the ruling class against the revolutionary masses?

Is that a question, or a synopsis of your senior thesis? Mr. Lewis wanted to know.

If this was a storm warning, Lewis's questioners, or rather inquisitors, were sublimely unaware.

Next question: If Mr. Lewis had not studied and absorbed—as obviously he had not—the theories of the leading antifascist philosophers, historians, and economists—John Strachey,[32] R. Palme Dutt,[33] Lewis Corey (author of *The Decline and Fall of American Capitalism,* who had lectured to us at Dartmouth a few days earlier in a voice of neo-Marxist doom),[34] if Mr. Lewis had not read Thorstein Veblen[35] and the precursors of the antifascists social scientists, then how could Mr. Lewis presume to write a book about fascism, even if it pretends to be a work of fiction?

From my place of honor as chairman I could see Red's jaw going tight. His weirdly mottled poison-ivy complexion seemed to grow even blotchier. His answers grew increasingly monosyllabic, shot through his teeth. He thought he had written a *novel,* a book to be *enjoyed,* not a goddamn Marxian tract. "And who the hell is R. Palme Dutt? Sounds like a character out of W. C. Fields!"[36] Red got his idea for Senator Buzz Windrip from Charlie Coughlin and Kingfish Huey, he told them, "not from some highly debatable, indigestible, and unpronounceable economic theory."

Lewis's short-tempered jabs were just what they wanted. My fellow Junto-ites closed ranks and pressed the attack. Is there anything more delicious for the callow intellectual pack than to bring down a literary lion? Or, to shuffle the menagerie deck, for the hagiology hounds to hold the great undoctrinaire stag at bay? I tried to head them off with a diplomatic parry, a safer, more purely literary question of my own. Too late, too late. A sociology honors student locally famous or notorious for his straight A's and his Engelsian[37] zealotry took dead aim on Red with a great bomb of a question "about Coughlin and silver and the business cycle linked to fascism and the final, repressive stage of capitalist imperialism?" Yes, that was a real fire-bomb of a question, fused with Lewis's ignorance, or defiance if you prefer, of economic theory and political cant.

"You little son of a bitch!" he answered. "All of you! Young sons o' bitches! You c'n all go to hell!"

There went my author, stomping out on those long, stilt-like legs. Exit Nobel Prize winner. A pox on Hands Across the Generations!

Some twenty minutes after the debacle, I followed Red to Ramon Guthrie's snug house across the Connecticut River in Norwich, Vermont. The fire in our honored guest was far from subsiding. In fact he had been stoking it with generous helpings of alcohol. With a tall Scotch in his hand he was telling the room, in that bellicose Middle American voice of his, exactly what he thought of those goddamn supercilious snot-nose know-it-all book-stupid theory-ridden little bastards. Oh ho, would he fix their wagons! *Now* he knew what this young generation was like the little smart-ass sons o' bitches! He was just lucky he had found out in time. Oh, those young smart-aleck Xz#"&'s.[38] [. . .] It was our Nobel Prize winner at his most emphatic if somewhat redundant self.

Thus was my missionary work undone. Back to Woodstock roared the literary lion, to lick his wounds and—Ramon Guthrie can substantiate this—revise his attitude and his book just as he had threatened. Out of this spleen came *The Prodigal Parents*—alas, one of the lesser efforts of Sinclair Lewis, a furious larruping of the young, cocksure, left-wing, out-of-kilter generation that *thinks* it knows more than its parents and is sadly and unforgivably mistaken. The hero of this unhappily shallow little novel was "Fred Cornplow," the name a giveaway to the heavy-handed and ill-conceived travesty in which the elder Cornplows are betrayed by the radical irresponsibility of their children. The Cornplows, whom Lewis sets up as American paragons, are comic-book rotarians, rural patriots who seem to have sprung from the pages of the Chamber of Commerce magazine. Searching in vain for the social satirist of *Babbitt* or the student of American values who created *Dodsworth,* I read it with a troubled heart. It seemed, in fact, as if the gifted parodist was playing a trick on us by engaging in self-parody. But sadly, the trick was on himself. Incredibly, Red Lewis, the friend of Debs, admirer of Darrow, and seeming convert of the young radical who had come from Dartmouth College to restore his faith, had crossed over to the side of the Babbitts and Hoover's Liberty Leaguers.[39] And in making that crossing he had seemed to leave his entire steamer trunk of talent behind him. Red Lewis had become Fred Cornplow. The rebel had become the philistine. In retrospect that process would seem to be organic and gradual. Could he ever have known his George Babbitts and Elmer Gantrys so well if he had not been their brother under the skin? Still it seemed to me at the time that on every page of *The Prodigal Parents* I could hear echoes of Red Lewis's Battle of the Junto.

I felt sick about it. As an influencer of great men I had struck out my first time at bat. Ramon Guthrie tried to console me: This switch was characteristic of Red, an intensely erratic, blow-hot-or-cold man, full of flashing intuitions, but with no guiding philosophy to hold him on course. That's why he could be a liberal, a radical, and a reactionary on three successive days. For him the only possible-ism was intuitivism.

As if to dramatize this description (thereby adding injury to insult), Red finally did go over to inspect the marble strike as I had asked him to, only to give what I considered aid and comfort to the enemy with his statement to the *Rutland Herald* that he was not particularly impressed with the marble workers' cause. Ramon Guthrie and I managed to get our easily exacerbated author to modify this rush to judgment so as not to do further damage to the marble workers.[40] We gathered that Red had not calmed down from his 100-proof rage when he sounded off against the strike in Rutland. It was not the strikers he was mad at. He simply lumped them impulsively with those goddamned Dartmouth brats and the Marxist manifestoes they used in place of human speech.

If this were fiction instead of fact, my narrative would come to a downbeat climax here with Lewis not only wreaking literary vengeance on the smart-ass generation that had done 'im wrong, but swearing to eat me alive if ever I climbed up his beanstalk again. The truth is somewhat less tumultuous. After the Junto fiasco I saw Lewis less often, but I still dropped in occasionally. A few days before graduation exercises I drove over to tell him the good news that Bennett Cerf,[41] the president of Random House, on one of his flying lecture tours, had stopped off at Dartmouth long enough to pick up my marble-strike series and had offered me a contract with a modest advance in case I "ever thought of doing a novel." I had published a couple of short stories in little magazines and was in that first happy flush of taking myself seriously as a writer. I told Red I was thinking of settling down near Dartmouth and taking a stab at my college marble-strike idea. Red thought that would be a damn-fool mistake. (That is always the way I remember him talking—profane, spontaneous, and violently opinionated.) "You come from one of the crazy American cities!" he shouted, "*Los Angeles*! What a novel there is in L.A.!" I should go home and write what I knew, the city I knew, not the marble strike that he looked on as a temporary affection or a passing phase. He hung on to that point, and a year or so later when I *was* back in Los Angeles, he wrote a pointed little essay in *Newsweek* that began: "There is in Hollywood, which is the beauty-factory of Jersey district of Los Angeles, a young man who graduated not long ago from a New England college, and who wants to go back to the little stone-walled fields and write fiction. Well, [. . .] if my young friend really wants to write fiction, he is deserting in Los Angeles a gold mine for which Balzac[42] or Frank Norris or even Dickens would have given anything—except possibly Dickens his fancy waistcoats."[43] [. . .] The piece was practically a playback of my graduation-week conversation with Red Lewis, without the choice four- and five-letter words, as he walked me out to my car and presented me with an inscribed copy of *It Can't Happen Here.* "To my fellow counter-revolutionist," he had written, "even though he doesn't know it." Another five years of Party-line convulsions were to pass before I was to find myself as disillusioned and later outraged by the doctrinaire left as he had been the night he was Red-Lewis-baited.

I took maybe half of Red's literary advice, which is about all one should expect of a very young man. I finally gave up the marble-strike project and for my first novel went back to my town and some firsthand responses to the film industry I had been exposed to since childhood. But I did find it more conducive to finish that book in the stone-fenced country of Vermont.

Although I continued to see Lewis now and then, I can't remember either of us ever mentioning *The Prodigal Parents* again. Like the five forgotten novels before *Main Street,* which put him and Main Street permanently on the map, *Parents* turned out to be one of his most appalling failures. I hardly could have felt more responsible if I had written the irascible work myself.

But even sadder to tell, this book was not a brief, angry aberration but an augury. There were other novels of Red Lewis's through the 1940s, but, with the possible exception of *Kingsblood Royal* [1947], they were put down as flabby Americana, difficult for a Lewis fan to place on the same shelf with the books our first winner of the Nobel Prize was writing in his thirties rather than his fifties. From age thirty-five to forty-five, Sinclair Lewis had performed the hat trick plus two, producing every other year a work of fiction that enhanced his reputation and lent vigor and definition to the American Novel. But by the time Red Lewis was fifty-five, he was, in the strange tradition of American letters, a burned-out old man. [. . .]

In the early forties, when my first book *What Makes Sammy Run?* appeared,[44] I'm afraid I already had begun to think of Sinclair Lewis not as a living inspiration (like the John O'Hara of *Appointment in Samarra* or the John Steinbeck of *In Dubious Battle*) but as a relic of our literary history. This fall from grace was further emphasized by the publication of *Bethel Merriday,* a novel that seemed to confirm the creative collapse that Red himself had predicted in his rainbow year of 1930. *Bethel Merriday* was a thinly disguised portrait of a teenage would-be actress with whom Red had been traveling on the straw-hat theater circuit [Marcella Powers], passing her off as his "niece"[45] after the inevitable breakdown of his marriage to Dorothy Thompson.

In this period Red and I met occasionally in the office of the editor whose friendship and solicitude we now happened to share; this was the selfless Saxe Commins,[46] who had brought Eugene O'Neill to Random House and nursed Bill Faulkner through his agonies. He had held Red's trembling hand on many occasions when the fireball of American letters, who may be the inventor of the modern American novel, was sinking into a bewildered darkness. When Red wrote a feeble play entitled *Angela Is Twenty-Two,*[47] embarrassingly tailored to the histrionic talents of his comely young protégé and her fifty-six-year-old protector, and insisted on touring with her in this unfortunate vehicle, I remarked to Saxe—regretfully, though perhaps with the arrogance of youth and the taste of my own early success—that Red Lewis appeared to be entering his second childhood.

Saxe Commins, an unsung St. Francis of the publishing world, long-suffering, infinitely patient, and immaculately discreet, expressed the hope that Red's lapses would prove to be only a passing phase—a bridge to a new period of productivity and maturity that would restore his friend to the pinnacle from which he had toppled.

There was to be a kind of last gasp with *Kingsblood Royal,* when Red tried to settle down to serious research in Duluth, returning in forlorn desperation to his Middle Western roots, to face a major social problem: the failure of our white culture to accept the Negro American into the mainstream of first-class citizenship. The issue still remains at the center of our efforts to prove the validity of our democratic experiment. Red had hold of a live one here, at least another *It Can't Happen Here,* an effective propaganda novel if less than a work of art. But for all its good intentions, the focus in *Kingsblood* is so soft, the author's grip on his material inadequate to the inherent force of that material. And Red's craftsmanship seemed increasingly weary or careless. I happened to be in Commins's office going over the galleys of my second novel when the *Kingsblood* galleys came in. Saxe had pored over the manuscript with Red at his new country home in Williamstown, but he knew that the writing was still uneven and he had queried many paragraphs in red pencil on the galleys. Red had answered Saxe with a note that confirmed my fears that he was letting his creative responsibilities go by proxy. The note simply permitted Saxe to make those changes and cuts he thought judicious. Engaged writers fight like tigers over every comma.

Red seemed to know, in appointing Saxe his surrogate, that *Kingsblood Royal* would never be the novel of social protest he had hoped to achieve. The novel of political idealism, the book Red Lewis all his life had wanted to write, and for which I once had been chosen to serve as a youthful model, had wound up as a bloodless tract. The fact that it touched a nerve, carried a glittering name, and achieved bestsellerdom despite negative reviews, only etched more deeply the predicament of a failed seer who came into his sixties with nothing more to say, his talent in disarray, his familiar American bridges collapsing behind him, his health destroyed through the excesses of escape. Who would have guessed that the irascible defender of "Write America First!" would wind down in Italy as the kind of driven expatriate he had ticked off so pitifully when I first met him in Vermont?

Just twenty years after the Nobel Prize had recognized the champion of the new American novel, the wreck of Red Lewis gave up the ghost in Rome. Destroyed by fame and self-destroyed by the bitter knowledge of the premature failure of his genius, he had been dying, slowly and terribly, ever since he finished *Dodsworth* at the age of forty-three. The speech in Stockholm that had rung out like a challenge to American philistinism, that had riled American traditionalists, and that had promised so much, turned out to have been his swan song.

89 / Fanny Butcher

Lewis's gift for mimicry apparently impressed the actress Helen Hayes, with unfortunate results.

Source: Fanny Butcher, *Many Lives—One Love* (New York: Harper and Row, 1972), 394–95.

One day, when he was in town [Chicago] very briefly, he asked Dick and me to stop in for a drink with Helen Hayes and her husband, Charles MacArthur.[48] Hal had never met Helen Hayes, although she had played the heroine of *Arrowsmith* brilliantly in the movies. (He once told me Dr. Sondelius was his favorite of the characters he created.) Charlie was an old friend of mine from his *Tribune* days, and of my husband's from their Rainbow Division days together in World War I. The ebullient Charlie rushed over to give me a smack and Dick a smashing pound on the back. In the doorway Helen waited, a tiny Griselda reluctant to intrude on what must have looked like old home week at dear Aunt Liza's. His enthusiastic greetings over, Charlie remembered Helen and said heartily, "Meet my squaw."

Soon Hal became, to the life, a real-estate man trying to make a deal with a woman for a four-room apartment, over her complaints about too little closet space. The realtor was privately gloating over his success in closing the deal, when the potential tenant casually mentioned her ten children. Hal put on a superb act, spurred to epic achievement by the presence of the great Helen Hayes. It is almost inevitable that everyone says to an incomparable mimic (as he was that night), "You ought to be on the stage." When those words were spoken with authority by Helen Hayes he accepted them as coming from on high—and I always thought that the reason Sinclair Lewis turned actor was the direct result of that brief encounter.

90 / Hallie Flanagan

Hallie Flanagan (1889–1969), playwright, author, director, producer, and director of the Federal Theatre Project, a division of the Works Progress Administration, worked with and knew many of the most significant figures in the theatrical world. In this excerpt from her autobiography, she reminisces about her collaboration with Lewis on the production of the theatrical version of *It Can't Happen Here,* which opened simultaneously on twenty-one stages in eighteen cities on October 27, 1936.

Source: Hallie Flanagan, *Arena* (New York: Duell, Sloan and Pearce, 1940), 115–16, 122–23, 127–29.

His play [*It Can't Happen Here*] was produced under the joint auspices of the Federal Government, Sinclair Lewis, Jack Moffitt,[49] their agents—Ann Watkins, Harold Matson, and Pat Duggan[50]—and the harassed staff of the Essex House,[51] which for several weeks moved in steady processional to the apartment of Mr. Lewis bearing libations of ice water, typewriters, and black coffee—not, I hasten to add—at government expense.

Written? Too mild a word. The play was produced by polygenesis. It was partly created by Mr. Moffitt who paced up and down in his apartment at the Essex House and threatened, if Mr. Lewis did not omit certain scenes and include others, various unusual reprisals; it was simultaneously springing almost visibly from the brain of Sinclair Lewis who, in another apartment of the Essex House, composed and acted every part differently every day. "Let's change the whole scene to an interior and have the Corpos beat Doremus almost to death—Bosworth, take the typewriter in the other room and pound out a rough draft and Hallie and I will just sketch through the details." At this point a note would be slipped under the door saying that Mr. Moffitt would appreciate it if I would communicate certain things to Mr. Lewis. Mr. Lewis would then communicate certain things to Mr. Moffitt, and since by that time I was the only acceptable medium of communication between the embattled collaborators, I would, on the way up to Mr. Moffitt with the message, communicate certain things to the Almighty, the only being in whom I could safely confide. [. . .]

Sinclair Lewis, writing all night, found time to work at casting by day. On the stage of the Adelphi he interviewed all applicants, heard them read, hand-picked the entire cast. Now he was distracted by the production details. At seven o'clock on Sunday morning, 25 October 1936, my telephone rang: "I haven't slept all night—for the matter of that as you know I haven't slept for weeks. Nobody can say I haven't given everything to the Federal Theatre. [. . .] Now it is all terrible—everybody has gone into a coma. [. . .] I want you to get right on the train and come to New York and postpone the play a week and get new people to do everything, or do it yourself. Why, the living room they have got up there on the stage looks like a cheap boarding house on Second Avenue. It doesn't look any more like the house of Doremus Jessup than I look like Jack Moffitt. It is all terrible. It is all a failure."

When I reached the Adelphi everyone was in a state of jitters except Kate Drain Lawson, Jack Lynds,[52] and Adams Rice, whose cool common sense endeared them to me forever. We went into a secret huddle in the alley back of the theatre.

"Is there any technical reason why the curtain can't go up Tuesday?" I asked. Adams Rice said no, and Jack Lynds said, "If it doesn't happen then it will never happen here." [. . .]

"It Can't Happen Here" seemed to have practically unlimited audience appeal: in New York City alone the Yiddish version played 86 performances to 25,160 people; the Adelphi version, 95 performances to 110,518; and the Suitcase version, touring the five boroughs, ran the play in repertory from the October opening to the following July, playing 133 performances to 179,209 people. The long tie-up of the Adelphi became an embarrassment, due to our other commitments. On 20 December [1936], Sinclair Lewis in one of his always memorable telephone calls said:

S. L. Well, Hallie, it's all over—I'm sorry but it's all over. Now don't say a word—I know it's not your fault, but you told me a week ago that I could have my own cast at the Adelphi; you know I gave the better part of my life to that cast; I trained them myself; I sat there day after day going without food, going without sleep. [. . .]

H. F. I know that, Sinclair. We all appreciate that.

S. L. I suffered, I tell you—nobody knows what I suffered. Why, I made that play out of my life's blood, and you know it's the only good play that the Federal Theatre ever did—am I right?

H. F. Well—

S. L. [. . .] The only play the Federal Theatre has ever had a chance at, and here it is, playing to packed houses, turning people away by the hundreds—and that, mind you, in spite of the fact that there's not a word in the papers about it—everybody in a conspiracy to keep anybody from knowing that a play of mine is on Broadway. And now you close it—you move it into a back alley somewhere—you take all my beautiful actors that I have trained with my own hands and put them in some other play. [. . .]

H. F. I've explained. . . .

S. L. I don't want explanations—I want my beautiful cast, the cast that I am devoted to, to the cast I trained myself [. . .] and you promised me last week that you had this all fixed up. [. . .]

H. F. Sinclair, we're not closing the play, just moving it to another house. You know at first you said we could only have it for three weeks and with that in mind we signed a contract with Barrie Stavis to put "The Sun and I" into the Adelphi on a certain date[53]—he's already waited weeks—he's holding us to our contract—I thought you agreed to all this at the meeting and I sent you a confirmation of this by letter.

S. L. Why do you send me all those thin carbon copies of letters—you are always sending me those thin letters and I can't read them. When you want to talk to me why don't you just call me up?

H. F. I don't call you up oftener because it costs a lot of money—you talk like a novel.

S. L. Well, I don't think I'm asking much for all I've done for Federal Theatre. I've been patient and reasonable, and you said yourself I had done more for Federal Theatre than any living person.

H. F. Did I say that?

S. L. It was in one of those thin letters; anyway, I am through now—absolutely through; there is nothing you can do. George Jean Nathan is here spending the night with me and he thinks . . .

Mr. Lewis relented. The play went on and on, not only in the original cities. [. . .] In an amazing variety of methods, in English, Yiddish, and Spanish, in cities, towns and villages, before audiences of every conceivable type. "It Can't Happen Here" played, under Federal Theatre, 260 weeks, or the equivalent of five years.

91 / Edward Robb Ellis

Edward Robb Ellis (1911–1998), journalist and diarist, whose life's work, *A Diary of the Century,* chronicles events of nearly every day from 1927 until 1995, recorded details of Lewis's visit to Oklahoma in 1937.

Source: Edward Robb Ellis, *A Diary of the Century* (New York: Kodansha International, 1995), 79–81.

Thursday, 28 October 1937. The other day when I learned that Sinclair Lewis was coming to town [Oklahoma City] I became excited and prayed I'd be assigned to interview him. He will go on to the University of Oklahoma in Norman to give a lecture entitled "The Novelist as a Prophet."

Sinclair Lewis has been a literary god to me ever since my college days when I twice read *Arrowsmith,* weeping each time. [. . .]

Well, the famous man arrived here today and I was lucky enough to be told to interview him. Lewis was staying in the home of Dr. Roy Rutherford, pastor of the First Christian Church. I arrived at the minister's home at 9:15 this morning with a *Times* photographer, Milt Mumblow. Two other reporters were there. When I said my photographer would like to take a picture, the minister fluttered like a bird in a bath and chirped:

"Oh, Sinclair, take this davenport over here—that's it!—and sprawl for these boys just as you did a moment ago. Boys, Sinclair is at his best when he is draped on the end of my davenport here. That's his real self—nonchalant, you know. That's it, Sinclair, right over here!"

Fighting the impulse to hold my nose, I wondered whether this candy-dandy minister was the model for Elmer Gantry, the hypocritical and unscrupulous evangelist in the writer's novel of that name. I also thought that his friends called him *Red.* He yanked himself out of a chair, walked over to the davenport and sat down on one end. I slipped into the seat at the other end because this placed me closer than the other reporters; he spoke toward me most of the time.

Lewis is taller than I had expected and has a belly like a basketball—something I'd not seen in photographs of him. Fifty-two years old, a prolific author, a

Nobel Laureate, world-famous, Sinclair Lewis is a very ugly man. His face looks like a skull.

"Well," he began, with a grin like a big crack, "and what can I tell you about the state of the nation?"

Dr. Rutherford slapped his knee, again and again, then roared:

"State of the nation! State of the nation! Did you get that? Best I ever heard! State of the nation, indeed!"

I wanted to vomit.

Ignoring the exuberant evangelist, Lewis began speaking.

"I am," he said, his tongue tucked into his cheek, "a reactionary. Or at least that's what they tell me—those who have read my latest book. It's to be out January 21. This book of mine tells about the revolt of the younger generation. I'm calling it *The Prodigal Parents.* My principal character, Fred Cornplow, is a middle-aged man who suddenly declares that he, too, might as well raise a little hell. He is just a shade more analytical than Babbitt was. Babbitt was introspective only when he had a hangover." Then he might possibly bring himself to the point of asking himself, "Why did I make such a damned fool of myself last night?"

Sinclair Lewis chattered with the speed of a machine gun. It was obvious that he likes to hear himself talk and, having gotten in a plug for his next book, he skittered from one subject to another and strayed so far afield that I interrupted him a few times to put some pertinent questions. The other reporters couldn't get in a word sideways, whereupon I became as smug as the pastor. Talk about *him* being an ass! Nonetheless, when Lewis mentioned Charles MacArthur I told two anecdotes about him that I'd read in Woollcott's *While Rome Burns,*[54] with Lewis keeping his eyes on me, and when I finished he guffawed in appreciation.

But he wanted to get back to his next novel, saying: "The chief editorial writer of the *Daily Worker* has abused and even threatened me for becoming a reactionary because, he says, my book is against communism.[55] This is stupid because it is not against communism. It is not even about communism. One of the characters just happens to be a communist for a time. She is a young girl who takes to communism temporarily as she might take to doing literary reviews for tea table women's clubs."

I asked how he gets the data he uses as the theme or background of his novels.

"I'm trying to get away from documentation," he replied. "I don't take voluminous notes. Notes don't serve any purpose but help one remember what he already knows. I overdid this documentation in *Arrowsmith.* There was too much bacteriology in the book. However, I guess I had more fun writing *Arrowsmith* than any other of my books because while getting the material I knocked around the Bahamas and down around there."

Aware that Lewis had been a reporter, I asked how he liked journalism.

With a grin he replied, "I was fired from a paper in Waterloo, Iowa, one in San Francisco, and the Associated Press."

"Why?"

"Why? [. . .] I was just naturally incompetent! If I liked the man I happened to have interviewed, I'd go back and write a dandy story. But if I didn't like him, my story would be a flop."

Dr. Rutherford walked over and put his hand on the arm of the author, then turned to us reporters and said: "Well, Sinclair has to go up now and get his shave. He must get some rest, too, you know. He has a busy day ahead of him. Better come on now, Sinclair."

Sinclair Lewis kept spouting words, gesturing with his free hand, eager to go on talking, but the minister tugged at his arm, so he arose and let himself be led out of the room, still chattering like a machine gun.

92 / John Hersey

John Hersey (1914–1993) was a Pulitzer Prize–winning author and journalist, whose article "Hiroshima" in the *New Yorker* for August 31, 1946, has been called one of the finest pieces of journalism of the twentieth century. He briefly worked as Lewis's private secretary during the summer of 1937.

Source: John Hersey, "First Job," *Yale Review* 76 (Winter 1987): 188–90.

Lewis's life [in 1937] was in a mess. But I was to have a marvelous summer, oblivious of his suffering. He never took a single drink while I worked for him; I remained in total ignorance of his history. I saw a surface that was gentle, kindly, boyish, and vividly entertaining. He treated me as a young friend, insisting that I call him Red. My work was fun. Taking his rapid dictation and reading it back to type it was like doing a crossword puzzle: I caught every fourth word with a squiggle of Gregg and had to figure out what went between.

He was endlessly playful. "He could no more stop telling stories than he could stop his hair growing," the historian Carl Van Doren once said. When we lunched alone, he would start a tale—either true or invented on the spur of the moment—and then, all for me, and of course for his own pleasure, he would jump up from the table and become the people in the story, switching from side to side as he conversed with himself in the telling. His improvisations were uncanny; one forgot his cadaverous face and *saw* John L. Lewis,[56] F.D.R., Huey Long, Father Coughlin. He could reel off astonishing footages of Milton, Blake, Edward Lear.[57] In company he organized games. Word and letter games were his favorites. He rattled off tongue twisters, spoonerisms, oxymorons. Once with John Marquand[58] and others he passed around pads and pencils and made everyone see how many names of rivers beginning with "M" they could write down. He would assign guests outrageous names from telephone books and tell them to converse in character with the names. He would hand out a set of end rhymes and get people writing sonnets with them against the clock; Schorer[59] records that Lewis's own best time was 3 minutes and 50 seconds. He hired a small donkey one day when two very tall people were to be at the house; for some reason he wanted to see them riding around with their feet dragging on the ground.

93 / Margaret Widdemer

Margaret Widdemer (1884–1978), Pulitzer Prize–winning novelist and poet, counted a wide range of literary eminences among her friends in her autobiography, including Lewis, Ezra Pound, F. Scott Fitzgerald, Thornton Wilder, and Edna St. Vincent Millay.[60]

Source: Margaret Widdemer, *Golden Friends I Had* (Garden City, NY: Doubleday, 1964), 236, 239–40.

I liked Dorothy and admired her. In spite of the common knowledge that Lewis drank too much, I liked, admired, and was sorry for him. There are men who can and do straighten up after drinking hard. He might have been one of them, given the right circumstances. [. . .]

Dorothy Thompson's breaking point was a high one; she could write, keep house, entertain, live with difficult people, and be comparatively nervously untouched. Hal's breaking point was low.

The climax of their parting—or perhaps it was the end of a string of climaxes—was a dinner party. It was a nice, civilized, well-organized dinner for some celebrated friend or other, who was just back from Europe full of laurels. Whether it was the party, or the laureled friend, or whatever, Lewis's breaking point snapped. He got drunk. And drink, as always, released in him all the things he was ordinarily too shy to do, plus all the things civilized people want to do and don't. You may, if shy, want to compensate by tramping through a crowded room, and dominate the conversation and shove everyone around. You may want to kiss all the women in the room and hit all the men. But you don't. The difference there is that when Lewis was drunk he did. The big frightened kid who couldn't dare make friends with anybody but a pitying faculty which appreciated brains was still inside the too-thin shell of the famous Sinclair Lewis. So, halfway through his own dinner party, he yelled insults at his guest of honor and presently hit him. The story got around. So did more of the sort. Presently there was news of a quiet divorce.

94 / George Seldes

As Lewis's career was in decline, Thompson's was skyrocketing.

Source: George Seldes, *Witness to a Century* (New York: Ballantine, 1987), 293–94.

Much talk about fellow writers. And experiences in the hinterland as a lecturer. One story ends: "And then the chairman introduced me as Upton Sinclair."

"I love Upton," said Lewis once, "but look what he says about me in *Money Writes!* [1927]. He says I am one of those writers spoiled by success, by big money. He says, 'Sinclair Lewis has a million dollars.'[61] I give you my word, George, I haven't more than $600,000 and he calls me a millionaire." The usual Lewisian sense of humor was not present.

When Red's marriage to Dorothy began to go bad, Red took the conventional road to alcohol. In his half-drunken times he would say cruel things about Dorothy, such as, "Tell me, George, why did I have to marry a *senator*?" And on one of our trips to Barnard [Vermont] in reply to frantic telephone calls from the Viennese couple who kept house for the Lewises—it was mid-April 1936—Red said, after my wife had fed him black coffee and partly sobered him, "George, you don't know anyone around here who is looking for a job as a mistress—at least a part-time mistress—do you?"

Strangely enough neither Sinclair Lewis nor Dorothy's first husband, whom I also knew—he was a Viennese poet whom my brother had published in America—ever suspected that the failure of their marriages was due to Dorothy's being bisexual, and at times, lasting years, wholly lesbian, as her recent biographer has disclosed.[62] Red thought she was a senator; her first husband told me one day that Dorothy had made his life unbearable by "dominating me—as a man would his employees."

Nevertheless, Sinclair Lewis owes several books to Dorothy, most notably *It Can't Happen Here,* written in 1934 and published the next year. She inspired the book, gave him the story of Nazi-Fascist dictatorships in Europe as she had experienced them, and invited her colleagues to Barnard to help Lewis.

As was his habit of pumping everyone for information, he especially pumped me on this subject. I had to relate every meeting with Mussolini, every glimpse of him, every day I could remember of the year and more in Rome under Fascism. He pumped day and night, lunch and dinner, cocktail hour and auto trips. In payment to several who helped him on this book he lists us on page 264 as journalists imprisoned by the American fascist dictator, "Buzz" Windrip.[63]

It was a brave thing for Lewis to take on Fascism at that time. The Un-American Activities Committee witch-hunts were directed always against the left, General Butler had testified to a fascist plot to seize Washington, and the news had been suppressed.[64]

Lewis has someone say to his crusading Vermont editor: "Why are you afraid of the word Fascism, Doremus? Just a word—just a word! And it might not be so bad [. . .] to have a real Strongman, like Hitler or Mussolini—Napoleon or Bismarck in the good old days—and have 'em really *run* the country and make it efficient and prosperous again." No one in the 1930s dared attack American fascism. (And few dare, even now.)

95 / Fanny Butcher

Just as she had recognized the problems in Lewis's first marriage, Butcher recognized the problems in his second one.

Source: Fanny Butcher, *Many Lives—One Love* (New York: Harper and Row, 1972), 393–94.

Perhaps poor Hal was never designed for marriage and fatherhood. His second marriage, to Dorothy Thompson, internationally famous as a commentator on the state of the crumbling world, ended, as did his first, in divorce. Their son Michael was not beside his father when he died, in a foreign country, as lonely as the last pine standing in a forest fire.

Sinclair Lewis repaid Dorothy by making her the talking woman in *Ann Vickers*. He told me once, after their marriage had been "Reno-vated," to steal one of Walter Winchell's favorite lines, that being waked up in the middle of the night by the telephone and having Dorothy reach across him to talk to Winston Churchill[65] made him feel as if he were married to the State Department.

96 / Fay Wray

Fay Wray (1907–2004), Canadian American actress, is most famous for her role as Ann Darrow in the 1933 classic film *King Kong,* in which she played the object of a giant ape's attention. Wray met Lewis in 1936 and later helped him with some of the stagecraft on *Angela Is Twenty-Two.* As Schorer explains, "she did no writing, and he did not always listen to her suggestions, but he nevertheless insisted that she have equal credit as author with him."[66]

Source: Fay Wray, *On the Other Hand: A Life Story* (New York: St. Martin's, 1989), 182–83, 196–97.

Sinclair Lewis, whom I had met earlier at a dinner party in Hollywood, was preparing to act in his own play, "It Can't Happen Here." He was unattractive in appearance—tall, gangly, and skeletal, his narrow face pockmarked, his teeth and fingers yellow from smoking. A small amount of hair justified the nickname "Red." He had fallen in love with the theater and saw it as a fresh life experience. He was enchanted with the cast of his play—Flora Campbell and Barry Sullivan[67] among others—and with all the young people at Cohasset [Massachusetts].

When I left Cohasset, letters from him followed me, then he followed, arriving at Saratoga when I was preparing to do *There's Always Juliet.* I could admire Lewis, admire his brilliance and the mind he himself defined as "chained lightning," but I wouldn't want him to come near me or touch me. When he convinced the theater's director, Harold Winston,[68] that he should play opposite me in the romantic comedy by John Van Druten,[69] a wave of desperation came upon me. It was Ethel Barrymore[70] who pulled me out from under by saying to Red, "Good God, are you serious? Do you think you can convince an audience that this woman could fall in love with you? Think of the audience—think of Fay Wray and all she went through in *that film*!"

It was Alexander Clark[71] who reported this. He should have known. He was asked to come from New York as quickly as possible to learn the long role even more quickly so that we could open on schedule. Lewis, who told him how Ethel had dashed his hopes, stayed on in Saratoga and began to write a play that *would* be suitable for him and me. At first he called it "Romeo is Fifty." It was to be about a young girl falling in love with an older man. This, too, had problems for me. But he persevered. He retitled it "Angela is Twenty-Two" and continued writing and eliciting my help. Mostly, what I did was to suggest thoughts that would develop dramatic structure and/or visually interesting moments. Dialogue was no difficulty for him. He could make people talk! [. . .]

In response to an invitation from the Lakewood Theatre management,[72] Sinclair Lewis arrived to do "Angela is Twenty-Two" with me. He had been playing summer theater himself, his name, if not his acting ability, great enough to be a box-office draw. While performing in *Shadow and Substance,* he had found a young friend, Marcella Powers, who had become his companion and would continue to share his life.

Around the lunch table someone mentioned that Clifford Odets[73] had recently been there. In a flash, Lewis was ready with a little verse:

> Clifford Odets, with his little moustache,
> Claims that soubrettes are exploited for cash.
> Then, at his most comradely, as soon as he's said it,
> Proceeds at once to exploit them on credit.

Funny, critical, but it was the speed that made it stick in my mind.

It just wasn't possible to realize any drama in working with Lewis. It was more like moving in an essay. Ideas were good, thoughts well-written, but there was no life, not even any certainty about where he would be on the stage at any moment. What had been rehearsed to play stage right was suddenly taking place stage left and we scrambled along for seven uncertain performances. But he was where he wanted most of all to be at that time in his life—in the theater.

97 / Kitty Carlisle

Kitty Carlisle (1910–2007), singer and actress, born Catherine Conn, was a strong advocate for the financial support of the arts. Among her early movies was the Marx Brothers' *A Night at the Opera* (1935). In March 1939, with her acting career foundering, she traveled to Hollywood for a screen test on the same train as Lewis, who was traveling to California to work on a screenplay of *Angela Is Twenty-Two,* eventually adapted under the title *This Is the Life.* Lewis was soon smitten. She married the playwright and theatrical producer Moss Hart in 1946 and never remarried after his death in 1961. She is best remembered as a panelist on the pioneering television game show *To Tell the Truth* (1957–78).

Source: Kitty Carlisle Hart, *Kitty: An Autobiography* (New York: Doubleday, 1988), 87–89, 90–91.

I went to California on the Superchief. In the dining car a man introduced himself as the director of the Goodman Theatre in Chicago.[74] He said he was sitting with Sinclair Lewis, who wanted to meet me.

Lewis, the first American writer to win a Nobel Prize, was a tremendous star at the time. He had lately turned to writing plays; he had with him the script of a work in progress, *Angela Is Twenty-Two,* and he asked me if I would look at it. I read it on the train, and I didn't think it was terribly good—he had a total lack of technical knowledge about the theater—but I was intrigued and in a way touched by his intense interest in it. He was like a stagestruck boy, and the reason he was attracted to me, I thought, was that I was an actress. We discussed *Angela* a great deal, and by the time we got to Pasadena he was trying to persuade me to do it. [. . .]

Sinclair Lewis—he was usually called "Red"—didn't seem to have many friends, and he had a lot of free time, so I spent most of every day with him. We drove to out-of-the-way places for lunch and afternoons we sat around in his bungalow at the Beverly Hills Hotel. What a talker he was; he never stopped the whole time I was with him. He was also working on a book, *Bethel Merriday,* and he showed me pages and pages of names he had jotted down for possible use. He had a wonderful knack for names, and I asked him how it felt to have created a generic name for a certain kind of person, Babbitt. He grinned: "I like it!" It was the shortest sentence I ever heard from him.

Red was tall and so thin that his clothes hung on him like a scarecrow. He never dressed casually à la California, but always as if he were going to a business appointment with his banker. Perhaps this was compensation for a distressing and painfully obvious problem—he had skin cancer.

Outside of his work, I knew very little about him—I didn't even know about his drinking problem, although he did drink an awful lot of iced coffee. We had no friends in common, not even the man who introduced us, whom I didn't know very well, and who never showed up again. It was as though our meeting on the train had somehow encapsulated us in another dimension.

I have an enormous curiosity about people, but for some reason I never asked Red about his life. I was too concerned about my own career; the screen test was as slow in coming as molasses in winter, and I was beginning to wonder what I was doing in California in the first place. Also, I think Red talked so much I never got a word in edgewise. I came away from all that time knowing as little about him as when I met him on the train. I never questioned the loneliness of his Hollywood life or why he was dependent on me for companionship.

I thought that companionship was all it was, until he astonished me by telling me he loved me. I didn't take him seriously, because I had told him about Decio.[75] Then he really frightened the wits out of me when he said he was going to tell his wife, Dorothy Thompson, that he wanted to marry me. Dorothy Thompson was a formidable creature—foreign correspondent, columnist, lecturer, and world figure. She had just arrived in California to make a speech, and Red said he was going to go to her lecture and give her this piece of news. I said if he told her any such thing I'd never speak to him again. All the time we were together he'd never asked me if *I* would like to marry *him,* or even if I loved him. It was Gershwin all over again:[76] I loved his talent, but I didn't love him. I liked him, and I was pleased that he cared to spend so much time with me, but the idea of sharing my life with him had never crossed my mind, and I was scared to think what an announcement of this kind could do to Miss Thompson. (Red obviously didn't say anything to her about marrying me, because I never heard from her.) [. . .]

In the end his affection for me dwindled because I could return so little of it. I never even managed to send the photographs he requested. But I treasure the time we spent together, the autographed books, *Babbitt, Arrowsmith, Main Street,* and photograph signed "To Kitty with Love."

13
The Slough of Despond
1939–45

Lewis's theatrical career—whether as playwright, actor, or producer—was critically and commercially unsuccessful. To be sure, he met the teenaged Marcella Powers (1921?–1985) on August 14, 1939, while they were working together with the Provincetown Players, and they remained friends and lovers until she married the journalist Michael Armine in 1947. Lewis even remembered Powers in his will. In general, however, these years were unhappy ones for Lewis, particularly after his son Wells was killed in World War II. He left Doubleday for Random House in September 1940 for the same reason he had left Harcourt a decade before: he alleged the publisher no longer promoted his books. Ironically, the novels he completed during this period, *Bethel Merriday* (1940) and *Gideon Planish* (1943), were negligible. In 1943, while living in Los Angeles, he tried to develop some film scripts with little success. In 1944 he inexplicably decided to live in Duluth the rest of his life—and stayed there less than two years.

98 / Edward F. Murphy

In a letter to Kitty Carlisle dated December 9, 1939, Lewis reported that he had been invited "to play (or play at) the Cedric Hardwicke part in *Shadow and Substance* with the Little Theater here [New Orleans]. I keep clear of the hectic social aspects of that institution, and they have a marvelous director: Bernard Szold."[1] Edward F. Murphy, SSJ (b. 1892), a Catholic priest, dean of the philosophy and religion department at Xavier University in New Orleans, and author of the novel *The Scarlet Lily* (1944), reminisced in his autobiography about Lewis's performances, though he neglected to mention that Marcella Powers had roles in both the play in New Orleans and *The Good Neighbor.* After tryouts in Stony Creek, Connecticut, and Baltimore, *The Good Neighbor* by Jack L. Levin opened at the Windsor Theatre on Broadway on October 21, 1941, and closed after one performance. Lewis lost over $25,000 on the venture. See also Richard Tuerk, "Directed by Sinclair Lewis: 'The Good Neighbor' by Jack L. Levin," *Journal of the American Studies Association of Texas* 17 (1986): 21–26.

Source: Edward F. Murphy, *Yankee Priest: An Autobiographical Journey* (Garden City, NY: Doubleday, 1952), 240–48.

One morning Mr. Bernard Szold,[2] the director of Le Petit Théâtre du Vieux Carré, phoned me to say, "I noticed in the papers that Eddie Dowling[3] has granted you first amateur rights to *Shadow and Substance.*[4] And this leads to a request. Sinclair Lewis, who's been making some stage appearances in other cities of late, was out sight-seeing here yesterday and stopped in at Le Petit. He approved everything, and when I told him we'd appreciate having him perform for us, he liked that too. But he said there's only one drama, one role, that he'd care to do—"Shadow and Substance" and the role of Canon Skerritt, which his friend Sir Cedric Hardwicke[5] played on Broadway. Well, there we are, Father. Would you consider letting us be the first group to do the show—with America's leading novelist as the star?"

Superfluous question. Xavier was busy on an opera. Le Petit, with a long record of successful offerings which had placed it in the front rank of little theaters, would be just right. And to think that my small hold on the play was enough to open a door like this! I readily gave Mr. Szold what permission I could, and gratefully he asked me to assist in the selection of a cast, to act as clerical adviser at rehearsals, and to let him bring Mr. Lewis and me together.

The chancery permitted me to have an active interest in the project because of the religious genre of the play, and then I was free for my first contact with him. We met at Le Petit Théâtre, near St. Louis Cathedral. [. . .] Now here he was before me, a tall, thin, gangly figure with corrugated brow, sparse hair combed flat, pale-blue agate eyes, a not too prominent nose, and mottled cheeks sloping to a vague, slightly bulbous mouth. And the instant I saw him, I liked him. [. . .] In our handclasp the feel of those frail, almost skeletal fingers that had dissected social hypocrisies and pretenses galore with a scalpel pen was strangely pleasant to me. [. . .] Soon it became evident to me that at least a part of Lewis's worldly success was an ability to plunge wholly [. . .] into a task. He was the first to report at Le Petit each evening and the last to leave; and he drained Bernard Szold, the director. [. . .]

Yet another night when Ethel Crumm Brett, expert designer of sets and effects, was training the spotlight on Lewis, his tired, watering eyes blinked in the glare. Any real actor would never have complained; but Lewis, just a novelist afield from his regular art and avid for the atmosphere of little theaters which were to be the theme of his next book, burst into a rage and, shouting that his vision meant more to him than this confounded play, stomped off the stage. I followed him. "Here everybody's bending backwards to please you," I rebuked in the privacy of his upstairs dressing room, "and you won't be pleased." His head slightly down, he gave me a sly, slant look which, to my astonishment, twinkled, and then he laughed. "Good act, wasn't it! Now I guess they'll admit I *can* perform when I let myself go." Two minutes later he was down on the stage again, and Szold was regarding me with the kind of awe that is usually reserved for wizards.

Only once did Lewis and I have a contention, and it amounted to nothing but a sprinkling of pepper and salt to season our harmony. As an Irish canon in the show, he had to wear a special cassock. I maintained that the pipings on it should be white, but he demanded red. "Don't you want to be ecclesiastically correct?" I asked. "I want to be theatrically effective," he returned, with a smile like a persimmon trying to be a peach. "Red is better for that. Anyhow I prefer it. Call me 'Red,' Father. All my friends do." And that closed the matter as far as we were concerned; but a report got out that he and I were at each other's throat, and echoes of the imaginary ruckus reached not only the local but even the metropolitan press. Little had I dreamed when I first read *Main Street,* away back in 1920, that I should ever share journalistic space with the author himself!

As for *Main Street,* he mentioned to me one night during a lull in the rehearsals that he remembered less the praises accorded him for that book than a certain wordless commentary. Shortly after publication he set sail for Europe and noticed, the second day out, that a large number of deck loungers had copies. One woman especially attracted his attention, for she kept beetling her brows and chewing her lips as she pored over the pages. Suddenly, mumbling to herself, she sprang up from her chair, leapt to the ship railing, and hurled *Main Street* with all her might into the sea. Recounting this to me, he chuckled as if it were just about the best criticism he had ever received.

In our few free moments I talked with him about religion, since he seemed so taken with the spiritual vistas of Carroll's play. Up in New York, Father (now Monsignor) Fulton Sheen[6] had recently converted Heywood Broun, and this prompted me one night to say to Lewis with affected casualness, "Why don't you do a 'Heywood Broun'?" He scrutinized me for a second and then, out of a quirk in the corner of his lips, suggested, "Why don't *you* do an 'Elmer Gantry'?" And no farther than that did we get, at that time, on the road to Damascus. But once, when rehearsal was over and we were having coffee in a nearby restaurant, we fell into a discussion of the role of the Church in an era menaced by Communism. "'Onward Christian Soldiers' may yet be drowned out by the 'Internationale,'" he said. And I thought, "Now I have him," because he sounded rather sad. My hope died, however; because he began to tease me by singing—low—the "Internationale" itself. His voice was so unsuited to any song, and his rendition of this one was so full of flaws, that I simply had to indulge in a little raillery: "Say, Caruso, the Catholic Church could probably save the world from Communism just by hiring you to chant the praises of Moscow on street corners. Every hearer would run to the arms of Rome for protection." And leering good-naturedly, he replied, "Just for that, Aquinas, I will henceforth be as silent and inscrutable as Eleanor Roosevelt."

After a month of rehearsals "Shadow and Substance" was ready, and yet we were not quite satisfied, so to try it out we put on a special performance for the clergy of the city. They liked it in the main, but some of them gave me a ribbing. Said one, "What a clerical adviser you are! Why, under your learned tutelage Mr. Lewis, as a priest, can't even bless himself." And I groaned within, because over and over again I had had Lewis practice the Sign of the Cross; but this simple act of faith was either too much for his genius or a resistance lurked in him to a symbol that he was not yet prepared to accept. But he played Canon Skerritt with conviction; and when we gave yet another trial performance, this time exclusively for Sisters, there was not the least criticism. They caught and laughed at every bubble of humor; and the laughter of nuns, as innocent as a child's, makes a music of its own. They wept at the pathos, as if every throb of it were personally theirs. "An audience of angels!" declared Lewis to me during intermission.

He was really moved, and I felt him now nearer to orthodoxy than ever before, for at last I saw him when the second act was in progress, making a perfect Sign of the Cross.

The night of the formal opening the thermometer was at a January low, and New Orleans society came perhaps reluctantly, certainly ashiver, to the little theater on St. Peter's Street. But once inside they found the season changed. Just as to old Broadway, so now to the Vieux Carré, "Shadow and Substance" wafted a breath of spring. Its plot unfolded with warmth and color, and its lyrical phrases were heather fresh. The bells of St. Louis Cathedral, sounding the hour, blended with the beauty of the production like a planned offstage effect; and it seemed to me, sitting in the orchestra rear, that a ghostly audience was smiling down on the spectacle of yesterday's God-challenger and today's still tough cynic portraying a minister of grace.

As a matter of record, Lewis's portrayal that night had sincerity but not much else. Still, it was far better than his singing of the "Internationale" had been, and I'd always resent—a little—a certain Manhattan critic's later witticism, "The real Red menace in the American theater is the acting of Sinclair Lewis."[7]

A few days later, after putting several questions to me about Negroes, he expressed a desire to visit Xavier; and I brought him there. Sister Frances, our new dean, attracted him instantly, and in the graciously warm atmosphere that nuns create, his wintry surface melted away. He asked that we let him confer with some of our colored teachers, which we gladly did. Wondering a trifle about his intent, but not questioning it, I absented myself from the conference after seeing it started, because somehow I felt that he preferred to have the group to himself. And not until some years later was I to understand the significance of that round table, for then there would appear a book, *Kingsblood Royal,* in which, with all his power, he'd champion the group I served. And then I'd know that at Xavier he had begun to learn about his subject from the very best of sources, Negro intelligence itself.

The day after his visit to our university, I brought him to meet Archbishop Rummel,[8] and they had a long conversation. It was his first contact with a Catholic prelate, and the effect on him was great. "A true man of God," he said after we left. Several times during the remainder of his stay in New Orleans he quoted His Excellency to me, and always with the same fondness and respect that I detected in his tone whenever he referred to the writings of Dorothy Thompson and the sayings of his close friend Dr. Cornelius Traeger. But it was rather embarrassing when, after praising me in a press interview, he went on to tell the reporters that the archbishop was "a swell guy too." I'd not have minded, had not the remark appeared in print exactly as he made it.

It was with real regret that I saw him off on the train for the North when the week of *Shadow and Substance* ended. But he promised to keep in touch with me, and so he did. From time to time he phoned or wrote, and I was glad to learn that, still fond of the play in which he had enacted a priest, he was touring the New England straw-hat circuit in the same role with a company emanating from New York. [. . .] Twice he returned to New Orleans; when he had a special personal worry which he felt I could ease, and when he and Lewis Browne were on a lecture jaunt. And once when I was on my way to earn a few dollars for my mission by delivering an address at Ford Hall Forum in Boston and stopped off in New York for a few days to visit Father Will, now filling the office of novice master at Epiphany College, I saw him yet again.

This time he was presenting a play, "The Good Neighbor," a comedy drama of "just plain folks," which he earnestly invited me to attend. As the curtain rose on the Broadway première, I leaned forward in my chair, eager for every word, glad to be present at the commencement of a new phase of Lewis' career, confident that he who had admired Paul Vincent Carroll's play so much would not permit a single reprehensible line or scene in this one. And I was right about the irreprehensibility; but the show itself—that was another matter. The first act, though well performed, seemed to zigzag on to nothing in particular, yet the audience applauded the close. I did not know whether this meant an approval of the play or a welcome to the intermission. George Jean Nathan, the most stringent of critics, whom I recognized from pictures in newspapers and magazines, left and did not return. This was ominous enough, but not conclusive, because Nathan was well known to have retched at many a production that the paying public found quite palatable. But the second act, as far as I could judge, showed no improvement on the first; though the final curtain, to my puzzlement, evoked even more applause. Did this indicate that the house was filled with Lewis's friends, or merely that pain—when it stops—amounts to pleasure? Anyhow, the exodus from the theater was cheerful, and not a few individuals, myself included, tarried in the lobby to offer Lewis congratulations.

He insisted that I join him at his hotel to await the verdict of the press in the early morning editions; and there in his suite I met Sylvia Sidney,[9] Luther Adler,[10] Dr. Cornelius Traeger, Dudley Digges,[11] Samson Raphaelson, and several other notables who had been merely names to me. A scintillant group they were, until a bellhop brought in the papers. Then a pall fell. But Lewis read the ghastly reviews stoically and winced only once.[12] That was when, trying to penetrate the gloom with an optimistic ray, I said, "Well, the critics are not the last word. Remember 'Abie's Irish Rose.'"[13] For the first and only time in our association, he gave me a dirty look.

I was with him the following night and wished I wasn't. We walked on Broadway, and as we approached the theater of "The Good Neighbor," so alive only twenty-four hours before, we saw comparative death. The foyer did not have a single light on, and not a customer was standing at the box office. We turned into the stage alley, which smelled of decay, and the members of the cast were hovering there like ghosts. Thanking them for having tried to make something out of nothing, he paid them off, his hand trembling a little. He had had far more success than most men of his time, but wasn't this now only making failure the harder to bear? I looked up at the stars over Broadway, all the bigger and brighter to me for the dreary well of an alley which served as a kind of telescope, and hoped that he would look up too. But he did not.

99 / James Branch Cabell

Lewis's relationship with Marcella Powers was punctuated by several separations and reconciliations like the one Cabell remembered.

Source: James Branch Cabell, *As I Remember It* (New York: McBride, 1955), 169–70.

Toward the end of March 1941, Hal Lewis of a sudden appeared in St. Augustine, and when among the cluttered and gaudy eighteen-eightyish splendors of the Hotel Ponce de León,[14] I passed a far more than saddening evening with him. He by this time was divorced from his second wife; and he could talk about nothing whatever consecutively except to tell me over and over again the unhandsome details of how very badly he had been treated by some young actress or another upon whom, throughout the last several months at least, he had centered his affections. She but that week had discarded him, as I remember matters, in Miami; and I found him, in the most kindly terms which I can now think of offhand, to be maudlin over the young so-and-so's ungratefulness after all he had done for and had spent upon her. [. . .]

Well, and after that, as it happened, I never any more saw Sinclair Lewis. I grant, though, I did not desire to see him again. The Hal Lewis whom I had known and had been fond of, and in whose genius I had invested a prophetic faith some twenty-odd years earlier, had been transformed by his famousness far too utterly and far beyond recognition.

100 / Fanny Butcher

The aide-de-camp to General John E. Dahlquist (1896–1975), Captain Wells Lewis, was shot and killed by a sniper in France on October 29, 1944. His father learned the news the evening of November 13. The next morning he sent a telegram to Grace, who regarded it as "so impersonal it could have been written by a stranger."[15] It read as follows: "On lecture trip. Did not get tragic news till last night. You must think only that you share in terrible but great honor and glory and not permit yourself any other memory." She wrote on the telegram, "What a message from the father to the mother! And quite phoney."[16] Lewis also telephoned her, though she "reproached him for his unforgivable irresponsibility as a father."[17]

Source: Fanny Butcher, *Many Lives—One Love* (New York: Harper and Row, 1972), 393.

On 14 November 1944, a date I cannot forget, Hal was in town overnight and had invited to dinner Lloyd Lewis and his wife, Kathryn; the Wilsons, Dorothy Thompson's sister and her husband;[18] a young girl from Duluth, Minnesota; Lewis Browne, author of *Stranger Than Fiction,* with whom Hal had been on a barnstorming lecture circuit, and my husband and me. All of us heard the news of Wells's death. Hal railed out at everybody because we felt deeply for him. When his ex-sister-in-law (he and Dorothy had been divorced a couple of years before) told him he ought to call Gracie, who, she said, must be going crazy, he reluctantly did telephone her, but came back more furious than before. Gracie was maudlin, he said, we were all maudlin. Death is death, he declared, and Wells was no different from any other American or German. He hated sentimentality he said, and Wells hadn't died a heroic death because he hadn't wanted to go to war anyway, and he, Hal, hadn't given a son to his country because he didn't want Wells to go to war either. Sinclair Lewis that night was a wild man and cursed the world.

101 / Dorothy Thompson

His former wife, Dorothy Thompson, supplies more details of the evening.

Source: Dorothy Thompson, "The Boy and Man from Sauk Centre," *Atlantic Monthly* 206 (November 1960): 41.

Sinclair Lewis had received the news of his older son's death in the fall of 1944 in a manner that seemed utterly feelingless. He was on a lecture tour en route to Chicago when the news came over the radio that Lieutenant Wells Lewis had been shot in Alsace by a sniper and killed instantly while studying a map with General Dahlquist, to whom he was aide-de-camp.

My gentle, sensitive sister, who was devoted to Sinclair Lewis and to Wells and of whom Lewis was fond, felt that the news which he might not have heard should be broken to him lovingly and went to the railroad station but missed him. He had scheduled a party for the evening, to which my sister and her husband had been invited. They phoned the Palmer House,[19] thinking it might have been called off. Lewis had already left for the party, and they went. There they found him in the liveliest possible mood. No one mentioned the death of Wells, but my brother-in-law, finding himself, for a moment, apart with "Red," quietly and simply expressed his sympathy and sorrow.

Sinclair Lewis flew into a biting rage. "People just love to be bearers of bad news." He snarled at Hal (Harrison) Smith, who had telephoned or telegraphed his friendship and sympathy. He attacked me because I had canceled my radio program when I heard of Wells's death a few minutes before I was scheduled to leave for it. "Dorothy's just putting on an act. She wasn't his mother. It's all self-dramatization."

Fanny Butcher, longtime literary critic of the *Chicago Tribune,* was there, and Lloyd Lewis, the newspaperman and historical writer, with his wife. Sinclair Lewis admired Lloyd and had collaborated with him on the play "Jayhawker," which had not been a success. When I ran into Fanny some months later, she was still shocked at Lewis's conduct that evening. Lewis bragged that he had heard the news just before he went to lecture and had never "been better in my life."

My sister, defending Hal Smith, said, "He is one of your oldest friends. He didn't want to bear bad news, but to offer you sympathy and comfort. And you know that what you say about Dorothy is not true. She loved Wells deeply, and he loved her. She was prostrated."

This reproof Sinclair Lewis took in silence. But my sister was not shocked. She was sorry. She knew only too well that Lewis's reaction to frustrations and griefs was to hit out at those who cared most for him, and often at those for whom he cared most. That was always the trouble: never knowing whether he really cared at all, for anybody or anything except his work.

102 / Harrison Smith

However stoic Lewis appeared, according to Smith the death of his son devastated him.

Source: Harrison Smith, "Sinclair Lewis: Remembrance of the Past," *Saturday Review of Literature,* January 27, 1951, 38.

I have always thought that the death of his son Wells in the war, though he rarely mentioned him, was a secret wound which he concealed even from himself. Wells was a strikingly handsome young man who was turning into a brilliant journalist and had published a novel just before he was killed. A friend of mine who met Lewis at Grand Central after he had heard the appalling news told me that his face was bland and expressionless, his answers to the gentlemen of the press courteous but curt. Wells Lewis might have been only a name of someone he remotely remembered. Another and almost a final object of human love and affection had been torn from him.

103 / H. L. Mencken

H. L. Mencken (1880–1956), journalist, essayist, and professional curmudgeon, was known during his lifetime as the "Sage of Baltimore." He was a literary critic for the *Smart Set* and later founded and edited, with George Jean Nathan, the *American Mercury.* He is remembered for his literary and cultural criticism as well as his ambitious multivolume study of spoken English in America, *The American Language* (1919, 1945, 1948). He met Lewis in 1920 and they remained close friends and correspondents for the next thirty years.

Source: H. L. Mencken, *My Life as Author and Editor,* ed. Jonathan Yardley (New York: Knopf, 1993), 344–49.

When he published *Bethel Merriday* in 1940 it got hardly any notice at all. Poor Red, by this time, seemed to be definitely done for. As Dorothy had gone up, he had gone down.

In July 1938, when a strange version of *It Can't Happen Here* was presented by a summer stock company in Cohasset, Massachusetts,[20] he appeared in the leading role, and after that, for several years, he was heard of, when he was heard of at all, mainly as an actor. During the winter of 1938–39 he actually went on the road with a company playing a piece called "Angela is Twenty-Two" which he had written in collaboration with Fay Wray, an obscure stock company actress [*sic*]. It never reached New York. [. . .] On 26 January 1941, he announced at Miami Beach, where he had been playing again in "Angela is Twenty-Two," that he was retiring from the stage to write a new novel. It was *Gideon Planish,* which came out in 1943 and fell dead. It bore the imprint of Random House, which is to say, of Bennett Cerf. Doubleday, Doran & Company had dropped him after the failure of *Bethel Merriday.* [. . .]

Since *It Can't Happen Here,* nothing that he had done has gotten much serious attention. Meanwhile, he has fallen into the net of another Delilah, a Jewish girl who called herself Marcella Powers, and there is every promise that she will do him more damage than even Gracie and Dorothy.

Red apparently encountered Marcella some time in 1940 during his days as an actor. She was then an actress, though later she took to literary endeavor, or, at all events, to jobs on magazines. She came to Baltimore in October 1941, as a member of a company presenting a preposterous play called "The Good Neighbor" by Jack Levin, a Baltimore advertising agent, and Red came with her. [. . .] When I heard Red was in town I invited him to Schellhase's restaurant[21] for an evening session, and he asked me to pick him up at 10 P.M. at Ford's Theatre, where "The Good Neighbor" was playing. [. . .]

It must have been plain to Red that I regarded La Powers as a piece of trash, and after that meeting in Baltimore I heard from him only a few times, and then very briefly. In November 1944, I learned that Wells, his son by Gracie, had been killed in action in France on October 29, and sent him a note of condolence, proposing that we have a meeting at some time in the not too distant future. He replied cordially, but [. . .] it was not until 18 April 1945 that we met. I then invited him to dinner at a French restaurant in West 46th Street, and asked George Nathan to come along. He insisted, without any suggestion from me, on bringing Marcella, and Nathan and I put in an uncomfortable evening. She had by now grown very confident and possessive, and it was plain that she was trying to show Nathan and me that she had poor Red in her pocket. [. . .]

Red's appearance when he came to the Algonquin[22] to meet Nathan and me before dinner was really shocking. [. . .] The black bumps were bad enough, but the red scales that surrounded them, covering his whole face, were even worse: they gave him the unearthly look of a scarlet lizard. [. . .]

It would certainly be an exaggeration to call Marcella attentive to him during our dinner in April; instead she basked complacently in his almost comic admiration, and, as I have said, tried to make it plain to Nathan and me that he was hers. We left the two of them very much depressed. Red had been a man of high achievement and even higher promise in his day, but now it was manifest he was done for. His next novel, he told us, would tell the love story of a young girl and an aging man, and Marcella's smirks made it plain that she was to be its heroine. Drink and two bad wives had wrecked him, and now he was on his way to the boneyard on the water-wagon, with an even worse wife preparing to climb up beside him. [. . .]

That he had something properly describable as genius in the *Babbitt* era I fully believe. I knew all the principal novelists of that time, and a few of them, notably Dreiser, had genius too, but the overwhelming majority of them were much inferior to Red. His powers of observation were really amazing, and he knew how to present his material with great effectiveness. He was never a stylist comparable to Hergesheimer or Cabell, and he failed constantly when he tried to be touching or profound, but he could tell a story with really extraordinary skill, and his sense of character was greater than that of any of his contemporaries.

But he was an old and worn-out man before he was fifty, and after that he did nothing even half good until *Cass Timberlane* [1945]. I urged him over many years to stick to the broad national types that he knew so well how to depict, and made many concrete suggestions to that end, but once he began to break up he found it increasingly difficult to handle them, and from *Dodsworth* onward the people he dealt with became less and less interesting. In *Cass Timberlane,* despite its revival of something of his old skill, they were not interesting at all, and many of them were not even credible. All that remained of him was a melancholy reminder that he had once been a first-rate man.

104 / Herbert R. Mayes

Herbert R. Mayes (1900–1987), editor and author, worked on several popular women's magazines for the Hearst Corporation starting in 1927 and published a sensational fictionalized biography of Horatio Alger, based on invented diaries, in 1928. He eventually became president and chief executive of the McCall Corporation. At Lewis's behest, he hired Marcella Powers as an editorial assistant in early 1943 and she lasted two years in the job.

Source: Herbert R. Mayes, *The Magazine Maze: A Prejudiced Perspective* (Garden City, NY: Doubleday, 1980), 43–45.

In his devotion to himself Sinclair Lewis was single-minded; about his greatness he had no misgivings. A sometime friend of Upton Sinclair, he could foam at the mouth if confused with him. Lanky, his face pocked with acne, his awareness of his ugliness affected most of his relationships. Now and then he could be amusing—more than now and then—and he was a grand mimic. I got along with him, found him generally kind, but suffered when he gave vent to rage, which also was more than now and then. His conduct could be irascible and irrational. During an evening I had taken him and Edith Haggard,[23] his literary agent, to a late supper, he became furious over some fancied slight on the part of the waiter, picked up a knife, and shattered a champagne glass to splinters. On another evening, in my home, he disrupted the dinner party by lashing out at Lester Markel,[24] then the Sunday editor of the *New York Times.* By his friends, Lewis always was called Red because of the color of his hair. He misunderstood and thought Markel had called him *a* red. [. . .]

Of the writers I *knew,* Sinclair Lewis was the most neurotic about punctuality. "What the hell makes you think you're more important than we are?" he snarled at Arthur McKeogh,[25] an associate of mine, who had been delayed for a few minutes in getting to a meeting with Lewis, Alexander Woollcott, and me at the Plaza, then rose abruptly and stalked out of the hotel. Woollcott, himself no benevolent soul, then said, "Who does Red think *he* is, leaving me here?" He didn't add "with the likes of you two," but that's what he meant, and he left also.

"A couple of rats," I said. McKeogh had known them longer. "A couple of bastards," he said, "and I'd slit their throats gladly." [. . .]

Though he was declared winner of the Pulitzer Prize for literature, which he rejected, and winner of the Nobel Prize for literature, which he accepted, not all of Lewis's novels, though always best sellers, were of first magnitude. I have thought of most of them as magnificent social histories in the form of fiction, with *Arrowsmith* the best. He saw himself genuinely a genius, and for half his writing life he *was* a genius. A short Lewis novel—"Harri" [*Good Housekeeping,* August 1943]—never saw the light of day as a hardcover book, and for good reason: it was twaddle. The author was usually willing to make reasonable changes, but this thing was hopeless, so bad that I had it rewritten in the office, rewrote part of it myself, without consulting him, which didn't make it much better. I knew Lewis wouldn't have taken the necessary time on that one. However, he didn't utter a complaining word; I had just done him a favor important to him—found a place on *Good Housekeeping* for a favorite young friend he had been trying to mold into an actress.

105 / Philip von Rohr Sauer

Dr. Philip von Rohr Sauer, a descendant of the pioneer pastor and leader of the Wisconsin synod Reverend Philip von Rohr, was a resident of Bemidji, Minnesota.

Source: Philip von Rohr Sauer, "The 1945 Lectures: A Happy Episode in Sinclair Lewis's Life," *Sinclair Lewis Newsletter* 4 (1972): 3.

During the summer of 1945 Lewis delivered a series of lectures at several colleges in Minnesota. [. . .] I had the privilege of being Sinclair Lewis's companion during his three-day sojourn in Bemidji. [. . .] The high point of Lewis's sojourn was, of course, his lecture. On July 11 at the newly erected Bemidji High School Auditorium he spoke to a large group of students, faculty, and townspeople. His topic for his lectures was to be "The Craft of Writing," but in Bemidji he changed his title at the last minute to "What Do You Know about Minnesota?"

Lewis's thesis was directed at potential local writers whom he strongly urged to remain in the Heartland rather than flee to the eastern metropolises as soon as they showed promise.

"In our small communities we have everything that travel can bring us," he said. "The German families have the customs and history of their country, the Norwegians their Viking sagas, and even the Mexican laborers bring the South American atmosphere."

Though he advocated travel and wide experience, he emphatically pleaded with young people to keep their roots in Minnesota. He then discussed some of the Minnesota writers who have stayed, as he put it, "in their own Bemidjis, Sauk Centres, and Moorheads," instead of rushing to New York where they are so lost among seven million that they find no one to hate or love.

14
Thorvale Farm
1946–49

Lewis's last home, perhaps the only home he had known since leaving Sauk Centre for Yale in 1903, was a 750-acre farm he bought in northwestern Massachusetts in June 1946 for $45,000. For most of the time Lewis lived there, he was able to control his drinking. Still, most of his companions during this period were his employees. As Lingeman notes, the farm consisted of 200 acres of woods, 120 acres under cultivation, a mansion, and a "seven room cottage" for the tenants, "a brook-fed swimming pool, a trout stream, a cow barn, a milk house, a 'sugaring-off' house, a sawmill," and the like.[1] But he was able to complete his last novel of any significance, *Kingsblood Royal,* which examined race relations in America and appeared the same year Jackie Robinson broke the color barrier in major league baseball.

106 / Harrison Smith

As Smith remembered, Lewis's life at Thorvale Farm was almost cloistered, if only unintentionally, partly because of its distance from New York, mostly because he had alienated so many of his friends.

Source: Harrison Smith, "Sinclair Lewis: Remembrance of the Past," *Saturday Review of Literature,* January 27, 1951, 37–38.

When Lewis's second marriage ended, the problem of companionship, of having somebody close to him became increasingly difficult. He moved restlessly around the country—a cottage in Stockbridge, a hotel apartment in New York, then one in Hollywood, a huge duplex on Central Park West, a city mansion that had once belonged to a millionaire in Duluth in his home state, and finally the great house called Thorvale Farm near Williamstown. There a few of his friends came to see him, Bennett Cerf, Carl Van Doren, and others, but it was too far from New York for people who had offices to return to on Monday. He had restored, decorated, and furnished the house, the farm down the hill was brought out of decrepitude, the farmer's house rebuilt, and the barns newly roofed and filled with cattle and farm machinery. He owned the mountain in back, a tennis court on which he could never play, and a guest house he did not need.

For years he had been adding to his large collection of books, and I often wondered if what appeared to be his passion for large dwellings was not the result of wanting space and a background for his library. His was a highly complex personality, but his needs were essentially simple. The one commodity he could not buy was companionship. All but his close friends he drove away from him, for he could not endure the casual, inane remarks that pass for conversation among most people. He would leap upon some innocent comment about the weather or his six-toed cat like a hawk swooping on a terrified rabbit. The polite people of Duluth, delighted to have in their midst a celebrated genius, finally shunned his house; and since he so often used people he met as objects of satire for his next book it was not astonishing that the college group in Williamstown considered Thorvale Farm an ogre's castle.

It is remarkable how little he had to do with the writers of the Thirties who were making a stir in the world. In one of his books Thomas Wolfe records a meeting with someone who could only have been Lewis;[2] but Steinbeck, Hemingway, Scott Fitzgerald, and the critics of the time, though he knew their books, were almost strangers to him. I can't remember meeting in his apartment in New York a single one of this vital group. In reading recently the biography of Scott Fitzgerald[3] I discovered that Lewis's name and his work are mentioned in only two sentences.

107 / Frederick Manfred

Frederick Manfred (1912–1994) was baptized Frederick Feike Feikema and early in his career published books as Feike Feikema. His most successful book, the novel *Lord Grizzly,* was a finalist for the National Book Award in 1954. While living in Duluth and working on *Kingsblood Royal* early in 1946, Lewis invited his fellow Minnesotan writer to visit him. See also Nancy Bunge, "The Minnesota School: Sinclair Lewis's Influence on Frederick Manfred," *North Dakota Quarterly* 70 (Winter 2003): 118–25.

Source: Frederick Manfred, "Sinclair Lewis: A Portrait," *American Scholar* 23, no. 2 (1954): 165, 166, 168–69, 170–71.

I knocked at his door at precisely four. It was cold, and I remember that I was all bundled up in a big greatcoat and a high fur hat. The door opened and a pair of luminous gray-green eyes topped by thinning white hair looked up at me, looked up even though the head was tilted forward and down. Pale, almost imperceptible brows had climbed halfway up a high blond forehead. [. . .] My eyes finally fastened on his face. And the face I saw was a face to haunt one in dreams. It was a face that looked as if it were being slowly ravaged by a fire, by an emotional fire, by a fire that was already fading a little and that was leaving a slowly contracting lump of gray-red cinder. [. . .]

As the tea was being poured by the housekeeper[4]—she had taken a seat to my right for a few moments—Red took a notebook out of his pocket and waited a moment for the talk to die down, then said, "Look, I'd like to get your reaction to these titles." He put down a nervous finger, traced the titles. "Kingson, Kingsblood, Kingsman. Which do you like best for a book that's about a man who believes in a family legend that somewhere way back one of the ancestors descended from royalty? When all along he's really got some Negro blood in him?"

All three of us chose Kingsblood. The unanimity surprised him. He looked around at all of us, nodded, said, "Good. I've got the title for my new book then. And now I can relax for the rest of your stay here. Next week I can begin work."

I had heard before about Red's way of letting others choose his titles for him, and sitting there I had the distinct feeling that he had taken our pulse, that with his finger on the pulse he was again his father, the country bedside doctor, the father he admired to idolatry. And I also had the feeling that Red was asking us to share in the responsibility—some would say guilt—for the kind of books he wrote. [. . .]

At the dinner that night he got going on the race question. He had spent some time in the South and had also hired himself a male colored cook, a cook who had excellent reading tastes. Red not only seemed to have explored the scenes of racial intolerance, but had also done a lot of reading on the subject. He probed us to see how we reacted to it all, but the only reaction he got from us was agreement. It was obvious, as we went along, that Red's interest was more than just casual, that in fact, as his list of titles suggested, he was about to explore the race question—which he did, of course, in his next novel, *Kingsblood Royal.*

108 / Barnaby Conrad

Barnaby Conrad (b. 1922), writer and artist, graduated from Yale in 1943 and served as American Vice Consul to Seville, Málaga, and Barcelona, Spain, from 1943 to 1946. He was Lewis's personal secretary and chess companion in the spring and summer of 1947. Among his books are *Matador* (1952) and *Dangerfield* (1961), the latter loosely based on his experiences with Lewis.

Source: Barnaby Conrad, *Fun While It Lasted* (New York: Random House, 1969), 282–83, 285, 302–3.

Four-and-a-half miles in back of Williamstown on Oblong Road, the 750 acres of field and mountain and woods of Thorvale Farm began. Mr. Lewis showed me around proudly. It was the most beautiful estate I had ever seen, complete with a trout stream, a purposefully rustic swimming pool set in a birch glen, guest houses, barns and a tennis court. The handsome manor house had a fine view of Mt. Greylock, seven bedrooms, five baths and was beautifully furnished. Bookcases were everywhere, even running up the stairs. Where there weren't books, there were valuable impressionistic paintings by Childe Hassam.[5] [. . .]

Mr. Lewis showed me his workroom upstairs off his bedroom, saying, "Here's the factory."

It was incredibly neat, with an almost sterilized feeling about it. A dozen freshly sharpened pencils were in an earthen pot on the L-shaped custom-built desk. Neat stacks of typed pages and notes on yellow legal paper were the only hints of the great activity that took place at that desk. Framed on the wall was a large detailed map of Lewis' mythical Midwestern town, the locale of so many of his books, with such labels as "Carol's house" or "Doc's place." There were half a dozen photos of Marcella, one of his son Michael, and one of Wells in uniform. [. . .]

That night I played chess with Mr. Lewis before dinner. I had studied chess for only a few weeks and had little talent for the game, but I managed to maneuver his king into a bad position fairly soon. I left to go to the bathroom, and when I returned I could swear the pieces had been moved to my disadvantage. But I didn't say anything and I managed to win anyway. He seemed upset. [. . .]

Part of the reason for his temperament at that time was not only the loss of Marcella, but the reception that *Kingsblood Royal* was getting. While it was commercially successful—a bestselling book—the reviews that were coming in were not what he had hoped for at all. When they would arrive in the mail from a clipping service, he will spill them out of the envelope contemptuously and pretend not to be interested in them. [. . .]

But one day a review came that was written by his longtime friend, Clifton Fadiman, a man he admired greatly. "Ah-hah!" said Lewis, as he tenderly held the clipping in his trembling fingers. "Let's see what old Kip has to say! His literary opinions are worth all the rest put together."

He read the first sentences and beamed. "Well, I'm delighted *somebody's* glad I'm 'still in the arena and still punching,'" he said. "Good old Kip! And you're damned right I did a lot of research on this book."

Then he read on, and he began to scowl. Soon the scowl twisted his red face and he began to talk back to the piece of paper, oblivious to my presence.

"What do you mean the characters don't live!" he muttered. "Why, they dance all over the pages!" And then, his eyes skipping down to the next paragraph, "Preposterous? Of course you'd think it was preposterous, Fadiman, what the hell do you know about the Negro? What do you know of the way he's treated, the way he lives? What the hell do you know about life, when you get right down to it—stashed away in your ivory cocoon!"

By the time he had ended the long and thoughtful review, the paper was twisted and torn. He started to crumple it up. Then, mechanically, he smoothed it out and gently placed it on the low table in front of him. He sat there looking at it in silence for a moment. Finally, he gave a low moan-like sigh. "Maybe," he murmured, "maybe it is [. . .] a bad novel."[6]

He dropped his face in his hands, and I took that moment to quietly leave the room.

109 / Betty Stevens

Betty Stevens, a Minnesotan journalist who had been formerly employed by a Southern CIO newspaper, was a friend to Lewis during the 1940s. They met while he was briefly teaching a course at the University of Minnesota in January 1942, and after she attended one of his lectures he invited her to visit him. She subsequently recorded her memories of several days she spent with him at Thorvale Farm in 1947.

Source: Betty Stevens, "A Village Radical: His Last American Home," *Venture* 2, no. 3 (1957): 35–46.

The New England land looked tidy and neatly combed, unlike the untamed prairie of Minnesota and the bleak wilderness of the rock red earth around the iron mine.

I was riding in a large black car with Sinclair Lewis. His chauffeur Joseph [Hardrick] drove us from the Pittsfield station to Lewis's New England farmhouse near Williamstown where I would be vacationing for the next ten days.

"Thorvale Farm," Lewis said. "You'll like it. Looks across a valley at Mt. Greylock. But it's not like the wheat farms back home."

When we arrived, he took my suitcases in his long hands, walking ahead of me, his tall, awkward body a rust-red exclamation point against the smooth green lawn. If his rangy and uncultivated look set him apart from the careful renovation inside, there was still that same wistful pride about his house that he had shown about his Duluth mansion two years before. I had been visiting Duluth relatives then, during the summer of 1945.

"Who-dunnits," he said, pointing to the bookcases in my room upstairs. "Some Agatha Christies,[7] too. Some people only confess to reading literature, but I like Agatha Christies, myself."

I noticed books everywhere, set in a whole wall of the living room, in the bedrooms, even tucked here and there near stair landings, as well as in the library and the upstairs study. Even the bright orange blocks on the dark blue of the early Lewis editions caught my eye. Without asking, I was sure he had finished with the Duluth house. I wondered if he had taken his books with him to each of his restless households, to all the cities and counties where he had lived since he first left Minnesota more than forty years before.

The white fringe that had edged the same dome of his head had now nearly overgrown the sparse red, and the lines in his face and hands were noticeably deeper than when I had seen him the year before in New York.

In the bright New England kitchen, he opened a family-size refrigerator and said, "If you're hungry after your trip, we can just help ourselves. Joseph won't mind. Supper will be a little later." It was more homelike than the Duluth kitchen, where haunches of beef and pork had hung behind sliding glass refrigerator doors.

From the kitchen, he led me through the long living room out onto a white-pillared porch. A young man flashed by us, and there were quick introductions. His name was Barney.

"My secretary," Lewis explained. "Gone to New York for the weekend. To see a girl, I think. I don't really need a secretary, but it gets lonesome up here, especially in the winter."

We stood there on the porch and looked out at the many acres of Thorvale Farm. So much land, and Lewis had not put in a crop.

"Bill," Lewis called to a young Negro man clipping bushes. "I want you to meet a friend of mine." There were first name introductions again, and I could see that Lewis didn't take to being a Lord of the manor. Bill was the gardener who lived with his father in a cottage on the grounds.

Kingsblood Royal had come out that year—1947—and I told him I had liked it, even if much of the literary press hadn't.

"I don't understand why most of the critics reacted the way they did," he said, and the lines on his pitted face dug deeper, as though scratched in by a rake. "Jane White[8] was up here visiting a few weeks ago. Lovely girl. I got to know the family when I was writing *Kingsblood.* Walter [White] was very helpful, gave me a lot of material from the NAACP files."

He talked on about how he had collected material for the book, and it was evident that he liked Kingsblood. "I went all over the country talking to people. Talked to Percy Greene,[9] down in Mississippi. And then, one time, I was with a group of Negro people, and one man leaned over to me and said, 'Red, you seem to understand the whole thing so well, you sure you weren't touched by the tar-brush yourself?'" He face relaxed with delight, then quickly turned thoughtful again. "They're Americans the same way I'm American. If I do understand, that's why."

His grandfather, a Canadian doctor, volunteered from Canada and served with the Union Army. He seemed quite proud of his grandfather, and he asked, "Anybody in your family volunteer?"

"Great-grandfather," I told him. "Went all the way through with Sherman from Atlanta to the sea."

"Lots of doctors in my family," he nodded. "My father, too, and now my brother, he's practicing in St. Cloud. I never quite get over the feeling that writing isn't much of a profession, compared with being a doctor, that it's not quite manly to be sitting there on the seat of your pants all the time. Those critics, though," he frowned, "that's something else. They've been telling me for thirty years that I can't write and never could."

It was almost dusk, and we watched the sun set out beyond Mt. Greylock. It was a gracious mountain, I thought, as this whole land was gracious and groomed from having been lived in for so much longer than any other part of the country.

Before I went up to my room he briefed me on the protocol of Thorvale Farm, in much the same way, I gathered, as he had all his other visitors. "I'm on a tight schedule up here," he began. "I get up very early and write until noon. But I'll see you at lunchtime. I take a nap every afternoon and write a few more hours. So, sleep late if you like, read anything you want. Or prowl around the grounds. Make yourself at home. There's a swimming pool over there. Do anything you like, child. This is your vacation."

That night we had supper together on the screened back porch and Lewis told me about a party he was planning for July Fourth. He had invited a girl from the bookstore in town [Ida L. Compton], and a few people from Williams College—"a nice English mathematician and his wife." Then he added, "Some of my lady relatives from home will be dropping by while you're here, maybe that weekend, but you'll understand them all right. Probably just like your own people."

Before dinner was over, Lewis asked me about my life in New York, what I'd been doing, about my friends and my job. I had only recently taken a job with a woman's fashion magazine, doing advertising copy, and I told him about it.

"Oh, advertising," he said, and he made a face. "Are you sure it's really moral for you? You know, with your principles about the labor movement and society? Are you sure it's really honest?"

I was defensive because I wondered the same thing.

"You'd be better off as a grocery clerk than writing advertising," he said. "But don't worry about it, you'll have to learn your own way. If you can't get back to the newspaper business, even publishing might be better. If you change your mind, let me know. I can speak to some publishers for you."

"I got fired trying to organize one place I worked," I told him, "and then I didn't have any New York references."

"References?" His head jerked sharply. "If you ever need references because you've been fired—especially for union activity—you just tell 'em you worked for me. Secretary, publicity, anything you like. The Lord knows I've had enough secretaries, one more won't make any difference. And, anyway," he added, "don't worry. All our girls from home get ahead when they come to New York."

As I looked about in the last big house where Lewis lived alone in his own country, I thought: he should have children and grandchildren to fill this house and to receive his shy, lonesome affection. And I was reminded of the college boy who came to Lewis while writing his Master's thesis on Lewis as a satirist.[10] They had discussed Lewis's social and literary views for hours, and later, Lewis wrote several letters to colleagues and helped the boy to get a good teaching job. I recalled, too, a young Minnesota writer who had been invited to take her ease and to write in peace at his home; and of another student he had taken behind the scenes of the Minnesota legislature to be instructed in the iniquitous machinations that took place there.

I believed all the stories I had ever heard, that Lewis was the softest touch in the world, and not only to people who really liked him. I wanted him to know, somehow, that I liked him because he was such a nice fellow, and such good company. I made up my mind I'd never ask him for a favor.

During the first days, I felt a bit timid as I wandered around the house, taking books off the shelves, nibbling at the good things in the refrigerator, sunning or swimming in the pool while Lewis wrote or napped. But pretty soon, I recognized the familiar small-town hospitality in the larger setting. I relaxed and enjoyed it, although occasionally it would startle me when Lewis would mention a certain book he had written. I'd been chatting with a friend from home and suddenly I'd look at a legendary figure who was the first American to be awarded the Nobel Prize for literature.

I was glad, too, that I had made a point of bringing a full supply of my own cigarettes, because Lewis noticed them one afternoon.

"Good," he said. "You brought your own cigarettes. If you need, say, a hundred dollars, just come up and ask me, I always say. But don't chisel cigarettes. If there's anything I can't stand, it's people who chisel cigarettes."

It seemed that Lewis had some idea of how a man of stature was supposed to act, and made a point of acting exactly the opposite. Back at almost the very start of our acquaintance, he insisted that I call him Red instead of Mr. Lewis, as I had been addressing him. Like some bankers I had known in small Minnesota towns where I lived and worked, who would have been deeply offended had a farmer or salesman along Main Street called him "Mister" instead of Ed or Bill.

Like my father, too, who never in his life had his shoes shined by a man who half-knelt at his feet with a shoeshine kit. He couldn't stand to see another man assume so undignified a position and he either blacked his own shoes or dropped them off at the shoe parlor.

During the third or fourth day at Thorvale, a telegram arrived from an old friend, telling him that their young son had died and that they wanted him to come to the funeral. "It's going to be a large public funeral," he told me, "and they actually want to talk about it. When Wells was killed, I didn't want to talk to anybody about it." His huge blue eyes were bare with bereavement. (His son, Wells, named after H. G. Wells, was the child of his first marriage, and was killed in World War II.)

There seemed to be no one in the world close to him then, no really close friends, and no one in his family. Except for an occasional *landsman,* like myself, passing through, a fellow refugee from Babbittry, with whom he might share his most poignant memory: home. If this was part sentiment, the memory surely had deeper roots, for Main Street was the source of his most inspired creative work.

When he was not working, we talked. We talked all the time, and he talked even more than I did. About politics, books, the East, the South, about the Midwest which was home, and about personalities. Often he used his talent for mimicry to change, before my eyes, into a person he created. And I remembered the brief visits with him in New York the year before, and the games he sometimes played, while we sat on a park bench or in a restaurant. "Look," he'd say, "that man over there. Looks like some Wall Street banker, doesn't he? Probably a salesman from Cincinnati, that's usually the way it is."

He still played those games, and he still talked with a high, flat nasal twang, a Minnesota accent as pure then as it had been the day he left the wheat town to go to Yale; even more pronounced than my own, and I had only recently left home.

On the fifth day, a couple of Lewis's lady relatives [his niece Virginia Lewis and her mother] did arrive from Minnesota. The older one came with her r's and small-town small-talk intact, her plump, pleasant face lively with the tourist enthusiasm of a woman locked all her life in the middle of a continent.

She talked about the weather, the road conditions, the land, the relatives, her town, the East, and what she would see in New York. She reminded me of my own relatives who had always overwhelmed me with their inexhaustible small-talk, and both Lewis and I fell into a deep silence.

I was worrying over whether or not I was being polite, when Lewis whispered to me, out on the porch, "Don't worry, child. It's hard talking to these older people." The woman was in her mid-fifties and Lewis was sixty-two, but suddenly he seemed as young as I was on a summer afternoon.

Later, the four of us had dinner together in a rustic roadhouse, and as we got out of the car, the others bustled up ahead, leaving Lewis and me to follow. There was a sharp look on the older woman's face as she passed us; the same sharp look my aunt would have flicked at any young girl who was visiting a divorced man and staying alone in the house with him.

"She can't understand what you're doing here," Lewis said in a low voice, holding in a sly, pleased laugh. "But why should I explain? I don't have to explain. Nobody's damn business, anyway."

I think I enjoyed being considered a bit of a Jezebel and it became a little joke between us. When the relatives left, you could tell that their firm impressions were packed away as neatly as the underthings in their bags. They were so much like the characters in his books that I wondered if what I had read was true: that Lewis had damned the whole lower middle class in America by such books as *Main Street* and *Babbitt.*

"No, no," he told me. "I didn't mean to damn anybody. I liked the people in those books. They were my children and I wanted to reform them. Gantry, too. Even Gantry wouldn't have been such a bad fellow if he'd been, say, a salesman. It's just that he was a minister and did the things he did."

The anger and violence against *Gantry* was a generation and a world away from this calm, easy time in New England. I remembered that I had read about a West Virginia minister who had actually invited Lewis south to be lynched, when *Gantry* came out. And there was the time back in 1926, when Lewis had denied God before the Kansas City Fundamentalists, asking God to strike him dead in ten minutes if He really existed.[11]

Now, twenty years later, Lewis still judged Gantry not simply as a minister but as a fraudulent minister. It occurred to me, with a sense of shock, that Lewis was an old Protestant atheist, and that he spoke of Gantry as an angry member in good standing of the Protestant community. But I didn't dare accuse him of it.

As I watched him then, an impish look sparked his small wry face. "Oh, you people," he called out sonorously toward the hedge around the house—a Gantry before his congregation. "I tell you, yes, I tell you, with all your fine cars and your fine clothes, and your fine cigarettes, and your fancy women, oh you people, I tell you, there's a day of reckoning coming, a day of reckoning!" He put his head back and laughed. But he quickly denied my observation that he had a fine satirical touch.

"Oh, no," he said, almost surprised. "I'm not a satirist. You take a man like Swift—he was a satirist because he exaggerated."[12]

During one of our afternoon strolls through Thorvale Farm, Lewis told me about how he'd become a socialist while at Yale, and had gone off to live for a while at Helicon Hall, Upton Sinclair's socialist colony in New Jersey, in 1906. It may have been no more than a curious coincidence that he told me about this just then, for that morning a book had arrived in the mail, a kind of Who's Who in American Literature. He had stared at the title and, with an apologetic look over at me for doing such an immodest thing, had turned to the section on Sinclair Lewis and had read it without looking up. Then he closed the book and set it on the coffee table without saying anything.

"I was the janitor," he said.

"It's no indignity being a janitor at a place like that," I said.

He agreed, and then he said, quite seriously, "But there's one thing I can never forgive Upton for." I leaned forward, anticipating an exposure of Upton Sinclair as a hard capitalist boss in a socialist utopia.

"For years," Lewis said, "every time I speak or lecture someplace, somebody in the audience always comes up to me and says, 'Oh, I so enjoyed your Lanny Budd series, Mr. Sinclair!'"[13]

Lewis's socialism was a writer's socialism, not a politician's, something all his own, like his writer's god was no one else's.

"I guess the kind of socialist I am is more like the German Social Democrats than anything else. I think the way we'll finally have socialism in America is that the state will take over more and more functions, the way it's taken over the post office. When I feel like it," he went on, "I'll vote for a Republican. I think Arthur Vandenberg[14] would be a good Presidential candidate in '48. I'm going to write and tell him so. I like Arthur. I think he is an honest man." He gave me a firm look as though he were trying to instruct me about an attitude.

"Oh, I know," he half-snorted, and his eyes sharpened upon me, "you'll probably be for Henry Wallace.[15] Frankly, I think Henry's got a Messiah complex. You mark my words, Henry'll never get more than a million votes. And going around talking about how he would accept the mandate of the American people. Whose mandate will it be, I'd like to know? Why, it's as though I were to go up to Hedy Lamarr[16] and say, 'I accept your hand in marriage.'"

Although I was singed by his scorn, I tried earnestly to defend Wallace and the Progressive program, pointing out mainly how it differed from other parties in foreign affairs. And since Lewis had never set himself up as an elder whose opinions were final, I told him about Madison Square Garden rallies of the Progressive Citizens of America,[17] and even started to suggest that he attend sometime, that he might even think about speaking.

It wasn't only Wallace, it must have been something about Madison Square Garden rallies, or maybe my overzealous approach, because suddenly his red face flashed brighter with rage. He sat upright, straight as a lever. His shout broke my sentence in two, and his thin body was shaking.

"Oh, I know what you're going to say now. I know. You're going to say that I'm not a good American. Don't you dare say I'm not a good American because I don't sign petitions or make speeches in Madison Square Garden. Don't you dare say I haven't fought for what's good in my country, and fought against what's bad. I've fought in all my books, for more than thirty years. And when it's said and done, they'll know by my work what I believed and what I stood for." Fury had taken his breath away, and his voice broke. He shook a long bony finger at me.

I sat there, close to tears, without saying anything for a minute or more. Finally, I whispered, "I never meant to say you aren't a good American. I never even thought such a thing."

"Come into the house," he said, "and I'll make you a nice, cool Tom Collins. It's getting hot out here." He got up quickly, looking ashamed of himself, as though he realized that it wasn't my fault if Henry had a Messiah complex.

I took the drink in silence and wandered over to one of the bookshelves, hearing him explain behind me that he didn't drink anymore, and adding, as he always did, "Used to be a drunk, you know."

One of the books took my attention, and he came up to look at it and then laughed. It dealt with the fleshly side of marriage.

"Oh, that's important, of course," he said. "But do young people in love ever stop and ask each other the really important things about marriage? Do any of them ever ask whether you like to sleep with the window open or closed? You'd be surprised at how important that is."

I fell in with it, and agreed that it was more important than love.

"And then all this talk about the role of the sexes," he said, shaking his head sadly, "and dominating women and all. Take me away from a dominating woman. Take me twenty miles away. If you don't, I'll marry her."

I was glad he had left his anger at Wallace out on the lawn, and was feeling mellow again. He told me that he had known two men whom all women loved: Charlie Chaplin and Bertrand Russell. "Nearly every woman who ever met either of them has taken someone aside to say now she's really met a man who understands her."

He remembered a dinner party he had gone to in England, at which Russell was also a guest, and how Russell had charmed the most attractive young woman there, without even seeming to try. And there was another time, when he had been having lunch in the Brown Derby with Charlie Chaplin and Cedric Hardwicke. A young girl had come in alone, and the three men had turned to look, but it was Chaplin who had sent a note with the waiter, asking if she'd like to join Chaplin, Lewis and Hardwicke for lunch. When she joined them, Lewis and Hardwicke were left completely to themselves once Chaplin started to talk to her. "And it wasn't really that Charlie was so much younger or handsomer than we were," Lewis sighed, wistfully.

He told me about other movie people he'd known when he was scriptwriting in Hollywood, and about one occasion with Adolphe Menjou.[18] "I went mountain climbing in Switzerland with Adolphe one time," he recalled. "Terrible stuffed shirt, Adolphe." I had a sudden wild picture of the two of them on an Alp, Lewis togged out in proper mountain climbing clothes, and Menjou coming up behind in a dress suit, mustaches waxed against the snow.

"I spent a while in the Soviet Union, too," he said, looking up at me slyly. "And you know what? I think Molotov[19] is a Babbitt. I can always tell, you know. I can just hear him. Suppose he has a young daughter, Tanya. I can hear him, 'Tanya, don't you dare smoke cigarettes. And don't stay out too late at the movies. A nice Soviet girl doesn't do such things.' I'm sure that's the way he is."

The labor novel that Lewis had talked about writing for nearly thirty years sat at the table with us at lunch one day. As long ago as 1930 he had petitioned the court to reduce his alimony to his first wife on the grounds that he would be writing a labor novel that year and it would reduce his income.

Friends who had been part of the CIO's organization of the steel industry in the mid-thirties had told me about Lewis and the union. He had considered the CIO an important and vital part of American life, and he wanted to see and understand it. They knew that Lewis was a man whose sympathies were to be trusted and they took him around to some of the secret organizing meetings held behind shade-drawn windows, while other union men kept watch for Steel Trust spies and guards.

Later, Lewis told the organizers that he had written some fifty thousand words about what he had seen, and then had given it up, because somehow he wasn't with it.

"People like those ladies at the Teachers' College," I remembered him telling me back in Duluth in 1945. "Maybe I don't agree with them, but I understand them. And the labor leaders and the workers, maybe I agree more with them, but I don't understand them. I don't know what to say to them."

By 1947, he had begun to think of the labor novel as a play, and during lunch that day he acted out some scenes for me. Part of the prologue was his reference to his membership in Actor's Equity, and mention of his roles both on Broadway and in Florida stock productions.

Although he usually just picked at the good food Joseph prepared, that day he left his lunch almost untouched, so nothing would interfere with the roles his hands would play. Everything about him was concentrated in the zeal of the storyteller, and the sun coming through the screens did very well as a spotlight.

"There's this factory. And there's this young radical whippersnapper of a labor organizer who's going to organize the workers. The owner's daughter is working in the factory for the summer, and she falls in love with the organizer. So they try to get the workers to join the union, but the workers won't vote for it. But the owner is a real American, a Dodsworth type of businessman who really believes in unions. So, in the third act, he gets up and makes a speech, telling the workers to join the union. And they do."

He picked up his fork with mild interest and began to pick at the food absently.

He never wrote either the labor novel or the labor play.

On the day after our Fourth of July picnic, which had featured a bonfire, wiener and marshmallow roasting, and no speeches, Lewis handed me a telegram he had received from the Joint Anti-Fascist Refugee Committee, asking his help in keeping Howard Fast[20] out of jail. (Fast, an officer in an organization which helped Spanish refugees, had refused to give names of those involved in the work of the group to an investigating committee.)

Lewis was sitting forward in his chair, staring out the wall of windows toward the mountain, the bleakness in his eyes dimming his whole face. "All right," he said, and he stood up firmly. "I'll write a letter for Howard. If they'd sent a petition, I wouldn't have signed it. But I'll write a letter. Howard's work is certainly true to the best American ideals."

He asked me to go with him to his study, and on the way up, he said over his shoulder, "Now, you take Howard. He isn't one of those parlor pinks. No, sir. He can't have been hanging around Village bars, chasing women and getting drunk all the time. Why, look at all the books he's written, and he's not even forty yet." And as we entered his study, Lewis said, "There's a young man who got up early and worked late. I know. I know how much work it is to write a book."

He typed out a letter, in which he said that Howard Fast was an important and deeply American writer, and that he, Lewis, was against sending him to jail. He made a typing error.

He took the paper out of the machine and pointed at the date. "See, I made it July 4th," and he winked. "More patriotic that way. And I started it by saying, 'On the anniversary of our country's birth.'"

After correcting the typing error in ink, he assured me that he could type without errors. "But when I write in my own corrections like this, they can say, 'See, the old man wrote this himself.'" He winked again.

"You mail it, child." He handed me the letter. "You'll be going back to New York in a few days."

Later, on the porch, he said, "You don't really think they'll send Howard to jail, do you?"

I thought they might.

"But if they do," and his voice was anxious, "they'll let him write, won't they? Won't they?"

I didn't know.

The worry on his face told me he was imagining himself in jail and not being allowed to write. "It's different for a writer," he said. "Take people like Foster and Davis and Gurley Flynn.[21] They're professionals, full-timers. I should think they'd consider going to jail an occupational risk. Especially Foster and Flynn, because they're both old Wobblies [members of the radical labor union IWW]. That's the way all the Wobblies I ever met figured it. Always talking about the jails they'd been in, how the food was in Butte, or the cells in Walla Walla. But not a writer. It's different for a writer."

And then he added, almost with embarrassment, "I hope people won't go around saying I wrote the letter because Howard was about the only one in the country who gave *Kingsblood* a good review." He sighed. "And I hope it'll be published someplace besides the *Daily Worker.*"[22]

110 / Ida L. Compton

Ida L. Compton, née Kay (1917–1985), was a student and journalist who befriended Lewis in 1947 and maintained a correspondence with him until his death.

Source: Ida Compton, *Sinclair Lewis at Thorvale Farm: A Personal Memoir* (Sarasota, FL: Ruggles, 1988), 3–5, 25–26, 41, 44–45, 46–47, 48–51.

My first meeting with Sinclair Lewis was quite by chance. It was in June 1947. He was living on his estate, Thorvale Farm, outside of Williamstown, Massachusetts, and had just completed his twentieth book, *Kingsblood Royal.* The book had received mixed reviews, some unfavorable, many lukewarm. But the literary world had been reminded that Sinclair Lewis was still a force to be reckoned with. At the time I was a graduate student at Williams College and helping to manage the bookstore in town. I had just started writing book reviews for the local newspapers and Lewis had read about my enthusiastic discussions of *Kingsblood Royal.* Through Barnaby Conrad, then Lewis's secretary-companion and later a very successful author in his own right, I was invited to Thorvale for dinner to meet the great man himself.

Lewis had been living in Williamstown for little over a year, but the town had seen very little of him. Rumor had it that he chose to be isolated, that he had no desire to meet anyone locally and that he wanted complete privacy to work and time to entertain his famous guests from out of town. Consequently the invitation to be his guest came as an exciting surprise. It also brought on some apprehension. I had read about his idiosyncrasies and decided that I should be on the alert for almost anything. Moreover, I, who ordinarily had no trouble talking, feared that I would become tongue-tied. [. . .]

On the arranged afternoon I walked up the side terrace of the house and found that I had interrupted a game of chess between Barnaby and a young lady houseguest. After a casual and relaxed introduction, Barnaby said Lewis was upstairs dressing and would be right down. I then became absorbed in their chess game and didn't notice when Lewis arrived at the screen door which led onto the terrace. "Oh, so you're Ida!" he said, as he swung the door open. [. . .] "Now, come around on this side of the house and tell me about yourself." I jumped up like a puppet whose strings had been pulled.

"Barnaby came back from town yesterday with glowing reports of his meeting with you," he said, as we walked along. And then after a pause, "Call me Red."

"Now come sit down," he said as he indicated a chair next to him. He spoke in a high pitched, clipped manner and turned toward me with a straightforward stare from compulsive blue eyes. His questions came in rapid fire order. "Who are you?" "Where did you come from?" "Where were you educated?" I found myself being a little disappointed at this inquisition. But I was to learn later that this famous author, a world traveler and center of many social and intellectual gatherings, was shy and felt socially uncomfortable until some kind of rapport was established with those whom he was meeting for the first time. [. . .]

As the evening progressed Lewis continued to be in great form: voluble, amusing, and charming. There wasn't any suggestion of formality. He was far easier to be with than most strangers. There was no hint of the loneliness which was so much a part of his life at the time.

It wasn't until later reflection that I realized that physically the man could be called ugly. His face was like a mask, badly pitted from frequent skin operations; his head was small for his over six foot gangling frame; his extremely long, skeletal hands protruded from his jacket sleeves and seemed to operate independently from his body. But he used them effectively and they were fascinating to watch. [. . .]

The summer of 1947 was a good one for Lewis despite many reasons for it to be otherwise. Marcella Powers, a young actress and literary agent with whom Lewis had had a liaison for over seven years, had left him and married a younger man during the previous spring. But enough things were happening in the newness of his surroundings to relieve the shock and pain. There had been enough attention paid to *Kingsblood Royal* so that he had swallowed the adverse criticism without too much resentment. He wasn't drinking and he was working on the beginning of *The God-Seeker* [1949].

He was surrounded by Joseph Hardrick, his cook and chauffeur, Alma and Wilson Perkins, who cleaned and took care of the estate, and Barnaby. Lewis was having his house redone to please his particular needs and the grounds were being cleaned and landscaped meticulously. He had frequent guests, including Max Flowers,[23] formerly of the Williams College Theatre department, and his wife Jo, who were heading up the student group at the Berkshire Playhouse in Stockbridge nearby. He was invited to the homes of neighbors William H. Vanderbilt, a former governor of Rhode Island,[24] O. Dixon Marshall, a local attorney, and Cornelia Stratton Parker, an author originally from California.[25] [. . .]

The summer when Barnaby Conrad was Lewis's secretary, Lewis felt a great warmth for this budding author, until he realized that Barnaby was not a worker as he, Lewis, always had been. When one night Barnaby complained of not feeling like writing the agreed upon number of words per day, Lewis flew off into a fury. "Barney! When will you learn that you write whether you feel like it or not? You'll never do anything if you wait until the mood moves you."

Barnaby protested mildly, "But what's the use of writing two chapters if I know that they're not what I want to say and they don't come up to the writing I've done before?"

This was enough for Lewis to go off in his high pitched voice, showing intense annoyance that someone could even aspire to be a writer and not follow the kind of routine he had imposed on himself all of his life. "No muse ever moved me. If I had waited for inspiration I would never have written even one book. You young writers don't know what it is to work. You all feel that there's something privileged about your ability. Just because you write one story and get it published, you think that you can sit back and wait for something else to happen. Well, it doesn't. You work for it and you sweat. You write words and pages and then you do them over again." [. . .]

Lewis had none of the pretentious approach to writing nor the commonly accepted version of the artist's way of life. He knew little about art, music, or the dance. He owned hundreds of recordings of which he recognized only a very few. He owned four original Childe Hassam paintings, but seemed to have no particular reason for having them. He had visited endless art galleries and famous cathedrals in Europe, but almost as a sense of duty and a means to an end. It added to the knowledge he might someday want. [. . .]

Most every actor before he becomes a star has an idol; most every painter aspired to another who has preceded him; most every writer has another writer before him as a model. Lewis's paragon was Charles Dickens. But on this matter as on others, Lewis was like a sensitive child who wants something but doesn't come out and ask for it directly. He hinted at it, talked around it, but hesitated to be explicit.

Prominent on his bookshelf in the living room at Thorvale was the beautiful Nonesuch Press edition of Dickens. Lewis often commented on the beautiful colors of the bindings and with pretended ridicule added that the books were in the living room because the colors blended with the décor. He would casually remark about the similarity of his choice of names for his characters and those Dickens used. He seldom missed an opportunity to mention the important role Dickens played in English letters and the high regard the English people had for him as a writer. He spoke of the brilliance of Dickens's style and the fact that he could read and re-read any of Dickens's books and always find something new and surprising. He once said jokingly, "Dickens and the Bible will never go out of print." And on another occasion, "When they have removed all authors from required reading in schools and substituted visual education, little boys and girls and young men and women will seek out Dickens, even if it is considered to be subversive literature, and he will be the savior of mankind."

I had hoped that sometime he would discuss what he thought about the relationship of his own writing to that of Dickens's; and eventually he did. It was after Norman Mailer's visit and we were discussing new authors and the value of their books. Lewis wanted to know how I felt about *The Naked and the Dead,* and the place it might finally have in American literature.[26] This led to the question of what makes an author live not only for his own age but for future generations. We had talked about this many evenings, but there was always something new to say.

"If my books are read fifty years from now," Lewis said, "it's because I did for America what Dickens did for England." [. . .]

His last book was originally written under the title of *Over the Body of Lucy Jade,* and was concerned with the relationships between an American girl and expatriate Americans in Italy. It was extremely sad to have it turn out poorly. He failed to make the characters convincing, and it was replete with unfortunate anachronisms, having his 1950s characters, for example, speak in the clichés of the 1920s.

Bennett Cerf, Lewis's publisher, read the manuscript at Thorvale shortly after Lewis finished it in the summer of 1949. Bennett found it to be almost unpublishable. He telephoned me for help.

"Ida, I wonder if you could come out this afternoon and read it. Then perhaps if you and I can get Red into a conversation about it, it will be easier for me to tell him what I think."

When I arrived it was immediately obvious that great tension permeated the house. Moreover, Lewis wasn't very enthusiastic about my reading the manuscript. But despite the stresses of the situation I managed to finish it by early evening, after we had dinner. When in the discussion which followed Bennett attempted to slide gently into some of his criticisms, Lewis quickly went into one of his ferocious rages. It was a nightmare: bitter, loud, personal, and also sad and pathetic. He stormed at Bennett and threatened to change publishers. It went on for a long time, but eventually he became exhausted and went off to bed.

The next morning he was a little more conciliatory. But for days after Bennett left, Lewis threw abusive insult after insult at him, Random House, and the world. He sank deeper and deeper into despair. But Bennett had done him a great service by refusing to publish it as it was. It would have been an embarrassment.

He eventually rewrote the book in Italy. In one of his letters from there the following spring he wrote, "I shall be busy with my book (which is so vast a change in and improvement of *Lucy Jade* that you will not recognize it. Even a different title)." It was published after his death as *World So Wide* [1951]. He went back to *Dodsworth* for some of his characters, returning to what had once made him famous. It became, probably without intention, a brilliant staging for his exit.

Lewis had been drinking heavily when he was in Europe during the winter of 1948–1949. His general health gradually worsened even after he returned to Williamstown. In early spring he was overcome by a severe attack of pneumonia. [. . .] By the middle of May Lewis had reasonably recovered. But after the *Lucy Jade* fiasco that summer he descended once again into a steady round of wine, gin, and whiskey, which was to mark the beginning of the last phase of his life. [. . .] It was a dreadful and uncertain time. [. . .] Although shaken and weak, he gradually resumed his walks and writing schedule. His thoughts turned to selling Thorvale and returning to Europe for good.

One day while dwelling on this subject as we walked along he turned to me and said, "Darling, you have added enormously to my life during these past few years." And then after a pause, "How about going to Europe with me as Mrs. Sinclair Lewis?"

His manner was casual and tentative. But I felt myself almost trembling with bewilderment. As our friendship developed Lewis had long since won my strong admiration for what he had accomplished and for what he still was, despite all the complexities. But marriage? I thought of the great differences in our outlooks and our ages and Lewis's persistent record of impulsiveness and unpredictability. And I thought of my other interests. Moreover, strong doubts pressed in about whether I would be up to handling what probably lay ahead.

When Lewis confided in Bennett Cerf that he wished I would marry him, Bennett, with his ever present humor quipped to me in private, "God, Ida, I can think of hundreds of beautiful chicks in New York alone who would grab the chance and scream 'aye' without having ever seen the man." And, not intending to be cruel, but just Bennett, he added, "You know it won't be for long, the way he's going. And you have so much to give each other." And then later, "Don't think of yourself, don't be that selfish, think of Red. You just might help to save the life of a great man."

In the end, however, my conservatism prevailed. And the immediate situation was eased when his brother Claude consented to go to Europe with Lewis. As a physician he could be especially important. But I continued to be haunted about the correctness of my decision.

Early in September Lewis and his brother left for Europe on what was to be Lewis's last sail across the Atlantic. Depressed, with a hatred of Williamstown, he remarked, "I've given my life to this country in the best way, and no one cares."

111 / Horace R. Cayton Jr.

Horace R. Cayton Jr. (1908–1970), scholar, journalist, government official, and educator, is probably most famous for his work with St. Clair Drake on their groundbreaking sociological study of Chicago, *Black Metropolis* (1945). He was the grandson of a Reconstruction US senator from Mississippi and the son of the journalist and Republican politician Horace R. Cayton (1859–1940). Like his father, he was a lifelong advocate for civil rights and proponent of social justice. Lewis mentioned Cayton in passing in chapter 53 of *Kingsblood Royal*. While he was at Yaddo, a writer's retreat near Saratoga Springs, New York, Cayton visited Lewis at Thorvale Farm.

Source: Horace R. Cayton Jr., *Long Old Road* (New York: Trident, 1965), 294–303, 308.

When *Kingsblood Royal* first came out, I reviewed the book favorably, although I realized it was not one of Mr. Lewis's best.[27] The Negro question was coming to a fast boil, and a man of his stature on our side was too valuable to subject to intensive literary criticism.

When I finished the review I had sent it to Mr. Lewis, thanking him for mentioning me in the book. He replied by return mail, suggesting that if I were ever in the neighborhood of Williamstown, Massachusetts, I should drop by and see him. So from Yaddo[28] I wrote and told him where I was, and it was arranged for me to visit him at his estate, Thorvale Farm.

The Lewis estate was large and lovely. His house was spacious and comfortable and stood on a large hill overlooking a beautiful valley. In addition to the main house, there were a couple of small cottages for servants and guests, a large swimming pool, a tennis court, and a farm. The establishment was run by three Negro servants.

Joseph, the chauffeur and cook, was about thirty or thirty-five. He was a competent, pleasant, and rather sophisticated man whom Lewis had found in New Orleans. He was fond of "the old man," as he sometimes called his employer, and very loyal and he told me on one occasion that Lewis had put him in his will. He knew that he had a good job and did his work well.

I never got the feeling that Joseph was sly or cunning, but he was something of an Uncle Tom, though a very high-class one. I suspected that Joseph had had a better education than he let on, and from conversations I had with him I don't think that he intended always to remain a servant. He was going to see this stint with Lewis through and then, depending on his inheritance, move on to a life more to his taste.

Alma was the maid, and Wilson, her husband, was the gardener-handyman. They had one small child. Alma was, I suspect, in her late twenties or early thirties, a light-colored creole from Louisiana who was plump and attractive. She seemed to dominate the quiet, easy-going Wilson and she outwardly accepted her position, kept her place, and did her work but she demanded and received respect. I got some insight into her character the first day I arrived.

Lewis and Joseph had met me at the train, some little distance from Williamstown. When we got to the house I stopped downstairs for a cup of coffee, and Joseph took my bags up to my room. When I finally got there, Alma had unpacked for me. She greeted me as I walked into the room. "Mr. Cayton," she said, "I am Alma."

But she was young and attractive, and I didn't want to treat her merely as a servant; I felt I should make her aware that I recognized we both were Negroes. "What is your last name?" I asked.

"Alma will do," she stated simply, letting me know that I was a guest and should stay in my place, as she would stay in hers. And that set the tone of my relationship with all the servants.

There was one other member of the household—Barnaby Conrad, Lewis's secretary—an extremely charming and talented young man who had just returned from Spain. He had been a bullfighter there and was engaged in writing his first novel. Lewis was helping him with it, and Barney was deferential and a little afraid of him. He was more of a companion than a secretary to Lewis, and so far as I saw obliged only to play chess with him after supper.

Barney, who was gifted in so many ways, was a poor chess player and hated it. He was delighted when I began to take his place in the after-supper games, and although I was also a poor player I managed to win about two out of three games. Everyone liked Barney; the servants all looked on him as a special friend.

Lewis was the master of his household, the complete master. I never heard him reprimand anyone or issue an order, but his control was absolute. Joseph might have been responsible for the efficient running of the household, but he was not some old retainer who in reality dominated his master; I never heard them, but he must have received sharp and definite instructions about all details.

I seldom saw Alma around the house but evidence of her work was ever present. I don't know whether she received her instructions from Lewis or from Joseph, but the house was kept spotless. Wilson kept up the grounds and served the meals on Joseph's day off. Apparently he knew what to do and did it well, as I never saw Lewis talking with him. Even Barney fitted his life into the Lewis rhythm so well that I never detected his duties, if he had any. Meals were always served on time—eight o'clock for breakfast, one o'clock lunch, and dinner at seven—and were announced by a large gong near the head of the stairs in the living room. I was warned by Barney that everyone was expected to be on time. The household followed Lewis's routine; people fitted into his mold. He was a stubborn man, set in his ways, and while living in his home one conformed to his pattern.

That it was important and necessary to Lewis for people to follow this pattern became evident to me the second day of my visit. Right after lunch he customarily took a nap, and the first day after we had finished eating and had talked for about a half-hour, he suggested that we go to our rooms and rest for a while. It had been a welcome suggestion, as I was tired from my trip. But the next day, taking it for granted that the routine had been firmly established, he made the same suggestion. Then followed what turned out to be a contest of wills between Lewis and myself.

"I don't think I'll nap today, Red," I said innocently. He had insisted that I call him Red an hour after I had first met him, and he called me by my first name. "Perhaps I'll walk down and see the farm."

"You'll feel much better after a little rest," he answered, seemingly solicitous of my well-being.

"Oh, I'm not a bit tired. How do I get to the farm?"

"I still think you should rest," he insisted, not answering my question.

It then occurred to me that he might not want me to see the farm, so I changed tactics. "Perhaps I'll take a walk up the stream instead."

"That's a beautiful walk, Horace. But it's much nicer in the cool of the afternoon. Why don't you rest for an hour or so and then take your walk?"

It would have been much easier at this point simply to have gone to my room and read for an hour to please him. He had been extremely pleasant and had put himself out to make my stay as enjoyable as possible. But I felt pushed; I didn't feel that I should give in. How I should spend my time was my affair, if it didn't interfere with the household routine.

"I don't want to rest, Red," I said. "I'll find something to do."

With that I left the table. I put on my swimming suit and walked down to the pool. I lay there for a couple of hours—sleeping, reading, and thinking. I was a little annoyed at the business over the luncheon table but after a while I forgot it.

In the latter part of the afternoon I saw Lewis coming down the rather steep hill from the house at an awkward old man's pace. When he sat down next to me he was as pleasant as ever. After a bit he said, "About that nap business, Horace, forgive me. I'm just an old bastard always trying to run people's lives. It's one of my faults."

Life at Thorvale Farm was actually extremely pleasant for me. The food that Joseph prepared was excellent, and the weather was perfect. Lewis was one of the most delightful conversationalists I have ever known. He knew something about everything; he talked on any subject well and on many brilliantly. At first, of course, it was the Negro question. He knew a number of Negro leaders and artists and commented on them with wise insight and occasionally with a bit of malice; he was far from a Negrophile.

He was pleased that *Kingsblood* had annoyed so many people and was extremely proud of the fact that in a film made from one of his books a Negro had been portrayed in a dignified way, since Hollywood usually made clowns of them. He described in detail the scene in *Arrowsmith* where the protagonist addresses a doctor who has been fighting the plague; the doctor's back has been to the screen, and when he turns, the startled audience sees that he is black. He seemed sympathetic to the Negro cause, like many other liberals of that period, except that he knew more about it and had written on the subject.

But just because he had written *Kingsblood,* he informed me, he didn't want to be thought of as the savior of the Negro race; he was a writer, not a politician or reformer. After a while we dropped the subject, and then our conversations ranged all over the course of contemporary life in America.

One thing that surprised me was that he talked little about literature. It may have been that he thought as a sociologist I was not interested, or was not particularly well informed. But when I would attempt to discuss some contemporary novel, he would make some remark about the author and drop the subject. He made no reference to his own work except to date some event by a book he had been working on at the time. In a sense he seemed defensive about his current position in American letters.

When I had first arrived from Yaddo, he had asked half curiously and half disdainfully what the young writers there were thinking about. I am sure what he really wanted to know was if they thought of him and if so, what. If I had answered truthfully it would have been embarrassing. The writers who came to Yaddo were concerned with Kafka,[29] Catholicism, and communism, Hemingway, Faulkner, and perhaps Robert Penn Warren,[30] but certainly not Lewis. When I had told a group of them that I was going to visit Lewis, they dismissed him as a journalist, dated and commercial.

But he talked about other things in the most delightful and interesting manner; sometimes I forgot that he was a world-famed author as we sat and joked at the table or as I beat him at chess.

There was one area of thought, however, where he was unsure, uninformed, and I dare say frightened. That was the subject of psychoanalysis. Every writer I had ever known had taken Freud for granted, so much so that many had not even bothered to read or understand him. Psychoanalysis had become part of the mass thinking of the country, perhaps in a vulgar and bastardized form, and it was even being accepted by the motion pictures. I was filled with the subject.

I had given Lewis a copy of an essay on the psychology of the Negro (later reprinted by Arnold Rose in his book *Mental Health*) in which I had attempted to combine some of the concepts of sociology and psychoanalysis in an attack on the problem.[31] I was prouder of this little essay than I was of the book Lewis had had in mind when he mentioned my name in *Kingsblood* and I was extremely anxious to talk with him about it.

I skirted the subject on several occasions (it is hard to come right out and ask a man what he thinks about your work after you have asked him to read it), but he seemed to be avoiding the subject. One day when we were sitting in the sun out in a field, I broached the subject directly. Carried away, I went on to develop my ideas about the unconscious feelings of both love and hate which the American Negro felt toward the white man and the variety of ways, consciously and unconsciously, in which many white men used the Negro to fill the unrealized, empty areas of their existence. It was an approach, I told Lewis, which would help explain the adolescent posturing and the casual cruelty of many whites toward Negroes; the irrational fear and hatred of the prejudiced whites; and the emotional defense of the liberal whites, which were sometimes equally as irrational.

Lewis let me finish, but I could see that he was either uncomfortable or bored. "I guess there's a lot in what you say, Horace," he said after a moment. "By the way, I read your essay and thought it was good. Well, let's get back to the house."

I was hurt and felt that I hadn't made myself clear for I was sure that what I had said deserved more consideration than he was giving it. I started in again but looked up to see him already headed toward the house. We never mentioned the matter again.

I had not been at Thorvale Farm long before I began to realize that Lewis was a lonely man. There were almost no visitors, only three during my stay—the mother of a young girl who had once lived with him and left him;[32] his agent; and Ida Kay, a young woman who ran a bookstore in Williamstown. Of course, I reasoned, a famous man might want to isolate himself so he could work. That was understandable. But why had he invited me, a stranger, and become so friendly with me in such a short length of time if he wanted privacy? Further, almost daily he sought me out at the pool for conversation and had hinted at an impossible plan by which I would live in one of his cottages so I could write. This wealthy, famous author was obviously without a friend, lonesome and hungry for company. It was puzzling.

One morning when I came down for breakfast, he was beaming. Before I sat down he said, "Lana and Spencer[33] are coming for dinner tomorrow."

"Good," I replied, then, on second thought, "who are Lana and Spencer?"

They were, as it developed, the movie stars who had had leading roles in a film made from one of his books, so the next day I allowed myself plenty of time to dress. Dinner was scheduled for eight, and the guests were expected late in the afternoon. But at seven Lewis and I were still sitting on the terrace waiting.

We talked casually for a while, but I could see that he was impatient. At seven-thirty he mentioned the guests for the first time. "I guess they got held up on the road."

We continued to talk, but less freely, while another half-hour passed. Again he mentioned the coming guests. "They'll phone any minute to tell me they've had traffic difficulties, I imagine."

The atmosphere was a bit strained, so I made some excuse and went to the kitchen and asked Joseph for a drink. Lewis was not drinking at the time and had not offered me one, but I could always get one from Joseph, whom I found sitting in the kitchen reading a magazine. When he had fixed it, he returned to his seat, and I perched myself on a high stool. "I wonder why the guests are so late."

"They aren't coming," Joseph replied. Then he decided to let himself go; it was the only time he ever criticized Lewis to me. "They aren't coming because they've gotten what they want from the old man. Oh, he was kingpin when we were in Hollywood talking about the picture—he had something to do with the casting. But they got their parts, they don't need him now."

"But it's a dirty trick if they don't come," I said.

"It's to be expected," Joseph replied. "He can't help it, but it's really the old man's fault. You just can't order people around, expect them always to come to you and not give them anything in return. He can give things but never himself."

A little later Lewis gave in and said that we might as well eat. It was a miserable meal. Later, in my room, I picked up an anthology of stories which contained one by Lewis. Turning to the back of the book, I found short sketches of the various authors.

In reading the one on Lewis, I realized with emotion for the first time since I had been there that I was in the home of a great writer, the first American ever to win the Nobel Prize in literature, a man who had added to the American language words like "Babbitt" and "Main Street." What had happened that such a person could be stood up by a couple of movie personalities and feel it so keenly?

It took me a longer time to find out how deep Lewis's sense of rejection was and how bitter he felt about it. We were at the breakfast table one morning, and he was in one of his more quiet moods. Joseph had brought our second cup of coffee, and I was intending to drink mine and then go for a walk. Without any sort of preliminaries, Lewis looked directly at me and said, "I know how it feels to be a nigger, Horace."

I looked up startled, then turned to see if Joseph had heard. We had not talked about the Negro question for some little time, and I was surprised that he had suddenly returned to it. Too, there was that little red surge of anger that always springs up in me when someone, in no matter how friendly a way, uses the word "nigger."

"When I was in England," he continued, apparently not giving a thought to my possible reaction, "I was taken up by society. I was a middlewestern hick to them, I guess, crude and uncultured. At first I took it as a compliment to be courted by these literary figures from the rich, cultured upper class, even the nobility. Then I realized that they looked upon me as if I were a freak, an ape that had been taught clever tricks. How to ride a bicycle. That's what I meant when I said I knew how it felt to be a nigger. For whatever a Negro may achieve in America, there are white men who will still look on him as an educated ape." [. . .]

After the writer left for Europe, Alma and Wilson remained at Thorvale as caretakers. Thorvale—ironically enough, for Lewis hated organized religion—was sold to the Carmelite Fathers as a retreat. Alma is there now as the cook. Wilson is working for an electric company, and Judy, their only child, attends the local high school. They live on the grounds in the same white cottage that they occupied when I knew them.

Joseph is dead. It was true that he was in Lewis's will; I had never completely believed it when he had told me. But the terms of that will were designed to keep him in a position of gentle bondage. Joseph was to receive one-sixteenth of the estate—certainly a generous sum—if he were in Lewis's service at the time of the author's death. But it just hadn't worked out that way.

Shortly after my visit to Thorvale Farm, the woman I had met there, the mother of the young girl Lewis had loved and failed to win, became a member of the household. As companion-housekeeper, she usurped some of Joseph's duties and authority. She accompanied the writer on one of his many trips to Europe, and Joseph was in charge of the luggage. When they sailed, two of her bags were lost in the confusion, and Joseph was discharged by letter. He wrote and begged Lewis to reconsider. Lewis's reply contained one word—"Fired."

112 / Allen Austin

A master's student at Columbia University, Austin was writing his thesis on Lewis as a satirist. He interviewed Lewis on June 20, 1948.

Source: Allen Austin, "An Interview with Sinclair Lewis," *University of Kansas City Review* 24 (1958): 199–210.

We sat down and Lewis began asking questions about me. It was some time before I managed to ask him what kind of work he had done before he was able to earn his living by writing.

"I worked for publishing houses mostly," he said, then immediately turned the topic of conversation back to me. "Let's see, you want to teach? You want a Ph.D.?"[34]

"Perhaps," I answered. "I don't know."

"If you want to teach," he said, waving his finger at me, "you've got to have one. It's like trying to become a doctor without an M.D. It's all bosh, but you've got to have one if you want to teach.

"I guess some people learn something," he continued, "but I know a lot of boneheads who have Ph.D's. I had a Ph.D. in drama up here [Max Flowers] and he didn't even know who Matthew Arnold was.[35] Oh, he knew vaguely. He'd heard of him—remembered reading something of Arnold's one time. He did know something about drama, but that's about all." Lewis paused and grinned slyly. "Anyway, English teachers are mostly frustrated writers."

I said that some teachers also wrote. I mentioned, as an example, Lionel Trilling's *Middle of the Journey* [1947],[36] which had recently been published.

"The reviews I read were good," Lewis said. "Is he English?"

I said that he was not.

"Lionel is an English name," Lewis remarked. "I wrote a story one time about a man named Lionel, an Englishman. He came over here to write a book on America. He was a regular Babbitt. I hope Lionel didn't think I was writing about him."

"I wouldn't think so," I said.

"It's not a common name, you know. Anyway, I had this man coming over on the ship, and he was trying to talk American lingo. He kept asking the Americans: 'What's your line? How do you get your dough?' And each time they would say, 'I beg your pardon.' Finally, he said, 'You know, you know, how do you dig it? How do you get your bread?' Each one told him, very sedately. One was a school teacher, one a banker, one a lawyer, etc. Lionel comes on over to America, and he likes the country very much. But he goes ahead and writes his book, criticizing us severely. The book sells well in England, and he makes a lot of money."

Mrs. Powers, whom I had forgotten, stood up and said she was going into the house for a while.

After she had left, Lewis told me that he would like to do a story on labor. "I don't know anything that's been done on a real labor leader, do you?"

"There's Steinbeck's *In Dubious Battle* [1936]. Of course, this is Steinbeck's portrayal of a Communist."

"I don't have that in mind," Lewis said. "I'm talking about a plain, hard-boiled labor leader."

"In Steinbeck's novel, the man organizes fruit pickers in California."

"I haven't read that. I don't know why. I've read most of Steinbeck. I've got it upstairs. I'll get it down and read it."

"In Dos Passos's *USA* there's a labor leader, but he's not an important character. Besides, he's an opportunist."

"Well, I don't want that. I want a hard-boiled labor leader and a hard-boiled factory president. You see, the new manager gets tough with labor, and a young radical in the labor movement keeps trying to stir up trouble. Finally, the president and the old labor leader get together and settle their difficulties."

I nodded my head.

"It sounds boring," Lewis remarked.

"It would probably be hard to translate into dramatic terms," I said.

"Yes. Maybe that's why it's never been done. I'll have to get that Steinbeck novel down and read it."

I felt that this was an opportunity to ask Lewis some questions about his own work. "Would you say, Mr. Lewis, that the main thing you are criticizing in American life is hypocrisy?"

"Yes," he answered, "a lack of honesty and integrity."

"But you like Babbitt. That is, in spite of your satire . . ."

"Yes, and in that way I'm different from Mencken. I think he despises the American people. Actually, I'm scolding them like children. I don't care about Jim Smith's children, but I want my children to be good."

"But you don't like Gantry," I said.

"Oh, no—Gantry is a hypocrite through and through. There's only one or two places where you can feel sorry for Gantry—for example, when he gets the church and decides to turn over a new leaf. Of course, he never does." [. . .]

"Why do you like Babbitt?" I asked.

"Babbitt wants to be honest. He tries to be independent, but he's just not man enough."

"Evidently," I said, "you see babbittry as typical of American society. What do you believe is the cause of babbittry?"

"I just don't know," Lewis answered. "I know our educational system is rotten. It fails to teach ideals of honesty and integrity."

"Why?"

"We've somehow drifted away from our early teachings," Lewis said. "We've forgotten the ideals of our fathers. You see, my father was a doctor and he hated the 'bedside manner,' though we now know that the 'bedside manner' can accomplish good. That's a paradox. Ethics from the devil. Anyway, my father didn't know this, and he was a man of complete honesty. Great stress was placed on this in my upbringing. And I've always tried to follow it.

"Let's see, you were writing at an early age?"

"Oh yes. I wrote a sonnet when I was fourteen and sent it off. I wish I had that sonnet. That indicates the man who wants to write—not just the writing of the sonnet, but the fact that it was sent off for publication. Of course, I thought it would set the world on fire."

Lewis stood up and suggested that we talk a walk to the swimming pool. After he had gone into the house and put on an old lopsided hat, we walked across the road and descended a flight of wooden steps which led to a small, white-tiled pool. We sat down in the lawn chairs facing the water, and I asked Lewis what he considered to be some positives qualities of American life.

"Well," he said, "although a man can't go out and buy up land at a penny an acre the way he once could, a young man can still get ahead in America—he can still make a good living."

"And the young people don't care as much about money as my generation," Lewis continued. "In fact, a millionaire is ashamed of his money. He apologizes for having it. And we are gaining in culture. We have more composers now than we ever had. Growth in this direction will take time. It took other countries hundreds of years. Why shouldn't it take us just as long? And another thing, we don't have a tradition of royalty. Even the labor government bows and scrapes before the King of England.[37] I'll admit that that poor Truman[38] is stupid, but the King of England can't even talk plainly—he stammers. He has the mentality of an eight year old. We don't have any of that nonsense here in America. A man is judged more by what he is, not what he owns or where he comes from. A lot of people don't see that I made babbittry an Anglo-American phenomenon. It exists in other countries, but not as strongly as in America and England. Why, Sir Edward Doaks[39] is as much a Babbitt as George Babbitt himself. I think America will outgrow it. We're a young country and we have a lot of advantages over other countries."

"What kind of society would you like?" I asked.

"I think socialism would be better than our present capitalism," he answered.

"Do you think socialism would eliminate babbittry?"

"Oh, no, I don't think it would."

"Do you think that socialism would affect morality?"

"It would probably increase the morality, but moral people can be awful babbitts sometimes." [. . .]

"Why do you want socialism?" I asked.

"It's more efficient. Instead of just a few people owning the wealth, everybody would own it, and we could produce what we need. I think it's very simple. The post office is a good example. We own the post office now. Next, we will own some other corporation. It will become clear that the state can operate it more efficiently. We'll keep taking over corporations until we have socialism."

"I know that when you were young you left Yale and went to Helicon Hall to join Upton Sinclair's community. You worked as a janitor. Did you go because you had been reading about socialism and wanted to see what a socialistic community was like?"

"No, no. It was a craving for adventure. During that time I also took two freighter trips."

"How did you like Helicon Hall?"

"I didn't like it very much. It was very inefficiently run. The pay was ridiculously low."

"Lower than outside?"

"Oh, much lower."

"What were your politics then?"

"Oh, I was a strong supporter of Debs. I knew old Gene—had a great admiration for him. Let me tell you about the first time I ever saw him. I was walking down in lower Manhattan, and I saw a man speaking to a crowd. It was old Gene. From that time on we were good friends. Gene was a real person, human through and through.

"Gene was also a fighter. But I think Gene was too emotional. He lacked theoretical foundation. He didn't have the combined qualities of [. . .] say, of Lenin.[40] I don't think he would have made a good president. He was all heart. It's no telling whom he might have appointed as a Cabinet—probably anybody he'd take a fancy to, regardless of their ability."

"You admire Lenin?" I asked.

"Yes. He was an excellent scholar—nothing phony about him. And I supposed the new boys coming up are scholars—Gromyko[41] and that bunch—scholars in a cold sort of way."

"You're for socialism," I said. "What parties or organizations do you support toward that end?"

"Definitely not the Communist party," he answered. "On the other hand, I don't support Norman Thomas.[42] He's no socialist. He's just a tired old man. If there were a real socialist party, I would support it. I'm inclined to think the early German Social Democrats had a good party."

"Mr. Lewis, when you wrote *It Can't Happen Here,* you thought America was close to fascism? What do you think the situation is today?"

"I don't think we're as close to fascism as we were then. People have jobs now, and there's not much violence, and there's no immediate dictator on the horizon. You see, I based my story on Huey Long. It's men like that who start dictatorships. Of course, they're backed up by the *lumpen* element. That's what the Communists fail to realize—that a large percentage of workers is *lumpen.*"

Lewis paused a moment and stared down at the ground. "And, you know, I think a lot of so-called progressives want to be martyrs. I'd like to do a story on that."

I asked whether such a portrayal would not be taken as typical of unorthodox thinkers.

"You'd always be accused of making it typical," Lewis said. "A lot of people could not understand why the man in *Kingsblood* told that he was a Negro. Some people are just honest. This man was honest. He'd fly headlong into injustice—the same way that an unarmed policeman will sometimes go after a burglar, even if he gets shot in the attempt. No, [. . .] you can't avoid being accused of making your people typical."

Lewis looked up at the sun. "I think it's about time for dinner," he said.

We stood up, and I asked, "Why did you satirize Upton Sinclair in *It Can't Happen Here*?"

"Did I say something about old Upton?"

"Yes. You have Upton and Bilbo as ambassadors to Russia."

"Really? Well, that was a dirty trick to play on Upton. I didn't know I said that about Upton. Are you sure?"

"Let's look it up when we get to the house," I suggested.

We started up the long wooden steps which led to the top of the hill. I said that I had recently heard a lecturer who maintained that Lewis's *Free Air* had had an influence in France.

"Well," Lewis said, "there was a man from Austria who told me that he enjoyed that book more than any he'd ever read." Lewis grinned. "Of course, he read it in prison, and my book is about the open countryside."

We paused about halfway up the steps. "Some critics," I said, "complain that Carol Kennicott is silly. I was under the impression that you meant her to be silly."

"Certainly. For example, I deliberately had her decorate a room in bad taste. A couple of critics used that to show what a fool I was."

"I notice that about the only positive characters you have for that period are Arrowsmith and Gottlieb. Of course, Arrowsmith is honest and a good doctor, but beyond that, he doesn't know much."

"Absolutely ignorant."

"On the other hand," I said, "Gottlieb is a good scientist and a man of some learning and culture. He is honest and completely devoted to his profession—in no way concerned with commercialism. In fact, he is an ideal."

"Yes, a scholar. He brings his background with him. America is still too raw to be conducive to that kind of development."

"Why did you make Gottlieb a Jew?"

"I think that's typical, don't you? Marx, Freud, and Einstein[43]—three of our greatest men—were Jews." [. . .]

We approached the house and stopped near the porch. "Would you call yourself a moralist?" I asked.

"Definitely."

"As Swift is a moralist?"

"No. I don't think Swift is a moralist."

I said that "A Modest Proposal," for example, is moral.

"Yes, that's moral. But Swift is a cynic. I'm not a cynic. I'm an old evangelist—a moral evangelist preaching to my people. I don't think many critics have caught that. In fact, I don't know any who have caught it." [. . .]

"That's what I am," Lewis continued, "an old evangelist giving them hell. Really, I should have been a preacher, [. . .] either a preacher or a doctor. I would like to be a doctor and write also."

"It worked well for Chekhov,"[44] I said.

"Oh, it's the ideal situation. You can't depend on writing even after you get four or five novels published. I also think the sea might be a good idea as a permanent job for someone who wants to write. He would have leisure and some good material. Conrad did well at sea."

At this point we got a call for dinner and went inside to the kitchen where Mrs. Powers was putting ice into glasses. I filled the glasses with water and took them out to a screened porch which afforded the same view as the terrace. Lewis put glasses of milk on the table, and Mrs. Powers brought out the food.

We sat down and the conversation soon turned to politics. Lewis remarked that he thought there was a strong desire in the American people for a political savior. "We Americans must have our messiahs," he said. "The story is that Lincoln, a common man, was just sitting around minding his own business when a committee of angels came down and said, 'Well, Mr. Lincoln, we've come to get you for the presidency. You're going to be a savior of the people.' 'Well,' Lincoln said, 'I ain't particularly hankerin' for the job, but I'll do my duty.' That's the belief. The truth is, Lincoln was a shrewd politician.

"We've got to have our messiah. I wonder if an attitude like that might not help the rise of a dictator."

"Aren't there more complicated forces behind the rise of a dictator?" I asked.

"Oh, I realize that!" Lewis exclaimed. "In *It Can't Happen Here* the *lumpen*—the American Legion type—play a big role. But H. G. Wells said that I didn't show enough the role of the N[ational] A[ssociation of] M[anufacturers]. He said that it would be the Babbitts who would be the leaders of fascism in America—backed by the Ku Klux Klan, the American Legion, and the N.A.M."

"Why is the leader of the anti-fascists a Republican?" I asked. "Did you mean to imply that such a struggle crosses all party lines?"

"Yes. But not so much that. The Republican represents the old school of honesty and integrity. It takes that kind of leadership to defeat fascism."

We had finished the main course of the meal and were having coffee and dessert. After a short pause in the conversation, I asked Lewis whether he found writing a lonesome occupation.

"No, that never bothered me," he answered. "Of course, I like to have people around in the evening."

"When you are writing a novel, do you begin with an idea and proceed from that point or do you begin with some person who interests you?"

"I generally begin with some idea, but I never undertake the writing until I find a person who represents that idea. All my characters are based on people I know."

"I've been wondering what you think of contemporary literature," I said. "Do you think anything significant has been produced in the 'forties?"

"Not much. I tried to get through that thing of Capote,[45] but I couldn't finish it. Homosexuals. I think preoccupation with that in writing represents something basically sick in our society, really degenerate. I've read one good thing—*The Naked and the Dead.* If you haven't read that, you want to get hold of it. It's the best novel that's come out recently."

"What do you think of Steinbeck?" I asked.

"I like Steinbeck. He hasn't done much recently. But he started off with a bang."

"What about Dos Passos?"

"Never read much of Dos Passos. Don't know why. Just never seemed to get around to it." [. . .]

"And [James T.] Farrell?"

"He bores me. I like him as a person, but he's no writer." [. . .]

Lewis stood up and suggested that we go into the living room. I followed him into a large room in which a divan faced a picture window which extended from the floor to the ceiling and looked out on the terrace and the valley. Two straight chairs and a table with a chess board and chess pieces were near the window. One wall was covered with bookshelves.

I walked over and looked at the books. I noticed a complete Nonesuch edition of Dickens and numerous novels by Wells. *Martin Chuzzlewit* was open on the table in front of the divan.

"You read a lot of Dickens," I said. "Of course, he was a strong influence."

"Yes, I was influenced mostly by Dickens and Wells. Also Thoreau."[46]

"There's something to this influence. But I think we make too much of it."

"Yes," Lewis agreed. "One time a critic had me influenced by [Flaubert's] *Madame Bovary.* He sounded very logical and convincing. But I'd never read the book."

"Would you mind if I looked at your library?" I asked.

"No. But most of my books are upstairs. I have some fiction and translations of my own novels down here."

I followed him into the library. "That's poetry and fiction," Lewis said, indicating the shelf on our left. "These books over here," he pointed at the shelf on the other wall, "are translations of my own books."

Lewis sat down and took *It Can't Happen Here* from the shelf.

"Maybe I can find that about Upton Sinclair," I said.

"I wrote the book," Lewis snorted. "I should be able to find it."

I laughed and took down [Alfred] Kazin's *On Native Grounds,* turning to the section on Lewis.[47] "Did you read this?" I asked.

He looked at me. "Oh, I never read criticism of my work. No, that is. It wouldn't do any good. It wouldn't change my way of writing. I'm too old now. It's like an old man who's been chewing tobacco for thirty years and suddenly marries a young woman. He won't stop chewing tobacco. He's too old and he's been doing it too long."

"Kazin has you listed with Sherwood Anderson under the heading of 'The New Realism.'"

"Well, that's about right, I suppose. But there's not much new about it. New in one sense, but in another, very old."

I put the book back on the shelf, and Lewis continued to thumb through *It Can't Happen Here.*

"Here it is," he said.

I looked at the passage where Upton Sinclair's name is linked with Bilbo's.[48]

"I wonder why I did that to Upton. I can't imagine. You know, Upton has written a lot of books, but I don't think they're much good."

"He's a good crusader," I said.

From the poetry shelf, I took down a volume of Yeats.

"A great poet," Lewis said. "One of the best."

"I had a teacher who maintained that's he's a much better poet than Shelley."[49]

"He's a good poet. I wouldn't say he's a better poet than Shelley. It's hard to make a comparison, like trying to compare ice cream with roast beef."

I put the book back on the shelf and pointed to a volume of Edwin Arlington Robinson.[50] "What do you think of him?"

"Just adequate," Lewis said. He then closed *It Can't Happen Here,* which he had been holding open in his lap. "I know why I might have made that crack about Upton. He spread the news that Jack London had committed suicide. It was being kept quiet. There was no reason why it should get out. But Upton spread the news around. I didn't like that. I always thought a great deal of Jack."

I said that London's work was full of contradictions, that evidently London was fascinated by violence.

"He likes violence," Lewis agreed. "That may be one of the reasons he never accomplished any more than he did."

"Hemingway also likes violence," I said.

"Well, I don't care for Hemingway's preoccupation with death, but he's a good writer—one of the best of our times."

"I think his short stories are better than his novels."

Lewis nodded his head. "He's tops with the short story. Excellent."

"I knew his brother Leicester[51] at *Look,*" I said. "It must be difficult to be the brother of a famous writer."

"Yes, that's a bad situation. Take Charley Norris, for example. Charley was the brother of Frank and the husband of Kathleen. He wore loud clothes, made more noise than anybody else. At a party, Charley had to be the center of attention.

"Kathleen was not a good writer, but she was famous. She was well known for her slicks. Quite a woman. Once she went to a small town in France. She always wore a long white dress and went to the cathedral every day. The rumor got around that she was the Virgin Mary. Oh, she enjoyed that tremendously. She had [. . .] I suppose you would call it verve. I remember her at a party. Some man, I forget who, came up and slapped her from behind. She turned around and grabbed him by the lapel and began screaming at the top of her voice. 'What am I going to do about our baby! You will marry me, won't you? Oh, how could you desert me and the baby! How could you be so cruel!' A crowd gathered around and gaped at them. The man looked somewhat sheepish. I'm certain he never bothered her again." [. . .]

I said, "You were one of the first in America to recognize [Thomas] Wolfe, weren't you, Mr. Lewis?"

"I don't know whether I was first or not. I thought he was a good writer, an original writer, and I said so."

"Lately, there's been a lot of criticism of Wolfe. Some critics are making much of his adolescence and his so-called search for a father."

"You can't depend on that type of criticism," Lewis said. "I've re-read Wolfe lately. He's still good, but I find him very repetitious in places. Perhaps it's just as well that he didn't write any more than he did."

I said that Wolfe, in spite of his subjectivity, often presents a vivid and realistic portrayal of life—for example, his description of Germany in the 'thirties.

"Wolfe had a perfect eye," Lewis remarked. "He made each paling in a fence stand out, made each one distinctive. But I don't think his description of me is accurate. He caught my nervousness and restlessness—that's about all. The place we went to is described as vivid, but incorrect. The man who owned the place was a poor hack writer. He didn't even have a chair to sit on while he was writing; he used a box. And Wolfe describes this as a sumptuous country home."[52]

"Wolfe strains life—wrings it, I should say—through his own consciousness. He is almost always everybody in his book. He is his brother, his mother, his father, and so on. Yet he often gives an essentially true picture of things."

"He's getting well placed in his niche," I said. "You get a phrase, 'the search for a father,' and there you've explained the writer's work."

"I don't like this categorizing." Lewis shook his head. "What was it that Kazin had me?"

"The New Realism."

"That's partly true. But you can't limit it there or you can't limit it to a decade."

"He says that you caught the vulgar salesmanship of the time."

"Yes, but what about Arrowsmith? What about Gottlieb?"

"Well, he does devote a lot of space to Arrowsmith and Gottlieb. He recognizes this aspect of your work."

"Some day, when I get a long white beard, I'm going to sit down and read what all these critics have to say about me."

"One of the main criticisms I have made against critics," Lewis continued, "is their division of literature into decades. That's mechanical. They put one writer in the 'twenties, another in the 'thirties, etc. How can you do that? Many of these writers are still writing. They don't belong to any one decade. In your thesis you should point out that the division into realist and satirist, although convenient, is mechanical. Also, you could point out that all categorizing, the decades included, is dangerous. I think that would be a real service.

"You take Wolfe and Hemingway—they're as different as writers could possibly be. If they ever met, they'd hate each other. Both of them have a touch of genius—but how different!"

I asked Lewis whether he thought that critics in general were capable of recognizing new talent.

"No, I don't think so." Lewis squinted his eyes and rested his chin in the palm of his hand. "That gives me an idea for a series of articles—a series of satires. We could have *Hamlet* produced for the first time. The ideas are lousy, the poetry is banal, and there is no characterization. I went all the way to Florida to see the only production of *Hamlet* ever staged."

I nodded.

"I don't think you see what I mean," Lewis said. "This is a brand new play, and it's lousy. [. . .] Say, maybe we couldn't make this a series. Maybe we'd have to limit it to one article. But I don't know who would publish it or who would read it. I think I could make a thing like that funny." [. . .]

Since it was about time for my visit to end, I wanted to get straight the question of the writer who had had the most influence on Lewis. "Getting back to a topic we discussed previously, would you say that the main influence on your ideas is Thoreau?"

"Yes, I've always had the greatest respect for Thoreau. Emerson's radicalism is respectable, but not Thoreau's. [. . .] But you can't take all that Thoreau says," Lewis went on. "You can't do that with any great man. [. . .] You know," he said, "Churchill is a good showman. I don't care much for him, but I have to admit that he did a good job during the war. He made the people work and fight."

"What was it? 'Blood . . .'"

"'Blood, sweat, and tears.' Oh, he is a master at speeches. 'We will fight them in the streets. We will fight them in our homes.' Right out of the Bible. When what's-his-name abdicated, he ended his address with 'God save the King!' Churchill wrote that." [. . .]

Lewis then turned to me and asked about an acquaintance who was considering a divorce from her husband. "She should go slowly," Lewis said. "Divorce is such a painful experience. I know; I've had two. I never want another one. That's one of the reasons why I'd be afraid to get married again." [. . .]

"Do you know much about Williamstown?" I asked. "Do you know many of the people?"

"Some. Occasionally people from the college come out. And the minister comes out sometimes. I made a speech the other day to the men's club at the church. I really surprised them. I had them gaping. I said the church needed to return to the old-time gospel. The church has become too secular. We needed gospel preaching. I put myself in the place of the minister and spoke as I thought he should. If you're going to believe in Christ—He probably never existed, but if you're going to believe in Him—you should preach about that and not make silly remarks about everything else."

113 / Bennett Cerf

Bennett Cerf (1898–1971), publisher and cofounder of Random House, was an advocate of good writing and a staunch friend to his authors, including Lewis. In 1933 he won the landmark anticensorship case *United States v. One Book Called Ulysses* and subsequently published an unabridged edition of James Joyce's masterpiece for a US audience. In 1940, after the commercial flop of *Bethel Merriday,* Lewis ended his relationship with Doubleday, or Doubleday wrote him off, and he signed with Cerf.

Source: Bennett Cerf, *At Random* (New York: Random House, 1977), 145–47.

Red had separated from Dorothy Thompson in 1938 after a stormy ten years of marriage, but he remained bitter about her even after he had found a new girl—an eighteen-year-old would-be actress named Marcella Powers. Red was crazy about her and remained so for the rest of his life. I suppose the great difference in their ages embarrassed him; when he first started taking her out he introduced her as his "niece," but he soon got over that. She left Red several times and he'd always scheme and plot out ways to get her back, including having her mother come and live with him so Marcella would have to call his house. Finally she left him for good. During the Marcella days Red was on the wagon and stayed on the wagon. [. . .]

That fall [1948], before he left for Italy, Red spent his last night before sailing at our house. Just as the three of us were finishing a quiet dinner at home, Bob Haas[53] phoned to say that Bill Faulkner was with them for the evening and asked if we'd like to join them. I was so sure Red would be delighted that I said yes without even asking him. But Red said, "No, Bennett. This is *my* night. Haven't you been a publisher long enough to understand I don't want to share it with some other author?" So I had to call Bob back and decline.

We sat and talked for a while; then Red, who had to get up at the crack of dawn, said goodnight and went upstairs to our guest room on the fourth floor. Since it was very early, Phyllis and I were still sitting in the living room, two floors below, when suddenly Red shouted down the stairwell, "Bennett! Bennett!" We were afraid something awful had happened, so I rushed to the stairs and called, "Red. What is it?" And he said, "I just wanted to be sure you hadn't slipped out to see Faulkner."

Red stayed in Italy about six months, and while there he began to drink heavily again. When he returned he went up to Williamstown and rapidly finished a novel, *Lucy Jade,* and I can't describe how bad it was. I was visiting him in Williamstown in July and I had to read it there, part of the time with him sitting across the room staring at me as I read. It was very hard under those circumstances to tell him what I thought of the manuscript, but I did, and he was very angry with me. He had sold the magazine rights to Herbert Mayes at *Cosmopolitan,* and he said he was going to let Mayes read it and see what *he* thought. When Mayes told him it was even worse than I'd rated it, Red actually agreed to write it all over again. But he so resented our criticism that he took off on a binge.

114 / Michele A. Vaccariello

Michele A. Vaccariello (1888–1971), then assistant professor of Italian at Williams College, instructed Lewis in the Italian language in 1949 prior to his final trip to Europe.

Source: Michele A. Vaccariello, "Tutoring Sinclair Lewis: A Personal Account," *South Dakota Review* 26, no. 2 (1988): 41–42.

Thursday, 30 June 1949. We had our lesson sitting at the table on the cool screened porch off the pantry. Mrs. Katherine Powers served us coffee and cookies. (Mrs. Powers was a more or less permanent house guest, a kind and loyal friend whom he had taken to Italy the year before.)

Sinclair Lewis found the moral attributes in grammars amusing when not irritating, although his irritation seemed to be always very much on the surface. [. . .] "Proverbs are damned lies, generally forced on the young," he said. "*When I was your age* is invariably the beginning of a lie."

The early bird catches the worm, I suggested, but there are so many more worms than birds in the world. "You're damned right," he laughed. "So it comes down to: are you a bird or are you a worm?"

Kathleen Norris, one of the sweetest and most pure-minded of women, told him once, anent proverbs, that they all became awfully indecent if you added "in the middle of the bed" to them. He illustrated and easily made his point.

The gems written in guestbooks were generally lies, he thought. At Burano he had written, when pressed, "*Cibo veneziano in bocca americana*" [Venetian food in the American mouth] over his signature. I complimented him on the simple statement of fact with an epigrammatic flavor.

15
World So Wide
1949–51

In fragile health, suffering from congestive heart failure, Lewis lived his final months in Florence, his favorite city in the world. He entertained few visitors, instead finishing his last novel with the help of a new personal secretary, Alexander Manson.

115 / Perry Miller

Perry Miller (1905–1963), literary critic, intellectual historian, and professor at Harvard University, was a highly regarded authority on Puritanism. He was the author of the groundbreaking two-volume Puritan intellectual history *The New England Mind* (1939, 1953) and he won the Pulitzer Prize in History posthumously for *The Life of the Mind in America* (1965). Miller spent the 1949–50 academic year teaching at Leiden University in the Netherlands.

Source: Perry Miller, "The Incorruptible Sinclair Lewis," *Atlantic Monthly* 187 (April 1951): 30–34.

The first night out of New York on the *Nieuw Amsterdam*,[1] 7 September 1949, my wife said, "That man going out of the bar looks like Sinclair Lewis." I caught a side glimpse—which I shall forever behold—of that long figure, its head tilted back, its narrow shoulders heightened and compressed, an elastic-jointed puppet held two inches off the deck by invisible strings, so that the longest pair of legs ever attached to so short a body jerked their way across the room in a motion that had nothing to do with the ordinary act of walking.

The obituaries, since his death on January 10, comment on the length of his legs and the convoluted patterns he made by intertwining them. Actually, he was not especially tall, and not preternaturally supple: it was the nervous compulsion inside the man that incessantly contorted his body as he talked or smoked or drank. It also sharpened his face and tormented his skin, drove him restless from place to place (made him hover, at last, over Italy like an exhausted hawk), gutted his loves and his friendships, kept him an obstinate adolescent at the same time that it wore him out; and finally it killed him.

I had the good fortune never to have met him before; hence we had never quarreled. When he had been working (if that is the word for what he did in preparation for the worst book he ever pieced together) upon *The God-Seeker*, he had wanted to consult an out-of-print work of mine on New England theology.[2] I offered, through the bookseller, to send him my own copy; he found another somewhere, and never replied. Now I was to discover that this sort of thing

Lewis did not forget. Of all the men I have ever known, his gratitude—for such a trifle—was the most profound and the most lasting. The point being that one thing really counted—his work. By which I mean that many observances which count much for other people, ruthlessly and magnificently and brutally, did not figure for him. Or rather, he had so schooled himself to not letting them matter that even when he stooped to acknowledge them he just did not any longer know how to cope with them. He and I were friends within five minutes, because we did not have to explain anything.

It took no astuteness to realize that Sinclair Lewis was dying. He had barely recovered from a siege of pneumonia (on this voyage he was not drinking): his hands shook, and the wavering of his legs meant that he was unsteady on them. With him was his brother, Dr. Claude Lewis of Saint Cloud, Minnesota—of whom Red had not seen much in recent decades, who was six years older than he, and who addressed him, to my never ending astonishment, as "Hal." Dr. Lewis looked a good ten years younger: Red's myth—to which he clung with inexhaustible solicitude—was that he was about to introduce Claude for the first time to the immemorial riches of Europe. He asked my advice morning and evening as to just how gradually and circumspectly he should spring the art galleries and cathedrals on brother Claude, so as not to heap too much into the initiation.

The whole business was slightly comic: Dr. Lewis is a distinguished surgeon, of eminent common sense, who can and does find his way about the world by his own native shrewdness. And when it comes to the conventional "sight-seeing," Red Lewis was about the most unperceptive and blundering of all the myriads of tourists this country annually exports. [. . .]

Still, all this was a clue: here was Sam Dodsworth casting himself, with outward bravado and considerable inward trepidation, as Virgil to a Dante who in fact was competently on his own. Sinclair Lewis was about to impart to his untraveled brother the immense stores of insight which to him, the much-traveled Odysseus, had become old stuff. One remembered the calculated brevity of the items Dodsworth finally enumerated as the sum total of what he was able to learn out of years of tourism.[3]

I had easily assumed that Lewis made up Dodsworth's list by looking down from a vast familiarity with Europe, as a device in "character study." The creature, not the creator, had obviously acquired no more out of Europe than a knowledge of timetables and the way to say "too much." My education took one vast stride forward when I discovered that the relation of this particular artist to that particular creation was not so disjunctive. It took another—a more tentative step—as I began to comprehend that nevertheless Dodsworth was not mere autobiography, not just an alias for Sinclair Lewis. It came momentarily to a dead halt when daily conversation (I pressed him unfairly) showed that if Dodsworth was in any sense Lewis himself, nevertheless the creator did know in what frame of reference he had set the man and that only thereafter had he become identified with the character. It took a final and immense leap when I realized that, although Lewis could not say it, and certainly would not, in the writing of that book, he had been (and still was) both in and out of it—not so much triumphantly as hopelessly. He had not mastered Dodsworth: he had presented him, and now was compelled to re-enact him.

I found that the secret was much the same when I got him onto *Main Street* and *Babbitt.* I then and there, with great relief, said good-by to the notion (which in the last weeks has been monotonously asserted in the obituaries) that Lewis was a "realist" and a "satirist." It does indeed become a curious comment on our age that lyrics and love songs which in any previous period would have been published frankly and freely as such, had to be composed, in our time, by this highly American artist under such elaborate disguises as his vast accumulation of the minutiae and the lingo of American life. What I have yet to learn—perhaps few of us yet understand or want to inquire too closely—is where did the love come from that could pour upon these things with a passion so concentrated that the only relief permitted it was to lash out against the very objects to which it was inescapably and irrevocably bound?

For the sake of the record, let me say that during Lewis's last year, I saw much of him—simply because I was in Europe and able to reach him. We perfected a little fiction between us that my wife and I, his newest friends, were his oldest and only friends. This gambit often grew rather harrowing as his perpetual mulling over the past disclosed the number of former friends who were now estranged, or at any rate out of touch. He received staggering quantities of mail, most of which (when he was with us) he never opened. In October he came to Holland and delivered a lecture at the University of Leiden. (Announced as an appearance for my class in American literature, it was attended by virtually the whole university, and had to be held in the great auditorium.) We drove him to Delft, Haarlem, and Alkmaar, to Antwerp and Brussels. We stayed with him in the spring at Florence, in the Villa di Costa with its vulgar spun-glass balustrades, and we last saw him in Zurich in August.

In December of 1949 he had found, in the Cook's Tourist Office at Florence, Alexander Manson,[4] who became his secretary, chauffeur, nurse, and interpreter. I gather that Aleck and his lovely Tina were with him to the end. I knew that Lewis had tried this "secretary" arrangement before, and that it had ended in repeated disasters; but Aleck Manson is something special: he knows Europe completely, speaks the languages, can repair a car or order a dinner, tell a story or comprehend a picture, and both he and his wife devoted themselves to Lewis with a disregard of self that would take all the recent history of Europe to explain. The beauty and poignancy of the story is that Aleck instantly knew, and never for a moment imagined anything else, what Lewis signified as an artist. I am a countryman of Sinclair Lewis, as Aleck is not; and I grew up with his novels a part—a very great part—of my experience; most of those who read this did likewise. It took me all these years, and then the illumination of his discourse, and after that Aleck's by no means blind consecration, to realize what a terrifying thing it is to be at the death of a lion. I used the word lion not in the flip sense of a target for hostesses: I mean it in the primitive sense of a leonine beast who roars his last defiance from a cave in the rocks.

You may think that this is a melodramatic overstatement as against some of the facts. Externally they are shabby enough. During the winter, while he worked on the novel which will be published this spring, he managed—with Aleck's help—to keep away from the bottle. As soon as he finished the manuscript, he started drinking, until his Florentine physician forbade him spirits. When I reached him in April, he was guzzling quantities of red wine, and despite Aleck's strenuous efforts, he generally succeeded in knocking himself out by afternoon. At a Florence restaurant he commanded the orchestra to play the sentimental tunes of his earlier escapades; he peeled off and flung about five-thousand-lira notes—Babbitt on a spree—until Aleck could get him out and pour him into the car. By August he was drinking only beer, but he had already had two serious heart attacks and should not have touched even that.

I suppose hundreds of people in three decades have seen Sinclair Lewis drunk; no doubt he made a vast public spectacle of himself. I cannot say what kept him going through the years of creativity; I do know that at the end of it, his back to the wall, facing himself drunk or sober, he did not flinch. There was something positively reckless about it. He was not drinking because he was miserable and wanted solace; neither was he what you would call a drunkard. He was no disenchanted, alcoholic Scott Fitzgerald, drinking compulsively. There may not have been much joy in what Red was doing, but there was still plenty of defiance. Remember, this was not Walter Scott[5] collecting his retainers about him in feudal glory; this was not Zola declining in the realization of an enshrined place in the Academy. This was just an American who had written himself out, to whom the Nobel Prize was no canonization but merely one of those things that happen, for whom the dignity of the artist had no external supports, and who yet somehow maintained it, as Poe and Whitman[6] did, on the terms which this nation imposes upon its artists—terms that Lewis gladly, as a matter of fact, imposed upon himself for fear he might otherwise take himself too solemnly.

This was something that ran deep and strong in him—his hatred for pomposity. I don't mean his treasuring the hypocrisies of Main Street or the sanctimoniousness of Elmer Gantry: that was something else entirely. I mean his attitude toward himself as a writer and toward writing in general. It was too serious a business to be taken solemnly. In the last months he had a game he would play with Aleck—it went on interminably—in which he was the stuffy, grandiose German Professor and Aleck was the trembling *Privatdocent,* the point of the game (aside from letting Lewis show off his German, for he was vain about his smattering of languages) was that the Herr Professor Dr. Geheimrat made a damn fool of himself. It was a way of throwing bricks at high silk hats. It was a Mark Twain gesture, it was deeply and embarrassingly American, but it was also more: it was a mythmaker thumbing his nose at those who would reduce myth to literalness.

Being a professor of literary history, I wanted to find out what he derived from. The answer was instructive: Dickens. He knew Dickens by heart. There was little to be gained by asking him about what had come in between, about realists and naturalists. He had read here and there, but most of them meant little to him, except Shaw and Wells, who to him were primarily writers that showed what might be done with Dickensian exaggeration in a modern situation. The most valuable and most plausible thing in his account of his own beginnings (you must understand that I seldom asked him a point-blank question) was the perfect naturalness and inevitability with which, it had seemed to him, a young writer of about 1910, with Dickens as a model, would proceed to make social comedy out of America.

Yes, he recognized that by now the generation of the twenties, himself the foremost, were being defined in historical terms and treated as radical departures, as collectively a great break with the past. He had no such sense of the story at all; as for most of the "influences" which, according to our historians, brought about the revolution, he was unaware of them or else heard about them only after their effect on his own work had been detected by some ingenious critic. He would agree that up to a point it had been a matter of the time and place; as he talked about the coming of the deep-freeze, television, and the high-powered automobile to Gopher Prairie, he saw that he had caught Main Street just at the turning point, at a now vanished point, and that his book was already a matter of history—and then he would take flight into fantasy, showing that he had never been and could never be capable of thinking in terms of history. He was in love with mythological and typological creations like Micawber and Gradgrind, and all his effort had been to evoke such genii out of the American bottle. It was a constricted and stoppered vessel he had—as he saw it—to work with, which is one reason he vented so much rage upon it. His incantations had to be more labored than those of Dickens, who was in a position to summon up, with a wave of the hand so to speak, a Pecksniff or a Mr. Squeers.[7] In America there had to be a vaster quantity of documented fact before Lewis could extract from it a Babbitt or a Gantry, just as there had to be all the knowledge of the River before Mark Twain could set Huck Finn afloat upon it.

Lewis listened to, and sometimes was impressed by, what the critics said of his books as providing a panorama of the civilization, but for him Babbitt and Gantry and Arrowsmith were creations; he was still trying the old art when he wrote such pathetically documented things as *The Prodigal Parents* or *Cass Timberlane.* He was still trying it even last winter, and told me with affected complacence, as though one should say that Winston Churchill had dropped in yesterday, that in the new book Mr. and Mrs. Dodsworth had reappeared.

In this view—I believe I am not overstressing it—the lecture he gave for my class in Leiden was immensely revealing: most of the students were bewildered, because it was not anything they expected or wanted Sinclair Lewis to say. He worked on it carefully, and his notes reside now in the University Library. It was his last effort of any such sustained discourse—in Florence he made one or two perfunctory appearances on platforms, when it took all of Aleck's immense diplomacy to keep him from attempting to deliver an address in Italian! At Leiden his argument was that America is not new, it is actually very old. He proved this first by dwelling on the antiquity of the Indian culture; how that was linked to the present American civilization so as to furnish us with its venerability never became quite clear. Secondly, he insisted, Americans all brought with them the civilization of Europe, and consequently their culture is as old as any European. He then blamed the Europeans for the antics of the Americans: because they expect us to act like wild Indians, we are obliged to put on a show for them. If you listen to the second half of a sentence uttered by the visiting American, he said, it will be a logical, sensible statement, but the first half will contain some "Oh boy" or "Gee whiz" or "What the hell"—to assist the European in keeping up his illusion.

This from the author of *Babbitt*! If I was amused, my students were puzzled, because the primary (and almost the only) assumption among literate Europeans is that the recent literature of America is a sociological report on the horrors of a materialistic order, that all our artists hate it and want, like Lewis, to escape to Europe. In part, Lewis's speech was sheer perversity: he got fun out of scandalizing the European stereotype. He, like all of us, was troubled over the charge that the American literature of protest, with himself as Exhibit A, was confirming Europeans in their anti-Americanism. But there was something else at work in him when he wrote his lecture, which I think is fundamental in his best work.

I stumbled upon it early in our friendship by telling him that as a boy in Chicago I had wanted to devote myself to the ancient history of the Near East. Nothing I ever said to him made his eyes shine so much. He too had wanted, more than anything in the world, to be an Egyptologist. Don't ask me if this is true (although Claude did remember that the boy Hal had spouted a lot about Babylonia): my point is only that he announced this to have been the great dream of his youth, and swore that it was the adventure yet to come. While his strength was visibly failing, even after the heart attacks commenced, he descanted on how he and Aleck were to set out in the fall, work their way through Sicily, then go to Egypt and Damascus and Assyria, and at last penetrate to Persepolis. I do not know how much history he read, but he loved to pontificate about Rameses II and the queen of Palmyra.

Was it a trauma of escapism? Maybe. In ordinary terms, I think it was something simpler: it was a thin little boy in Sauk Centre dreaming (over an unfinished book) about the gorgeous panoply of Ashur-bani-pal. Remember how many times the majestic syllables of ancient history are involved in his ironic addresses to America, how "Ur of the Chaldees" had for him a magic sound, and how it seemed the supreme comment upon the tin Lizzie standing before the Bon Ton store that for this the pyramids were built and Hannibal crossed the Alps.

I said good-bye to him one night in Zurich; Aleck was taking him the next day to Turin, and he and I knew that we would never meet again. The next morning, before breakfast, he telephoned: he wanted me to tell him whether Rangoon[8] is a port for ocean-going vessels and the precise dates when Generals Lee and Grant died.[9]

I suppose he knew that he would never get to Egypt. He probably would have been as restless before the pyramids as he was in the cathedral of Antwerp, and would have distracted his attention from the sublimity of the pile by finding some detail off to one side, or by looking at his watch and worrying about whether he could get back to the hotel on time. But that is not what concerns us. One of the most perceptive of my friends in Leiden came from his lecture exhilarated; when I asked her what she liked about it, she replied with unhesitating emphasis, "His fanaticism." That, she said, is what Europe needs, and she went on to contrast him and Dodsworth with Henry James; where James made so exquisite an effort to comprehend the special essence of every European place, to stretch his sensibility into the fine web that would catch the slightest reverberations, Lewis (like Dodsworth) stood intransigent and incorruptible. For this listener, and several others, his lecture had not been what he may consciously have intended it, the rebuttal of a flimsy European stereotype about America; it was much more: it was a revelation of the sources of his energy as an artist, of the act of dedication he had performed so thoroughly that he could never, whether flamboyant or, as now, sick and battered, do anything but exemplify it. My friend said that she was reading *Babbitt* with new eyes.

The difficulty is that too few in America have read him with such eyes. Perhaps I might put my contention more bluntly (although it loses much if stated so flatly): it is all very well to call Lewis a realist because he heaped up the furnishings of the Kennicotts' parlor or because he could mimic to the last grammatical atrocity the jabberings of the man who knew Coolidge, but at the heart of him Lewis was what we must call, for lack of a better word, a romancer. He loved telling stories, and even in this last year, in the ebb of his powers, could start with almost anything and make the draft of a novel out of it. I have never heard anything so fascinating, and it made the Dickens clue trebly revelatory.

Lewis could have earned a comfortable living writing stories for magazines; in fact, before *Main Street* he was doing exactly that. He might well have become another Hervey Allen or a Kenneth Roberts.[10] What kept him from being just a spinner of yarns was not something more sophisticated in him—not any doctrinal adherence to, or even comprehension of, the tenets of realism or naturalism—but something more primitive. The scrupulous documentation was the working of a conscience. This organ does not operate so strenuously in easy living or in facile writing; it becomes tormenting only when there is some deep psychic dislocation, some wrong done—or some hurt felt.

I gather that few of Red's friends got along with him for any period without certain stormy scenes. I had mine the night before his lecture, when we were invited for dinner by the Rector Magnificus of Leiden University. Professor van Groningen is a civilized, gentle classicist; his wife is witty and, fortunately, comprehends the world. They both had behaved with quiet heroism in the war, and are what in Holland is known as "conservative" on the Indonesian question (which means that they regret the American policy), but I never had any difficulty discussing it with them.

This night, I started the dinner off by remarking that the Amsterdam paper had called Claude the younger brother. (There is no way I can tell this story that reflects the slightest credit on me.) At the table, the van Groningens intimated their attitude toward Indonesia, whereupon Red launched into a patriotic tirade, of the sort he had voluminously burlesqued, in which the embattled Indonesians became American patriots at Valley Forge and his Dutch hosts supercilious Tories in London of 1776. I completed the ruin of the evening by asking the Rector to have Dr. Lewis escorted through the Faculty of Medicine on the morrow, managing by an inspiration of stupidity to say that Claude had heard his brother before and did not need to hear him again. The resulting scene was Red Lewis at his most histrionic: we were all denounced and assured that the lecture would never be delivered. The situation was saved only by the wit of Mevrouw van Groningen, who told funny stories, mostly at her own expense, while Lewis sulked like a child, until he came out of it, put his hand on my arm, and said of his hostess, "Wouldn't Frans Hals[11] have liked to paint her!"

Somehow, my wife and I got them back to the hotel. Claude pulled me aside and whispered as he went up to bed, "He's been like that since he was a boy."

Lewis was contrite, but of course wouldn't admit it; he took us into the bar, and then the confession came. It's been that way from the beginning, he said. I wanted to write, and I've worked like hell at it, and the whole of Sauk Centre and my family and America have never understood that it is work, that I haven't just been playing around, that this is every bit as serious a proposition as Claude's hospital. When you said that Claude did not want to hear my lecture, Lewis told me, you set up all the resentments I have had ever since I can remember.

If much of this sounds petulant, it was. It was also the story of the artist in America. It was a revelation of the sources of what the perceptive Dutch woman found his redeeming fanaticism. It may have been bad manners but it was freedom, passionate and consuming. It was the *élan* that went into the writing of the great novels of the twenties, which makes them, in the guise of ferocious attacks upon America, celebrations of it. For at the end of the lecture on the next day, he said something which I believe he seldom brought himself to avow, which certainly he never put in print: "I wrote *Babbitt* not out of hatred for him but out of love."

Schlegel's Julius once swore to his Lucinda that man is a serious animal and that we must attack this abominable propensity from all sides. "To that end ambiguities are also good, except that they are so seldom ambiguous. When they are not and allow only one interpretation, that is not immoral, it is only obtrusive and vulgar."[12] I am afraid that in the books of his later years Sinclair Lewis wrote much that allows only one interpretation. All this immense America had to be poured through him; there was too much of it, and finally he took merely to reporting it, as Whitman, when his vitality flagged, catalogued it. But Lewis never got altogether away from the ambiguity that informs his five triumphs of the 1920s.

Over and over again, after he had mailed the manuscript of his last book, when he would try to enjoy Italian scenery or the Swiss Alps, he would come back, with the reiteration of obsession, to asserting that he had written twenty-three novels about America, that nobody could ask more of him, that he had done his duty by his country. "I love America," he would shout into the unoffending European atmosphere; "I love it, but I don't like it." As a closing statement on the career of Sinclair Lewis, this assuredly does not, whatever else you say about it, allow of only a single, and certainly not of a literal, interpretation.

116 / Alexander Manson

Alexander Manson, who was of Polish ancestry and who had served in British military intelligence, was Lewis's last private secretary. Lewis paid for his divorce so he could marry Tina Lazzerini and later hired her to be an assistant secretary and editor. Accounts of the couple's honesty and competence vary widely, but Lewis apparently trusted them and considered them friends. Shortly after Lewis's death, Manson and his wife vanish from the record.

Source: Alexander Manson, "The Last Days of Sinclair Lewis," *Saturday Evening Post,* March 31, 1951, 110–12.

From December 1949 until Lewis was taken to the hospital on 31 December 1950, I was never separated from him for a single day. In all that time he drank nothing but wine, and then, except on a few occasions, only in reasonable quantities.

However, at sixty-five he was not a healthy man. He had no appetite, his pulse was irregular, and he was extremely weak. At first he refused to see a doctor, but I finally persuaded him to. The doctor was not optimistic; he said that Lewis had ruined his health by excesses and that his heart had been bad for years. We put him on an extensive vitamin diet, and almost immediately he began to pick up weight and his appetite improved. Within a month he had gained fifteen pounds.

This period, January and February 1950, was one of the best of Lewis's final year. We spent days walking around Florence, visiting churches and museums. His favorite was the Monastery of San Marco, which contains the Fra Angelico frescoes. Red rarely entered San Marco without spending at least a half hour looking at the Great Crucifixion, most famous of all the artist's works. He became so fond of Fra Angelico that he made him our patron saint. Whatever he wanted, if nothing more than good weather instead of bad, he would whimsically appeal to Fra Angelico for it.

Red really loved only one city, and that was Florence. He never spoke of his "hometown," except to mention now and then that he had been born in Sauk

Centre, Minnesota. In Florence he said he had the impression of being in the Middle Ages, which pleased him because he had a deep interest in the history of that period. He knew the city better than the Florentines themselves—every museum, church, old building, café and restaurant. His favorite eating places were in Maiano and Rotolino on the outskirts of the city. At first he had frequent contacts with the American colony there, but later—except for a few friends—lost touch because what he called the "clannishness" of the Anglo-Americans in Florence irritated him. He said they lived geographically in Italy, but had nothing to do with Italy; that they surrounded themselves by the high wall within which they kept their own national caste. [. . .]

He flew into a rage whenever he saw Americans abroad who, he thought, were behaving tactlessly or giving Europeans reason to laugh at them. Loud-voiced Americans in hotels infuriated him. Although he himself had made almost a profession of criticizing Americans he writhed in discomfort when he heard Europeans criticizing them. He was like a father with a wayward child; he himself could get angry with Americans, but God help anyone else who did.

In his last press interview at the end of 1949, he said, "I'm a diagnostician, not a reformer."[13] I disagree with this statement, because I think his deep desire was to reform. He wanted Americans to rise to a cultural maturity higher than in any other nation, and for this reason he prodded them with his satire. The fact that many Americans resented this hurt him deeply.

He hated all kinds of snobbery, particularly title manias, and was extremely annoyed because some of the biggest "title snobs" in Florence were Americans. He also hated intellectual snobbery and what he called "literary people," who liked to preside over literary salons and tried to add him as their *pièce de résistance.*

In March 1950, when he was finishing his last book, *World So Wide,* he began to overwork. He spent nine or ten hours a day at his typewriter, tiring himself so that he couldn't eat or sleep; smoking three to five packages of cigarettes daily, and drinking wine almost constantly. In April, when he had completed the book, the state of his health was discouragingly bad. As early as January he had begun to plan that in May we would take a European trip and then spend the winter in Sicily. As soon as the final page of his manuscript had been sent off, we started out—Lewis, my wife Tina, whom he affectionately called "Little Monkey," and myself.

For the next three months we chased over Europe, pursuing we knew not what, and moved only by Red's irrepressible restlessness. After we left Florence he cut down on his smoking and wine drinking, and his physical condition improved rapidly. We traveled through Tuscany and Umbria and moved north through the Dolomites to Lake Garda. He loved out-of-the-way places, and he always read up on towns before we visited them. We planned to spend a fortnight on Lake Garda, but after five days of it he was bored. One morning he told me he wanted to go to France.

We left Gardone and traveled through Genoa and San Remo and spent five days at Nice. Then he couldn't stand that either, so we moved on to Marseille and Montpellier, drove through the Loire Valley and as far north as Versailles. After five or six days there, with a few one-day trips into Paris, he grew restless again and decided to go to Switzerland. His plans were never followed out and places where he expected to spend a week he often couldn't bear for more than one night.

Through Neufchâtel we moved on to the Swiss resort of Grindelwald in the Bernese Oberland, stayed there twelve days, then drove to Zurich, where we spent a month. This was in July, and I insisted that he have a rest. He finally agreed. [. . .]

A specialist told him that unless he quit smoking cigarettes altogether, reduced his wine drinking to a minimum, stayed under strict medical supervision and stopped traveling about, he would jeopardize his life. Red's first reaction was to make him give me his word I would not tell anyone about his heart attacks.

"Rather than become an invalid locked up in four walls, I prefer to live the way I like, and make it short," he told me.

Then he abruptly decided that he wanted to go to Taormina, the Sicilian seaside resort, and from there to North Africa. After that he planned to go to Spain and Portugal, and then through Scandinavia, Scotland, Wales, and England. It was as though something kept driving him onward, as though he were trying to cram half a lifetime into a few months' time.

I drove him over the St. Bernard Pass and we stopped in Turin for sixteen days, where he rested, saw another specialist, and again got intensive vitamin treatments. The results were good, and we decided to proceed slowly to Taormina. But when we reached Naples he was so obviously exhausted that I refused to continue the trip and said we would go where he could have proper medical attention. On the twenty-fourth of September we came back to Rome.

Red disliked Rome as much as he loved Florence and the rest of Italy. He didn't like the atmosphere, particularly the American colony, which he said was completely nonrepresentative of what was best in the American people. He said Rome was showing increasing signs of what he called "Chicagoism," which to him meant the ruthless modernization and mechanization of a city. He admired Chicago, but was terrified of it and said that "Chicagoism" and the traditional spirit of Rome could not be merged, and hence a discord was being created in the city. [. . .]

Often he spoke of Wells Lewis, his son by his first wife. He was greatly shaken by Wells's death in World War II and was never able to discuss it. But I think he was equally fond of Michael, his son by Dorothy Thompson. Michael visited him in Rome shortly before his death, and Lewis was much worried about Michael and the war situation.

Lewis had absolutely no sense of money values or of business; he didn't know the difference between five cents and fifty dollars. To him, money was only a means to an end, and whether the proportion between the means and the end was justified or not didn't matter. He had very little idea what his income was; and knew nothing of stocks and bonds. It was torture for him to discuss financial matters.

Although at times he was willing to economize, he felt that economy was a brake on his personality. To him, it was like being handcuffed. He would cut down expenses for two days and then feel so fettered by it that he would immediately spend some fantastic amount to make up for it. [. . .]

After we settled in Rome at the end of September, he was under constant medical care. By November he had so disciplined himself that he drank nothing but milk and never smoked more than fifteen cigarettes a day. In November he was working very hard, preparing notes for his new novel. He never worked less than five or six hours a day. [. . .]

Late in November—presumably from overwork—he became highly nervous. He had always had a habit of waking in the night and making himself some coffee and smoking while drinking the coffee. But this time he began to hate to be left alone. For a fortnight I arose with him to keep him company. Then at the doctor's suggestion, we got a night nurse—purposely a non-English-speaking one, so that he wouldn't tire himself by talking. But in the daytime he worked as hard as ever, and was working almost to the moment of his final attack.

On December thirty-first, he worked from six to eight A.M., and then had his usual big breakfast of porridge, honey, bread and butter, and sat in the living room. Suddenly he staggered to the door of my room and said, "Alec, something terrible is happening. I am going to die." I led him to a big chair, and there he buried his head in my arms like a frightened child. Those were his last fully conscious words.

117 / Frederick Manfred

After Lewis's death of a heart attack on January 10, 1951, his body was cremated per Manson's instructions and his ashes returned to Sauk Centre for burial on January 19.

Source: Frederick Manfred, "Sinclair Lewis's Funeral," *South Dakota Review* 38 (Fall 2000): 89.

I stood immediately behind the family. It was terribly cold out, 22 below zero. A small digging had been cut into the ground. A stack of some of Lewis's books had been placed in the bottom of the grave. Dr. Claude Lewis, Red's brother, snipped the red ribbon seals on the silver urn with a scissors, opened the urn, and poured the ashes over the books in the grave. There was a difference of some 90 degrees between the warmth caught inside the urn (it had just come out of the warm high school) and the terrible cold outdoors, and the moment the urn was opened a plume of steam resembling human breath puffed up—in fact the plume resembled a puff of steam as from a deep cough. The plume rose swiftly and wisped away as the wind carried it across the prairie. I couldn't help but remark, *sotto voce,* to myself, "Well, they tried to bring Red home, but at the last second there he still got away."

List of Reminiscences

See the Bibliography for complete listings.

Part 1. Sauk Centre: 1885–1903

Hazel Palmer Lynam, "The Earliest Lewis."
Isabel Lewis Agrell, *Sinclair Lewis Remembered,* 35–36.

Part 2. New Haven and New Jersey: 1903–7

Chauncey Brewster Tinker, "Sinclair Lewis, a Few Reminiscences."
William Lyon Phelps, "Men Now Famous."
Henry Seidel Canby, *American Memoir,* 307–9.
Leonard Bacon, *Semi-Centennial,* 44–46.
Upton Sinclair, *The Cup of Fury,* 64–66.
Emile Gauvreau, *My Last Million Readers,* 43.

Part 3. Bohemia: 1907–19

William Rose Benét, "The Earlier Lewis."
Charles Hanson Towne, *Adventures in Editing,* 85–87.
Mary Heaton Vorse, *Time and the Town,* 95–96.
Harrison Smith, "Sinclair Lewis: Remembrance of the Past."
Edna Ferber, *A Peculiar Treasure,* 191–92.
William E. Woodward, *The Gift of Life: An Autobiography,* 187–88, 197–98.
Elizabeth Jordan, *Three Rousing Cheers,* 339–43, 356.
W. D. Inglis, "Where Lies the Hope of the Average Man?"
Albert Payson Terhune, *To the Best of My Memory,* 195.
Harrison Smith, "Sinclair Lewis: Remembrance of the Past."
William Rose Benét, "The Earlier Lewis."
Alfred Harcourt, *Some Experiences,* 27–28.
Fanny Butcher, *Many Lives—One Love,* 383–87.
Grace Hegger Lewis, *Half a Loaf,* 79–81.
Burton Rascoe, *Before I Forget,* 367–69.
Grace Hegger Lewis, "When Lewis Walked Down Main Street."

Fanny Butcher, *Many Lives—One Love,* 387–93.
George H. Doran, *Chronicles of Barabbas,* 339–41.

Part 4. Main Street: 1919–21

Alfred Harcourt, *Some Experiences,* 35–36, 54–58.
James Branch Cabell, *As I Remember It,* 166–67.
Grace Hegger Lewis, *With Love from Gracie,* 145–46, 190.
Heywood Broun, "Hewing to the Line."
Kathleen Norris, *Family Gathering,* 205.
George Jean Nathan, *The Intimate Notebooks of George Jean Nathan,* 8–10.
Fanny Butcher, *Many Lives—One Love,* 396.

Part 5. Zenith: 1921–22

Frazier Hunt, *One American and His Attempt at Education,* 248–54.
Charles Phillips Russell, "Sinclair Lewis Declares Americans, More Than Britons, Ruled by Main-Street Idea."
Charles Breasted, "The 'Sauk-Centricities' of Sinclair Lewis."
C. R. W. Nevinson, *Paint and Prejudice,* 236–38.
Harold Loeb, *The Way It Was,* 84–86.
Lilian T. Mowrer, *Journalist's Wife,* 98–100.
Alfred Kreymborg, *Troubadour: An American Autobiography,* 297–98.
George Jean Nathan, *The Intimate Notebooks of George Jean Nathan,* 10–14.
Alfred Harcourt, *Some Experiences,* 58–59.

Part 6. Hartford and England: 1922–25

Emile Gauvreau, *My Last Million Readers,* 74.
Morris Fishbein, *Morris Fishbein, M.D.: An Autobiography,* 99–103.
Alfred Harcourt, *Some Experiences,* 79–81.
Frazier Hunt, *One American and His Attempt at Education,* 254–56.
Paul De Kruif, *The Sweeping Wind: A Memoir,* 65–66, 75–76, 85–86, 102–3, 108.
George Jean Nathan, *The Intimate Notebooks of George Jean Nathan,* 14–16.
Morris Fishbein, *Morris Fishbein, M.D.: An Autobiography,* 105–6.

Part 7. Paris: 1925

Harold E. Stearns, *The Street I Know,* 204–6.
Samuel Putnam, *Paris Was Our Mistress: Memoirs of a Lost and Found Generation,* 101–02.
George Slocombe, *The Tumult and the Shouting,* 215–17, 219.
Nina Hamnett, *Laughing Torso,* 237–38.
Robert McAlmon, *Being Geniuses Together 1920–1930,* 32–34.
Sisley Huddleston, *Paris Salons, Cafés, Studios,* 113–15.

Part 8. Katonah: 1925–26

Grace Hegger Lewis, *With Love from Gracie,* 324–25.
Matthew Josephson, *Life among the Surrealists,* 303–4.
James Branch Cabell, *As I Remember It,* 167–68.
George Jean Nathan, *The Intimate Notebooks of George Jean Nathan,* 16–19.

Part 9. Kansas City to Berlin: 1926–27

Samuel Harkness, "Sinclair Lewis's Sunday School Class."
George Seldes, *Witness to a Century,* 292–93.
Charles Breasted, "The 'Sauk-Centricities' of Sinclair Lewis."
Ramon Guthrie, "Sinclair Lewis and the 'Labor Novel.'"
Vincent Sheean, *Personal History,* 278–79.
Claud Cockburn, *Cockburn Sums Up: An Autobiography,* 43.

Part 10. At Large: 1928–30

Charles Breasted, "The 'Sauk-Centricities' of Sinclair Lewis."
Vincent Sheean, "The Tangled Romance of Sinclair Lewis and Dorothy Thompson."
Eileen Agar, *A Look at My Life.* 80–82.
Alfred Harcourt, *Some Experiences,* 83–85.
Ramon Guthrie, "Sinclair Lewis and the 'Labor Novel.'"
Morley Callaghan, *That Summer in Paris,* 68–70, 74.
Gordon Sinclair, *Will Gordon Sinclair Please Sit Down,* 25–26.
William E. Woodward, *The Gift of Life: An Autobiography,* 342–44.

Part 11. Stockholm: 1930–31

H. Allen Smith, *Low Man on a Totem Pole,* 39–41.
George Jean Nathan, *The Intimate Notebooks of George Jean Nathan,* 20–21.
Carl Van Doren, *Three Worlds,* 267–68.
Dorothy Thompson, "At the Court of King Gustaf."
Fanny Butcher, *Many Lives—One Love,* 396–97.
Louis Adamic, *My America 1928–1938,* 97–98.
Harrison Smith, "Sinclair Lewis: Remembrance of the Past."

Part 12. Grub Street: 1932–39

William L. Shirer, *20th Century Journey: A Memoir of a Life and the Times,* 449–50, 451–52.
Dorothy Thompson, "Sinclair Lewis: A Postscript."
Fanny Butcher, *Many Lives—One Love,* 394.
George Seldes, *Witness to a Century,* 289–90, 292.

Malcolm Cowley, *The Dream of the Golden Mountains,* 296–97.
Benjamin Stolberg, "Sinclair Lewis."
Ramon Guthrie, "Sinclair Lewis and the 'Labor Novel.'"
Budd Schulberg, *The Four Seasons of Success,* 31–53.
Fanny Butcher, *Many Lives—One Love,* 394–95.
Hallie Flanagan, *Arena,* 115–16, 122–23, 127–29.
Edward Robb Ellis, *A Diary of the Century,* 79–81.
John Hersey, "First Job," 188–90.
Margaret Widdemer, *Golden Friends I Had,* 234, 236, 239–40.
George Seldes, *Witness to a Century,* 293–94.
Fanny Butcher, *Many Lives—One Love,* 393–94.
Fay Wray, *On the Other Hand: A Life Story,* 182–83, 196–97.
Kitty Carlisle, *Kitty: An Autobiography,* 87–89, 90–91.

Part 13. Slough of Despond: 1939–45

Edward F. Murphy, *Yankee Priest: An Autobiographical Journey,* 240–48.
James Branch Cabell, *As I Remember It,* 169–70.
Fanny Butcher, *Many Lives—One Love,* 393.
Dorothy Thompson, "The Boy and Man from Sauk Centre."
Harrison Smith, "Sinclair Lewis: Remembrance of the Past."
H. L. Mencken, *My Life as Author and Editor,* 344–49.
Herbert R. Mayes, *The Magazine Maze: A Prejudiced Perspective,* 43–45.
Philip von Rohr Sauer, "The 1945 Lectures: A Happy Episode in Sinclair Lewis's Life."

Part 14. Thorvale Farm: 1946–49

Harrison Smith, "Sinclair Lewis: Remembrance of the Past."
Frederick Manfred, "Sinclair Lewis: A Portrait."
Barnaby Conrad, *Fun While It Lasted,* 282–83, 285, 302–3.
Betty Stevens, "A Village Radical: His Last American Home."
Ida L. Compton, *Sinclair Lewis at Thorvale Farm: A Personal Memoir,* 3–5, 25–26, 41, 46–47, 48–51.
Horace R. Cayton Jr., *Long Old Road,* 294–303, 308.
Allen Austin, "An Interview with Sinclair Lewis."
Bennett Cerf, *At Random,* 145–47.
Michele A. Vaccariello, "Tutoring Sinclair Lewis: A Personal Account."

Part 15. World So Wide: 1949–51

Perry Miller, "The Incorruptible Sinclair Lewis."
Alexander Manson, "The Last Days of Sinclair Lewis."
Frederick Manfred, "Sinclair Lewis's Funeral."

Additional Sources

The following sources were omitted from the bibliography below for reasons of brevity, redundancy, or relevance, though they are worthy of study by readers of Lewis.

Aaron, Daniel. "The Proud Prejudices of Sinclair Lewis." *Reporter* 4 (August 1953): 37–39.

Acheson, Dean. *Morning and Noon.* Boston: Houghton Mifflin, 1965, 43–45.

Austin, Mary. *Earth Horizon: Autobiography.* New York: Literary Guild, 1932, 342–43.

Barrymore, Ethel. *Memories: An Autobiography.* New York: Harper and Brothers, 1955, 258–59.

Baum, Vicki. *It Was All Quite Different.* New York: Funk and Wagnalls, 1964, 306–8.

Benét, William Rose. *The Dust Which Is God.* New York: Dodd, Mead, 1941, 71–73.

Bottome, Phyllis. *The Goal.* New York: Vanguard, 1962, 184.

Cabell, James Branch. *Preface to the Past.* New York: McBride, 1936, 217–18.

Clemens, Cyril. "Impressions of Sinclair Lewis." *Hobbies* 56 (April 1951): 138–39.

Conrad, Barnaby. *Dangerfield.* New York: Harper, 1961.

Fadiman, Clifton. *Party of One.* Cleveland and New York: World Publishing, 1955, 50–53.

Gough, Marion. "Sinclair Lewis's Apartment Is a Man's Idea of Home." *House Beautiful* 86 (January 1944): 40–41, 58–59.

Lewisohn, Ludwig. *Mid-Channel: An American Chronicle.* New York: Harper and Brothers, 1929, 6–7, 182.

Sheean, Vincent. *Dorothy and Red.* Boston: Houghton Mifflin, 1963.

Shirer, William L. *A Native's Return, 1945–1988.* Boston: Little, Brown, 1990, 196–97.

Sinclair, Upton. *My Lifetime in Letters.* Columbia: University of Missouri Press, 1960, x–xii, 1–11, 253, 296, 298.

Wolfe, Thomas. *You Can't Go Home Again.* New York: Grosset and Dunlap, 1940, 574–76.

Notes

Introduction

1. Sinclair Lewis, *The Man from Main Street: Selected Essays and Other Writings, 1904–1950,* ed. Harry E. Maule and Melville H. Cane (New York: Random House, 1953), 272.

2. George Killough, "German Catholicism, Sauk Centre, and Sinclair Lewis," *American Literary Realism* 39 (Winter 2007): 109–25.

3. Lewis, *Man from Main Street,* 51.

4. Ibid., 54.

5. E. M. Forster, *Abinger Harvest* (New York: Harcourt, Brace, 1936), 127.

6. At www.randomhouse.com/modernlibrary/100bestnovels.hml.

7. Ernest Hemingway, *Green Hills of Africa* (New York: Scribner's, 1935), 8.

8. Mark Schorer, *Sinclair Lewis: An American Life* (New York: McGraw-Hill, 1961), 553.

9. Schorer, *Sinclair Lewis,* 799.

10. Granville Hicks, "Sinclair Lewis' Stinkbomb," *New Masses,* January 25, 1938, 19.

11. Alfred Kazin, *On Native Grounds* (New York: Reynal and Hitchcock, 1942), 205–26.

12. Lewis, *Man from Main Street,* 15.

13. Ibid.

14. Schorer, *Sinclair Lewis,* 501.

15. Ibid., 245.

16. Richard Lingeman, *Sinclair Lewis: Rebel from Main Street* (New York: Random House, 2002), 101.

17. Lewis, *Man from Main Street,* 45–46.

18. Lingeman, *Sinclair Lewis: Rebel from Main Street,* 291–92.

19. Stephen S. Conroy, "Sinclair Lewis's Sociological Imagination," *American Literature* 42 (November 1970): 348.

20. Lingeman, *Sinclair Lewis: Rebel from Main Street,* 553, 481.

21. Lewis, *Man from Main Street,* 38.

22. Schorer, *Sinclair Lewis,* 270.

23. Ibid., 181.

24. Ibid., 410.

25. Valerie Eliot, ed., *The Letters of T. S. Eliot* (San Diego: Harcourt, Brace, Jovanovich, 1988), 618.

26. Constance Rourke, *American Humor* (New York: Harcourt, Brace, 1931), 286.
27. Schorer, *Sinclair Lewis,* 286.
28. Lewis, *Man from Main Street,* 153–64.
29. Ibid., 48.
30. Lewis, *Man from Main Street,* 13.
31. Dorothy Thompson, "The Boy and Man from Sauk Centre," *Atlantic Monthly* 206 (November 1960): 42.
32. Lingeman, *Sinclair Lewis: Rebel from Main Street,* 191.
33. Ernest Hemingway, *Across the River and Into the Trees* (New York: Scribner's, 1950), 113, 119, 87.
34. Thomas Wolfe, *You Can't Go Home Again* (New York: Harper and Brothers, 1940), 546.
35. Quoted in Lingeman, *Sinclair Lewis: Rebel from Main Street,* 50.
36. Ibid., 95.
37. Ibid., 259.
38. Ibid., 552.
39. Ibid.
40. Ibid., 311.
41. Schorer, *Sinclair Lewis,* 579, 587, 588, 595.
42. Ibid., 813.
43. Schorer, "My Life and Nine-Year Captivity with Sinclair Lewis," *New York Times Book Review,* August 20, 1961, 7.
44. Irving Howe, "The World He Mimicked Was His Own," *New York Times Book Review,* October 1, 1961, 34.

Part 1

1. Lewis, *Man from Main Street,* 49.
2. Launched in 1926, this French passenger ship was one of the most elegant vessels of the period.

Part 2

1. See headnote to chapter 7.
2. Lewis compared the American poet Arthur Upson (1877–1908) to John Keats and Thomas Chatterton, two famously gifted poets who also died young.
3. George Santayana (1863–1952) studied with William James (1842–1910) and Josiah Royce (1855–1916) at Harvard and taught with them in the Harvard Department of Philosophy.
4. Algernon Charles Swinburne (1837–1909), controversial and innovative English poet and critic, is known for technically masterful work that is, by contemporary standards, florid.
5. In his satirical poems, Bacon often targeted his friends—including Lewis, who

seems to be the butt of "To One Who Ran Down Pope" (Leonard Bacon, *Lost Buffalo and Other Poems* [New York: Harper, 1930], 100).

6. Harold Beers Randall (1889–1971) completed an engineering degree at Yale in 1911.

7. "The Ballade of the Golden Horn," *Yale Literary Magazine* 649 (January 1908): 174.

8. William Pepperell Montague (1873–1953) joined the faculty of Barnard College in 1903 and the graduate faculty at Columbia University in 1907.

9. William Noyes (1862–1928) of Columbia Teachers' College and his wife, Anna G. Noyes (b. 1873), manager of the colony.

10. Edwin Björkman (1866–1951) translated four volumes of plays by the Swedish dramatist August Strindberg (1849–1912) between 1912 and 1916.

11. The "minor novelists" included Grace MacGowan Cooke (1863–1944), author of *Their First Formal Call* (1906) and *The Power and the Glory* (1909).

12. Dr. Charles H. Castle (b. 1860) was an eye, ear, nose, and throat specialist in Cincinnati, Ohio.

13. Among the other residents were the sculptor Jo Davidson (1883–1952) and the author-editor Michael Williams (1878–1950), who collaborated with Upton Sinclair on *Good Health and How We Won It* (1909) and founded the Catholic magazine *Commonweal* in 1924.

14. Upton Sinclair, *Sylvia* (Philadelphia: John C. Winston, 1913).

15. Arthur J. Sloane, managing editor of *New Haven Journal-Courier.*

16. Waldo Frank (1889–1967) graduated from Yale in 1911 and became a novelist, historian, and literary and social critic. He was also associate editor of *Seven Arts* and the first president of the left-leaning League of American Writers.

Part 3

1. Martin Light, *The Quixotic Vision of Sinclair Lewis* (West Lafayette, IN: Purdue University Press, 1975), 11.

2. The Sheffield Scientific School, founded as the Yale Scientific School in 1847 and renamed to honor railroad executive Joseph E. Sheffield in 1861, is dedicated to science and engineering instruction.

3. See headnote to chapter 103.

4. "Barney McGee," from *More Songs of Vagabondia* (1896), is a poem by Richard Hovey (1864–1900). It celebrates its eponymous hero as a mischievous and amiable vagabond.

5. Allan Updegraff (1883–1965), American novelist and translator, was one of the first authors to settle in Woodstock, Vermont. He was one of the "optimistic rebels" to whom Lewis dedicated *The Trail of the Hawk.*

6. Henry Martin Hoyt (1887–1920) was the younger brother of Elinor Wylie and their father's namesake.

7. George Sterling (1869–1926), Californian bohemian poet whose fame was well

established in northern California, but remained localized. See Schorer, *Sinclair Lewis,* 147: "Sterling had discovered the domestic uses of the abalone and it became the standard culinary fare in the colony."

8. Edith Wharton (1862–1937), novelist and short-story writer, developed a literary style principally distinguished by humor and dramatic irony. She received the Pulitzer Prize for *The Age of Innocence* in 1921, when the jury's original decision to grant the award to Lewis for *Main Street* was overturned by the trustees of the prize fund. Her letter of consolation to Lewis, whose work she admired, inaugurated their friendship.

9. Alice MacGowan (1858–1947), prolific novelist and short-story writer, is perhaps best known for her novel *The Last Word* (1902).

10. Helen MacGowan Cooke (1895–1944), daughter of Grace MacGowan Cooke and niece of Alice MacGowan, was a northern California writer. They all lived for a time at Upton Sinclair's Helicon Hall and were among those injured in the fire that destroyed the building in March 1907. For a little over a year Lewis lived in a shack on the beach near their Carmel-by-the-Sea home that came to be known as "Cooke's Cove."

11. The novelist and playwright Henry Leon Wilson (1867–1939) married Helen MacGowan Cooke in 1912. They divorced in 1927.

12. Benét alludes to the poem recited by Ora Weagle in chapter 1 of *Work of Art* (1935).

13. The American novelist F. Scott Fitzgerald (1896–1940) coined the phrase "Jazz Age" and was the author most famously of *The Great Gatsby* (1925).

14. Max Eastman (1883–1969) and Floyd Dell (1887–1969) were editors of *The Masses,* a journal that was openly critical of US participation in World War I and was ultimately forced to close as a result of charges brought against it under the Espionage Act of 1917. Eastman was a supporter of progressive causes and patron of the Harlem Renaissance. Dell, a promoter of American literature and a lifelong poet, is remembered as the author of popular novels such as *Moon-Calf* (1920) and the Broadway play *Little Accident* (1928).

15. John Masefield (1878–1967), English poet, propagandist, and author of children's novels, served as Poet Laureate of the U.K. from 1930 until his death.

16. Emma Goldman (1869–1940), an anarchist and feminist activist, was celebrated by her defenders as a proponent of free speech and condemned by her critics as a supporter of politically motivated violence. Her abiding interest in politics and women's issues did not prioritize women's suffrage the way that first-wave feminism did, but instead sought ways to incorporate gender into anarchy.

17. Frances Perkins (1880–1965), secretary of labor from 1933 to 1945, was the first woman to serve in the US Cabinet. She championed the causes of labor and unions, worked for Roosevelt's New Deal, and fought against efforts to draft women into the military so that they could join the civilian workforce in greater numbers.

18. Edna Kenton (1876–1954), feminist writer and editor, was elected to the ex-

ecutive board of the Provincetown Players in 1916. She read plays and wrote some brochures for the group and later wrote the history of the theatrical company from 1915 to 1922.

19. See headnote to chapter 13.

20. John Reed (1887–1920), American journalist and poet, was a socialist activist famous for his controversial and influential firsthand account of the Russian Revolution of 1917, *Ten Days That Shook the World* (1919). After his death, he was buried at the Kremlin Wall necropolis in Moscow's Red Square. He is the only American to be interred at the Kremlin Wall.

21. George M. Cohan (1878–1942), American entertainer, composer, playwright, and producer, was known in the decade before World War I as "the man who owned Broadway" and is considered the father of American musical comedy. He was also a founder of the American Society of Composers, Authors, and Producers. On Lewis's musical comedy, *President Pip,* see also Schorer, *Sinclair Lewis,* 200–202; Lingeman, *Sinclair Lewis: Rebel from Main Street,* 47; and Lewis, *Man from Main Street,* 215n1.

22. Paul W. Beck (1876–1922), pioneering aviator, was the fourth American to be awarded the 1913 Military Aviators' Badge while serving as a captain in the US infantry.

23. Lewis published *Hike and the Aeroplane* under the pseudonym Tom Graham in 1912.

24. Schorer, *Sinclair Lewis,* 638.

25. William d'Alton Mann (1839–1920), American soldier, businessman, and editor, purchased *Town Topics* in 1891 and founded *Smart Set* in 1900 and *Transatlantic Tales* in 1905. Lewis was on the staff of the latter magazine from March to October 1907.

26. Arthur Sullivant Hoffman, editor of the pulp magazine *Adventure,* was responsible for publishing some memorable writers, including Lewis, Harold Lamb, and T. S. Stribling.

27. See Lewis's "How I Wrote a Novel on Trains and Beside the Kitchen Sink," *American Magazine,* April 1921; rpt. *Man from Main Street,* 198–206.

28. See headnote to chapter 26.

29. The first line of Robert Browning's poem "Memorabilia" (1855).

30. See headnote to chapter 15.

31. Schorer, *Sinclair Lewis,* 189.

32. The lifelong friends Susan Glaspell (1876–1948), writer and actress, and Lucy Huffaker, actress and later a Chicago journalist, were Washington Square Players. Glaspell married George Cram Cook (1873–1924) in 1913 and the two of them founded the Provincetown Players in 1915. Huffaker married director Edward Goodman, one of the founders of the Washington Square Players.

33. Hutchins Hapgood (1869–1944), journalist, author, and free love advocate, was a prominent New York bohemian. Neith Boyce (1872–1951), novelist and playwright, was a founding member of the Provincetown Players. They married in 1899.

34. Wilbur Steele (1886–1940), American short-story writer and playwright.

35. Joseph O'Brien (d. 1915), journalist, labor activist, and second husband of Mary Heaton Vorse.

36. Kibbe Cook House, owned by Vorse, was built in the mid-eighteenth century in Provincetown.

37. Mack Sennett (1880–1960) was a Canadian-born American actor, entertainer, and film director famous for innovations in slapstick.

38. The illustrator Art Hutchins collaborated with Lewis on *Hike and the Aeroplane.*

39. George Soule (1887–1970), Yale alumnus and American political intellectual, wrote *The Coming American Revolution* (1934).

40. George Bernard Shaw (1856–1950), Irish playwright, social critic, and advocate for the Fabian Society, was a satirist much admired by Lewis throughout his life.

41. H. G. Wells (1866–1946), English author, was known for his political and sometimes satirical novels but is primarily remembered for his popular work in the science fiction genre. In 1917 Lewis named his first son Wells in honor of the author, and in 1931 he nominated the author for the Nobel Prize in Literature.

42. The vaudeville comedians Joe Weber (1867–1942) and Lew Fields (1867–1941) were famous for their "Dutch act" in which they caricatured German immigrants.

43. Rodman Gilder (1877–1953), American author and businessman, was the son of Richard Watson Gilder (1844–1909), Civil War soldier, poet, founder of the *Newark Register,* and editor of *Scribner's,* later renamed *Century,* until his death.

44. The fashionable Brevoort House was located at 11 Fifth Avenue at the southeast corner of Fifth Avenue and East Ninth Street.

45. Edgar Van Slyke (1894–1957) was advertising solicitor for the book page of the *New York Post* in addition to his work with the Publishers' Newspaper Syndicate.

46. See headnote to chapter 22.

47. George Horace Lorimer (1867–1937), editor of the *Saturday Evening Post* from 1899 until 1936.

48. The headquarters of the publishing company Harper and Brothers was located at 331 Pearl Street fronting Franklin Square in lower Manhattan.

49. Lewis published his breakout novel *Main Street* with Alfred Harcourt at Harcourt, Brace, and Company.

50. This reference alludes to a line in chapter 2 of *Our Mr. Wrenn,* to "the five thousand princes of New York" who "protect themselves against the four million ungrateful slaves."

51. John McGraw (1873–1934), manager of the New York Giants of the National Baseball League from 1902 until 1932.

52. This reference alludes to a line in chapter 31 of *The Trail of the Hawk:* Terhune is a "big newspaperman who lives at Pompton, N.J."

53. Owen Johnson (1878–1952), novelist and short-story writer, remembered for his Dirk Stover novels.

54. In 1927 the aviator Charles Augustus Lindbergh (1902–1974) became the first person to fly nonstop across the Atlantic Ocean, from Long Island to Paris. His father,

Charles August Lindbergh (1859–1924), represented a Minnesota district in Congress from 1907 to 1917.

55. See headnote to chapter 20.

56. The old Waldorf-Astoria hotel was built in 1893 at Fifth Avenue and Thirty-Fourth Street, now the site of the Empire State Building.

57. Dale Carnegie (1888–1955) self-help guru, author of *How to Win Friends and Influence People* (1937). See also Lewis's "Car-Yes-Man," *Newsweek,* November 15, 1937, 31.

58. See headnote to chapter 23.

59. Tanglefoot Flypaper was patented by a company in Grand Rapids, Michigan, in 1887 and heavily advertised during the early twentieth century.

60. Marie Doro (1882–1956), a lithe and delicately beautiful stage and silent film actress; Carrie Nation (1846–1911), a famously large and stern member of the temperance movement; Eleonora Duse (1858–1924), an introverted and quiet Italian actress who was the first woman featured on the cover of *Time* magazine (1923); Queen Victoria (1819–1901), longest-reigning British monarch; and Eva Tanguay (1879–1947), a brassy, uninhibited, and extravagant Canadian-born vaudevillian actress and singer.

61. Schorer, *Sinclair Lewis,* 207.

62. Irvin S. Cobb (1876–1944), Kentucky-born author and local-color humorist, several of whose short stories were made into films. "Phoebe Snow," the official face of the Lackawanna Railroad's "Road of Anthracite," was a character portrayed by the model, dancer, and actress Marion (Marie) E. Murray, the pin-up phenomenon of her era; her image was used to sell the idea of clean train travel with "sootless" anthracite fuel beginning in 1900.

63. Sherwood Anderson (1876–1941), novelist and short-story writer, famous still for the collection *Winesburg, Ohio,* was a significant influence on the early careers of such eminent American writers as Ernest Hemingway (1899–1961), William Faulkner (1897–1962), and John Steinbeck (1902–1968), all recipients of the Nobel Prize for Literature.

64. Harry Hansen (1884–1977), later (post-1920), literary editor of the *New York World-Telegram;* Keith Preston (1884–1927), poet, columnist, and critic; Jerome Frank (1889–1957), judge and legal philosopher influential in the "legal realism" movement; Gene Markey (1895–1980), author, screenwriter, and producer.

65. In his Nobel Prize acceptance speech, Lewis offered this tribute: "Thomas Wolfe, a child of, I believe, thirty or younger, whose one and only novel, *Look Homeward, Angel,* is worthy to be compared with the best in our literary production, a Gargantuan creature with great gusto of life" (Lewis, *Man from Main Street,* 17). At the press conference on the day his receipt of the prize was announced, Lewis also commended *Look Homeward, Angel:* Wolfe "may have a chance to be the greatest American writer. [. . .] In fact, I don't see why he should not be one of the greatest world writers. His first book is so deep and spacious that it deals with the whole of life" ("Nobel Prize Goes to Sinclair Lewis," *New York Times,* November 6, 1930, 27).

66. Boston Store: a chain of department stores founded in 1897 and headquartered in Milwaukee, Wisconsin.

67. Lewis refers to a pair of negative reviews of *The Job.* In "Cheap and Chippy," the reviewer for the *New York Tribune* (March 3, 1917, 7) condemns "its all-pervading slang and vulgarity" and compares the novel to "a weed patch or a compost heap." In "Critical Reviews of the Season's Latest Books" (New York *Sun,* March 3, 1917, 6) the reviewer avers that "Lewis has chosen to express himself in that form of realism that dwells on the sordid and sees only the unpleasant side."

68. Coningsby Dawson (1883–1959), Anglo-American novelist and soldier, was literary advisor to the George H. Doran Publishing Company from 1906 until 1910.

69. Joseph Addison (1672–1719), English poet and essayist, cofounder with Richard Steele (1672–1729) of the *Spectator.*

70. Arnold Bennett (1867–1931), English journalist, novelist, and businessman, known for *Tales of the Five Towns* (1905) and *The Old Wives' Tale* (1908).

Part 4

1. Quoted in Schorer, *Sinclair Lewis,* 298.

2. Heywood Broun, "Books," *New York Tribune,* October 20, 1920, 8: "*Main Street,* by Sinclair Lewis, [. . .] is a novel about American life which is good enough to stand beside Zona Gale's *Miss Lulu Bett* and Willa Sibert Cather's *My Ántonia.*"

3. Womrath was the name of an important chain of bookstores in New York City with a key location at Madison Avenue and Forty-First Street (a Fifth Avenue and Twenty-Eighth Street location opened in March 1921).

4. Schorer, *Sinclair Lewis,* 258.

5. In Lingeman, *Sinclair Lewis: Rebel from Main Street,* 143.

6. Rockbridge Alum Springs, which became famous in the 1860s, was a health resort in the Shenandoah River valley fifteen miles west of Lexington, Virginia.

7. Carl Van Doren (1885–1950) had suggested in his essay "The Revolt from the Village" in the *Nation* for October 12, 1921 (407–12) that Lewis in the writing of *Main Street* had been influenced by Edgar Lee Masters's *Spoon River Anthology* (1915).

8. Schorer, *Sinclair Lewis,* 284.

9. Lewis's play "Hobohemia," written in collaboration with Daniel Reed (b. 1893) and produced in Greenwich Village, was based on a story he published in the *Saturday Evening Post* for April 7, 1917. Here "epizoötic" refers to a disease, especially a plague among cattle. See also Lingeman, *Sinclair Lewis: Rebel from Main Street,* 110–11.

Part 5

1. Kazin, *On Native Grounds,* 219.

2. Lingeman, *Sinclair Lewis: Rebel from Main Street,* 199.

3. Ray Long (1878–1935), editor of *Cosmopolitan,* 1918–31, president of Hearst's International Magazine Company.

4. Carl Eric Bechhofer (1894–1949), who published as Bechhofer or Bechhofer Roberts and who is cataloged under the name Roberts, wrote several historical studies of Russia and revolution and translated *Five Russian Plays, with One from the Ukrainian* (1916).

5. Savage Club: a "gentleman's club" founded in London by Richard Savage in 1857. Among the American writers who had addressed the club over the years were Mark Twain (a.k.a. Samuel L. Clemens) (1835–1910), Bret Harte (1836–1902), Stephen Crane (1871–1900), and Artemus Ward (a.k.a. Charles Farrar Browne) (1834–1867).

6. José Doroteo Arango Arámbula (1878–1923), a.k.a. Pancho Villa, was a Mexican Revolutionary general whose tactics were studied by the US government as well as the filmmakers of Hollywood and also adapted by later guerilla leaders.

7. Walter Fuller (d. 1927), British poet and antiwar activist, was Max Eastman's brother-in-law. He had recently returned to England from an extended trip to the United States and was in search of editorial work.

8. Hunt was writing a series of articles for *Collier's Weekly* under this title about the relation of big business to Prohibition.

9. The American journalist Albert Curtis Brown (b. 1866) founded the Curtis Brown literary agency in London.

10. See headnote to chapter 52.

11. Sir Philip Gibbs (1877–1962), English journalist and novelist, was literary editor of the *Daily Mail* and one of five official British reporters during World War I. A[rthur] S[tuart-] M[enteth] Hutchinson (1880–1971), British novelist and short-story writer, whose *If Winter Comes* (1921) was a best-selling novel in America in 1922 and was adapted as a feature film in 1923. Hutchinson's subsequent novels were also very popular in the United States.

12. Anthony Comstock (1844–1915), secretary of the New York Society for the Suppression of Vice; and John S. Sumner (1876–1971), who succeeded to the office upon Comstock's death. Lewis and seven other writers published a letter in the New York *World* on August 20, 1922, protesting the censorship activities of Sumner and the society (Schorer, *Sinclair Lewis*, 341).

13. Joseph Hergesheimer (1880–1954) wrote floridly descriptive novels about decadence among wealthy Americans.

14. George Peabody Gooch (1873–1968), British historian, journalist, and politician, edited the *Contemporary Review* from 1911 until 1960.

15. Sir Hermann Gollancz (1852–1930), British rabbi and Hebrew scholar, taught at University College London. In 1923 he became the first rabbi to receive a knighthood.

16. Maxwell Armfield (1881–1972), English artist, illustrator, and writer, whose 1901 self-portrait was adopted as the cover illustration of the 2006 Oxford edition of Oscar Wilde's *The Picture of Dorian Gray.*

17. Cyril Scott (1879–1970), English composer, wrote four hundred works, most of which are characterized by predominantly romantic and impressionistic qualities.

18. Edmund Dulac (1882–1953), French illustrator, continued his artistic career

mainly as an illustrator for periodicals and caricaturist following the decline in deluxe illustrated editions after World War I.

19. John Galsworthy (1867–1933), English novelist and playwright, received the Nobel Prize in Literature in 1932. He is remembered for *The Forsythe Saga* (1906–22) and its sequels.

20. Claude Lovat Fraser (1890–1921), English artist and author, designed decorative books and, after World War I, increasingly contributed to theater and costume design as well.

21. Sir J[ames] M[atthew] Barrie (1860–1937), Scottish novelist and dramatist, is best known for *Peter Pan* (1904).

22. Joseph Conrad (1857–1924), Polish-born English novelist and short-story writer, was a major precursor to modernist literary style.

23. W[illiam] Somerset Maugham (1874–1965), English novelist, playwright, and short-story writer, was among the most popular and highest paid authors of the 1930s; Syrie Wellcome (1879–1955), English interior decorator, married Somerset Maugham in 1917; Edward Knoblock (1874–1945), German American dramatist and novelist, anglicized his name (Knoblauch) and became a British subject in 1916; Charles McEvoy (1879–1929), British playwright and novelist, was a realist author who had originally been trained as a journalist; Sir Osbert Sitwell (1892–1969), English writer, dedicated his life to art and literature, as did his famous siblings, Dame Edith Sitwell and Sir Sacheverell Sitwell; Sir Edward "Eddie" Howard Marsh (1872–1953), British polymath, translator, and civil servant, was a major patron of the arts.

24. William Maxwell Aitken, 1st Baron Beaverbrook (1879–1964), Canadian-born British politician and writer, owned a chain of English newspapers and, through them, wielded tremendous power.

25. Empress, Alberta, named for Queen Victoria who was also Empress of India, is a Canadian village on the Alberta-Saskatchewan border; it connected major cities by the Canadian Pacific Railway.

26. Blaise Cendrars (1887–1961), Swiss-born novelist and poet, was a major influence on modernist literary style.

27. "Lily" is most likely Kathleen "Kitty" Eaton Cannell (1891–1974), Paris-based American dance and fashion reporter, who was having an affair with Harold Loeb (1891–1974) during this period. In Hemingway's *The Sun Also Rises,* Loeb is the ostensible model for Robert Cohn and Cannell the model for Frances Clyne.

28. Ford Madox Ford (1873–1939), English editor and novelist, best known today for *The Good Soldier* (1915).

29. Rebecca West (1892–1983), English author, journalist, literary critic, and travel writer, was recognized for her cultural contributions by being made first Commander (CBE) and then Dame Commander (DBE) of the British Empire late in life. She had an affair for several years, beginning in 1913, with H. G. Wells, with whom she had a son, Anthony Panther West (1914–1987).

30. Irene Castle (1893–1969), American dancer and actress, starred in many silent films between 1917 and 1924.

31. The Russians Prince Felix Yussupov (1887–1967) and Grand Duke Dmitri Pavlovich (1891–1941) are best known for their parts in the murder of Grigori Rasputin (1869–1916), peasant faith healer and mystic.

32. This trattoria, Al Vero Alfredo, is identified in chapter 15 of *Babbitt:* "there's a little trattoria on the Via della Scrofa where you get the best fettuccini in the world."

33. See headnote to chapter 77.

34. Kaiser Wilhelm II (1859–1941) wore a distinctive upturned moustache to which Lewis refers.

35. The Hotel de Russie in Rome is a luxury hotel on Via del Babuino, between the Spanish Steps and Piazza del Popolo.

36. Ludwig Lewisohn (1882–1955) was a Jewish American novelist and critic.

37. Alfred Henry Lewis (1858–1914) was an American journalist and novelist who wrote about social issues.

38. May Sinclair (1863–1946), a.k.a. Mary Amelia St. Clair, popular and prolific English novelist, poet, and critic, was politically active and committed to the suffrage movement.

39. These are novels by Edith Wharton, Charles Dickens, Gustave Flaubert, Arnold Bennett, and Charlotte Brontë respectively.

40. Like Dickens, Lewis had a penchant for book titles that were names (e.g., *Babbitt, Arrowsmith, Elmer Gantry, Dodsworth, Gideon Planish, Bethel Merriday, Cass Timberlane, Kingsblood Royal, Ann Vickers*). As he elsewhere noted, "nothing has been more successful than names for titles" (Sinclair Lewis, *From Main Street to Stockholm: Letters of Sinclair Lewis, 1919–1920,* ed. Harrison Smith [New York: Harcourt, Brace, and World, 1952], 88).

41. George Franklin Babbitt (1848–1926), a graduate of Harvard College and a longtime columnist for the *Boston Herald,* threatened legal action.

42. Hugh Walpole (1884–1941), New Zealand-born English novelist, short-story writer, and playwright, was popular during his lifetime but has been largely neglected since his death.

Part 6

1. Schorer, *Sinclair Lewis,* 357.

2. Quoted in ibid., 338.

3. The only notice of *Main Street* we have located in the Chicago *Daily News* is Gladys Nelson Muter's "There's a Main Street in Every Town," October 27, 1920, 12.

4. "Book Notices," *Journal of the American Medical Association,* December 11, 1920, 1167: "Physicians who read this book will like it, even though every now and then it causes an inward wincing because of some of the satirical thrusts at their faults. [. . .] For the physician, [it] is more than a first class piece of fiction—it is a commentary on the social side of medical life."

5. Dr. Simon Flexner (1863–1946), physician and scientist, taught experimental pathology at the University of Pennsylvania. As the first director of the Rockefeller In-

stitute for Medical Research and a trustee of the Rockefeller Foundation, he fired Paul De Kruif.

6. Dr. Arthur J. Cramp (1872–1951) was director of the Bureau of Investigation of the American Medical Association.

7. Dr. Anna Mantel Fishbein was married to Morris Fishbein.

8. Eugene V. Debs (1855–1926), one of the founders of the American Railway Union and organizer of the Pullman strike in 1894, was a Socialist candidate for president in 1900, 1904, 1908, 1912, and 1920. He was imprisoned in 1919 during the first Red Scare and died in a sanitarium in Elmhurst, Illinois.

9. Carl Sandburg (1878–1967), poet, editor, and biographer, received three Pulitzer Prizes, two for poetry and the third for his biography of Abraham Lincoln. His work often focused on the city of Chicago and the American Midwest.

10. First built in its current location in 1894, the Bismarck, named for Germany's first chancellor, is a luxury hotel located at 171 West Randolph Street in Chicago, Illinois. During World War I the hotel was rechristened the Randolph. It reopened as the Bismarck in 1926.

11. Lewis wrote Grace Hegger Lewis on November 8, 1925, that the "voyage down was easy; a little rough the first night, but nothing to speak of" (Speer Morgan and William Holtz, "Fragments from a Marriage: Letters of Sinclair Lewis to Grace Hegger Lewis," *Missouri Review* 11, no. 1 [1988]: 71–98, at 77).

12. Donald C. Brace (1881–1955), cofounder of Harcourt, Brace in 1919.

13. Quoted in Schorer, *Sinclair Lewis,* 362.

14. Ibid., 368.

15. Ibid., 372–73.

16. William Norman "Trilby" Ewer (1885–1976), British journalist, wrote in support of Guild Socialism and was involved with various left-leaning associations. He is reputed to have spied for the Soviet Union during the 1920s.

17. Schorer, *Sinclair Lewis,* 407.

18. The *Arrowsmith* character Max Gottlieb was modeled on Jacques Loeb (1859–1924), celebrated German-born American physiologist, and Frederick Novy (1864–1957), De Kruif's bacteriology professor at the University of Michigan.

19. Stuart Sherman (1881–1926), conservative critic and educator, feuded publicly with H. L. Mencken over American modernism for years, until he moved slightly toward the political center near the end of his life.

20. John Drinkwater (1882–1937), English playwright and poet.

21. Philip Guedalla (1889–1944), English barrister and travel writer.

22. The Prussian Eugen Sandow (1867–1925), born Friedrich Wilhelm Müller, was the father of modern bodybuilding.

23. Karl Harriman (1875–1935) had edited *Redbook* and its sister publications *The Blue Book* and *The Green Book* during the period that Lewis had contributed work to the magazine.

24. The movie *Mantrap* (1926; dir. Victor Fleming) starred Clara Bow (1905–1965).

25. Bartlett Cormack (1898–1942), playwright, most famous for *The Racket,* a 1927 play adapted as a 1928 movie; Henry Justin Smith (1875–1936), managing editor

of the Chicago *Daily News;* Ben Hecht (1894–1964), screenwriter, playwright, director, and novelist; and James Weber Linn (1876–1939), professor of English at the University of Chicago.

Part 7

1. Lewis Galantière (1895–1977), American playwright, journalist, and translator of French literature, worked for the International Chamber of Commerce in Paris from 1920 to 1927.

2. The high-modern novelists James Joyce (1882–1941) and Gertrude Stein (1874–1946). Lewis paid a backhanded compliment in his Nobel Prize acceptance speech to the modernists "in the tradition of James Joyce, who, however insane they may be, have refused to be genteel and traditional and dull" (Lewis, *Man from Main Street,* 17).

3. Robert H. Davis (1869–1942), novelist and poet, worked for the Frank A. Munsey Company in New York City and edited *Munsey's Magazine* in 1903–4.

4. Walter Duranty (1884–1957), Moscow bureau chief for the *New York Times,* 1922–36, and a recipient of a controversial Pulitzer Prize in 1932.

5. Stacy Aumonier (1887–1928), British writer, is best known for his short fiction in the suspense genre, which was adapted for television and film.

6. Dr. Frederic C. Howe (1867–1940) served as commissioner of the Ellis Island Immigration Center during World War I.

7. The French writer Gustave Flaubert (1821–1880) is regarded as one of the greatest Western novelists.

8. Djuna Barnes (1892–1982), author and bohemian, is remembered for her novel *Nightwood* (1936). Her stylistic innovation was important for the development of literary modernism, and there has been a resurgence of interest in her work since her death.

9. Mina Loy (1882–1966), poet, novelist, and artist, was "recovered" near the end of the twentieth century and is highly regarded, especially for her poems.

10. Harriet Monroe (1860–1936), editor and critic, was the founder and editor of the little magazine *Poetry* (Chicago) in 1912.

11. The American novelist Henry James (1843–1916) was the author of *Daisy Miller* (1878), *The Portrait of a Lady* (1881), and *The Ambassadors* (1903).

12. The American novelist John Dos Passos (1896–1970) was also the author of *Manhattan Transfer* (1925) and the trilogy *U.S.A.* (1930–36).

13. Anthony Trollope (1815–1882), English novelist, remains one of the most respected Victorian writers.

14. The Russians Georgy Chicherin (1872–1936), Maxim Litvinov (1876–1951), C. G. Rakowsky (a.k.a. Chaim Rakeover) (b. 1873), and Leonid Krassin (1870–1926) were Marxist revolutionaries, Soviet politicians, and diplomats.

15. G[ilbert] K[eith] Chesterton (1876–1936) was an English journalist, novelist, poet, and Christian apologist.

16. Bertrand Russell (1872–1970) was an English philosopher, historian, and social critic.

17. Philip Wylie (1902–1971), American author, best known for his collection of essays, *Generation of Vipers* (1942).

18. James Stephens (1882–1950) was an Irish poet and novelist.

19. James Whistler (1834–1903) was an American expatriate painter.

20. Café du Dôme on the Left Bank in Paris opened in 1898. Lewis satirized this favored meeting place for intellectuals in chapter 14 of *Dodsworth* as the "Café Novgorod, the favorite of the more arty Americans."

Part 8

1. See headnote to chapter 85.

2. Émile Zola (1840–1902) was the exemplary figure for the development of naturalism in French literature and theater.

Part 9

1. Schorer, *Sinclair Lewis,* 468.

2. Theodore Dreiser (1871–1945) was a journalist and novelist involved with the early development of American literary naturalism.

3. The politician and author William Allen White (1868–1944) was editor of the *Emporia* (Kansas) *Gazette.*

4. Probably the publisher, industrialist, and politician Walter S. Dickey (1862–1931).

5. Gary Alan Fine and Amy Campion, "Sinclair Lewis, *Main Street,* and Community Reputation," in *Difficult Reputations: Collective Memories of the Evil, Inept, and Controversial,* ed. Gary Alan Fine (Chicago: University of Chicago Press, 2001), 232–58, at 245.

6. Maxwell Bodenheim (1892–1954), American poet, so-called king of the Greenwich Village bohemians in the 1920s.

7. Carl Van Doren's brother, Mark Van Doren (1894–1972), was a literary critic, Pulitzer Prize–winning poet, and a particularly influential Columbia University professor.

8. Laurence Stallings (1894–1968) was an American playwright, critic, and novelist.

9. Lewis Browne (1897–1949) was an author and lecturer.

10. William Seabrook (1884–1945) was an occultist, explorer, and journalist.

11. Arthur Hopkins (1878–1950) was a Broadway theater director and producer.

12. Lewis actually published twenty-three novels, including the pseudonymous *Hike and the Aeroplane* (1912).

13. Ferdinando Nicola Sacco (b. 1891) and Bartolomeo Vanzetti (b. 1888) were Italian-born laborers and anarchists who were accused of armed robbery and murder in 1920 and executed in 1927. Their guilt has never been conclusively established, though the prejudice of the judge who sentenced them in a famously unfair trial has.

14. In two paragraphs in chapter 21 of *Dodsworth,* the protagonists travel from Paris to Italy, Turkey, Spain, back to Italy, before continuing to Austria, Hungary, and Germany.

15. *Imitation of Christ* by Thomas à Kempis (ca. 1380–1471) is one of the best-known books of Christian devotion.

16. Clarence Darrow (1857–1938) was an American lawyer and civil libertarian famous for his defenses of Leopold and Loeb during their murder trial and the teacher John Scopes when he was tried for teaching evolution in Tennessee in 1925.

17. James B. McNamara (1882–1941) and his brother John J. McNamara (1876–1941) were convicted of dynamiting the *Los Angeles Times* building in 1910; J. B. confessed to what was then touted as the "crime of the century," was sentenced to life imprisonment at San Quentin, and consistently refused to file parole requests. Clarence Darrow had represented them. Lewis signed the petition for J. B.'s parole when he was dying in prison.

18. Vachel Lindsay (1879–1931), American populist poet.

19. Henry Wadsworth Longfellow (1807–1882), a popular American poet, best known today for such narrative verse as *Evangeline* (1847) and *The Song of Hiawatha* (1855).

20. Alfred, Lord Tennyson (1809–1892), poet laureate of England, wrote in a wide variety of styles but is often remembered for the insistent iambic rhythm that prompted James Joyce to refer to him as "Lawn Tennyson, gentleman poet."

Part 10

1. Jonathan Cape, British publisher, was one of Lewis's oldest friends and published his work in the United Kingdom from 1921 until nearly the end of Lewis's career. Their friendship dissolved after Cape's critique of *The God-Seeker.*

2. Savoy Chapel or Queen's Chapel of the Savoy is located on the Strand in the West End theater district.

3. Dora Black (1894–1986), English author and feminist, hastily became the second Mrs. Bertrand Russell (later Lady Russell) when she returned, six-months pregnant, from Russell's and her yearlong stay in China. Their son, John Russell, was born in 1921.

4. Anita Loos (1888–1981) was an American screenwriter, playwright, and comic novelist best remembered for *Gentlemen Prefer Blondes* (1925).

5. Gilbert Frankau (1884–1952) was a British novelist, short-story writer, and poet.

6. Born Diamant József, Joseph Bard (1882–1975), expatriate Hungarian novelist, was Dorothy Thompson's first husband (1922–27). He married Eileen Agar in 1940.

7. Lewis, *From Main Street to Stockholm,* 302.

8. Lingeman, *Sinclair Lewis: Rebel from Main Street,* 362.

9. See headnote to chapter 86.

10. Mikhail Bakunin (1814–1876), Russian revolutionary, was the principal theorist of collectivist anarchism. Karl Liebknecht (1871–1919), German socialist, cofounded with Rosa Luxemburg the Spartacus League and the Communist Party of Germany.

11. Jack London (1876–1916), novelist and short-story writer, was one of the first Americans to make a lucrative living from his writing. On Lewis's sale of story plots

to London, see Franklin Walker, "Jack London's Use of Sinclair Lewis Plots, Together with a Printing of Three of the Plots," *Huntington Library Quarterly* 17, no. 1 (1953): 59–74.

12. "Since these reminiscences were written, Grace Hegger Casanova has told me of two letters to her from Sinclair Lewis describing his meeting with Eugene Debs in Chicago, which indicate that the germ of the labor novel was probably in his mind as early as August 1922" (Guthrie's note).

13. Schorer, *Sinclair Lewis,* 512.

14. Louis E. Florey was Lewis's sometime secretary, valet, and drinking companion from 1925 until 1937.

15. Eleanor Wilson McAdoo (1889–1967), daughter of Woodrow Wilson, married American lawyer and politician William Gibbs McAdoo (1863–1941) in 1914 and divorced him in 1934.

16. Louis Bromfield (1896–1956), Pulitzer Prize–winning novelist and conservationist, is remembered for his innovative work in grass-based sustainable farming. He received a Pulitzer Prize in 1926 for his novel *Early Autumn.*

17. Rose Wilder Lane (1886–1968), journalist, novelist, and political theorist, helped to found and support the American libertarian movement.

18. Samson Raphaelson (1894–1983), screenwriter and playwright, taught playwriting at Columbia University.

19. Woodward alludes to the temperance novel *Ten Nights in a Barroom* (1854) by T. S. Arthur (1809–1885).

Part 11

1. Sherwood Anderson, *Sherwood Anderson: Selected Letters,* ed. Charles E. Modlin (Knoxville: University of Tennessee Press, 1983), 128.

2. Croswell Bowen (1905–1971) was an American journalist, biographer, and documentary photographer.

3. Louis Sherwin (1883–1978) was a British journalist and drama critic.

4. Leopold Stokowski (1882–1977) was a British-born American orchestral conductor.

5. John J. "Black Jack" Pershing (1860–1948), general in the US Army.

6. Thornton Wilder (1897–1975) was awarded three Pulitzer Prizes, for his novel *The Bridge of San Luis Rey* (1927) and his plays *Our Town* (1938) and *The Skin of Our Teeth* (1942).

7. Michael Gold (1893–1967), editor of the *New Masses* and proletarian author of *Jews without Money* (1930).

8. All of these figures are mentioned in this sequence in the final paragraph of Lewis's Nobel speech (Lewis, *Man from Main Street,* 17). Did Van Doren merely lift the names from this source? Ironically, Lewis allowed in his interview with Allen Austin (see chapter 112) that he "never read much of Dos Passos."

9. Schorer, *Sinclair Lewis,* 615.

10. Thomas Mann (1875–1955), German novelist, recipient of the Nobel Prize for Literature in 1929.

11. Dr. Karl Landsteiner (1868–1943), Austrian biologist and physician, received the Nobel Prize for Medicine and Physiology in 1930.

12. Francis Brett Young (1884–1954) was an English novelist, playwright, and composer.

13. E[dward] M[organ] Forster (1879–1970) was an English novelist, short-story writer, essayist, and librettist.

14. Willa Cather (1873–1947) was a Pulitzer Prize–winning American novelist. Lewis praised her in "The Greatest American Novelist," *Newsweek,* January 3, 1938, 29.

15. Eugene O'Neill (1888–1953), American playwright, recipient of the Nobel Prize for Literature in 1936.

16. Paul Morand (1888–1976) was a French diplomat, novelist, playwright, and poet.

17. André Maurois (1885–1967) was a French author of novels, histories, biographies, and children's books.

18. Lion Feuchtwanger (1884–1958) was a German-Jewish playwright and novelist.

19. Several American journalists were skeptical about the conferral of the Nobel Prize on Lewis, though perhaps none quite matched the vehemence of Irish-born American critic Ernest Boyd (1887–1946) in the *New Freeman.*

20. *Drottningholm,* a Swedish transatlantic ocean liner, was built in 1905 for the Allan Line of Canada, sold in 1920 to the Swedish American line, and sold again in 1948 to the Home Lines of Italy.

21. Rabindranath Tagore (1861–1941), Bengali author, recipient of the Nobel Prize for Literature in 1913.

22. Folke Bernadotte (1895–1948), Swedish diplomat and nobleman, married American heiress Estelle Romaine Manville (1904–1984) on December 1, 1928.

23. Lewis Gannett (1891–1966) was an American journalist and author who for many years wrote the daily book review column for the New York *Herald Tribune.*

24. Henry Hazlitt (1894–1993) was an American journalist and libertarian economist.

25. Walter White (1893–1955), African American novelist and activist, served as executive secretary of the NAACP from 1931 until his death. Lewis had blurbed White's novel *The Fire in the Flint* (1924), after which they began to correspond. See also Charles F. Cooney, "Walter White and Sinclair Lewis: The History of a Literary Friendship," *Prospects* 1 (1975): 63–79.

26. V. F. Calverton, a.k.a. George Goetz (1900–1940), was an American Marxist literary critic and historian.

27. In *The Liberation of American Literature* (1932), Calverton reiterates that "Lewis' whole approach to the American scene [. . .] has been from the petty bourgeois point of view" (V. F. Calverton, *The Liberation of American Literature* [New York: Scribner's, 1932], 431).

28. "Book Marks for Today," *New York World-Telegram,* March 23, 1931, 23: "By now Sinclair Lewis ought to realize that whatever he does is first-page stuff. His irritation because bookmen have been speculating in print on his next publishing connection is amusing, in view of Lewis' own publishing experience. Two houses have asked me not to mention that they are negotiating with Lewis, for fear it will antagonize him. But my sympathies are somewhat with Lewis."

29. Dr. Charles E. Rush (1885–1958) was associate librarian of the Sterling Library at Yale from 1929 to 1938.

Part 12

1. Lingeman, *Sinclair Lewis: Rebel from Main Street,* 549.

2. Klaus Mann (1906–1949) founded the German language *Die Sammlung* in Amsterdam (Querido Verlag), September 1933–August 1935.

3. Ernst Rowohlt (1887–1960) founded his publishing house in 1908.

4. Lloyd Lewis (1891–1949) was a historian, drama critic, sportswriter, and popular columnist for the *Chicago Daily News.*

5. *The Jayhawker* premiered in Washington, DC, on October 15, 1934. It opened on Broadway in New York on November 5 and closed November 26.

6. Paul Osborn (1901–1988), playwright and screenwriter, is best known for his film adaptation of *East of Eden.*

7. Gilbert Seldes (1893–1970), American writer and cultural critic, edited *The Dial* from 1922–23 and was the New York correspondent for T. S. Eliot's *The Criterion.*

8. Quoted in Lingeman, *Sinclair Lewis: Rebel from Main Street,* 158.

9. Genevieve Taggard (1894–1948), American poet and cofounder with the playwright Maxwell Anderson of the little magazine *The Measure.*

10. John's Restaurant, established in 1908, is located at 302 East Twelfth Street in the East Village. During the 1930s its ads in the *New Masses* read, "A place with atmosphere where all radicals meet" (Schorer, *Sinclair Lewis,* 611).

11. Horace Gregory (1898–1982) was professor of English at Sarah Lawrence College from 1934 until 1960.

12. Sidney Howard (1891–1939) was nominated for an Academy Award for his adaptation of *Arrowsmith* in 1932. He also adapted *Dodsworth* for stage in 1934 and was nominated again for an Academy Award for his screenplay of *Dodsworth* in 1936.

13. Joseph Goebbels (1897–1945) was the Minister of Propaganda in Nazi Germany.

14. The first fight between Joe Louis (1914–1987) and Max Schmeling (1905–2005) was a politically charged contest that for many pitted American (and African American) pride against the claims of eugenic superiority of Nazi Germany. Although the seemingly unbeatable Brown Bomber lost the June 19, 1936, fight by knockout in round twelve, he won their June 22, 1938, rematch with a convincing first-round knockout.

15. Charles Coughlin (1891–1979), a Catholic priest and popular pundit known as the father of hate radio, began his broadcasting career as a supporter of Franklin D. Roosevelt and the New Deal, but ultimately moved to the far right in both his political and economic opinions.

16. Schulberg had been raised in Hollywood and had known such writers there as Nathanael West, Fitzgerald, Faulkner, William Saroyan, Dashiell Hammett, and Dorothy Parker.

17. Charlie Chaplin (1889–1977), English film actor, famous for visual comedy routines, especially mime and slapstick, in silent features.

18. Schickelgruber: the ostensible birth name of Adolf Hitler (1889–1944).

19. Huey Long (1893–1935), the "Kingfish," served as Governor of Louisiana and US Senator. He was assassinated in the Louisiana State Capitol in September 1935 by the son of a political enemy. William Dudley Pelley (1890–1965) was an American extremist and spiritualist; Fritz Kuhn (1896–1951), a German-born American Nazi and anti-Semite.

20. Gauleiter: the leader of a regional branch of the Nazi party.

21. "*Company House,* a would-be Odetsian one-actor produced in the Dartmouth Little Theater in 1935" (Schulberg's note).

22. Benito Mussolini (1883–1945), Fascist leader of Italy from 1922 until 1943.

23. "'The cause of the marble workers is in the great tradition of Vermont's struggle for freedom. I believe that this cause should be ours as well.' MacLeish jotted this down on a piece of brown paper I have saved to this day" (Schulberg's note). Archibald MacLeish (1892–1982), author and librarian of the Library of Congress, was politically active with anti-Fascist causes and received three Pulitzer Prizes.

24. The New Hampshire Proctors, the progeny of Redfield Proctor (1831–1908), are a wealthy and influential family.

25. The Irish American novelist James T. Farrell (1904–1979) is famous for his *Studs Lonigan* trilogy (1932–35).

26. John O'Hara (1905–1970), a novelist and short-story writer, had an exacting sense of dialogue and often wrote about class and status differences as well as social ambition.

27. Herbert Hoover (1874–1964), thirty-first president of the United States (1929–33), was in office at the start of the Great Depression.

28. William Gropper (1897–1977), American artist, illustrator, and radical, contributed caricatures and cartoons to many leftist publications, including *New Masses.*

29. King "Kingfish" Levinsky (1910–1991) was a heavyweight boxer who froze in his August 7, 1935, bout with Joe Louis, which he lost by knockout in the first round.

30. Tom Mooney (1882–1942), American labor leader imprisoned for over twenty years after a show trial in 1916.

31. Joseph Stalin (1878–1953), leader of the Soviet Union from 1922 until his death.

32. John Strachey (1901–1963) was a British Labour Party leader and writer.

33. R. Palme Dutt (1896–1974), author of *Fascism and the Socialist Revolution*

(1935), was a leading journalist and Stalinist theoretician for the Communist Party of Great Britain.

34. Lewis Corey (1894–1953), an Italian-born American writer and popular economist of the Left during the 1930s, began his radical career as Louis C. Fraina, a founding member of the American Communist Party in 1919, disappearing two years later after an alleged misappropriation of funds.

35. Thorstein Veblen (1857–1929), sociologist and economist, best known for *The Theory of the Leisure Class* (1899).

36. The movie comedian W. C. Fields (1880–1946) played screen characters with such names as Elmer Prettywillie, J. Effingham Bellwether, Augustus Q. Winterbottom, and Ambrose Wolfinger.

37. Friedrich Engels (1820–1895), one of the earliest theorists of modern communism and coauthor with Karl Marx (1818–1883) of *The Communist Manifesto* (1848).

38. "One of our lesser Jewish fistic heroes of the period" (Schulberg's note).

39. The American Liberty League was organized in 1934 to promote free-market principles by conservative Democrats who were opposed to the New Deal.

40. Jack Wilgus discusses these events in detail in "Sinclair Lewis Visits a Strike," *New Masses,* January 14, 1936, 10–11.

41. See headnote to chapter 113.

42. Honoré de Balzac (1799–1850), French novelist and playwright, was a key figure in the development of realism in European literature.

43. Schulberg cites Lewis's column, "Gold, Inc.," *Newsweek,* February 21, 1938, 21.

44. Schulberg's *What Makes Sammy Run?* (1941), his first novel, is a rags-to-riches narrative about a copy boy who finds success but not satisfaction as a Hollywood screenwriter. The novel was adapted as a live television drama and a long-running Broadway musical, and has been criticized for perpetuating Jewish stereotypes.

45. Carl Van Doren later observed that "Red took her out to Palm Springs and introduced her as his niece. By the time they'd left she was *everyone's* niece" (Lingeman, *Sinclair Lewis: Rebel from Main Street,* 479).

46. Saxe Commins (1893–1958) was an editor at Random House from 1933 until 1955.

47. Lewis's play *Angela Is Twenty-Two* opened in 1930 with Lewis as director and male lead; the film version, *This Is the Life,* was released in 1944.

48. Helen Hayes (1900–1993), American actress, was known as the "first lady of the American stage," and her husband Charles MacArthur (1895–1956) was an American playwright.

49. Jack Moffitt (1901–1969), screenwriter for Paramount, where he worked with such famed directors as Fritz Lang, Raoul Walsh, and Michael Curtiz.

50. Ann Watkins (1885–1967) was briefly Lewis's agent; Harold Matson (1898–1988) was also a literary agent; and Pat Duggan (1910–1987) was a producer.

51. The Essex House, a luxury hotel on Central Park South in New York, opened in 1931.

52. Kate Drain Lawson (1894–1977), American actress, was the wife of John Howard Lawson; John "Jack" Lynds was an American actor and stage manager.

53. The dramatic version of *It Can't Happen Here* opened at the Adelphi Theater at 152 West Fifty-Fourth Street (currently the George Abbott Theatre) in October 1936 and closed there on January 16, 1937. It reopened three days later at Daly's Sixty-Third Street Theater. *The Sun and I* by the American playwright Barrie Stavis (1906–2007) opened at the Adelphi in February 1937 and closed after seventy-four performances in May 1937. Like *It Can't Happen Here,* it was sponsored by the Federal Theatre Project.

54. Alexander Woollcott (1887–1943), American critic and author of *While Rome Burns* (1934), a collection of essays and anecdotes, was a member of the Algonquin Round Table.

55. See Schorer, *Sinclair Lewis,* 635: "The Communist press, between sneers and rage, denounced [*The Prodigal Parents*] as a crime against humanity."

56. John L. Lewis (1880–1969), aggressive and effective American leader of organized labor, was president of the United Mine Workers (1920–60).

57. John Milton (1608–1674), English Puritan poet, author of *Paradise Lost,* is associated with the development of political liberalism; William Blake (1757–1827), English poet, painter, and printmaker, was a prophetic figure associated with Romanticism and a political radical; Edward Lear (1812–1888), English poet and artist, attained considerable fame for his popular limericks and "nonsense" verse.

58. John Marquand (1893–1960), American novelist and short-story writer, received a Pulitzer Prize in 1938 for his novel *The Late George Apley.*

59. Mark Schorer (1908–1977), American critic and writer, is best known for his scholarship on Lewis, especially the biography *Sinclair Lewis: An American Life* (1961). He also published short stories in such venues as the *Atlantic Monthly, Esquire, Harper's,* and the *New Yorker.*

60. The American poets Ezra Pound (1885–1972) and Edna St. Vincent Millay (1892–1950).

61. Upton Sinclair, *Money Writes!* (New York: Boni, 1927), 67: Sinclair Lewis "lived in the kennel for many years, but jumped over the fence."

62. Marion K. Sanders, *Dorothy Thompson: A Legend in Her Time* (Boston: Houghton Mifflin, 1973).

63. "Among these imprisoned celebrities were so many journalists: Raymond Moley, Frank Simonds, Frank Kent, Heywood Broun, Mark Sullivan, Earl Browder, Franklin P. Adams, George Seldes, Frazier Hunt, Garet Garrett, Granville Hicks, Edwin James, Robert Morss Lovett."

64. General Smedley Butler (1881–1940), the only soldier to be awarded the Marine Corps Brevet Medal and two Medals of Honor, testified before a congressional committee in November 1934 that he had been urged by a group of wealthy businessmen to lead a military coup against the Roosevelt administration. The *New York Times* dismissed Butler's allegations as a "gigantic hoax" ("Credulity Unlimited," November 22, 1934, 20). Butler later complained in a radio interview that the names of the alleged conspirators had been omitted from the committee report, even though it also found credible evidence of a plot.

65. Winston Churchill (1874–1965), British politician, was twice elected prime minister of England (1940–45, 1951–55).

66. Schorer, *Sinclair Lewis,* 641.

67. Flora Campbell (1911–1978) later played the lead opposite Lewis in *Angela Is Twenty-Two,* and Patrick Barry Sullivan (1912–1994) had a successful career as a supporting actor.

68. Harold Winston was a director and performer on Broadway as well as a voice director for some notable Hollywood films from the later 1930s through the middle 1940s.

69. John Van Druten (1901–1957) was an English playwright and director.

70. Ethel Barrymore (1879–1959) was an American actress.

71. Alexander Clark (1901–1995) was an American actor. In 1945 he married Frances Tannehill, who had performed a bit part in the 1934 production of *Dodsworth.*

72. Lakewood Theatre, five miles north of Skowhegan, Maine, was founded in 1901, and is the oldest summer theater in the United States. From 1925 to 1941 it was the premier summer stock venue for Broadway hopefuls.

73. Clifford Odets (1906–1963), socialist American playwright best known for *Waiting for Lefty* (1935), *Awake and Sing!* (1935), and *The Golden Boy* (1937).

74. The Goodman Theater at Monroe and Columbus Drive in Chicago opened in 1925. The man in the dining car may have been Maurice Gnesin (1896–1957), who became head of the Goodman School of Drama in 1931.

75. Carlisle had an affair with Decio de Moura, the Brazilian ambassador's assistant and secretary, ending when Moura was recalled to his home country. Beyond this notorious affair, which drew occasional comments in gossip columns, little is known about Moura.

76. George Gershwin (1898–1937), American composer and pianist, was one of many theater men—including Irving Berlin, Kurt Weill, and Oscar Hammerstein—who professed love for Carlisle.

Part 13

1. Sinclair Lewis, *Selected Letters of Sinclair Lewis,* ed. John J. Koblas and Dave Page (Madison, WI: Main Street Press, 1985), 78.

2. Bernard Szold (1894–1960) was an American stage director, actor, and drama coach.

3. Eddie Dowling (1889–1976) was an American writer, performer, and composer.

4. *Shadow and Substance* is a four-act play written in 1937 by Irish playwright Paul Vincent Carroll (1900–1968).

5. Cedric Hardwicke (1893–1964) was a celebrated English actor. He was knighted in 1934 at the uncommonly young age of forty-one.

6. Fulton Sheen (1895–1979), later an archbishop in the Catholic Church.

7. See George Jean Nathan, "Red Menace," *Newsweek,* August 22, 1938, 22.

8. Joseph Rummel (1876–1964) was archbishop of the Archdiocese of New Orleans from 1935 until his death.

9. Sylvia Sidney (1910–1999) was an American actress.

10. Luther Adler (1903–1984) was an American actor and director.

11. Dudley Digges (1879–1947) was an Irish character actor.

12. Brooks Atkinson's review in the *New York Times* ("'Good Neighbor,' a Drama of American Tolerance," October 22, 1941, 26) may be representative: "If Mr. Lewis' play is apprentice work, Mr. Lewis' direction is a beginner's job also. The performance looks like Monday evening in a second-rate stock company." According to Fanny Butcher (*Many Lives—One Love* [New York: Harper and Row, 1972], 395–96), Murphy was more forthcoming in private: he "admitted to me that he was afraid Sinclair Lewis wasn't meant to play a Catholic priest any more than to be one."

13. Ann Nichol's play *Abie's Irish Rose,* despite poor reviews, was a commercial hit, running on Broadway from May 23, 1922, to October 1, 1927.

14. The Hotel Ponce de León was a luxury hotel that was opened in January 1888 in St. Augustine, Florida.

15. Lingeman, *Sinclair Lewis: Rebel from Main Street,* 485.

16. Morgan and Holtz, "Fragments from a Marriage: Letters of Sinclair Lewis to Grace Hegger Lewis," 97.

17. Schorer, *Sinclair Lewis,* 723.

18. Dorothy Thompson's sister, Margaret "Peggy" Thompson Wilson (b. 1897) married Howard Wilson.

19. Palmer House is a luxury hotel at the corner of State and Monroe Streets in Chicago.

20. Lewis took a house for the summer in Cohasset, Massachusetts, as he prepared to play Doremus Jessup in a summer stock production of "It Can't Happen Here." The play opened on August 22, to a sold-out house and was carried over for an extra week.

21. Schellhase's restaurant was located at 412 North Howard Street near the theater district in Baltimore.

22. The Algonquin is a luxury hotel at 59 West Forty-Fourth Street in New York. It opened in 1902.

23. Edith Haggard (1903–1995) was for a time Lewis's literary agent in the Curtis Brown office.

24. Lester Markel, editor of the Sunday *New York Times* from 1923 until 1964.

25. Major Arthur McKeogh (1890–1937), World War I hero and decorated officer of the "Lost Battalion," was managing editor of *Good Housekeeping.*

Part 14

1. Lingeman, *Sinclair Lewis: Rebel from Main Street,* 502.

2. See headnote to chapter 66.

3. Arthur Mizener, *The Far Side of Paradise: A Biography of F. Scott Fitzgerald* (Boston: Houghton Mifflin, 1951).

4. This is most likely a reference to Lillian Harkison, who served as Lewis's housekeeper in Minneapolis as well as Duluth.

5. Childe Hassam (1859–1935) was an American impressionist painter.

6. In fact, Fadiman reviewed *Kingsblood Royal* much more favorably than Conrad

reports. See "The American Problem," *Saturday Review of Literature,* May 24, 1947, 9–10: "It will arouse fury, indignation, resentment, passion, and, above all, thought."

7. Agatha Christie (1890–1976) was an English mystery writer.

8. Jane White (1922–2011), daughter of Walter White, is an Obie Award–winning African American actress.

9. Percy Greene (1897–1977) was an African American civil rights activist in Mississippi.

10. See headnote to chapter 112.

11. See Schorer, *Sinclair Lewis,* 447–48; Lingeman, *Sinclair Lewis: Rebel from Main Street,* 276–77.

12. Jonathan Swift (1667–1745), Anglo-Irish author, critic, and dean of St. Patrick's Cathedral (Dublin), is the foremost prose satirist of the English language.

13. Upton Sinclair wrote eleven novels featuring Lanny Budd (1940–53). He received the Pulitzer Prize for *Dragon's Teeth,* the third book in the series, in 1943.

14. Arthur H. Vandenberg (1884–1951), who began his career as an editor and publisher, was a Republican senator from Michigan (1928–51) who contributed to the formation of the United Nations; he capitulated to most of the early New Deal measures, opposed the second wave of reforms in 1935, and refused to allow the Republicans to nominate him for vice president in 1936.

15. As a Democrat, Henry A. Wallace (1888–1965), formerly a liberal Republican, was the thirty-third vice president of the United States (1941–45). In 1948 he ran unsuccessfully for the presidency on the Progressive Party ticket.

16. Hedy Lamarr (1914–2000), an Austrian-born Hollywood beauty famous in the late 1930s and '40s.

17. The Progressive Citizens of America (1946–48), the precursor of the Progressive Party of 1948, grew out of a working-class base and had the support of the unions as well as early civil rights activists (such as W. E. B. Du Bois and Paul Robeson). Known as the third progressive movement, it was a precursor of contemporary progressivism.

18. Adolphe Menjou (1890–1963) was an American actor.

19. Vyacheslav Molotov (1890–1986), Soviet foreign minister under Stalin and a signatory of the Soviet-Nazi nonaggression pact in 1939.

20. The novelist Howard Fast (1914–2003) joined the Communist Party USA (CPUSA) in 1944.

21. William Z. Foster (1881–1961), general secretary of the CPUSA from 1929 to 1932; Benjamin J. Davis (1903–1964), a leftist African American lawyer; Elizabeth Gurley Flynn (1890–1964), member of the International Workers of the World and founding member of the American Civil Liberties Union.

22. The review of *Kingsblood Royal* in the *Daily Worker* was not by Fast but by Samuel Sillen: "Sinclair Lewis Takes Lid Off Jimcrow in 'Kingsblood Royal,'" May 23, 1947, 11. See instead Fast's review in the *New Masses:* "The Broadaxe of Sinclair Lewis," June 10, 1947, 23.

23. Max Flowers (b. 1908) directed the student theater at Williams College and was Lewis's guest at Thorvale Farm after he lost that position as a result of faculty politics.

24. William H. Vanderbilt III (1901–1981), governor of Rhode Island from 1939 to 1941.

25. Cornelia Stratton Parker (1885–1972) was a prolific American magazinist and the author of *An American Idyll: The Life of Carleton H. Parker* (1921), a biography of her late husband, and *Working with the Working Women* (1922).

26. Lewis observed in an interview less than a year before his death that "the best novel he had read lately was Norman Mailer's *The Naked and the Dead*. 'I think Mailer will be all right,' he said, 'unless he gets into a left-wing compulsion and won't write anything'" (Joseph A. Barry, "Sinclair Lewis, 65 and Far from Main Street," *New York Times*, February 5, 1950, 153).

27. In "Kingsblood" (*Pittsburgh Courier*, national edition, June 7, 1947, 7), Cayton imagines a conversation among African Americans about Lewis's novel. They are dumbfounded that a man passing as white would voluntarily reveal his black ancestry.

28. Yaddo is a 400-acre artists' community near Saratoga, New York, founded by financier Spencer Trask and his wife, Katrina, a poet, in 1900.

29. Franz Kafka (1883–1924), German novelist and short-story writer, is one of the most influential fiction writers of the twentieth century.

30. Robert Penn Warren (1905–1989), American poet, novelist, and critic, was one of the founders of the school of New Criticism.

31. Horace R. Cayton Jr., "The Psychology of the Negro under Discrimination," in *Mental Health and Mental Disorder: A Sociological Approach*, ed. Arnold Rose (New York: Norton, 1955), 377–92.

32. Katherine Powers, Marcella's mother, had "supported her daughter and herself in threadbare circumstances by running a boardinghouse in East Orange, New Jersey." Lewis once explained to Carl Van Doren why he had hired Mrs. Powers: "She enjoys everything, never complains about anything, will talk or shut up as you prefer" (Lingeman, *Sinclair Lewis: Rebel from Main Street*, 440, 528).

33. Spencer Tracy (1900–1967) and Lana Turner (1921–1995) starred in a movie adaptation of *Cass Timberlane* in 1947. Lewis had socialized with Tracy in Hollywood in 1943 (Lingeman, *Sinclair Lewis: Rebel from Main Street*, 476).

34. "The words given as Lewis's are not his in every detail, but I have tried to record his statements, his manner of speaking, and phrases as accurately as possible. I am sure that I have come extremely close to his language" (Austin's note).

35. Matthew Arnold (1822–1888) was an English poet and critic.

36. Lionel Trilling (1905–1975) was an American educator, literary critic, and novelist.

37. The reign of King George VI of England (1895–1952) lasted from 1936 until his death.

38. Harry S Truman (1884–1972), thirty-third president of the United States (1945–53).

39. Sir Gerald Doak is a character in *Babbitt;* this reference, presumably, is to him.

40. Vladimir Lenin (1870–1924), Russian revolutionary and leader of the Soviet Union from 1917 until his death.

41. Andrei Gromyko (1909–1989), Soviet ambassador to the United States (1943–

46) and later Soviet representative to the UN Security Council. He was also Soviet foreign minister from 1957 until 1989.

42. Norman Thomas (1884–1968) was a leading American socialist and pacifist who campaigned for president during six elections on the Socialist ticket, filling the vacuum left by Eugene Debs's death in 1926.

43. Karl Marx (1818–1883), political theorist and revolutionary; Sigmund Freud (1856–1939), the founder of modern psychoanalysis; and Albert Einstein (1879–1955), theoretical physicist.

44. Anton Chekhov (1860–1904) was a Russian playwright, short-story writer, and physician.

45. Truman Capote (1924–1984) was known as a writer of short stories prior to the publication of *Other Voices, Other Rooms* (1948), the novel Lewis denigrates.

46. On Lewis's opinion of Thoreau (1817–1862), see "One Man Revolution," *Newsweek,* November 22, 1937, 33; rpt. *Man from Main Street,* 240–42. See also Julian Mason, "Sinclair Lewis's Copy of *Walden,*" *Thoreau Society Bulletin* 173 (Fall 1985): 7.

47. Alfred Kazin (1915–1998) was an American author and literary critic. Chapter seven of his *On Native Grounds* (1942) addresses what he terms "The New Realism" in American fiction through the work of Sherwood Anderson and Lewis.

48. Lewis repeatedly satirized Upton Sinclair in *It Can't Happen Here,* particularly in chapter 15.

49. Percy Bysshe Shelley (1792–1822) was a British romantic poet and political radical.

50. Edwin Arlington Robinson (1869–1935), American poet, received three Pulitzer Prizes.

51. Leicester (pronounced Lester) Hemingway (1915–1982), the younger brother of Ernest Hemingway, published six books, including a biography of his brother.

52. "Mark Schorer has called my attention to the fact that Lewis and Wolfe visited their British publisher's home, which is accurately described by Wolfe. Either Lewis did not remember correctly or he felt—if I may apply to him his interpretation of Wolfe—that a 'vivid' example is more important than an accurate one" (Austin's note).

53. Robert K. Haas (1890–1964), Yale '11, was Faulkner's publisher, the junior partner in the firm of Smith and Haas (1932–36) and later vice president of Random House.

Part 15

1. *Nieuw Amsterdam* was a luxury ship of the Holland America line that was commissioned in 1937.

2. Miller refers to his book *The New England Mind: From Colony to Province* (1939).

3. Miller alludes to a brief passage at the close of chapter 31 of *Dodsworth.*

4. See headnote to chapter 116.

5. Walter Scott (1771–1832) was a Scottish historical novelist.

6. The American poets Edgar Allan Poe (1809–1849) and Walt Whitman (1819–1892).

7. The Dickens characters Lewis recalls are nearly allegorical, as their names often imply: Micawber, from *David Copperfield,* is poor but eternally optimistic; Gradgrind, from *Hard Times,* is cold and interested only in facts; Pecksniff, from *Martin Chuzzlewit,* is unctuous, sanctimonious, and hypocritical; Mr. Squeers, from *Nicholas Nickleby,* is an abusive and cruel schoolmaster.

8. Rangoon is the former capital of Burma.

9. Robert E. Lee (1807–1870) and Ulysses S. Grant (1822–1885) were respectively the commanders of the Confederate and Union armies during the American Civil War.

10. Hervey Allen (1889–1949) was an American novelist and author of *Anthony Adverse* (1933); and Kenneth Roberts (1885–1957) was an American historical novelist.

11. Frans Hals (ca. 1580–1666), a Dutch painter.

12. Karl Wilhelm Friedrich von Schlegel (1772–1829) published *Lucinde* in 1799. In the novel, which caused a scandal, the character Julius stands in as the alter ego of the author, and Lucinde represents Dorothea Veit (1763–1839), a divorcée with whom he lived in Berlin and Jena.

13. Barry, "Sinclair Lewis, 65 and Far from Main Street," 13. Elsewhere, Lewis calls himself a "cheerful pathologist" (Lewis, *Man from Main Street,* 104).

Bibliography

Adamic, Louis. *My America, 1928–1938.* New York and London: Harper, 1938.

Agar, Eileen. *A Look at My Life.* London: Methuen, 1988.

Agrell, Isabel Lewis. *Sinclair Lewis Remembered.* Crosslake, MN: privately printed, 1996.

Anderson, Sherwood. *Sherwood Anderson: Selected Letters.* Edited by Charles E. Modlin. Knoxville: University of Tennessee Press, 1983.

Atkinson, Brooks. "'Good Neighbor,' a Drama of American Tolerance, Directed for the Stage by Sinclair Lewis." *New York Times,* October 22, 1941, 26.

Austin, Allen. "An Interview with Sinclair Lewis." *University of Kansas City Review* 24 (1958): 199–210.

Bacon, Leonard. *Lost Buffalo and Other Poems.* New York: Harper, 1930.

———. *Semi-Centennial.* New York: Harper, 1939.

Barry, Joseph A. "Sinclair Lewis, 65 and Far from Main Street." *New York Times,* February 5, 1950, 153.

Batchelor, Helen. "A Sinclair Lewis Portfolio of Maps: Zenith to Winnemac." *Modern Language Quarterly* 32 (December 1971): 401–7.

Benét, William Rose. "The Earlier Lewis." *Saturday Review of Literature,* January 20, 1934, 421.

Breasted, Charles. "The 'Sauk-Centricities' of Sinclair Lewis." *Saturday Review of Literature,* August 14, 1954, 7–8.

Broun, Heywood. "Hewing to the Line." *Woman's Home Companion* 58 (February 1931): 26.

Bunge, Nancy. "The Minnesota School: Sinclair Lewis's Influence on Frederick Manfred." *North Dakota Quarterly* 70 (Winter 2003): 118–25.

Butcher, Fanny. *Many Lives—One Love.* New York: Harper and Row, 1972.

Cabell, James Branch. *As I Remember It.* New York: McBride, 1955.

Callaghan, Morley. *That Summer in Paris.* New York: Coward-McCann, 1963.

Calverton, V. F. *The Liberation of American Literature.* New York: Scribner's, 1932.

Canby, Henry Seidel. *American Memoir.* Boston: Houghton Mifflin, 1947.

Carlisle, Kitty. *Kitty: An Autobiography.* New York: Doubleday, 1988.

Cayton, Horace R., Jr. *Long Old Road.* New York: Trident, 1965.

Cerf, Bennett. *At Random.* New York: Random House, 1977.

Cockburn, Claud. *Cockburn Sums Up: An Autobiography.* London: Quartet, 1981.

Compton, Ida L. *Sinclair Lewis at Thorvale Farm: A Personal Memoir.* Sarasota, FL: Ruggles, 1988.

Conroy, Stephen S. "Sinclair Lewis's Sociological Imagination." *American Literature* 42 (November 1970): 348–62.

Cooney, Charles F. "Walter White and Sinclair Lewis: The History of a Literary Friendship." *Prospects* 1 (1975): 63–79.

Conrad, Barnaby. *Fun While It Lasted.* New York: Random House, 1969.

Cowley, Malcolm. *The Dream of the Golden Mountains.* New York: Viking, 1980.

Davison, Richard Allan. "Sinclair Lewis, Charles G. Norris, and Kathleen Norris: An Early Friendship." *Modern Fiction Studies* 31 (Autumn 1985): 503–10.

De Kruif, Paul. *The Sweeping Wind: A Memoir.* New York: Harcourt, Brace and World, 1962.

Doran, George H. *Chronicles of Barabbas.* New York: Harcourt, Brace, 1935.

Eliot, T. S. *The Letters of T. S. Eliot.* Edited by Valerie Eliot. San Diego: Harcourt, Brace, Jovanovich, 1988.

Ellis, Edward Robb. *A Diary of the Century.* New York: Kodansha International, 1995.

Fadiman, Clifton. "Party of One." *Holiday* 11 (February 1952): 11–12.

Ferber, Edna. *A Peculiar Treasure.* New York: Doubleday, Doran, 1939.

Fine, Gary Alan, and Amy Campion. "Sinclair Lewis, *Main Street,* and Community Reputation." In *Difficult Reputations: Collective Memories of the Evil, Inept, and Controversial.* Edited by Gary Alan Fine, 232–58. Chicago: University of Chicago Press, 2001.

Fishbein, Morris. *Morris Fishbein, M.D.: An Autobiography.* Garden City, NY: Doubleday, 1969.

Flanagan, Hallie. *Arena.* New York: Duell, Sloan and Pearce, 1940.

Forster, E. M. *Abinger Harvest.* New York: Harcourt, Brace, 1936.

Gauvreau, Emile. *My Last Million Readers.* New York: Dutton, 1941.

Grebstein, Sheldon. "The Education of a Rebel: Sinclair Lewis at Yale." *New England Quarterly* 28 (September 1955): 372–82.

Guthrie, Ramon. "Sinclair Lewis and the 'Labor Novel.'" *Proceedings of the American Academy of Arts and Letters* n.s. 2 (1952): 68–73.

Hamnett, Nina. *Laughing Torso.* New York: Long and Smith, 1932.

Harcourt, Alfred. *Some Experiences.* Riverside, CT: privately printed, 1935.

Harkness, Samuel. "Sinclair Lewis's Sunday School Class." *Christian Century,* August 5, 1926, 938–39.

Hemingway, Ernest. *Across the River and Into the Trees.* New York: Scribner's, 1950.

———. *Green Hills of Africa.* New York: Scribner's, 1935.

Hersey, John. "First Job." *Yale Review* 76 (Winter 1987): 184–97.

Hicks, Granville. "Sinclair Lewis's Stinkbomb." *New Masses,* January 25, 1938, 19.

Howe, Irving. "The World He Mimicked Was His Own." *New York Times Book Review,* October 1, 1961, 34.

Huddleston, Sisley. *Paris Salons, Cafés, Studios.* Philadelphia: Lippincott, 1928.

Hunt, Frazier. *One American and His Attempts at Education.* New York: Simon and Schuster, 1938.

Hutchisson, James M. "Sinclair Lewis, Paul De Kruif, and the Composition of *Arrowsmith.*" *Studies in the Novel* 24 (Spring 1992): 48–66.

Inglis, W. D. "Where Lies the Hope of the Average Man?" *Lexington* (Kentucky) *Herald,* May 12, 1915, 13.

Jordan, Elizabeth G. *Three Rousing Cheers.* New York: Appleton-Century, 1938.

Josephson, Matthew. *Life among the Surrealists.* New York: Holt, Rinehart and Winston, 1962.

Kazin, Alfred. *On Native Grounds.* New York: Reynal and Hitchcock, 1942.

Killough, George. "German Catholicism, Sauk Centre, and Sinclair Lewis." *American Literary Realism* 39 (Winter 2007): 109–25.

Kreymborg, Alfred. *Troubadour: An American Autobiography.* New York: Boni and Liveright, 1925.

Lewis, Grace Hegger. *Half a Loaf.* New York: Liveright, 1931.

———. "When Lewis Walked Down Main Street." *New York Times Sunday Magazine,* July 3, 1960, 10.

———. *With Love from Gracie.* New York: Harcourt, Brace, 1955.

Lewis, Sinclair. *From Main Street to Stockholm: Letters of Sinclair Lewis, 1919–1920.* Edited by Harrison Smith. New York: Harcourt, Brace, and World, 1952.

———. *The Man from Main Street: Selected Essays and Other Writings, 1904–1950.* Edited by Harry E. Maule and Melville H. Cane. New York: Random House, 1953.

———. "Mr. Lorimer and Me." *Nation,* July 25, 1928, 81.

———. *Selected Letters of Sinclair Lewis.* Edited by John J. Koblas and Dave Page. Madison, WI: Main Street Press, 1985.

Light, Martin. *The Quixotic Vision of Sinclair Lewis.* West Lafayette, IN: Purdue University Press, 1975.

Lingeman, Richard. *Sinclair Lewis: Rebel from Main Street.* New York: Random House, 2002.

Loeb, Harold. *The Way It Was.* New York: Criterion, 1959.

Lyman, Hazel Palmer. "The Earliest Lewis." *Saturday Review of Literature,* April 14, 1934, 628.

Manfred, Frederick. "Sinclair Lewis: A Portrait." *American Scholar* 23 (1954): 165–71.

———. "Sinclair Lewis's Funeral." *South Dakota Review* 38 (Fall 2000): 89.

Manson, Alexander. "The Last Days of Sinclair Lewis." *Saturday Evening Post,* March 31, 1951, 110–12.

Mayes, Herbert R. *The Magazine Maze: A Prejudiced Perspective.* Garden City, NY: Doubleday, 1980.

McAlmon, Robert. *Being Geniuses Together, 1920–1930.* 1938; rpt. Baltimore: Johns Hopkins University Press, 1997.

Mencken, H. L. *My Life as Author and Editor.* Edited by Jonathan Yardley. New York: Knopf, 1993.

Miller, Perry. "The Incorruptible Sinclair Lewis." *Atlantic Monthly* 187 (April 1951): 30–34.

Morgan, Speer, and William Holtz. "Fragments from a Marriage: Letters of Sinclair Lewis to Grace Hegger Lewis." *Missouri Review* 11, no. 1 (1988): 71–98.

Mowrer, Lilian T. *Journalist's Wife.* New York: Readers League of America, 1940.

Murphy, Edward F. *Yankee Priest: An Autobiographical Journey.* Garden City, NY: Doubleday, 1952.

Nathan, George Jean. "Art of the Night." *Saturday Review of Literature,* November 28, 1936, 9.

———. *The Intimate Notebooks of George Jean Nathan.* New York: Knopf, 1932.

Nevinson, C. R. W. *Paint and Prejudice.* New York: Harcourt, Brace, 1938.

Norris, Kathleen. *Family Gathering.* Garden City, NY: Doubleday, 1959.

Orwoll, Mark. "A Battle in Bohemia: The Sinclair Lewis-Harold Stearns Feud." *Lost Generation Journal* 9 (Fall–Winter 1989): 2–5.

Phelps, William Lyon. "Men Now Famous." *Delineator* 117 (September 1930): 94.

Putnam, Samuel. *Paris Was Our Mistress: Memoirs of a Lost and Found Generation.* New York: Viking, 1947.

Rascoe, Burton. *Before I Forget.* New York: Literary Guild of America, 1937.

Rourke, Constance. *American Humor.* New York: Harcourt, Brace, 1931.

Russell, Charles Phillips. "Sinclair Lewis Declares Americans, More Than Britons, Ruled by Main-Street Idea." (Portland) *Oregonian,* October 9, 1921, 3.

Sanders, Marion K. *Dorothy Thompson: A Legend in Her Time.* Boston: Houghton Mifflin, 1973.

Sauer, Philip von Rohr. "The 1945 Lectures: A Happy Episode in Sinclair Lewis's Life." *Sinclair Lewis Newsletter* 4 (1972): 3.

Schorer, Mark. "My Life and Nine-Year Captivity with Sinclair Lewis." *New York Times Book Review,* August 20, 1961, 7.

———. *Sinclair Lewis: An American Life.* New York: McGraw-Hill, 1961.

Schulberg, Budd. *The Four Seasons of Success.* Garden City, NY: Doubleday, 1972.

Seldes, George. *Witness to a Century.* New York: Ballantine, 1987.

Sheean, Vincent. *Personal History.* Garden City, NY: Garden City Publishing, 1937.

———. "The Tangled Romance of Sinclair Lewis and Dorothy Thompson." *Harper's* 227 (October 1963): 136–38.

Shelton, Frank W. "Thomas Wolfe and Sinclair Lewis." *Thomas Wolfe Review* 12, no. 1 (1988): 7–12.

Shirer, William L. *20th Century Journey: A Memoir of a Life and the Times.* New York: Simon and Schuster, 1976.

Sinclair, Gordon. *Will Gordon Sinclair Please Sit Down.* Toronto: McClelland and Stewart, 1975.

Sinclair, Upton. *The Cup of Fury.* Great Neck, NY: Channel Press, 1956.

———. *Money Writes!* New York: Boni, 1927.

Slocombe, George. *The Tumult and the Shouting.* New York: Macmillan, 1936.

Smith, Harrison. "Sinclair Lewis: Remembrance of the Past." *Saturday Review of Literature,* January 27, 1951, 7–8.

Smith, H. Allen. *Low Man on a Totem Pole.* Garden City, NY: Doubleday, Doran, 1941.

Stearns, Harold E. *The Street I Know.* New York: Lee Furman, 1935.

Stevens, Betty. "A Village Radical: His Last American Home." *Venture* 2, no. 3 (1957): 35–46.

Stolberg, Benjamin. "Sinclair Lewis." *American Mercury* 53 (October 1941): 450–53, 459.

Terhune, Albert Payson. *To the Best of My Memory.* New York: Harper, 1930.

Thompson, Dorothy. "At the Court of King Gustaf." *Pictorial Review* 32 (April 1931): 17, 45, 50.

———. "The Boy and Man from Sauk Centre." *Atlantic Monthly* 206 (November 1960): 41.

———. "Sinclair Lewis: A Postscript." *Atlantic Monthly* 187 (June 1951): 73–74.

Tinker, Chauncey Brewster. "Sinclair Lewis, a Few Reminiscences." *Proceedings of the American Academy of Arts and Letters* n.s. 2 (1952): 65–67.

Towne, Charles Hanson. *Adventures in Editing.* New York: D. Appleton, 1926.

Tuerk, Richard. "Directed by Sinclair Lewis: 'The Good Neighbor' by Jack L. Levin." *Journal of the American Studies Association of Texas* 17 (1986): 21–26.

Updike, John. "No Brakes: A New Biography of Sinclair Lewis." *New Yorker,* February 4, 2002, 77.

Vaccariello, Michele A. "Tutoring Sinclair Lewis: A Personal Account." *South Dakota Review* 26, no. 2 (1988): 41–42.

Van Doren, Carl. *Three Worlds.* New York: Harper, 1936.

Vorse, Mary Heaton. *Time and the Town.* New York: Dial, 1942.

Walker, Franklin. "Jack London's Use of Sinclair Lewis Plots, Together with a Printing of Three of the Plots." *Huntington Library Quarterly* 17 (November 1953): 59–74.

Widdemer, Margaret. *Golden Friends I Had.* Garden City, NY: Doubleday, 1964.

Wilgus, Jack. "Sinclair Lewis Visits a Strike." *New Masses,* January 14, 1936, 10–11.

Wolfe, Thomas. *You Can't Go Home Again.* New York: Harper and Brothers, 1940.

Woodward, William E. *The Gift of Life: An Autobiography.* New York: Dutton, 1947.

Wray, Fay. *On the Other Hand: A Life Story.* New York: St. Martin's Press, 1989.

Index